Applied Computing

Springer

London
Berlin
Heidelberg
New York
Barcelona
Hong Kong
Milan
Paris
Singapore
Tokyo

The Springer-Verlag Series on Applied Computing is an advanced series of innovative textbooks that span the full range of topics in applied computing technology.

Books in the series provide a grounding in theoretical concepts in computer science alongside real-world examples of how those concepts can be applied in the development of effective computer systems.

The series should be essential reading for advanced undergraduate and postgraduate students in computing and information systems.

Books in this series are contributed by international specialist researchers and educators in applied computing who draw together the full range of issues in their specialist area into one concise authoritative textbook.

Titles already available:

Deryn Graham and Anthony Barrett
Knowledge-Based Image Processing Systems
3-540-76027-X

Derrick Morris, Gareth Evans, Peter Green, Colin Theaker
Object Orientated Computer Systems Engineering
3-540-76020-2

John Hunt
Java and Object Orientation: An Introduction
3-540-76148-9

David Gray
Introduction to the Formal Design of Real-Time Systems
3-540-76140-3

Mike Holcombe and Florentin Ipate
Correct Systems: Building A Business Process Solution
3-540-76246-9

Jan Noyes and Chris Baber
User-Centred Design of Systems
3-540-76007-5

Arturo Trujillo
Translation Engines: Techniques for Machine Translation
1-85233-057-0

Ulrich Nehmzow
Mobile Robotics: A Practical Introduction
1-85233-173-9

Fabio Paternò
Model-Based Design and Evaluation of Interactive Applications
1-85233-155-0

Tim Morris
Multimedia Systems: Delivering, Generating and Interacting with Multimedia
1-85233-248-4

Arno Scharl

Evolutionary Web Development

Springer

Arno Scharl
Department of Information Systems, University of Economics and Business
Administration, Augasse 2-6, A-1090 Vienna, Austria

Series Editors

Professor Ray J. Paul, BSc MSc PhD
Dean of the Faculty of Science, Brunel University,
Uxbridge, Middlesex UB8 3PH, UK

Professor Peter J. Thomas, MIEE MBCS CEng FRSA
Centre for Personal Information Management, University of the West of England,
Frenchay Campus, Bristol BS16 1QY, UK

Dr Jasna Kuljis, PhD MS Dipl Ing
Department of Information Systems and Computing, Brunel University,
Uxbridge, Middlesex UB8 3PH, UK

ISBN 1-85233-310-3 Springer-Verlag London Berlin Heidelberg

British Library Cataloguing in Publication Data
Scharl, Arno
    Evolutionary web development. - (Applied computing)
    1.World wide web 2.Web-site design
    I.Title
    005.2'76
    ISBN 1852333103

Library of Congress Cataloging-in-Publication Data
A catalog record for this book is available from the Library of Congress

Typesetting: PostScript files by author
Printed and bound by Athenæum Press Ltd., Gateshead, Tyne & Wear
34/3830-543210 Printed on acid-free paper SPIN 10765393

Preface

With the continuing evolution and convergence of previously disparate technologies around electronic commerce, the World Wide Web is increasingly pervasive in the corporate value chain. Most business processes, from procurement and inbound logistics to marketing and after-sales service, create and use information (Porter 1998, 167f.). They are connected via networked information systems, which have become the basic infrastructure for global transaction-oriented applications. Every transaction process occurring in such an electronic marketplace goes hand in hand with the access, absorption, arrangement, and selling of information in heterogeneous ways (Zakon 1999).

Despite these technological and organizational changes, the customers' information needs provide a uniform purpose for Web information systems. Accordingly, developers of such systems have to analyze the requirements of the newly empowered and technologically savvy customers in order to exploit the potential of online trading of information, services, and physical goods.

This book presents a methodology for analyzing and developing Web information systems that considers the structural changes in electronic markets outlined above. Chapter 1 defines the field and introduces the term "ergodic literature" for textual material whose access and utilization requires non-trivial efforts by the reader. It identifies navigational and textual features of interactive Web applications, a subset of ergodic literature, and compares these features with those of printed media. An analysis of the multifaceted term "interactivity" then sets the stage for Chapter 2, which investigates the life-cycle economies and diffusion characteristics of traditional and Web-based applications. The subsequent sections delineate the evolution of electronic markets in general and the World Wide Web in particular from both Darwinian and methodological perspectives. To investigate this process, an evolutionary framework based on system adaptivity and the underlying communication patterns is introduced. It classifies Web information systems and analyzes their ability to support the various phases of electronic business transactions. Only advanced system architectures can fully leverage the potential of the World Wide Web to deliver additional customer value. The framework specifies the following four categories: Static Web information systems that provide basic information of limited value for the average customer (↪ Chapter 3), interactive systems that enable explicit customer feedback and transaction processing (↪ Chapter 4), adaptive systems that instantly and automatically generate the hypertext structure according to embedded user models (↪ Chapter 5), and agent-mediated architectures that allow individual negotiations regarding product and non-product attributes (↪ Chapter 6).

Chapter 3 summarizes the characteristics of static Web information systems. These collections of rudimentary hypertext documents are still common for many small and medium-sized companies. More in line with current business practices of larger organizations, Chapter 4 focuses on gathering customer feedback and its immediate analysis within an iterative cycle of design, implementation, usage, and analysis. The emergent attributes of modern organizations suggest such an evolutionary approach to Web development. Analytic activities are no longer captured within the early stages of a system's life-cycle but represent a continuing task of system maintenance. Analysis, operation, and maintenance activities become parallel but highly interrelated processes. Cyclical planning is rendered obsolete, since the results of the ongoing analysis are continuously fed into the maintenance phase. Section 4.2 outlines the current state of Web engineering with special regard to design methodologies, conceptual modeling approaches, and related visualization techniques. It introduces a symbolic modeling language for the construction of both reference and customized models during the development process of commercial Web information systems (↪ Section 4.3). This graphical notation helps analysts to visualize individual and aggregated access patterns of online customers derived from log file data of corporate Web servers. It enhances the limited, statistically oriented representations of commercially available Web-tracking software with a map-like overview similar to customer tracking in traditional retailing outlets (↪ Section 4.4).

Numerous tools support the structured design of Web information systems, ranging from rudimentary layout products for individual documents to sophisticated Web site management solutions that facilitate conceptual authoring-in-the-large. Structured analysis, by contrast, has largely been neglected by both theory and practice but belongs to the most relevant questions in formulating business strategies for electronic commerce. This comes as a surprise, since analysis is less constrained by the technical limitations of existing architectures. Section 4.5 intends to fill this gap by suggesting a methodology for the automated analysis of Web information systems. The chapter summarizes empirical results covering several business sectors, namely information technology, travel and tourism, retail banking, and environmentally oriented non-profit organizations. Classifications, comparative sector assessments, longitudinal studies, and exploratory textual analyses help practitioners chart the industry evolution and compare the performance of their own Web information system with those of competing organizations.

Chapter 5 introduces adaptive Web information systems that promise a sustainable competitive advantage in an environment where information redundancy becomes increasingly evident. Such a competitive advantage can only be achieved through customizing products, services, and communications. Key elements of customization are the separation of product and process life-cycles as described in Section 5.1. The resulting "classic loop of adaptation", delineated in Section 5.2, is founded on the continuing gathering of information regarding the customers' current needs and preferences. Sections 5.3 and 5.4 compare explicit and implicit acquisition methods and describe ways to combine the various information sources and transform the resulting body of knowledge into consistent user models. On the basis of such embedded user models, adaptive Web information systems can automatically generate the content of documents, the primary navigational system comprising links between and within these documents, and supplemental navigational systems such as index pages, trails, guided tours, or interactive site maps. Many prototypes that incorporate adaptive components are developed without a clear model of the components' functionality. Therefore, Section 5.5 provides a conceptual guideline for the development process by classifying the various mechanisms into content-level, link-level, and meta-level adaptation.

In the fourth and last stage of Web evolution, which is portrayed in Chapter 6, efforts to automate and optimize electronic business-to-consumer transactions gradually transfer certain tasks from adaptive Web information systems to agent-mediated architectures. Many deployed applications use content-based information agents and collaborative filtering systems for general information retrieval or specific product recommendations (↪ Sections 6.1 and 6.2). By contrast, most transaction agents are only available as prototypical implementations up until now (↪ Section 6.3). Transaction agents allow multidimensional negotiations regarding a variety of product and non-product attributes. Once the necessary infrastructure is in place (↪ Section 6.4), their customizability and remarkable flexibility promise to change the inherent characteristics of doing business electronically.

Acknowledgements

I have been helped in various ways with the conceptual planning of this book, the gathering of the empirical data, the compilation of results, and with the production of the final manuscript. My first debt of gratitude is to Hans Robert Hansen and Hannes Werthner for encouraging and helping me through the process of writing this book. Their suggestions and critical observations have led to innumerable improvements. I also owe special thanks to Bernard Glasson and Arie Segev for their generous support during my time as visiting research fellow at the Curtin University of Technology and the University of California at Berkeley, respectively.

The successful completion of a project such as this is not possible without the feedback of many colleagues. First of all, I would like to mention Christian Bauer, to whom I am greatly indebted for his invaluable help. Several analyses presented in this book originate from our joint research efforts over the last two years. I would also like to thank my home institution, the Information Systems Department of the Vienna University of Economics and Business Administration, for granting me the resources and intellectual support necessary to finish this project. The cooperation with my colleagues Martin Bichler, Roman Brandtweiner, and Marion Kaukal contributed to important aspects of my research. Thanks also go to Judith Gebauer, with whom I have been fortunate to work at the University of California at Berkeley.

I apologize to the people I have omitted to acknowledge, and also – in the event that their ideas have been misrepresented – to those whom I have acknowledged. I would also like to recognize the considerable financial support from the Austrian Science Fund and the Austrian National Bank. Finally, I would like to thank Rebecca Mowat and the staff at Springer London for their support and help in the materialization of this book.

Vienna, July 2000   *Arno Scharl*

Table of Contents

1 Introduction

The definitions presented in the following sections represent a hierarchical structure, which is depicted in Figure 1.1. To analyze this semantic hierarchy, the chapter starts with the delineation of *text* as the most general term, a description of its characteristic metaphysics, and an analysis of the observable media influences on written textual material. The wide range of this material is then divided into two categories, identifying the reader's non-trivial efforts to traverse the text as the essential quality of *ergodic literature*. These efforts distinguish *hypertext* as one specific form of ergodic literature and its applications from traditional (broadcast) media. The focus on distributed hypertext systems implies that other forms of ergodic literature such as computer-generated narratives, textual game genres, or participatory simulations are not considered in this book. The history of hypertext research is presented, describing the sequence of ideas, prototypes, and implementations until the early 1990s, when prior efforts culminated in the specification of the *World Wide Web*. Evolving so quickly that previous versions become obsolete within a few years, the World Wide Web provides a dynamic and distributed platform for interactive business applications. It has begun to make the barriers between different forms of communication more permeable than ever by functionally melding elements of mass, organizational, and interpersonal communication. The term *Web information system* denotes the result of this integration. It comprises a heterogeneous set of networked systems of variable complexity, from simple collections of static hypertext documents to sophisticated adaptive architectures and agent-mediated transaction environments. Evidently, the navigational and linguistic characteristics of Web information systems, described in the Sections 1.4.4 and 1.4.5, depend on the their level of sophistication.

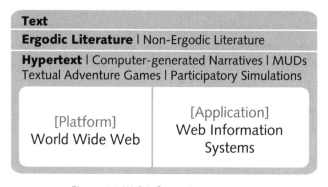

Figure 1.1. Web information systems as
subcategory of (electronic) textuality

1.1 FORMAL DEFINITIONS OF TEXT

The term *text* has been given a variety of definitions both in linguistics
and in information systems research. As an outward manifestation of a
communicative event, it generally denotes a structured object with the
primary function to relay verbal information. The electronic storage
and dissemination of such an object is causing diverse and sometimes
contradictory assertions as to its significance for the representation and
transmission of knowledge (Sutherland 1997, 1). There is little disagreement, however, regarding the fact that quantitative changes in the
amount of textual information available to an individual or the speed of
its transmission promote a qualitative change in the processes of constructing knowledge and understanding (Burbules and Callister 1996).

1.1.1 The Metaphysics of Written Text

Language can be defined as a "set of signs as well as instructions for
their use such that (1) the signs can be produced by purposeful individuals, (2) the signs are semantically and pragmatically efficient for a
significant portion of those who use them, (3) the signs are environmentally and socially general in the semantic and pragmatic sense, and
(4) the instructions signify ways of permuting and combining signs in
the set to form sign complexes that also satisfy conditions (2) and (3)"
(Ackoff and Emery 1972, 177). Most linguists regard both spoken and
written language in combination with visual images and corresponding
sound effects as parts of a text (Fairclough 1995, 17). Spoken language
traditionally entails a copresent listener who is able to directly affect the

speaker's flow of discourse. Usually, spoken language broadcast by mass media does not allow that (Garrett and Bell 1998, 2). In the context of this book, therefore, only the written category is taken into account, for which considerations of structure, presentation, and (visual) impact are increasingly salient. Consequently, a written text must not be reduced to the information it transmits, as it entails a set of powerful metaphysics, the concepts of reading, writing, and stability being the most important of them (Aarseth 1994, 53):

- A text is what is read, the words and phrases that the reader sees before her eyes and the meanings they produce in her mind – in addition to the script (visible words and spaces), a text includes a practice, a structure, and a ritual of use.
- A text is a message, imbued with the values and intentions of a specific writer in the context of a specific genre and culture.
- A text is a fixed sequence of constituents (beginning, middle, and end) that cannot change, although its interpretations might.

Critics and enthusiasts alike discuss issues such as the nature and extent of authorial property, the stability and fluidity of text, or its relation to material form and reading practices (Sutherland 1997, 1). Similar controversies can be observed with regard to other forms of social discourse and interpersonal communication in particular. Despite the fact that textual computer-mediated communication has been claimed to be incoherent in various ways (fragmented, agrammatical, and interactionally disjointed), users enthusiastically flock to the Internet. As an answer to this obvious discrepancy, Herring proposes that "the degree of interactional coherence[1] characteristic of a communication medium and the popularity of that medium are essentially independent phenomena that can inform one another in complex ways" (Herring 1999a; Herring 1999b).

Nowadays, pure technological determinism postulating that it is technology that shapes the forms of society and organizations is generally refused (Jones 1999, 289). However, unless we are determined to think of texts as no more than their linguistic codes (words with only an accidental relation to their material means of presentation), there is no way of denying that the meaning of texts is indeed influenced by available technology and its representational capacities. Texts are cross-products between a set of matrices (Aarseth 1994, 59) – linguistic (the

---

[1] Language users generally assume *coherence*, expecting that what is said or written will make sense in terms of their normal experience of things. More formally, coherence can be defined as "the familiar and expected relationships in experience which we use to connect the meanings of utterances, even when those connections are not explicitly made" (Yule 1996, 127).

script), technological (the representational capacities), and historical (the socio-political context). When dealing with electronic textuality and issues such as portability or denatured physicality, the experience of reading a text, therefore, must not be confused with the particular technology on which it is read. With regard to computer text encoding, four distinct representational strategies are identified by (Renear 1997, 108ff.): orthographic, pictorial, format-based, and content-based strategies. Simple orthographic representational strategies, on the one hand, treat text as a sequence of linguistic entities and a few related paralinguistic items such as blanks and punctuation marks. They ignore layout devices and critical structural features of the text, which both represent vital components of robust textual encounters. Pictorial representations such as bitmaps or digital images, on the other hand, are arguably not textual at all and are usually embedded in more sophisticated structures. To overcome the shortcomings of early orthographic approaches, format-based strategies include interspersed codes indicating formatting information about the content and are a prerequisite for the development of content-based strategies. The latter rely on taxonomies of markup which usually include descriptive markup to classify an interval of text (e.g., normal paragraphs, headers, citations, or footnotes), procedural formatting markup, and presentational markup to indicate font shifts, white spaces, composed lines, and so forth. The *Standardized Generalized Markup Language (SGML)* and its more popular subset, the *eXtensible Markup Language (XML),* are meta-grammars for defining such markup structures (↪ Chapter 4: The Emergence of Interactivity).

1.1.2 Technological Implications for the Discursive Space

There is no such thing as a non-technological environment for creative processes like reading, writing, or editing. Each new medium creates its own public, which is often more interested in the provided technology than in the medium as a vehicle of information. To a certain extent, therefore, the medium determines its own content (Deledalle 1997, 51f.). The traditional metaphorical system governing our conceptualization of these processes is still transparently dependent on the print medium, which is just one of many possible conventions to express our problems and make sense of our subjective reality (Rosello 1994, 123). The influence of new technologies on the representational capacity has important implications for the formulation and reformulation of the discursive space. Computer programs, for example, are complex sign systems that follow the rules of their own syntax and semantics. The nature of their extremely abstract layout usually requires expert knowledge to understand and interpret their functionality (Ipsen 1997, 560f.).

Computer programs commonly have two kinds of receivers in mind: machines and software developers. This double standard of aesthetics balancing efficiency and clarity is drastically demonstrated by some authors who replace the scansion and rhyming conventions of traditional poetry by the rigid rules of computer programming languages. This "formalized" category of poetry, which does not necessarily produce any meaningful output, provides a balance between familiarity and strangeness, stasis and innovation. The nature of most existing computer programming languages, where most of the available (reserved) words are procedural commands, forces the author to write in the imperative voice, a technique that is otherwise usually avoided (Hopkins 1992). One rather popular example of this category is the poem "*Listen*" by Sharon Hopkins (Economist 1995), written entirely in *Perl*, the *Practical Extraction and Report Language* (↪ Chapter 4: The Emergence of Interactivity).

1.2   ERGODIC LITERATURE

When accessing electronic texts users effectuate semiotic sequences. Aarseth describes this selective movement as a work of physical construction and uses the term *ergodic literature* for texts that require a non-trivial effort to allow the reader to traverse the text (Aarseth 1998, 1ff.). More specifically, ergodic literature is characterized by the presence of four distinct user functions: (a) *interpretative* – user reflects about the meaning of the text, (b) *explorative* – user must decide which path to take, (c) *configurative* – scriptons are temporarily chosen or created by the user, and (d) *textonic* – user may permanently change or annotate the text (↪ Figure 1.2). This distinction corresponds to the three different types of readers as defined by Slatin: the reader as browser who reads for pleasure, as user who accesses the hypertext with a clear purpose, or as co-author who is actively involved in the creation of an evolving document (Slatin 1991, 153ff.; Snyder 1996, 72).

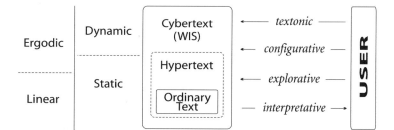

Figure 1.2. User functions and textual categories (adapted from Aarseth 1998, 64)

Being appropriated from physics, the term *ergodic* is derived from the Greek words *ergon* (work) and *hodos* (path). With hypertext being the most prominent category, the term includes computer-generated narratives, participatory simulation systems, textual adventure games, or socially constructed multi-user dungeons.[2] In either case, the functional and structural differences between different technologies play a defining role in determining the aesthetic processes of authoring and accessing the text.

1.3 HYPERTEXT AND HYPERMEDIA

Hypertext was conceptually developed by Vannevar Bush in his landmark 1945 magazine article *"As we May Think"* in the context of a machine called *Memex (= Memory Extender)* for storing, annotating, retrieving, and linking information. "The summation of human experience is being expanded at a prodigious rate, and the means we use for threading through the consequent maze to the momentarily important item is the same as that used in the days of square-rigged ships" (Bush 1945, 102). Coined by Theodor H. Nelson in 1965 for describing nonlinear text, the term hypertext was an audacious choice: The *hyper-* prefix has "a bad odor in some fields and can suggest agitation and pathology, as it does in medicine and psychology. But in other sciences *hyper-* connotes extension and generality, as in the mathematical hyperspace, and this was the connotation I wanted to give the idea" (Nelson 1965, 84ff.; Nelson 1992, 49).[3] Current terminology employs the term to signify at least three different but interrelated concepts:

- Systems relying on a rather simple information technology to perform high-speed, branching transactions on textual chunks via associative relationships (Conklin 1987, 17ff.; Lowe and Hall 1999, 30). Some authors use the term *protohypertext* when referring to paper-based texts with paths or similar spatial devices (Aarseth 1998, 75).
- A body of text embedded in and defined by such a system, which can be viewed and accessed in a variety of ways and represents a subcategory of ergodic literature as depicted in Figure 1.1 (Ledgerwood 1997, 549).
- The underlying "science of relationships" (i.e., the interrelationships among objects or pieces of information) and how people can access information using these relationships (Aarseth 1994, 67f.; Landow 1994, 1; Burbules and Callister 1996; Bieber 1997, 1f.).

---

[2]   http://mudlist.eorbit.net/~mudlinks/
[3]   http://www.sfc.keio.ac.jp/~ted/

As an unfortunate result, many assumptions made about the general nature of hypertext confuse these categories and only refer to specific implementations. On top of that, some authors restrict the term hypertext to verbal information and use hypermedia when describing multimedia structures accommodating not only text but also digital sound, graphics, animation, video, or virtual reality (Snyder 1996, ix; Wenz 1997, 576; Díaz and Melster 1999). Due to a lack of convincing reasons to reserve a special term for text-only systems, the term hypertext is used for the structure and content of both types of information throughout this book. As an immediate result of hypertext's capacity to permit the reuse of information, networked structures are created, often distributed logically and geographically over various locations (Landow 1994, 23). The majority of current research efforts focus on such distributed hypertext systems and particularly the World Wide Web, in contrast to stand-alone architectures like Apple's *HyperCard*. From the user's perspective, such environments generally grant only limited privileges to add, modify, or reorganize published documents and are synonymously referred to as read-only, broadcast, or exploratory hypertext (Landow 1994, 9; Snyder 1996, 30; Aarseth 1998, 60).

1.3.1 History

The 1980s as the golden era of hypertext research culminated in the first release of Apple's *HyperCard* and the first major conference on hypertext in 1987. Table 1.1 delineates the history of hypertext, starting with its conceptual foundations back in 1945 (Nielsen 1990, 29ff.; Lowe and Hall 1999, 40). Describing the sequence of ideas, prototypes, and applications until the early 1990s, when prior efforts culminated in the specification and implementation of the World Wide Web, it concludes with a summary of emerging, Web-based standards for encoding hypertext documents (compare with Figure 2.6 of Section 2.2.1: Stage Models for Describing Web Evolution).

Table 1.1. From the Memex to the World Wide Web – The History of Hypertext

Year	Description
1945	Vannevar Bush proposes the Memex (= Memory Extender), a device that would mechanize a more efficient and human mode of retrieving and annotating fact and imagination (Landow 1997, 8).
1965	Theodor H. Nelson coins the term hypertext and envisions a global repository for everything that anybody has ever written, a truly universal hypertext (Xanadu).[4]

---

[4] http://www.xanadu.net/

Year	Description
1967	The world's first true hypertext system is implemented on IBM mainframes: the Hypertext Editing System and FRESS (= File Retrieval and Editing System).
1968	Douglas C. Engelbart demonstrates the NLS (oN-Line-System), part of the Augment project, at the Fall Joint Computer Conference (Engelbart and English 1968, 395ff.; Bardini 1997).[5]
1975	Prototype of the KMS (Knowledge Management System) for military maintenance manuals is developed and later installed on the aircraft carrier USS Carl Vinson in 1983.
1978	The MIT Architecture Machine Group introduces the first hypermedia system, the Aspen Movie Map based on videodiscs.
1983	Various research projects result in a number of prototypes including Hyperties (University of Maryland), Filevision (Telos), Notecards (XeroxPARC), Symbolics Document Examiner (Janet Walker), and Intermedia (Brown University).
1986	The first commercial hypertext system, Guide by Office Workstations Ltd., is released and soon available for both the Macintosh and the IBM PC.
1987	Apple's Hypercard is released and becomes the most famous hypertext product in the late 1980s. At the same time, the first ACM conference on hypertext (Hypertext '87) is held at the University of North Carolina.
1989	The inaugural issue of "Hypermedia", the first scientific journal devoted to hypertext, is published (since 1995: "The New Review of Hypermedia and Multimedia").[6]
1990	Work on the definition of hypertext interchange formats is started through informal meetings of the so-called Dexter Group, which is named after the inn in New Hampshire where it has its first meeting (Lowe and Hall 1999, 68ff.). After the hypertext standardization workshop in 1990, work on hypertext reference models continues through more formal activities at the U.S. National Institute of Standards and Technology (Nielsen 1995, 134).
1991	Tim Berners-Lee and colleagues at CERN, the European Laboratory for Particle Physics near Geneva, present the specifications for the World Wide Web and introduce the Hypertext Markup Language (HTML 1.0).
1993	Mosaic is made available by the National Center for Supercomputing Applications (NCSA) and – prior to the rise of Netscape's Navigator and Microsoft's Internet Explorer – temporarily becomes the most popular browser for accessing the World Wide Web.
1994	In collaboration with CERN, the World Wide Web Consortium (W3C) is founded at the Massachusetts Institute of Technology. W3C's mission is to lead the evolution of the World Wide Web by promoting and developing a software environment that permits each user to make the best use of the resources available, considering the novel legal, commercial, and social issues raised by this technology.[7]
1995	HTML 2.0 becomes proposed standard of the Internet Engineering Task Force (IETF).[8] Divided into several working groups, the IETF is an open international community of network designers, operators, vendors, and researchers concerned with the technical evolution of the Internet architecture.

[5] http://www.csl.sri.com/history/augment.shtml
http://www.histech.rwth-aachen.de/www/quellen/engelbart/
[6] http://www.comp.glam.ac.uk/~NRHM/
[7] http://www.w3.org/Consortium/
[8] http://www.ietf.org/

Year	Description
1996	Responding to the need for an updated specification, the W3C endorses the HTML 3.2 specification as a recommendation. The recommendation represents the consensus on HTML features for 1996 and is published in January 1997. While providing backward compatibility, HTML 3.2 adds widely deployed features such as tables, applets, or text-flow around images.
1997	HTML 4.0 is released as a W3C recommendation in December 1997. In comparison with HTML's previous versions, HTML 4.0 supports additional multimedia options, scripting languages, and style sheets.
1998	The eXtensible Markup Language (XML 1.0), a subset of the Standard Generalized Markup Language (SGML) becomes a W3C recommendation. It is intended to facilitate implementation and to enable interoperability with both SGML and HTML ($\hookrightarrow$ Chapter 4).[9]
1999	To allow advanced information retrieval and provide interoperability between applications that exchange machine-understandable information, the W3C issues the Resource Description Framework (RDF) as an official recommendation in May 1999 (Flammia 1999, 21).
2000	Reformulating HTML 4.0 in XML 1.0, the eXtensible Hypertext Markup Language (XHTML 1.0) is published as W3C recommendation, together with three Document Type Definitions (DTDs) corresponding to the ones defined by HTML 4.0.[10] XHTML is a content language that conforms to XML and operates in HTML-compatible user agents.

1.3.2 Adaptability versus Adaptivity

Adaptivity and hypertext have for a long time been considered as two mutually exclusive approaches, distinguished basically according to navigational control. By avoiding rigid structures or policies governing system behavior, adaptive hypertext systems intend to bridge the gap between these two approaches ($\hookrightarrow$ Chapter 5).

Hypertext systems are traditionally seen user neutral. They provide the necessary tools to navigate freely through complex information spaces. In such an environment, users are responsible for creating and managing their personalized views via bookmarks and the client's default settings. This process, usually referred to as *adaptability*, tends to be confused with the term *adaptivity* (Brusilovsky 1998, 28; Paternò 1999, 89). *Adaptation* represents the intended result, while adaptability and adaptivity are to two different ways to achieve this result. Adaptable systems, on the one hand, encourage human intervention by allowing users to define parameters of the system and its interface representation. Truly adaptive hypertext systems, on the other hand, automatically customize information and present the most relevant material. They reflect some features of individual or stereotypical users including their common access patterns in central, explicitly represented collections of

---

[9] http://www.w3.org/XML/
[10] http://www.w3.org/TR/xhtml1/

data commonly referred to as *user models*. Thereafter, these collections are processed to tailor the content, the navigational system, the interface representation, and various other behavioral aspects of the system to the unique characteristics of those users (↪ Section 5.5: Adaptive Web Presentation Techniques).

Milosavljevic cites the instant generation of the network and its nodes on request of the user as one of the key elements in any *dynamic* hypertext system (Milosavljevic 1998, 29f.). Static structures are replaced entirely, and there may not even be any pre-existing conceptualizations of what could be documents within the system. According to Milosavljevic's definition, *adaptive* hypertext systems require a predefined network of documents and utilize a user model to control the exact sequence of documents to be presented to the user (↪ Section 1.4.5.2: Mapping Textons to Scriptons). However carefully the user's path is tailored, it is always contained within a predefined matrix of possibilities (Snyder 1996, 95). From an external perspective, the distinction between dynamic and adaptive hypertext is hard to verify for deployed systems. As most implementations rely on hybrid approaches, both types of system will be referred to as adaptive hypertext throughout this book. The term dynamic will be used in its more general sense for components and processes whose characteristic attributes change over time. Several authors provide comprehensive summaries of available prototypes and deployed systems in this area (Knott et al. 1996, 151ff.; Brusilovsky 1997, 12ff.; Milosavljevic 1998, 30ff.; Milosavljevic and Oberlander 1998).

1.4   WEB INFORMATION SYSTEMS

Nowadays, there is little disagreement about the fact that information represents a key economic resource and an organizational asset critical to survival. Like other assets, information has both a cost and a value, but with rather unique characteristics (Moody and Walsh 1999, 499ff.). Etymologically, the Latin *"informare"* means to bring something into form, and so in a bizarre way is related to the Greek root *"morph"* as in morphology. Many attempts at defining the term failed (e.g., defining information as the aspect of novelty contained in a message only replaces one vague term by another) with a few notable exceptions. Based on thermodynamic foundations, Shannon and Weaver succeeded to "separate information from semantics by retaining from novelty only the aspect corresponding to indetermination" (Marcus 1997, 16). From a thermodynamic perspective, information is identified with order and organization as opposed to disorder and chaos. The second law of thermodynamics, for example, prescribes that irreversible processes in ordered systems favor destruction of existing order and ultimate decay (Apter 1969, 187; Von Bertalanffy 1974, 11; Mainzer 1997, 5; Marcus 1997, 19).

1.4.1 Theories of Communication

The basic theorem in Shannon and Weaver's theory articulates five components that determine the characteristics of any communication process: *message, source, code, channel,* and *noise* (Shannon and Weaver 1964, 7). It portrays communication as the transmission of a message through a channel having particular technical characteristics and performance. The amount of information transmitted can be defined as the number of bits needed to identify an event that occurs with a certain probability (Mladenic 1998, 42; Bolisani 1999, 31). Noise is synchronously caused by the process and inherent in the object of communication (Ackoff and Emery 1972, 182). *Syntactic noise* emanates from structural differences between a message sent and the message received. *Semantic noise* describes ambiguity in the denotation or connotation of a message. *Pragmatic noise* refers to anything that appears in a message or its environment that was not produced by the sender and that decreases the probability of the receiver's responding in the way intended by the sender (↳ Section 4.5.8: Exploratory Textual Analysis).

Shannon and Weaver's theory asserts that if the entropy of the source is not larger than the capacity of the channel, then there exists a coding mechanism which makes the message safe up to a limited, predefined number of acceptable transmission errors (Shannon and Weaver 1964, 16ff.; Rosie 1969, 154; Sampson 1976, 12). Consequently, Wiener defines information to be the negation of entropy (Wiener 1961, 11). It can be regarded as a measure of a system's degree of organization. Other authors follow a more pragmatic approach and contrast information with two related terms, data and knowledge (Turban and Aronson 1998, 111; Bolisani 1999, 28; Lowe and Hall 1999, 46ff.):

- *Data.* Objective facts about events, activities, or transactions that are recorded, classified, and stored as a vehicle for conveying information.
- *Information.* Data that have a meaning to the recipient within a context set by a priori knowledge and whose form, content, and time of transmission and reception are suitable for a particular use.
- *Knowledge.* Information that guides actions and decisions. Knowledge combines ideas, rules, and procedures to convey understanding, experience, and expertise as they apply to a current problem.

Syntax and semantics have to be defined in advance to deduce knowledge from the information transmitted by means of rational formal methods (Bolisani 1999, 33). In this context, an *information system* can be defined as a linked and related system of entities (including one or more information devices) that provides access to one or more bodies of knowledge and acts as a communication mechanism. The term comprises users interacting with each other and the information device, the designers who create the device, and the information specialists who select and organize the data, and who interact with the users as intermediaries (Allen 1996, 19).

Web information systems represent such linked and related systems of entities. They provide access to organized collections of functionally heterogeneous documents that are publicly available via the World Wide Web and maintained by an organizational entity, although individual and cooperative projects are equally common (Terveen et al. 1999, 81). Web-based applications continually grow in size and feature increasingly complex functionalities. As cooperative development efforts are often necessary, they tend to show a lack of central structure and formal control. By definition, they are meant for a wider user base than traditional applications, whether within an organization (*Intranet*), across a number of organizations (*Extranet*), or over the *Internet*. Not surprisingly, the changed environment leads to a number of concerns about the quality and reliability of such applications (Deshpande et al. 1999) and necessitates modifications to the underlying communication models (↪ Section 2.2.1: Stage Models for Describing Web Evolution).

In most frameworks for applying electronic business models, three application types are usually distinguished (Jutla et al. 1999a, 70): business-to-business, business-to-consumer, and consumer-to-consumer. The term *Web information systems* as used throughout this book is focused on business-to-consumer transactions, although it also comprises Web-based Electronic Data Interchange (EDI) and consumer-to-consumer transaction systems such as *Kasbah | Market Maker* or *eBay* (↪ Section 6.3: Transaction Agents; (Zacharia et al. 1999)).[11] In contrast to systems supporting EDI or wholesale trading, Web-based mass information systems exclusively target individual customers. Mass information systems in general are systems that support online information retrieval and routine tasks by way of self-service for a large number (thousands or millions) of occasional users who are spread over various locations (Hansen 1995, 125; Hansen and Scharl 1998, 994). Web information systems seen as a subcategory of mass information systems –

---

[11] http://maker.media.mit.edu/
       http://www.ebay.com/

next to interactive television, kiosk systems, or automated teller machines, for instance – rely on the distributed hypertext functionality and transfer mechanisms of the World Wide Web. Being characterized by interactivity, dynamic updating, hypertextuality, and global presence they are very similar to the concept of electronic product catalogs, which include any online document whose aim is to convey information about the products and services a commercial entity offers (Segev et al. 1995, 11; Palmer 1997, 6ff.; Milosavljevic 1998, 26).

1.4.2   Media Characteristics of the World Wide Web

No medium can operate in isolation, because it must enter into hierarchical relationships of respect and rivalry with other media (Bolter and Grusin 1999, 98). Thus the content of any medium always represents another type of medium, as every system can be conceptualized as part of another and larger system (McLuhan 1964, 15f.; Ackoff 1974, 29). Emerging media founded on advanced technologies, for example, often do not substitute but enrich and incorporate those that came before. Since computer technology can sustain a multitude of media types and genres with very distinctive characteristics, all the major representational formats of the previous 5000 years of human history are now being translated into digital form (Snyder 1996, 2; Murray 1997, 27).

While the philosophical discussion has continued sporadically, innovations in communication technologies and, more specifically, in the World Wide Web have begun to make the barriers between different forms of communication more permeable than ever (↳ Section 1.4.6: Interactivity). By functionally melding elements of mass, organizational, and interpersonal communication (Rogers 1995, 194ff.; O´Sullivan 1999), the World Wide Web has created "a plethora of design opportunities that are only gradually understood" (Werthner and Klein 1998, 285). *Mass media channels* are essential in disseminating initial information about an innovation. *Organizational channels* and their substantial economic value ensure a continuous supply of resources for establishing the basic infrastructure. Most importantly, *personal channels* are essential to ensure the long-term acceptance of an innovation. Web information systems can be regarded as a true medium as defined by Bentley and Dourish, going beyond rudimentary mechanisms for transmitting structured data (Bentley and Dourish 1995). They provide the unique advantage of simultaneously supporting all three types of channels. Analogous to most successful technologies, Web information systems will eventually become transparent. Users will lose consciousness of the medium and see neither a document nor a computer screen but only the power of the text itself. "If digital art reaches the same level of expressiveness as ... older media, we will no longer concern ourselves with how we are receiving the information. We will only think about what truth it has told us about our lives" (Murray 1997, 26; compare with Nielsen 1999, 67).

1.4.3   Evolving Web Genres

Rhetoricians since Aristotle have attempted to classify recurrent communicative events into genres of similar attributes (Schaeffer 1995; Marcus 1997, 15f.; Eriksen and Ihlström 2000). Web genres, characterized by the triple {content, form, functionality}, facilitate the recognition of similar items in the midst of the great diversity found in the field of electronic communication (Shepherd and Watters 1999). Due to the highly dynamic evolution of the World Wide Web, the boundaries among Web genres tend to be fuzzy. Under the influence of new technologies, they may evolve into new variants of the original genre (Shepherd and Watters 1999). Naturally, organizational goals such as providing access, advertising and selling products, informing the public, creating discussions, or nurturing communities have a strong impact on this evolution of Web genres (Shneiderman 1997a, 12).

Developers of Web information systems usually try to find ways to conceptualize the new medium *World Wide Web* as a platform for evolving (variants of) genres with rather unique features. The familiar layout of a physical store, for example, becomes "a maze of pull-down menus, product indices, and search features. Now more than ever, the promise of electronic commerce and online shopping will depend to a great extent upon the interface and how people interact with the computer" (Lohse and Spiller 1998, 81). Other examples of emerging genres on the World Wide Web are search engines, homepages, link collections, or lists of frequently asked questions (FAQs), to mention a few. Web genres share common aspects of form, content, editorial objects, or socially recognized communicative purpose, such as an inquiry, letter, memo, or meeting (Crowston and Williams 1999). By contrast, general textual categories (narrative, argumentative, descriptive, or instructive) are not genres but can be understood as "pre-genres" that are broadly genre-like in being a way of using language associated with a particular category of purposeful social action. Due to their pervasive character and the multitude of different types, however, it would be misleading to treat these categories as ordinary genres (Fairclough 1995, 90; Titscher et al. 1998, 41).

Once recognized as being of the same genre, the assessment and comparison of information products is facilitated substantially, even if they turn out to be composites of two or more of these genres. Unfortunately, there are no definitive lists of genres and no automatic procedures for deciding what genres are operative in a given document. However, in many cases even basic attributes such as the total number of documents may serve as good indicators for particular Web genres and their complexity (Shneiderman 1997a, 10). Independent of the genre's size and complexity, Fairclough distinguishes three different conceptions of genre in terms of their analytical value:

- *Schematic genres.* Schematic structures made up of obligatory or optional stages, which occur in a fixed or partially fixed order.
- *Heterogeneous genres.* Sequential and embedded forms of textuality, where different generic types alternate within a text, or where one is embedded within the other.
- *Polyphonic genres.* Mixed intertextuality with configurations of non-congruent and sometimes contradictory linguistic features.

While heterogeneous and polyphonic genres are of obvious value for linguistically motivated studies, the schematic perspective will be favored throughout this book as its reduced complexity simplifies longitudinal and comparative analyses (↪ Section 4.5.1: Overview and Analytical Objectives). Nevertheless, it is important to keep in mind the limited value of examining single documents, because most complex genres span multiple documents (↪ Table 1.2). This division of content and the resulting pattern of links affect document form, although there is a class of changes to form related to pagination rather than purpose that does not affect genre (Crowston and Williams 1999).

Table 1.2. Approximate number of documents characteristic for certain Web genres

Documents	Genres
1-10	Personal Bio, restaurant review, project summary, course outline
5-50	Scientific paper, photo portfolio/exhibit, conference program, organization overview
50-500	Book or manual, city guide, corporate annual report, product catalog, advertisement
500-50,000	Photo library, museum tour, technical reports, music/film database
5,000-50,000	University guide, newspaper/magazine
50,000-500,000	Telephone directory, airline schedule
> 500,000	Congressional digest, digital library
> 5,000,000	Library of Congress, NASA archives

1.4.4 Structure and Navigation

Creative metaphors proliferate in science and express the way in which some pioneering fields or challenges make their appearance. Not surprisingly, most information fields are guided by such metaphors

(Marcus 1997, 33). The metaphorical term *navigation* in the context of distributed hypertext systems, for instance, refers to "the ongoing observation of environmental attributes, adjustments to the mental problem representation based on these observations, and the resulting behavioral actions" (Marchionini 1995; compare with Rumpradit and Donnell 1999). These behavioral consequences inevitably lead to questions such as how the powerful but extremely primitive logic of the hyperlink will affect our discursive methods (Aarseth 1994, 81).

Primary and supplemental navigational systems of Web information systems allow the user to experience pleasures specific to intentional navigation: orienting herself by landmarks, mapping a virtual space mentally to match her experience, and admiring the juxtapositions and changes in perspective that derive from moving through an intricate environment (Murray 1997, 129). The *primary navigational system* of a hypertext includes contextual links embedded in the textual information of a document and local non-contextual links (all kinds of links independent of page content such as a set of buttons or pop-up menus). In electronic environments, the user can also verify the relation between different virtual spaces by retracing her steps or employing *supplemental navigational systems* such as indexes, overview diagrams, or guided tours (↪ Section 5.5.4: Meta-Level Adaptation).

Many forms of spatial metaphors common in the real world (navigation, net, maps, paths, trails, signposts) and spatial imagery (three-dimensionality, textual landscapes, topography) inspired the early designers of hypertext systems and are still implemented for reasons of comprehensibility (Wenz 1997, 577; Wexelblat 1999). However, this rhetoric fails to hide the fact that "pure" hypertext is among the least topographical modes of non-linearity and as such is characterized by discontinuity and the sudden displacement of the user's position in the text (Aarseth 1994, 69). The travel metaphor in terms of the frontiers of knowledge as territory to be established, therefore, is problematic when used to characterize the retrieval of unstructured hypertextual information or the access of structured databases (Rosello 1994, 129).

1.4.4.1 *The Myth about Linearity*

Linearity is an important background assumption concerning the structure and presentation of text that is routinely violated when users access electronic media (Gray 1993, 1). Thus the question of linearity is frequently raised as part of the rhetoric of liberation associated with hypertext. It can be asked about a text itself, about different versions of the same text, and about the paratextual material, which consists of conventions for the presentation of a text and its editorial apparatus (Lamont 1997, 57).

"A non-linear text is an object of verbal communication ... in which the words or sequence of words may differ from reading to reading because of the shape, conventions, or mechanisms of the text. ... Linear text may be seen as a special case of the non-linear in which the convention is to read word by word from beginning to end" (Aarseth 1994, 51). Analyzing their relationship, Aarseth describes a peculiar semiotic power of the linear text over the non-linear: The non-linear text cannot lie and pretend to be linear (Aarseth 1994, 54). The linear, however, can flirt with non-linearity – consider, for example, William Gibson's *Agrippa: A Book of the Dead* (Gibson 1992), which was published in a very special and limited edition. It was a set of engravings and a computer diskette including a poem in encrypted form. The engravings were chemically treated to fade away with time. The decrypting program deleted each line of the script after it was displayed at a fixed scrolling pace on the screen, effectively destroying its traversal function after that one projection: "I hesitated before untying the bow that bound this book together" (Gibson 1992).

On the one hand, most standard definitions of a (hyper-)link delineates it as mechanism to connect two pieces of semantically related information within and between documents. On the other hand, every link may be seen as a self-reflexive structure, a place or moment of detour that operates on two planes. In the meta-discourse of the interface, it is the signature of a pause. Phenomenologically, it traces a pure interval, spatiality deferred in time. Reading across the link introduces a discontinuity, an "irreducible gap in the fabric of digital narrative" that cannot be accounted for in a spatial model of the text's narrative structure (Harpold 1994, 196; Barbatsis et al. 1999). "Electronic linking, which provides one of the defining features of hypertext, also embodies Julia Kristeva's notions of intertextuality, Mikhail Bakhtin's emphasis upon multivocality, Michel Foucault's conceptions of networks of power, and Giles Deleuze and Félix Guattari's ideas of rhizomatic,[12] nomad thought" (Landow 1994, 1; Landow 1997, 35ff.).

1.4.4.2 The Labyrinth Metaphor

Writing about the navigational characteristics of hypertext entails the description of an anti-linear style of writing and technology by means of linear text (Snyder 1996, xi). In his *"Philosophical Investigations"*, Ludwig Wittgenstein reveals the difficulties encountered when trying to

---

[12] The aesthetic vision of post-modern hypertext authors often relates to philosopher Gilles Deleuze's *"rhizome"*, a heterogeneous root-like system spreading in all directions, in which any point may be non-hierarchically connected to any other point (Burbules and Callister 1996; Murray 1997, 132).

present complex contents in a linear manner: "My thoughts were soon crippled if I tried to force them on in any single direction against their natural inclination. And this was, of course, connected with the very nature of the investigation" (Wittgenstein 1953, vii; in: Liestøl 1994, 87). Many textbooks and monographs face such difficulties and have to develop effective strategies to maintain structural consistency and avoid confusion of the reader. To post-modernist writers, however, confusion appears to be acceptable; often it is "not a bug but a feature" (Murray 1997, 58). For many of them, *"The Garden of the Forking Paths"* by Jorge L. Borges, telling the story of a seemingly meaningless act of murder, represents the quintessential multiform narrative (Borges 1981, 44ff.; Bolter 1991, 139; Murray 1997, 30ff.). Its permutations inspired several other authors – compare, for example, Stuart Moulthrop's *"Victory garden"*, an interactive hypertext novel intentionally echoing the title of the original short story (Douglas 1994, 160; Murray 1997, 82).

Web information systems are frequently associated with such a virtual labyrinth. In contrast to unicursal labyrinths with only one winding and turning path, usually toward a center, our present idea of a labyrinth is more similar to the Borgesian (multicursal) structure of the forking paths. The multicursal labyrinth symbolizes a bewildering chaos of passages and critical choices that lead to countless directions but never directly to our desired goal. Complex hypertext structures as the manifestation of a multicursal labyrinth require sophisticated means of navigation. Many current tools, however, are insufficient to mitigate the inflexibility caused by the author-imposed fragmentation and fail to overcome "the reader's textual claustrophobia as he skims the *déjà-lu* nodes" (Aarseth 1998, 79). Consequently, like a ship bereft of nautical instruments or maps, users may encounter the frequently cited phenomenon of being *"lost in hyperspace"* – i.e., lose a coherent path through the information due to a lack of understanding of the document's local and global context (Conklin 1987, 17ff.; Horn 1989, 156f.; Ipsen 1997, 570; Kaplan et al. 1998, 46f.; Vassileva 1998, 209; Lowe and Hall 1999, 154ff.).

1.4.5 Textual Characteristics

Traditional texts have created an expectation of structural stability as an inherent feature of the (physical) object text (Wenz 1997, 576). This expectation is misleading, since the elements of meaning, of structure, and of visual display are fundamentally unstable in electronic environments (Bolter 1991, 31). The phenomenon hypertext is constructed by both writers (authors) who initially create the content including link structures and readers who decide which threads to follow. Location of specific information and comprehension are the two principal reading tasks (Guthrie and Kirsch 1987, 220ff.; Boyle 1998, 82). Instead of carefully reading the complete text of retrieved documents, users tend to follow a less strictly coded reading path. They merely scan the document – i.e., visually grasp it as a whole, pick out headings and links most relevant to them, and only read selected paragraphs (Nielsen 1999, 68). Corporate homepages represent the most apparent example. Similar to newspaper front pages, they are complex signs that invite and require an initial reading as one sign. More specific reading then draws its initial orientation from the first reading of the large sign (Kress and Leeuwen 1998, 187f.).

Such a reading strategy has a number of implications for writing and structuring Web documents. Turning around traditional ways of writing, journalists have long adhered to the *inverted pyramid style*: start the article by telling the reader the conclusion, follow by the most important supporting information, and end by giving the background. This approach is equally useful for Web documents, as readers can stop at any time and will still have accessed the most important parts of the document. Only interested readers will scroll, and these "few motivated souls will reach the foundation of the pyramid and get the full story in all its gory detail" (Nielsen 1997).

In this dialogic view of the World Wide Web, the inherent openness of textual information can be turned to advantage. "If it is generally true of reading that a reader imposes an idiosyncratic texture or order on what she takes from a text; if it is generally true that a hermeneutic cycle of interpretation continually changes the understanding of each part as the reader comes to understand others; and if it is generally true that every text is implicitly linked (or linkable) with a virtually infinite variety of other texts; then the technical capacities of hypertext, [which] … are especially suited to incorporate and organize such textual openness, should be exploited to structure it intelligibly" (Burbules and Callister 1996).

In many ways hypertext confirms what deconstructionists and other contemporary literary theorists have been saying about textual instability and the decreasing authority of the writer (Bolter 1991, 153; Snyder 1996, 41). "In 1968 Roland Barthes famously declared the author to be dead, and although creditable attempts at resuscitation have been made, the health of the patient cannot be taken for granted" (Barthes 1977; in: Lamont 1997, 52). The widespread recognition of authorship results from the reader's preference for material of legitimate origin. Authorship as social category depends on its recognition and requires configurative power over not merely content but also over a hypertext's genre and form (Rosello 1994, 145; Aarseth 1998, 164). By reconfiguring the roles of readers and writers and blurring the functional boundaries between them (Snyder 1996, 62; Gay et al. 1999), virtual textuality substantially differs from print textuality. Situated within the complex of cultural practices, the described convergence furthers the impossibility of textual, literary, and cultural critics assuming and defending their self-imposed insularity and separateness of their activities (Ledgerwood 1997, 548; Sutherland 1997, 3f.). Representing a "simulacrum for which no physical instantiation exists" (Landow 1994, 6), hypertext as a new form of textuality is "conspicuously non-print, unheavy, undark, dry, unimprinted, prone to sailing off" (Joyce 1992, 86).

Complexity and comprehensiveness as the very virtues of hypertext make implicit authorial choices all the more essential for the usability of texts and yet all the more difficult for critics to detect. Large Web information systems simply offer too many documents for critics ever to read. They remove mastery and authority, for one can only sample, not master, their documents (Landow 1994, 34f.). "Instead of asking, *What have I read?* the critic might become preoccupied with the question, *Have I read all?* and come to identify the task of interpretation as a task of territorial exploration and technological mastery" (Aarseth 1998, 87). Significant absences, silences, or exclusions in hypertexts are unlikely to be seen or noticed by the vast majority of users. Their high complexity will make hypertexts "all the harder to diagnose and criticize, except by readers of comparable expertise – who, by definition, will be rare" (Burbules and Callister 1996).

1.4.5.1 *Differences between Printed and Electronic Media*

"The stability of paper-based documents is as much a product of our metaphysical belief in a transcendental text as an inherent quality of the physical object" (Aarseth 1994, 55). When confronted with printed media, readers encounter sequentially ordered text as it is structured by the sequence, style, and organization conceived by the author. Occasionally, explicit references are made to other texts within the narrative, but these materials exist outside the body of the document (= the primary text). Distributed hypertext systems lack appropriate cues to mark this division between the primary text and paratextual material. Without such cues, the structure of electronic media begins to blur the idea of what constitutes the primary text, gradually destroying its authoritative vantage point and univocal voice (Burbules and Callister 1996; Jackson 1997). Using the words of Harpold, the "spatial field dividing the textual from the paratextual – concrete in the printed volume, figural in the digital volume (though perhaps no less inevitably a component of how we conceptualize the form of these texts) – is contaminated by, subordinated to, the detour's temporality" (Harpold 1994, 195).

The relative decline of the importance of sequentially ordered text and the observable move towards hierarchically structured textual resources are not trivial phenomena but instances of a more general trend away from certain forms of textual order and coherence (Kress and Leeuwen 1998, 206). Hypertextual non-linearity, as an alterity of textual linearity (mono-sequentiality), can be seen as a topological concept, defined formally and not metaphorically in terms of nodes and links (Aarseth 1998, 43). Hypertexts, however, are usually not so much experienced as non-linear but as multi-linear or multi-sequential (Snyder 1996, 16; Wenz 1997, 581). Computerization organizes sequential engagement with non-sequential forms of knowledge and experience – "immediate encounters with abstract or complexly mediated forms" (McGann 1997, 22). In such an environment, linearity becomes a "quality of the individual reader's experience within a single lexia and his or her experience of following a particular path, even if that path curves back upon itself or heads in strange directions" (Landow 1992, 104). In other words, the act of reading reduces the multidimensional non-linearity of space to the one-dimensional linearity of time (Liestøl 1994, 103ff.; Wenz 1997, 577). The temporal dimension is in itself far from trivial, as accessing Web information systems can create vast differences between the perceived time sphere of the virtual world on the one hand and the user's personal working time on the other. Ipsen categorizes these differences into *acceleration, retardation,* and *repetition* (Ipsen 1997, 569).

Unlike a certain page of a book, the complete work is not reassuringly available to the user during the time she is reading a particular document. By linking only between a document and its intended successor, authors can enforce the perception of a single narrative rather than allowing users to move around at random. Such a predetermined path actually provides the user with fewer navigational choices than a printed version of the same text would offer (Sutherland 1997, 12; Crowston and Williams 1999). Although its printed sequence is suggestive and controlling and readers are expected to begin at a clearly marked point (Snyder 1996, 68), every book can be read out of order. Depending on the category a particular book belongs to, this "random access" may happen quite frequently (e.g., encyclopaedias, reference manuals, textbooks, or experimental fiction). The same holds true for the daily newspaper, which exemplifies a document composed of discrete subjects grouped according to certain subject categories (Landow 1994, 24). Not surprisingly, electronic newspapers were amongst the first customizable applications to be found on the World Wide Web.

1.4.5.2 Mapping Textons to Scriptons

Every body of hypertext consists of a varying number of textual segments. Those segments are called *"lexias"* and are generic chunks of
information that occupy a virtual space – preceded by, followed by, and
placed next to an infinite number of other lexias (Murray 1997, 55).
They are "units of local stability in the general flux of the hypertext"
(Snyder 1996, 46). Textons and scriptons represent two different subsets
of lexias. Aarseth defines a *texton* as an arbitrarily long string of graphemes (letters) being identified by its relation to the other units as constrained and separated by the conventions or mechanisms of their
mother text (Aarseth 1994, 60). A *scripton* is an unbroken sequence of
one or more textons as they are projected by the text during the reading
process. The reader has the choice to read the whole scripton or only
parts of it before following a link. As a consequence, scriptons are not
necessarily identical to what readers actually read, but what an ideal
reader would read by strictly following the linear structure of the textual
output (Aarseth 1998, 62).

This manipulation and imposing of a different order *(ordo artificia-
lis)* upon the given structure of stored textons *(ordo naturalis)* may be
characterized as an operation of the orator (hypertext reader) within the
boundaries established by the enabling technologies (Liestøl 1994, 100).
In addition to its textons, therefore, a text has to comprise one or more
traversal functions that combine and project textons as scriptons to the
user of the text. In terms of the *Dexter Hypertext Reference Model*, this
process maps the underlying storage layer to the presentation layer,
actually linearizing textons as entities of a spatial, networked configuration of nodes and links (Halasz and Schwartz 1994; Wenz 1997, 581).
Adaptive hypertext generation supports this process by providing dynamic and highly customizable traversal functions (↪ Section 5.5:
Adaptive Web Presentation Techniques). After retrieving a number of
relevant textons being stored in the back-end databases, these techniques transform textons into hypertext documents (= customized sets
of scriptons). Applied to the topology of a text, non-linearity is found
when scriptons are not presented in one fixed sequence, whether temporal or spatial, but in an arbitrary sequence through cybernetic agency.

Aarseth presents seven attributes that characterize traversal functions of textual communication (Aarseth 1994, 61f.; Aarseth 1998, 62ff.),
which will also be employed to analyze the evolutionary stages of Web
information systems in Chapters 3-6:

- *Dynamics.* Nodes and links constantly appear, disappear, or evolve,
  creating a network of multiple discursive sequences (↪ Section 2.1:
  Darwinian versus Technological Evolution). This dynamic process,

which is characterized by the changing contents of scriptons, requires permanent management. The number of textons can either remain fixed (intratextonic dynamics) or may vary as well (textonic dynamics).

- *Determinability* (stability of the traversal function). A text is determinant if the adjacent scriptons of every scripton are always the same.

- *Transiency.* If the mere passing of the user's time causes scriptons to appear, an electronic document is called transient.

- *Perspective.* Texts with a personal perspective require the user to play a strategic role in the (virtual) world described by them. The majority of Web information systems can be regarded as impersonal textual communication. They usual favor the language's textual function (i.e., creating well-formed and appropriate text) and ideational function (i.e., representing thought and experience in a coherent way), putting less emphasis on its interpersonal function to initiate and maintain social interaction between author and reader (Fairclough 1995, 58; Yule 1996, 83).

- *Access.* This attribute distinguishes random access to all scriptons and controlled (arbitrary) access that limits the availability of documents at a given time (↪ Section 1.4.4: Structure and Navigation).

- *Linking.* If semantic associations between lexias are established, they can be implemented as explicit or conditional links.

- *User functions.* (a) *Interpretative* – user reflects about the meaning of the text, (b) *explorative* – user must decide which path to take, (c) *configurative* – scriptons are temporarily chosen or created by the user, and (d) *textonic* – user may permanently change or annotate the text (↪ Section 1.2: Ergodic Literature).

1.4.6   Interactivity: An Ambiguous Term

Many authors are particularly effusive in their praise of the World Wide Web's interactive features (Bucy et al. 1999). Consequently, the rather vaguely and pervasively used term *interactivity* is also heavily stressed in commercial rhetoric. It denotes a "theoretical construct that grapples with the origins of captivation, fascination, and allure that can be inherent in computer-mediated groups" (Rafaeli and Sudweeks 1997). The term interactivity becomes less ambiguous when used in a clarifying context. Interactive visualization, for instance, is a very specific area of research. It is concerned with view types and their effective transformation, enabling users to exert control over particular graphical interface representations (↪ Section 5.5.4: Meta-Level Adaptation). Originally derived from the physical sciences, interactivity involves reciprocal action or influence. It represents mutual and simultaneous activities on the part of two or more actors, not necessarily human. Despite the disparities in the respective positions of the machine and the human, the use of the term *interactivity* for describing informational processes between them is well supported by the "reactive, linguistic, and internally opaque characteristics of machine-based artifacts" (Suchman 1987; Gray 1993, 21).

Although being required for a number of real-time applications, most definitions do not include the actors' co-presence in time as an inherent characteristic. For humans, interactivity applies to a very large number of quite different social encounters (Yule 1996, 71). Focusing on information systems, Murray characterizes interactivity as an attribute of procedural, participatory environments (Murray 1997, 71ff.). While the term *procedural* stands for the ability to execute a series of rules, only *participatory* systems allow the user to induce this rule-generated behavior.

Several attempts have been made both in scholarly and popular literature to operationalize the concept of interactivity. Nevertheless, curiously few formal definitions are available. The majority of these definitions focus on specific aspects of interactivity. Accordingly, the following sections describe three important determinants of interactivity: media permeability, communication patterns, and discourse structure.

1.4.6.1 Media Permeability

Interactivity is related to permeability, which may involve different sense modalities and occur in one or several dimensions. The type and possible direction of this permeability are important attributes to characterize different media (Sonesson 1997, 73f.; O'Sullivan 1999). The telephone, for example, offers two-way permeability to audio information via non-mediated messages between a very small number of participants (usually two), who have knowledge of each other. Television offers one-way permeability to simple audio-visual information of fixed format via mediated messages delivered to large, undifferentiated audiences. By providing multi-way permeability to complex audio-visual information of variable format, the World Wide Web effectively melds the elements of various other types of media (↪ Section 1.4.2: Media Characteristics of the World Wide Web). Thus it is not an exaggerated prediction that the Internet, spurred on by the World Wide Web, will someday supersede these other forms of communication (Choi et al. 1997, 10).

1.4.6.2 Communication Patterns

Rogers defines communication as the "process in which participants create and share information with one another in order to reach a mutual understanding. This definition implies that communication is a process of convergence (or divergence) as two or more individuals exchange information in order to move toward each other (or apart) in the meanings that they give to certain events" (Rogers 1995, 6). Consequently, interactivity is not just a condition. It is a continuum, a dynamic variable of responsiveness that measures the extent to which communication reflects back on itself, feeding on and responding to the past (Newhagen and Rafaeli 1996; Rafaeli and Sudweeks 1997). Interactivity delineates the "media's potential ability to let the user exert an influence on the content and/or form of the mediated communication" (Jensen 1998, 201). Seen as a process variable based on the relatedness of sequential messages, it is an "expression of the extent that, in a given series of communication exchanges, any third (or later) transmission (or message) is related to the degree to which previous exchanges referred to even earlier transmissions" (Rafaeli 1988, 11; in: McMillan 1999a).

1.4.6.3 Discourse Structure

Emphasizing the procedural character of communication, interactivity can be understood as a formal element of conversations, both unmediated and mediated. It is limited neither to two people nor to face-to-face communication (Schultz 1999). An interactive hypertext system, for example, allows the reader to physically change the discourse in a way that is interpretable and produces meaning within the discourse itself. The reader's interaction is an integrated part of the system's sign production (Andersen 1990, 89; Aarseth 1998, 49).

A sound theoretical framework for the World Wide Web's interactive features is provided by discourse analysis, in its most general sense covering "constructions or significations of some domain of social practice from a particular perspective" (Fairclough 1995, 94). The term includes an extremely wide range of activities, from narrowly focused investigations of word usage to the study of dominant ideologies in a culture (Yule 1996, 83). The related term *conversation* can be understood as a set of linguistic units that are larger than a sentence and involve at least two participants (Schiffrin 1989; Jasper et al. 1998). While *syntax* is the study of language patterns at the sentence or utterance level (↪ Section 4.5.8: Exploratory Textual Analysis), *discourse analysis* is the study of such patterns at the conversation level. When restricted to Web information systems, discourse analysis is mainly used to de-

scribe the structures of such "conversations" between authors of published documents and their target audience (Jasper et al. 1998). As single user requests provide less information than the functional group
with which those requests are associated, utterances are either examined as pairs or larger groups of utterances (↪ Section 4.4.3: Units of
Analysis).

2 The Evolution of Electronic Markets

The term "paradigm" gained prominence after the original publication of *The Structure of Scientific Revolutions* by Thomas S. Kuhn in 1962 and has since been applied in multiple contexts, scientific and otherwise (Earman 1993, 19; McMullin 1993, 56ff.; Kuhn 1996). Information technology is consistent with this paradigm-shifting view of scientific revolution. Electronic commerce, the newest addition to the succession of information technology paradigms, grows progressively on an unprecedented scale. Momentous changes in the performance of deployed systems, the organizational structure, and the corporate value chain strongly influence this new paradigm (Beam and Segev 1996; Brandtweiner and Scharl 1999b, 8). The unprecedented success and rapid evolution of electronic commerce is not only grounded on the World Wide Web's simple means for authoring documents and accessing its vast resources, but also in its effective support for a variety of communication models of diverse complexity. The evolution of mediated forms of communication rarely leads to their extinction. Unsurprisingly, computer-mediated environments such as the World Wide Web are no exception. However, whereas deployed systems and established communication models may not go into instant extinction, they will be radically transformed by the emergence of new technologies.

This chapter presents a conceptual framework based on distinct communication patterns that classifies information systems according to their level of technological sophistication and their customizability. Necessary preconditions for an adequate consideration of customer-specific parameters in adaptive system solutions for electronic commerce will be identified. This primarily inductive process includes the:

- Detailed description and analysis of the evolution of the infrastructure for electronic markets in general and Web-based applications in particular; and the
- Classification of system adaptability and adaptivity with regard to conceptual design and implementation – from client-side browser preferences for formatting documents to highly complex server applications involving the use of decision support systems, adaptive negotiation support systems, and distributed artificial intelligence (Segev et al. 1997).

2.1 DARWINIAN VERSUS TECHNOLOGICAL EVOLUTION

The Darwinian theory of evolution describes the emergence and growth of species on earth for several billion years, providing a causal explanation of the morphological similarities among living organisms that are characterized by caloric, chemo-dynamic, cellular, and cybernetic processes. This organismic perspective became widely accepted in other disciplines as well, replacing the term "organism" by "organized entity", which includes a variety of heterogeneous concepts such as social groups, personalities, or technological devices. These entities are definable only by cohesion in a broad sense, that is, the interactions of their constituting elements. {Node, connector, resource} triads are not only typical for ecosystems {species, foodweb interactions, biochemicals} or biological systems such as the central nervous system {nerve cells, nerve cell interconnections, pulses}. They also characterize networked computing environments {computer stations, cables, messages} or, more specifically, the World Wide Web {nodes, hyperlinks, documents}. In this sense, Web information systems are just as real as biological organisms (Von Bertalanffy 1974, 12ff.; Holland 1995, 23).

Thus in the mathematical framework of complex systems, the term *evolution* does not generally refer to genetic mechanisms and the particular process of biological evolution. In a complex system, evolutionary equations describe the dynamics of its elements, which may be elementary particles, atoms, molecules, organisms, humans, organizations, or documents (Mainzer 1997, 282). For this reason the concept of evolution has been extended to other areas of human discourse like sociopolitical theory or economics to explain dynamic change over time, sometimes with "an implicit gradualness to distinguish it from revolution" (Fabian 1998, 1). The crucial issue here is how to delineate, analyze, and design complex systems that feature emergent behavior and evolve unpredictably from an initial set of simple elements. For eons, the earth has constantly been changing and evolving. These environmental changes were the driving force behind biological evolution. Compared to this fundamental process, the history of the World Wide Web and its applications spanning approximately ten years seems both rather insignificant and far beyond Darwin's primary concerns at the same time.

At first glance there are few common processes or evident similarities that could guide conceptual Web design. By applying general biological terminology to adaptive Web representations, however, a number of analogies can be identified (↪ Table 2.1). *Ontogenesis* stands for the individual development of organisms (= life-cycles of an organization's published documents). On a larger scale, *phylogenesis* refers to the evolution of the whole species (= genre of documents). A *genome* is the complete collection of an organism's *genes* (= underlying database system) – i.e., the set of instructions that genetically determine an organism's ontogenesis. Consequently, genes (= textons stored in the database) are the biochemical units that carry hereditary characteristics from parent to offspring. Found in every nucleus of an organism's many trillions of cells, they consist of tightly coiled threads of deoxyribonucleic acid (DNA) and associated protein molecules (= textual content). *Genotype* refers to an organism's genetic constitution (= database representation), while *phenotype* denotes the individual's observable characteristics or traits (= hypertextual Web representation), as determined by the genotype and the environment (= user and task models).

Table 2.1. Comparison of Darwinian and technological terminology

Term	Darwinian Evolution	Web Evolution
Ontogenesis	Individual growth of organisms	Life-cycle of Web documents
Phylogenesis	Evolution of species	Evolution of Web genres
Genome	Complete set of genetic information	Underlying database system
Genotype	Genetic constitution of organism	Database representation
Phenotype	Observable characteristics of organism	Hypertext representation

The dynamic change within the population (= deployed Web information systems), therefore, may be regarded as the ongoing competition between various pieces of information (= textons) and their representation in hypertext documents (= scriptons) for the user's attention, which is limited in front of such a wealth of information. This attention usually correlates with the perceived utility that the documents provide regarding the user's current tasks and goals. Even the agent-mediated architectures of Chapter 6 conform to this conceptualization, with each selling agent proactively defending its principal's particular interest. The agent's parameters regarding competence, performance, and relevance determine the perceived utility and the outcome of this competition (Geldof 1997). Design Darwinism, as coined by Nielsen, will tend to drive out flamboyant documents of poor content (or agents of poor functionality), and concentrate traffic at documents with higher selective value – e.g., those that follow certain usability principles (Nielsen 1999, 67). Documents that do not deliver any additional value to customers will be eliminated from the hypertext structure in the long run (= natural selection). The fitness function is replaced by the perceived utility function (Holland 1995, 89; Fogel 1997, 277), which can be approximated by analyzing access patterns or acquiring explicit user feedback (compare with Section 2.3.2: Redefining the Customer-Delivered Value). Thus the information regarding the documents' specific appeal to the envisioned target group plays a vital role in updating (= mutation) and restructuring (= recombination) the content of Web information systems.

The analogy between Darwinian and technological evolution provides an intuitive but only partial explanation for the dynamic character of the World Wide Web. Since biological mutation, defined as suddenly appearing and well-defined inheritable variation, is a random process, changes can be useful, unfavorable, or neutral to the individual's survival. Conceptual Web design, however, can hardly be described as a random process. Even adaptive hypertext documents do not act and reproduce; they are authored, redesigned, or eliminated by the Web designer or the department(s) responsible for the content of a particular domain. In contrast to the rise of biological species, the development of Web information systems requires creativity and intelligent planning during the pre-deployment phase (initial analysis, design, and implementation). This phase is referred to as *internal (r)evolution* in Figure 2.1 (Österle 1995, 23; Scharl 1997b, 54; Bauer et al. 1999a, 55). The diagram contrasts the initial investment with the processes that characterize the succeeding maintenance phase *(= external evolution)*.

To acknowledge the importance of creativity and intelligent planning, Martin introduces the term *intelligent evolution* (Martin 1996, 217). With special emphasis upon corporate business behavior, he compares three types of evolution with the classic Darwinian evolution based on the survival of the fittest (or *differential reproduction* in modern terminology):[13]

---

[13] Describing the mechanisms of natural selection as antithetical to the idea of species as stable systems, Charles R. Darwin incorporated the term "survival of the fittest" into later editions of *On the Origin of Species by Means of Natural Selection* (Darwin 1859; Eldredge 1995, 174). Nevertheless, it was the social philosopher Herbert Spencer who originally coined the term (Caudill 1997, 71).

- Internal (r)evolution:
    - First-order evolution modifies Web information systems according to continuously changing market requirements. Predesigned processes ensure conformity with the existing corporate structure. This concept resembles Utterback's definition of product innovation (Utterback 1996). Frequently, multiple product innovations are required at the same time to be adopted by the envisioned target group (Rogers 1995; Treloar 1999, 155).
    - Second-order evolution modifies the development process, the chosen methodology, or the fundamental design of work. Utterback uses the term process innovation to describe this organizational change, which usually aims at reducing costs or raising quality (Utterback 1996).
- External evolution:
    - Third-order evolution considers external factors outside the corporation such as relationships with customers, other companies, governmental institutions, or standardization committees.

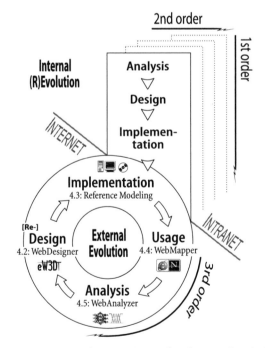

Figure 2.1. Distinction between internal and external evolution

First-order evolution mirrors the classic approach of systems analysis and design methodologies. Frequently, predesigned processes and static corporate structures are considered as independent variables not subject to evolutionary change. Propagating second-order evolution helps developers overcome the limitations of this traditional approach such as lack of continuity or the consideration of system evaluation and quality control as post-hoc processes (Allen 1996, 291). Companies should optimize and extend their development methodologies, reengineer the corresponding processes, and question established concepts and theories regarding the organizational integration and strategic importance of Web information systems.

2.1.1 Alternative Life-Cycle Economies

Definition, development, and maintenance of corporate information systems can be structured in various ways. The traditional *systems development life-cycle (SDLC)*, often referred to as the *waterfall model*, prescribes a number of consecutive stages. While most authors do not use a uniform terminology and often present variations of the standard model, they usually agree on the following general sequence: (a) project identification, (b) requirements specification, (c) analysis, (d1) architectural design, (d2) logical design, (d3) physical design, (e) coding and unit testing, and (f) operation and maintenance (Senn 1987, 603ff.; Avison and Fitzgerald 1988, 13; Hansen 1996b, 136; Dix et al. 1998, 149; Hoffer et al. 1999, 24ff.; Kendall and Kendall 1999, 7ff.; Lowe and Hall 1999, 19; Noyes and Baber 1999, 86f.).

Even though some of these phases inevitably overlap, many of the early models assumed that a new phase could only be initiated when a *milestone* (availability of a pre-specified set of artifacts) had been reached. Even popular object-oriented process frameworks such as the *Rational Unified Process* continue this tradition (Fowler and Scott 1997, 14ff.; Jacobson et al. 1999, 11). By assuming such sequential and orderly projects, conventional life-cycles tend to be inaccurate and simplistic. They neglect that the real world is subject to various constraints, interruptions, distractions, emotions, personalities, and politics (Rubinstein and Hersh 1984; Noyes and Baber 1999, 84). Thus the waterfall model gives no indication of how *exceptional situations* can be handled (↪ Section 2.3.1: Evaluating Transactional Infrastructures).

2.1.1.1 Prototyping

In the early 1980s, *prototyping* was introduced to bypass the rigid stages of the waterfall model (Naumann and Jenkins 1982, 29ff.). Often relying on *computer-aided software engineering (CASE)*, a prototype allows the interface to be tried and tested before the final system has been constructed. Prototyping can be characterized along two dimensions:

- *Modeling approach.* Possible alternatives range from minimal paper-based approaches to computer-based conceptual designs to elaborate simulations of part or all of the system.
- *Temporal extent.* This dimension describes the temporal continuum covered by a particular prototype (Dix et al. 1998, 174; Turban and Aronson 1998, 294f.).

  □ *Throwaway.* Prototype is built, tested, and then discarded.
  □ *Incremental.* Components of the prototype are built separately. The final system is being released as a series of products.
  □ *Evolutionary.* The prototype is not discarded, but refined iteratively over a longer trial period and then released.

If enough representative functions are implemented to make the prototype resemble a real system, feedback about the proposed system and about how readily it is fulfilling specific requirements can be elicited from the potential users (↪ Section 5.2: Classic Loop of Adaptation). For Web-based applications and their a priori anonymous audience, however, it is generally challenging to generate a representative sample of users prior to the actual deployment of the system.

Some authors cite the lengthy process with numerous iterations or the adoption of inadequate systems as disadvantages of prototyping, especially when it is embedded into the standard development life-cycle (Kendall and Kendall 1999, 209). This applies to traditional information systems for which updates are only released at certain intervals. By contrast, Web information systems are never regarded as "complete". They are continually modified and extended, which distinguishes evolutionary Web development from prototyping and related approaches. Even though initial design steps prior to deployment often enlarge the system's functionality, Web development efforts are not necessarily additive. Frequently, superficial designs are only replaced by more detailed and sophisticated ones (Jacobson et al. 1999, 7).

2.1.1.2 Organizational Emergence

Traditionally, the long life span and low volatility of corporate information systems hinder organizational emergence, inhibiting rather than facilitating organizational change. Non-evolutionary prototyping, participatory design, end-user development, object-oriented approaches, open systems connectivity, or business process reengineering are only partial solutions to this problem. The dynamic nature of electronic markets requires more fundamental approaches that redefine the role of commercial organizations. Such an organization represents "a purposeful system that contains at least two purposeful elements which have a common purpose relative to which the system has a functional division of labor; its functionally distinct subsets can respond to each other's behavior through observation or communication; and at least one subset has a system-control function" (Ackoff 1974, 37).

Commercial organizations participating in electronic markets are no longer stable, but have to adapt continuously to their rapidly shifting environment. This adaptation refers to both the functional division of labor (including the system-control function) and prevalent communication models. Modern organizations can said to be "in a state of constantly seeking stability, while never achieving it" (Truex et al. 1999, 117). Thus there is a need to radically rethink (Web) information systems development. Web-based applications require a continuous and evolutionary (re-)development perspective. Such a perspective comprises iterative cycles of evaluation and refinement. The number and frequency of these iterations depends on the type of application, the users' expectations, and the desired degree of perfection.

2.1.1.3 Types of Maintenance

Claiming up to 80 per cent of the information systems budget, maintenance remains the largest systems development expenditure for many organizations (Pressman 1996; Hoffer et al. 1999, 805; Kendall and Kendall 1999, 12; Lowe and Hall 1999, 293). Therefore, minimizing maintenance efforts represents a highly valued goal of traditional information systems development, trying to recoup soaring initial costs over the long period of low-cost operation (Truex et al. 1999, 119). In such an environment, which focuses on minimizing costs and lacks the fierce competition and changing customer demands of global electronic markets, early approaches to software evolution and rapid prototyping had only limited impact on general business practices (Belady and Lehman 1976; Luqi 1989; Arthur 1991).

The maintainability of applications, defined as the ease with which software and its components can be understood, corrected, adapted, and enhanced (Hoffer et al. 1999, 812), is crucial in Web-based environments. Developers should not have to worry about "the effects of the change reverberating unexpectedly throughout the system" (Jacobson et al. 1999, 64). Figure 2.2 contrasts types of system maintenance and their relative importance in the traditional systems development lifecycle with the changed requirements of evolutionary Web development. Maintenance activities are grouped into four distinct categories (Andrews and Leventhal 1993, 21; Hoffer et al. 1999, 810ff.; Lowe and Hall 1999, 189):

- *Corrective maintenance*, which repairs defects in the design, coding, or implementation of the system, is the only category that adds little or no value to the organization or its customers (↪ Section 2.3.2: Redefining the Customer-Delivered Value). Nevertheless, most defects need to be resolved immediately to curtail possible interruptions in normal business activities. As defects tend to surface soon after installation or major system changes, evolutionary approaches to Web development, which do not require such regular discontinuities, substantially reduce the need for corrective measures.

- *Adaptive maintenance* evolves the system's core functionality to accommodate changing business needs, additional user requirements, or technological advances (Kendall and Kendall 1999, 11f.). To compete successfully in dynamic electronic markets, the relative increase of adaptive maintenance as depicted in Figure 2.2 is necessary and complies with the postulations of evolutionary Web development.

- *Perfective maintenance* enhances performance or interface usability, two important criteria that influence the perceived quality of Web information systems.

- *Preventive maintenance* safeguards the application from possible future failures by adding or updating components to (a) handle anticipated changes such as a soaring access frequencies, or to (b) increase flexibility and the system's capability to handle unexpected situations – i.e., extending the system's "area of validity" (↪ Section 2.3.1: Evaluating Transactional Infrastructures).

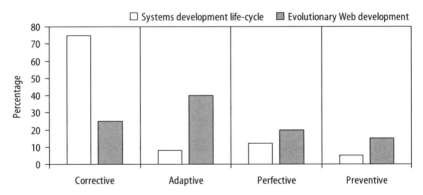

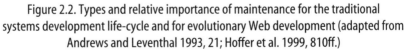

Figure 2.2. Types and relative importance of maintenance for the traditional systems development life-cycle and for evolutionary Web development (adapted from Andrews and Leventhal 1993, 21; Hoffer et al. 1999, 810ff.)

For functional components of Web information systems, the time-to-market lag from conception to delivery (publication) can be as short as a few hours. This necessitates an evolutionary approach to their pro-

duction with multiple-staged deliveries throughout their life-cycle
(Norton 1999). Lengthy analysis, centralized design, and rigid process
infrastructures are poor investments in such a volatile environment,
which calls for development plans that optimize for high maintenance
characteristics. The accelerated nature of electronic markets does not
support long periods of low volatility and minimum maintenance.
Profits go to the quick and responsive players who are able to leverage
emerging technologies (Mena 1999, 9). Section 2.3.1, Evaluating Transactional Infrastructures, introduces a formal model to analyze and
evaluate alternative process infrastructures throughout their lifetime,
considering the impact of automation on process flexibility, maintainability, and customer value.

2.1.1.4 Stable System Drag

Porter characterizes innovation in the traditional product life-cycle as
both a response to incentives created by an industry's overall structure
and a shaper of that industry. "Through successive product innovation
and imitation, the uncertainty about appropriate product characteristics is reduced and a dominant design emerges. Growing scale makes
mass production feasible, reinforced by the growing product standardization. Technological diffusion eliminates product differences and
compels process innovation by firms in order to remain cost competitive. Ultimately, diminishing returns to process innovation set in, reducing innovative activity altogether" (Porter 1998, 195). High initial
costs, which are characteristic for such a scenario, seem counterproductive in constantly changing environments; they tend to increase the
stable system drag. Truex et al. use this term for a condition in which
the organization has to deal with both its dynamically changing environment and its outdated information infrastructure (Truex et al. 1999,
118). Stable system drag as depicted in Figure 2.3 can be eliminated by
continuously redeveloping Web-based applications. The goal is to prevent diminishing returns to process innovation as described above,
which usually lead to the application's obsolescence. Traditionally,
many organizations tried to determine how long they should maintain
their information systems (Hoffer et al. 1999, 806; Kendall and Kendall
1999, 12). This question is becoming increasingly irrelevant. By not
allowing a system to "decay beyond its economic rescue point" (Truex
et al. 1999, 122), the need for termination at the end of its planned life-
cycle is eliminated. To what extent the initial investment can be reduced
(thin dotted lines) largely depends on both business sector and organizational structure.

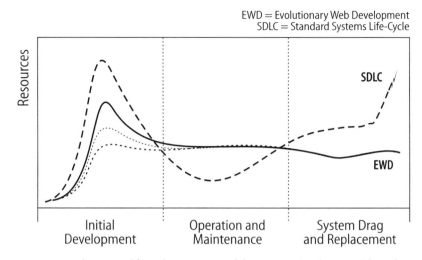

Figure 2.3. Alternative life-cycle economies of the systems development life-cycle and evolutionary Web development (adapted from Truex et al. 1999, 119)

2.1.2 Electronic Business Ecosystems

"The virtual economy, by its very nature, facilitates – and in some ways requires – convergence in products, processes, infrastructure, and market space" (Choi et al. 1997, 553). Many consumer products converge since digital formats have made it unnecessary to distinguish between different representations. The same trend is responsible for process and infrastructure convergence (↪ Section 2.3.1: Evaluating Transactional Infrastructures). Handling digital transmissions, for example, can be implemented and optimized regardless of the data format being transmitted. Most importantly, global network structures imply a spatial and organizational convergence of markets, grouping together formerly independent market participants.

Especially third-order (external) evolution relies on this concept of a *business ecosystem*, comprised of several independent organizations. The term is based on the ecology-oriented framework proposed by Moore, which aims at analyzing the complex dynamics of modern companies. Moore concludes that businesses are not just members of certain industries, but parts of a particular business ecosystem that incorporates a whole bundle of different industries. The driving force is not pure competition but *co-evolution,* sometimes also referred to as *co-opetition* (Martin 1996, 147), implying that companies work cooperatively and competitively at the same time. Both Charles R. Darwin and the social philosopher Herbert Spencer accommodated cooperation as well as competition in evolution (Caudill 1997, 72).

Formally defined, a business ecosystem represents "an economic community supported by a foundation of interacting organizations and individuals – the organisms of the business world. This economic community produces goods and services of value to customers, who themselves are members of the ecosystem. ... Over time they co-evolve their capabilities and roles, and tend to align themselves with the direction set by one or more central companies" (Moore 1997, 26). Members of the ecosystem center their efforts on innovation and the development of new products to create and satisfy individual customer needs (Moore 1993). Even if advances in technology do not yield competitive advantage to any one company, they may positively affect the industry's structure and its overall profit potential (Porter 1998, 172).

2.1.2.1 Autopoietic Self-Reference

In systems theory, two principal ideas were advanced to deal with the problem of order and organization in complex non-linear systems. One was the comparison with man-made machines. The other was to conceive of order as a product of chance, expressed by the evolution of probabilistic distributions and the Darwinian idea of natural selection (Von Bertalanffy 1974, 11; Mainzer 1997, 3).

Maturana and Varela emphasize the second aspect. They use the term *autopoiesis* to characterize systems that maintain their defining organization throughout a history of environmental perturbation by continuously regenerating their components (Maturana and Varela 1980; Whitaker 1995). Similar to most organizational entities, business ecosystems are characterized by autopoietic self-reference, which is based on the notion that the significance of a given system's character or behavior is meaningful only with respect to itself. Business ecosystems use their own identity and socially constructed reality as the primary point of reference when reconstructing themselves (Truex et al. 1999, 118). Unlike their biological counterparts, however, they have a predefined, carefully planned purpose and a long-term vision for the future (Martin 1996, 144).

2.1.2.2 Chronological Development and Demarcation

By analyzing the chronological development of business ecosystems, four distinct stages can be identified (Moore 1993; Moore 1997): Birth, Expansion, Authority, and Renewal (or Death). In the *pioneering stage* (Birth), cooperative behavior usually represents the preferable option. In the *expansion stage,* the ecosystem has to broaden its concept to reach a global audience. Grim and costly fights for supremacy and control in the particular business ecosystem characterize the *authority stage.* In the *renewal stage*, tracking new trends and anticipating them with corporate strategies deserves highest priority. Comparing the evolution of the Web infrastructure as outlined in Section 2.2.1: Stage Models for Describing Web Evolution with Moore's sequential approach, strong similarities are revealed.

In addition to companies with their active and potential customers, the business ecosystem also includes government agencies, regulatory organizations, and a number of additional stakeholders mentioned in the shaded areas of Figure 2.4 (compare with Scharl 2000b, 107). All members of such an ecosystem are responsible for the prosperity of this particular system. For establishing a new business ecosystem, even competitors have to cooperate. They are allies in the competition with other business ecosystems, but rivals within the boundaries of their own system. Martin concludes that leading corporations have to evolve rapidly the ecosystems in which they participate so that those ecosystems develop a need for the types of products in which they can claim a competitive advantage (Martin 1996, 217). Thus business ecosystems constantly broaden and shrink, particularly under the influence of emerging technologies. Web information systems, for instance, enlarge the geographical scope of many markets, blur organizational boundaries, and fold whole industries together. They often introduce or enhance products, thereby bringing new customers and competitors into the virtual marketplace (Porter 1998, 175).

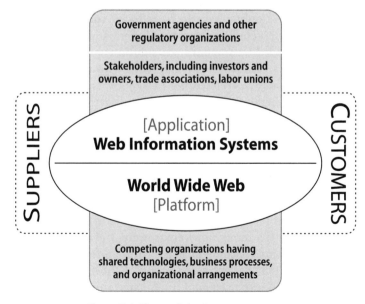

Figure 2.4. Electronic business ecosystems
(adapted from Scharl and Brandtweiner 1998a, 41)

2.1.2.3 Critical Mass of Content and Adopters

Assuming that the development of electronic markets follows the stages identified by Moore (with Web information systems representing the primary enabling technology), we currently find ourselves at the beginning of the expansion stage. One of the most important findings of the *"Web 2000 Growth report"* (Smithson 2000) is that many of the world's largest and best-established enterprises undergo substantial changes and rapidly develop into the most successful proponents of electronic commerce. This phenomenon reflects the superior resources of big companies. Among the most important challenges for these companies are the conversion of antagonistic relationships into mutualistic ones (Martin 1996, 147), the support of cross-corporate teams, and the creation of a worldwide critical mass of both content and adopters. The concept of a critical mass is derived from physics, where it is defined as the amount of radioactive material necessary to produce a self-sustaining nuclear reaction. Applied to the number of customers participating in electronic markets, it helps us to understand the nature of collective customer behavior and the size of the audience needed for a new technology to be considered successful (Morris and Ogan 1996; Damsgaard and Scheepers 1999, 103). The critical mass occurs at the point at which enough individuals have adopted an innovation that the innovation's further rate of adoption becomes self-sustaining (Rogers 1995, 333). To create a critical mass of customers, the marginal costs of doing business online have to be reduced substantially in comparison with traditional retailing networks (Tenenbaum 1998). These reductions may be provided by standardized solutions and customizable distribution networks, which have to co-evolve with the changing and heterogeneous demands of electronic markets. "There is no doubt that … reliance on iterative design and evolutionary change is better than waiting for the revolution that never comes" (Nielsen 1995, 65).

2.2 A BRIEF HISTORY OF WEB ADAPTIVITY

Since its emergence in 1991, the World Wide Web is an energetic, chaotic, and largely anonymous environment evolving so quickly that its previous versions become obsolete within a few years. Indeed, it is this very quality that has attracted many of the Internet trail-blazers who first developed, explored, and propagated this new frontier (Bucy et al. 1999; Psoinos and Smithson 1999, 14). To a large extent, the rapid acceptance of the World Wide Web is based on the simple but effective communication architecture of the Hypertext Transfer Protocol

(HTTP), and on the graphical user interfaces provided by browsers like Netscape's *Navigator* or Microsoft's *Internet Explorer*. Web clients are generally distributed at no cost. They represent essentially substitutable platforms for rendering hypertext documents (most applications do not exclusively rely on a particular product), sitting on top of non-substitutable operating systems (Treloar 1999, 153). The escalating succession of unilateral extensions by several manufacturers, however, or the added functionality provided by proprietary scripting languages, introduce a number of difficulties for the information provider who tries to develop systems in a platform-independent format (Lyardet et al. 1999, 294).

Despite the anonymous nature of the World Wide Web, adaptability and interactivity have always represented two of its inherent features. As such they provide the vertical dimension of the evolutionary stage model presented in the next chapter, stressing the criticality of a technology's underlying specifics when studying its evolution, acceptance, and diffusion (Damsgaard and Scheepers 1999, 101). Although the underlying technologies may almost certainly be eclipsed by future innovations, they have popularized and commercialized the concepts of interactivity, adaptability, and adaptivity (McMillan 1999a). The discrepancy between the potential capabilities of the medium and the actual functionality of deployed applications reveals that many organizations are not taking full advantage of the technology's unique characteristics.

Stage models offer insights into how new technologies evolve over time, describing an organization's progress through a number of successive and identifiable stages. Available technologies to create Web information systems can be categorized into four stages according to their technical sophistication, organizational maturity, and adaptivity. Adaptive systems and communication models that reach beyond the simple automation of operations are necessary to manage the informational requirements of highly demanding, technologically savvy customers. In a general sense, these requirements can be associated with problem perception, alternative identification, or alternative selection. Not all of them can be satisfied fully by only one application (Allen 1996, 49). This constraint should urge organizations to remember their core competencies and to focus on their primary target groups. Changing communication models as introduced in the following Section 2.2.1 raise the need for equivalent modifications and extensions of design paradigms, techniques, and tools. Parameters influencing this evolutionary process from innovation to maturity are then described in Section 2.2.2: Diffusion of Web Technology.

2.2.1   Stage Models for Describing Web Evolution

Traditional Web information systems that combine a set of static hypertext documents embody the simplest type of communication. This
characterization does not imply that such applications rely on outdated
technologies. On the contrary, the features provided by HTML, client-
side plug-ins, or scripting languages offer quite complex options for
structuring content and user interface representations. However, no
analysis of user information is taken into account for designing and
optimizing the system. Obviously, such applications do not exploit the
full potential of the World Wide Web's architecture. Most developers
avoid such one-way communication, which normally belongs to the
domain of broadcast-oriented mass media. Alternatively, they consider
two channels of user feedback: explicit and implicit. The term *feedback*
in this context is defined as "information obtained by any functional
entity about the product of its behavior" (Demczynksi 1969, 14; Ackoff
and Emery 1972, 187). A cybernetic feedback loop as introduced by
Norbert Wiener in *"Cybernetics or Control and Communication in the
Animal and the Machine"* is a form of system control that is used by
organizations to manage their resources effectively (Wiener 1961;
Kitching 1983, 16; Kendall and Kendall 1999, 29). Negative feedback, on
the one hand, has a corrective function, helps to maintain the system
within a critical operating range, and reduces unintentional performance fluctuations. Positive feedback, on the other hand, reinforces the
attributes of a system, causing it to continue its performance and activities without change (Senn 1987, 67f.). Both types of feedback are
vital for self-correcting and self-regulating information systems that do
not repeatedly require decisions on typical occurrences (↪ Section
2.3.1: Evaluating Transactional Infrastructures).

  Naturally, some implicit information is always transmitted with every
user request. Its utilization involves gathering such data, analyzing it,
and reacting accordingly. Some developers, however, may choose not to
exploit this source of information due to various reasons, which range
from lack of competencies, incurred cost, or available resources to
questions of user acceptance, privacy concerns, and conformity with the
organization's business model. The four distinct Web communication
models used in this book are based on the relative importance of implicit and explicit feedback channels whose characteristic attributes and
information flows are presented in Figure 2.5. The models incorporate
two sets of parameters (McMillan 1999a): perceptions of the *participants* (explicit and/or implicit user control, user activity, and perceived
purpose of communication) and perceptions of the *medium* (information flow, time sensitivity, and sense of place).

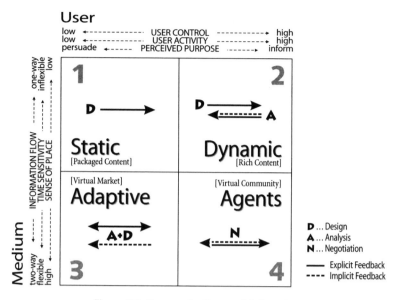

Figure 2.5. Communication models based on
explicit and implicit channels of feedback

The communication models show a number of similarities to McMillan's analysis of cyber-interactivity (McMillan 1999a). Drawing on a number of previous scholarly approaches (Bordewijk and van Kaam 1986, 16ff.; McQuail 1994; Fidler 1997; Jensen 1998, 185ff.), she uses the terms *packaged content, rich content, virtual market,* and *virtual community* for describing computer-mediated communication models. The characteristics of these models closely resemble those of the four main categories of deployed Web information systems:

- Static Web information systems (↪ Chapter 3), correspond to McMillan's category *packaged content*, which comprises corporate brochures created to attract an audience, promote products and services, or perform persuasive but non-selling communication functions.

- Dynamic Web information systems (↪ Chapter 4) are similar to *rich content*, which denotes online environments that provide in-depth searchable content such as databases or archived information.

- Adaptive Web information systems (↪ Chapter 5) focus on active environments that facilitate the execution of online transactions (*virtual markets*). Examples include the sale of customized products, solicitations for membership, individual customer support, and so forth.

- Commercial manifestations of *virtual communities*, defined as environments where participants build shared communication and their roles as either sender or receiver become indistinguishable. While

McMillan only lists simple examples such as chat rooms and bulletin boards; the agent-mediated architectures of Chapter 6 complement this category on a more sophisticated level.

Each stage of the evolution process shifts the focus and the timing of design and user feedback analysis into a new context. The model depicted in Figure 2.6, however, does not represent a dogmatic view in the sense that all organizations must necessarily go through all these stages in sequence. The nature of their business model may induce companies to leave out certain stages of this framework altogether. Deployed systems may also cross the boundaries of the model's stages. More realistically, the framework can be seen as a continually refined and extended set of communication models that rely on methods and technologies of increasing technical sophistication. In line with the organization's actual goals, the optimal tool is usually chosen based on criteria such as expected utility, costs, required resources, or available know-how. Figure 2.6 visualizes the stages, lists examples of enabling technologies, which will be explained in the corresponding chapters, and summarizes the changes these technologies introduce (compare with Hansen and Tesar 1996; Scharl 1997b, 22; Scharl and Brandtweiner 1998a, 42). It demonstrates the implications of the underlying feedback channels for designing Web information systems (D), analyzing implicit and explicit customer data (A), and implementing negotiation mechanisms (N).

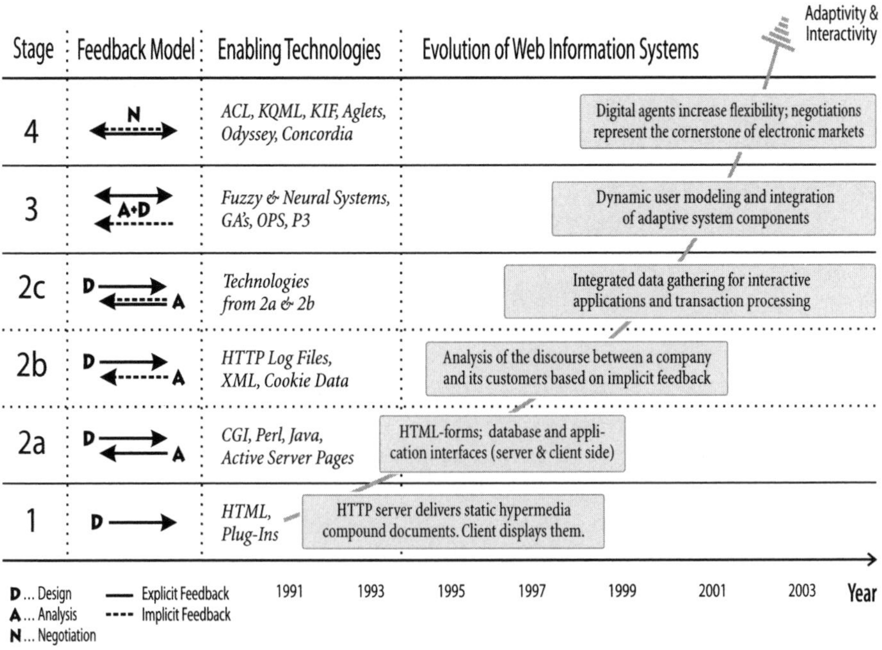

Figure 2.6. Evolution of the infrastructure for Web information systems

2.2.2 Diffusion of Web Technology

In the majority of cases, a one-size-fits-all approach to information systems design is less successful in achieving usability than customized solutions (Allen 1996). Another way to look at Figure 2.6, therefore, is the increasing consideration of the human user and her requirements. Traditionally, there is a variety of conceptual approaches to the design of information systems (Olson and Olson 1991, 62f.):

- *Technology-driven design.* Systems are built because the technology exists.
- *Rational design.* Systems are built by prescription in order to change the way people behave.
- *Intuitive Design.* Systems are built because it seems intuitive that the new functionality represents an advantage.
- *Analogical design.* Systems are built to resemble non-electronic objects that people presently use.
- *Evolutionary design.* Systems are built to iteratively extend the capabilities of other systems that people already use.
- *User-centered design.* Systems are built on the basis of detailed considerations regarding the users' tasks and capabilities.

Quantitative advancements in Web technology almost always represent a qualitative improvement as well, because more efficient and effective exchanges of information between an application and its users become possible (Bolisani 1999, 27). Thus the diffusion of the World Wide Web advances on an unprecedented scale. It follows predictable curves as the underlying technologies move from innovation to maturity. The acceptance and adoption rate of both customers and organizations follow similar curves and track the technology itself (Treloar 1999, 152).

2.2.2.1 *Temporal Pattern of the Diffusion Process*

Gordon E. Moore, co-founder of Intel, observed that the number of transistors per square inch on integrated circuits had doubled every year since the integrated circuit was invented (Moore 1965, 114ff.). In 1965, when writing an article for the 35th anniversary edition of *Electronics Magazine*, he quantified the astounding growth of the new technology of semiconductors and predicted that this trend would continue for the foreseeable future. In subsequent years, the pace slowed down. Component densities from 1975 forward were plotted with a gentler slope; one in which density doubled every 18 months, but which still behaved in a log-linear fashion. This is the current definition of *Moore's*

Law. Beginning as a simple but remarkably accurate observation of trends in semiconductor device complexity, Moore's Law has become an explanatory variable for the qualitative uniqueness of information technology and a metaphor for technological progress on a broader scale (Schaller 1997, 52ff.).

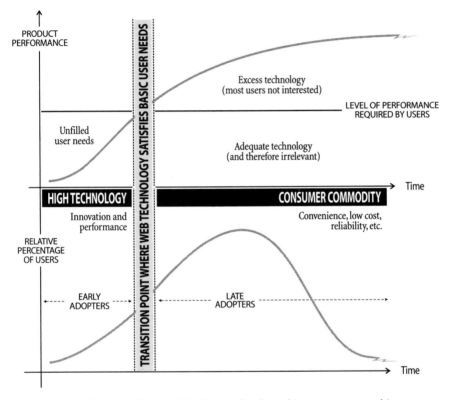

Figure 2.7. The transition from technology-driven to customer-driven products (adapted from Norman 1998, 155; Treloar 1999)

Although not obvious at first sight, Moore's observation supports the diffusion framework of Rogers, who classifies stages in a technology life-cycle by the relative percentage of customers who adopt the technology at this particular stage. Diffusion is defined as the "process by which an innovation is communicated through certain channels over time among the members of a social system. It is a special type of communication, in that the messages are concerned with new ideas" (Rogers 1995, 5). The adoption of innovations among a population is described using a bell-shaped curve that depicts the density function of the time taken by different segments of the population to adopt the innovation (↪ Figure 2.7). The integral of this curve results in the typical S-shaped temporal pattern of the diffusion process (Damsgaard and

Scheepers 1999, 103f.). Considering the relative youth of products shaped by information technology, the basically linear character of their temporal diffusion as described by Moore is not surprising. The shift from the original prediction of 12 months in 1965 to the more conservative estimate of 18 months in 1975 serves as a good indicator that the correlation is not perfectly linear and will probably resemble Rogers' S-shaped pattern in the long run.

Innovators and early adopters seek to be the first to introduce technical changes that support their generic strategies (Porter 1998, 181). While they are concerned with basic mechanisms and new possibilities to differentiate and create cost advantages, late adopters (early majority pragmatists, late majority conservatives, or laggards) are more interested in convenient solutions and their usability. Technological followers adapt the product or its delivery system more closely to buyer needs by learning from the innovator's experiences. According to Geoffrey A. Moore, many high-technology companies concentrate on excess technology and never successfully cross the transition point where available performance and functionality satisfy basic customer needs. This transition point is represented by the grey area in Figure 2.7 (Moore 1999a).

2.2.2.2 Rate of Adoption

The dominance of high technology companies in the creation process of electronic markets may be one of the reasons why the importance of customer preferences and requirements has been underestimated for years. Many features of deployed applications belong to the category *excess technology*, which is only of limited interest to the ordinary user. Several authors regard this failure to view evolving media from the user's perspective as the "blind spot in the study of interactivity" (Morrison 1998, 149ff.; McMillan 1999a). Besides its social acceptance, the rate of adoption depends on a number of system attributes (Nielsen 1995, 280; Rogers 1995, 250):

- *Costs and relative advantage* refer to the degree to which an innovation is perceived as better than the idea it supersedes and to the costs incurred to achieve this improvement. Depending on the provision of additional functionality and utility, the relative advantage determines the customer-delivered value in the case of commercial applications (↪ Section 2.3.2: Redefining the Customer-Delivered Value).

- *Compatibility* is the degree to which an innovation is perceived as consistent with existing values, past experiences, and the needs of potential adopters.

- *Trialability* and *observability* are both positively related to the rate of adoption. Trialability describes the degree to which an innovation may be experimented with on a limited basis – e.g., software that is freely distributed on a trial basis with the understanding that the user may need or want to pay for it later. Observability refers to the degree to which the results and relative advantage of an innovation are visible to others.

- *Usability* is the "extent to which a product can be used by specified users to achieve specified goals with effectiveness, efficiency and satisfaction in a specified context of use" (Smith et al. 1997, 68; Paternò 1999, 142).[14] This definition originates from ISO 9241-11 on ergonomic requirements for office work with visual display terminals. It includes the visual appeal of contents, hypertext structure, and interface. Generally speaking, usability is negatively correlated to an innovation's *complexity* (= the degree to which it is perceived as relatively difficult to understand and use). Current Web information systems included in the *"1999 Worldwide Web 100 Survey"* of the London School of Economics perform quite well on their *ease of use* and *innovation* dimensions (Psoinos and Smithson 1999, 12). Experienced developers consider usability in the initial steps of the design process, rather than treating it as a secondary *ex post* criterion. Summarizing a number of earlier definitions, the term *usability* comprises the following attributes (Nielsen 1995, 279; Noyes and Baber 1999, 148ff.):

  - *Relevance.* Extent to which the system's functionality matches the user's current needs.

  - *Learnability.* Ease of learning for initial use and remembering the system's basic methods.

  - *Efficiency.* High levels of productivity and flexibility when using the system.

  - *Safety.* Low likelihood of errors and effective methods to recover from them (e.g., an "undo" function).

  - *Contentment.* Engendering of positive attitudes towards the system based on the user's subjective satisfaction when accessing it.

From an organization's perspective, *maintainability* and *portability* represent important quality characteristics as well. While being highly relevant for corporate users in business-to-business scenarios, however, they are generally of little concern to the ordinary Web user (Olsina et al. 1999). On the corporate side, the adoption rate is dictated by factors such as perceived costs and benefits, complexity, compatibility with existing systems, or ease of implementation and use (Nambisan and Wang 1999, 98). But for successfully participating in electronic markets,

---

[14] http://www.iso.ch/cate/d16883.html

it is not enough for companies to be willing to adopt new communication models. Without superior technical and specific managerial expertise, organizations are not able to successfully assimilate and exploit
advanced Web technologies ahead of the industry curve (Jutla et al.
1999a, 74).

2.3 ELECTRONIC MARKET TRANSACTIONS

Generally speaking, electronic markets facilitate the exchange of information, goods, services, and payments associated with market transactions (Bakos 1998, 35). Three core phases of such a transaction can be
distinguished: information, negotiation, and settlement (Gebauer 1996;
Schmid and Lindemann 1998; Ware 1998; Werthner and Klein 1998). In
the first phase, buyers identify and evaluate their needs and possible
sources to fulfill them. At the same time, sellers arrange to provide their
goods and identify potential customers.[15] To a large extent, these steps
evolve around the exchange of information. Subsequently, prospective
buyers and sellers negotiate the terms of the intended transaction by
jointly identifying possible solutions with the goal of reaching a consensus, usually in the form of a contract. Eventually, the contract is executed, and goods and financial compensation are exchanged according
to the conditions previously stipulated.

Several descriptive models and theories such as the Nicosia model,
Engel-Blackwell model, Bettman information-processing model, or the
Andreasen model seek to capture the customer's actions and decisions
involved in buying and using goods and services. These models share
six fundamental stages that guide consumer behavior (Guttman et al.
1998; O´Keefe and McEachern 1998; Maes et al. 1999):

- *Need identification.* Product information causes the buyer to become aware of some unmet need.
- *Product brokering.* Retrieved information and personal criteria such
  as preferences or specific quality requirements enable the buyer to
  evaluate product alternatives, and to specify a so-called "consideration set" of products.
- *Merchant brokering.* The consideration set of the preceding stage is
  used to evaluate merchant alternatives, again based on buyer-
  provided criteria such as price, warranty, availability, delivery time,
  or reputation.

---

[15] The term *buyer* describes someone looking for a particular object of commercial
value. It is synonymous with *purchaser* and *customer*. A person or organization
that offers goods and services via the World Wide Web is referred to as *seller*, a
term synonymous with *vendor* (Miles et al. 1999, 132).

- *Negotiation.* The exact terms of the transaction are stipulated, with varying degrees of duration and complexity depending on the specific market and the relative power of the transaction partners.

- *Purchase and delivery.* If the negotiation turns out to be satisfactory for both parties, the predefined exchange of information, money, and commodities takes place. Otherwise, the transaction is terminated.

- *Product service and evaluation.* This last stage involves after-sales product support, customer service, and the evaluation of the transaction's outcome.

As these abstract stages can only represent an approximation and simplification of complex market behavior, they usually overlap and are linked in non-linear and iterative ways (Maes et al. 1999, 83). The first five stages can be subsumed under the three transaction phases *information*, *negotiation*, and *settlement*. Stage six (product service and evaluation), however, introduces a new aspect. Given the importance of after-sales support and *ex post* transaction analysis in today's buyer-dominated markets, they are incorporated as a fourth phase into the transaction model depicted in Figure 2.8. The diagram highlights the relative importance of implicit and explicit feedback channels for managing business-to-consumer transactions. Regardless of the level of sophistication, a large amount of information is processed and communicated between the market participants. Catalog data, third party product evaluations, buying contracts, and shipping documents are being exchanged in addition to basic information about offerings and requests.

Due to the complexity of modern marketplaces, it is usually not feasible for companies to acquire all necessary information via direct communication with customers. Implicit information about consumer preferences and needs, therefore, is used to complement explicit sources. It is made available by secondary analysis of past internal records, online monitoring, or the integration of external sources from market research institutions such as *Acxiom, Applied Geographic Solutions, CACI Marketing Systems, Claritas, Equifax, Experian, Polk,* or *Trans Union* (Mena 1999, 228ff.).[16] Compared to traditional (offline)

---

[16] http://www.acxiom.com/
http://www.appliedgeographic.com/
http://demographics.caci.com/
http://www.claritas.com/
http://www.equifax.com/
http://www.experian.com/
http://www.polk.com/
http://www.tuc.com/

transaction schemes, Web information systems extend the possibilities of implicit communication quite significantly. They offer new ways to improve the effectiveness of marketing activities and help establish individualized customer support.

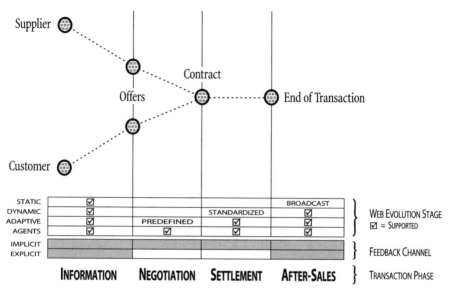

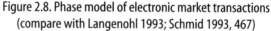

Figure 2.8. Phase model of electronic market transactions
(compare with Langenohl 1993; Schmid 1993, 467)

The first costs for the potential customer arise during the information phase in the form of resources spent on locating an organization's online presence, searching for specific information within that system, reading and pondering it. Locating an organization's online presence can be facilitated if it actively advertises its existence and benefits (Kaukal and Simon 1999, 55). Searching for specific information is supported by practically every Web information system, independent of its level of technical sophistication (compare with the evolutionary stage model of Section 2.2.1). As soon as all relevant information has been gathered and evaluated, potential transaction partners can be contacted.

Matching supply and demand (i.e., reaching a mutually satisfactory agreement regarding a transaction's terms and conditions) is generally more challenging, from both technical and organizational points of view. Negotiation mechanisms may be defined as computer-assisted forms of "decision-making where two or more parties jointly search a space of possible solutions with the goal of reaching a consensus" (Rosenschein and Zlotkin 1994; compare with Guttman et al. 1998). Systems belonging to one of the first two stages fall short in providing the necessary functionality. Potential customers benefit in the information phase

of the transaction and may place simple orders but have to refer to traditional sales channels to request products or services that differ from
standardized offerings. The adaptivity of stage three applications,
therefore, is a prerequisite for explicit agreements (= "predefined" negotiation). Support of the whole transaction by integrated business
solutions such as Netscape's *MerchantXpert,*[17] Intershop's *Enfinity,*[18] or
Broadvision's *One-to-One Commerce,*[19] to mention a few, eliminates the
need to refer to other media or traditional communication models.
While the investments to provide the infrastructure necessarily increase, the costs of standard operations are reduced substantially. The
extended area of validity ensures that very few cases have to be handled
manually.

Only digital agents of stage four enable real-time negotiation on a
truly individual level (as compared to a predefined set of conditional
offers, which is typical for stage three). Ideally, the technology disap-
pears and becomes a natural "extension of man" (McLuhan 1964;
Damsgaard and Scheepers 1999, 110). Implementing this functionality
requires rather complex algorithms, which may be one of the reasons
why even the simplest type, price negotiation, is very scarce amongst
deployed systems (Psoinos and Smithson 1999, 11). To compensate for
high initial investments, the cost parameter for exceptional operations
is practically eliminated from the evaluation model. Advanced agent-
mediated transaction systems simultaneously support a high number of
dynamic business relationships with previously unknown customers. In
such an environment organizations will be "at their most agile, and
marketplaces will approach perfect efficiency" (Maes et al. 1999, 91).

Short-term infrastructure requirements for the settlement phase and
eventual secondary transactions are easier to meet. Standardized solutions become feasible in the second stage, but are considerably enhanced by customized process control in stage three (e.g., personalized
delivery or payment arrangements). Stage two offers a limited area of
validity without adequate mechanisms for spontaneous, peer-to-peer
negotiations during the preceding agreement phase. General terms and
conditions such as the availability of alternative payment methods,
therefore, should already be addressed in the information phase.

From a marketing perspective, after-sales activities predominantly
serve the purpose of maintaining and deepening the relationships to
customers (Werthner and Klein 1998, 56). Only satisfied customers
become long-term loyal clients. The after-sales phase has to satisfy the
customers' latent need for continued reassurance that they made a good

---

[17] http://home.netscape.com/merchantxpert/
[18] http://www.intershop.com/products/
[19] http://www.broadvision.com/

decision in choosing the company and its product (Porter 1998, 145). Due to the heterogeneity of this task, its characterization in terms of typical activities is problematic. Related efforts range from simple electronic mail services (e.g., notifying customers of product upgrades) to sophisticated helpdesks, comprehensive and highly cross-referenced electronic maintenance manuals, user communities, or exclusive services for valued customers (Mathé and Chen 1998, 171f.). According to the *"1999 Worldwide Web 100 Survey"* of the London School of Economics, value-adding customer service and related measures to increase the loyalty of online customers are still lacking in most business sectors (Psoinos and Smithson 1999, 12). With their limited broadcast functionality, stage one solutions are restricted to transferring static information. The last transaction phase, however, relies on the organization's ability to target its marketing efforts precisely. The required interactive dialogs and customized services become available with the implementation of more advanced technologies and benefit from the interactive nature of extended communication models.

2.3.1   Evaluating Transactional Infrastructures

Emerging information systems provide unprecedented support for business processes, especially in the case of electronic market transactions where they reach beyond organizational boundaries (Rockart and Short 1991; Clemons et al. 1993; Fulk and DeSanctis 1995). Gebauer and Scharl specify an evaluation framework to help deploy information systems in a way that ensures streamlined operations without compromising organizational responsiveness (Gebauer 1996; Gebauer and Scharl 1999). The framework evaluates the overall efficiency of a process throughout its lifetime. It takes into account both short-term effects from the automation of operations and the resulting impacts on process flexibility and customer value (↪ Section 2.3.2: Redefining the Customer-Delivered Value).

The model depicted in Figure 2.9 provides a generic tool to describe, analyze, and evaluate the organizational structure of business processes. Business processes are defined as corporate subsystems that generate a predetermined output – e.g., providing prospective customers with offers that exactly match their preferences. The output of a process is specified not only in quantitative terms such as provided utility or time of delivery, but also by certain quality standards. For the time being, it is assumed to be constant.

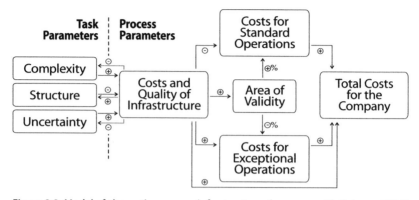

Figure 2.9. Model of alternative process infrastructures (compare with Gebauer 1996)

The framework supplements traditional methods of evaluating the costs and benefits of information systems and organizational process structures. The measurement of lead times and operation costs, for example, is usually carried out independently of the process changes that accompany them (Powell 1992; Remenyi et al. 1993; Hess and Brecht 1995; Hornback 1995). According to Moody and Walsh (Moody and Walsh 1999, 507), methods are chosen based primarily on their validity, reliability, and cost (i.e., effort to apply). The concepts of *reliability* (consistency, stability, reproducibility, and accuracy of results) and *validity* (quality of the approximation of true economic value) are inextricably intertwined, with reliability often being regarded as a precursor to validity (Potter and Levine-Donnerstein 1999).

In a broad sense, the deployment of process infrastructure refers to all initial activities that are repeatedly leveraged for day-to-day process operations. In the context of electronic transactions, infrastructure-related measures often refer to the flow of information and imply the introduction of additional communication channels, the establishment of appropriate database connectivity, and the development of integrated online ordering systems. Throughout its entire lifetime, the infrastructure has a substantial impact on process efficiency by simultaneously determining the levels of automation and process flexibility. The objective is to choose an infrastructure that maximizes this efficiency, understood as the resources expended in relation to how accurately and completely a certain goal is achieved.

Day-to-day operations can be divided into two groups, standard situations and exceptions (Kieser and Kubicek 1992). *Standard situations* allow the use of the infrastructure in its regular way. Fully automated tasks ensure low costs of operation and high short-term efficiency. The more flexibly a system has been designed initially, the more situations are covered. *Exceptional situations* are not supported by the infrastructure at justifiable costs. Processes have to be handled manually and require organizational adjustments or extended negotiations. Exceptions also apply to situations where the actual use of the infrastructure leads to poor results that have to be improved *ex post* to match desired quality standards. The more flexibly a system is constructed, the lower the costs that unforeseen (exceptional) situations may cause.

The long-term efficiency of a process is determined by all three kinds of expenses (infrastructure, management of standard situations, and exception handling) throughout the entire period that the infrastructure is used. The dynamics of the process environment determines, among other factors, the length of this period. Many evaluations of process performance do not include this important parameter and also neglect the specific characteristics of a task. The model of Figure 2.9 assumes that the expenses necessary to build up a certain level of process infrastructure mainly depend on three interrelated features of a task:

- *Task complexity* is determined by the number of sub-processes and organizational units, and their interdependency with the process environment. Building an infrastructure for repeated use deals with complexity *ex ante* and thus reduces it during later operations.
- *Task structure* refers to the specific type of task (Picot and Reichwald 1987). *Routine tasks* occur regularly in similar form and can be structured easily. In contrast, the degree of freedom involved when performing *innovative tasks* limits their automation. *Administrative tasks,* a hybrid category, combine the mentioned attributes in various ways.
- *Task uncertainty* results from the instability of the process environment and from the unpredictability regarding the organizational elements' dynamic behavior. Through the establishment of rule-based process control, uncertainty is reduced by prescribing specific patterns of behavior for certain situations.

2.3.2   Redefining the Customer-Delivered Value

Integrated communication is a frequently used term to describe the combination of different marketing instruments for analyzing and manipulating information retrieval, decision processes, and usage patterns of active and potential customers (Belz 1997). By customizing Web information systems, companies attract prospects, convert prospects into shoppers, convert shoppers into buyers, and retain existing buyers. Optimally, they can offer tailored products at the right time, use appealing representations (Link and Hildebrand 1995), and address customers with a terminology appropriate to their current level of expertise (↪ Section 2.3.4.1: Customizing Corporate Communication).

Unfortunately, most of these efforts are only based on their notional value, as people consider the outcome beneficial but are unable to quantify their assessment (Moody and Walsh 1999, 498). Therefore, more operational approaches are needed. Kotler and Armstrong (Kotler and Armstrong 1998, 552), for example, recommend to maximize the *customer-delivered value*, which is calculated as the difference between the *total customer value* (product, services, personnel, and image values), and *total customer costs* (monetary, time, energy, and psychic costs). Other authors suggest similar approaches, defining customer value as the market-perceived product and non-product quality adjusted for the relative price of the product (Gale and Wood 1994, xiv; Cleland and Bruno 1996, 3). Kaukal and Simon present a literature review and comparison of various customer value definitions and their applicability to electronic markets (Kaukal and Simon 1999, 65).

The evaluation model introduced in Section 2.3.1 assumes that the output of a business process is invariable. Different forms of technical infrastructures are being evaluated in terms of their impact on overall process expenses. With regard to Web information systems, this assumption does not conform to reality. Cost-centered decision support deals, at best, with those facets that maintain competitive parity and misses the point about the strategic role and long-term impact of Web information systems (Psoinos and Smithson 1999, 32). Due to relatively low investment requirements, many companies implement Web-based applications to deliver additional customer value and leverage the technology's high popularity among potential customers (Nambisan and Wang 1999). The new differential functionality of innovative Web technologies extends traditional forms of customer support and adds significant value to business-to-consumer transactions. It increases the overall output level and the quality of (information) products. This improvement refers not only to the product itself but also to its representation, corresponding services, and the automated packaging with complementary goods (non-product quality).

To account for these effects, the original model is extended by introducing the notion of value that is delivered to the customer. This parameter denotes the monetary worth of the technical, economic, and social benefits a customer receives in exchange for the price of a market offering (Anderson and Narus 1998, 54). It correlates with the market-perceived quality of goods, which itself relies on both product and non-product attributes. Perceived quality grows out of individual expectations of how a product and the company supplying it will positively affect the buyer's value chain. Real value is ultimately created only when customers actually use products with attributes that match their specific needs. However, buyers will not pay for real value they do not perceive. They use indications (= signaling) such as advertising, reputation, market share, packaging, public appearance, attractiveness of facilities, and information provided both traditionally or via electronic sources to infer the expected value of a product (Porter 1998, 139). Naturally, it is hard to generalize or compute a variable that is dependent on such a broad range of external factors.

Figure 2.10. Customer-delivered value

Four distinct categories of product and non-product attributes can be identified (Kambil et al. 1996, 13): *basic attributes* are mandatory elements so that the product can serve its purpose; *expected attributes* are those that all players within a specific industry typically deliver; *desired attributes* are usually offered by another segment of the industry, but cannot be delivered for the price the customer is willing to pay; *unanticipated attributes* provide value but have not yet been considered by either the customers or the competition. Similarly, Albrecht distinguishes expected utility (shortcomings in this category result in immediate loss of users) from desired and unexpected utility (Albrecht 1993, 155ff.). Developing products that provide unexpected utility is an excellent way to enhance a company's competitive position.

Section 2.2.2: Diffusion of Web Technology describes the high potential of new technologies such as Web information systems to satisfy latent customer needs. The boundaries between the utility categories described above, however, are dynamic and necessarily change with the technical evolution of the World Wide Web. In competitive environments, unexpected utility tends to become expected utility in a rather short period of time (Kaukal and Simon 1999, 55).

The total cost for the consumer depends on the direct and indirect costs of using the product (e.g., labor, fuel, maintenance, required space, impact of the product on other value activities, expected cost of product failure, and so forth). Obviously, it also includes search costs (e.g., opportunity cost of time spent searching or associated expenditures caused by driving, telephone calls, or magazine subscriptions), costs of minimizing transaction risk, and costs of delivering, installing, and financing the product (Bakos 1998, 36; Porter 1998, 135; Strader and

Shaw 1999, 83). In the case of information systems, the total cost can be lowered through a number of measures, such as eliminating redundant data entry, improving navigational functionality, streamlining user interfaces, or limiting the need to search for suitable product alternatives. Costs of redundant data, for example, result from re-keying data into multiple systems, increased storage requirements, additional system extensions (e.g., interfaces to keep data consistent), or manual reconciliation efforts (Moody and Walsh 1999, 500).

"Everything is worth what its purchaser will pay for it" (Publilius Syrus, "Sententiae", circa 50 B.C. in: (Anderson and Narus 1998, 53)). Analogous to traditional markets, it can be assumed that online customers buy products and services from the (information) provider that they believe offers the highest customer-delivered value (Bakos 1998, 36; Scharl and Brandtweiner 1998b, 454). But no simple series of steps will cure complacency and create real customer value, which is hard to determine from a methodological perspective. In most cases, the only feasible solution to measure the customer-delivered value is to directly obtain estimates from active customers. In soliciting perceptions, however, companies would do well to remember that customer expectations are formed relative to competitive substitutes in terms of cost, time, and convenience. Customer opinions provide little meaning without reference to available alternatives. Moreover, people are generally better and more experienced at making comparative judgements than at expressing absolute values (Naumann 1994, 20; Anderson and Narus 1998, 59).

The most effective organizational strategies to increase customer-delivered value must flow from a company's culture, values, management style, and reward systems. They should be focused on enhancing and sustaining product and non-product quality, rather than on production equipment, system performance, or excess technology as defined in Section 2.2.2: Diffusion of Web Technology (Moody and Walsh 1999, 498). In summary, the following customer value basics can be identified (Naumann 1994, 24; Cleland and Bruno 1996, 31):

- The customer defines the appropriate product and non-product qualities, and the reasonable price. Companies should not regard customer-delivered value as secondary to shareholder value.
- Customer value expectations are hard to measure and are formed relative to competitive offerings. Product and non-product needs are dynamic and continually move higher.
- Product and non-product qualities are delivered by and are the responsibility of the whole channel, not just the manufacturer (compare with the definition of electronic business ecosystems in Section 2.1.2).

- Maximizing customer-delivered value requires total organizational involvement and commitment. Companies have to build integrated customer value strategies and allocate resources to the highest combined value.

2.3.3   Extending the Evaluation Model

The preceding sections analyzed the procedural structure of electronic market transactions and the organization's efforts to maximize the customer-delivered value. At the same time, companies try to limit both their initial investment and the resources required for operating and maintaining their systems. By introducing efficiency as an additional parameter, Figure 2.11 combines both aspects. Formally defined, a production plan is technologically efficient if there is no other plan within the short-run production possibility set that would produce more output (= customer-delivered value) with the same input (= the company's total costs) or produce the same output with less input (Varian 1992, 4).

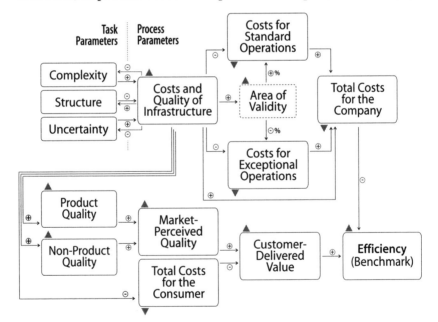

Figure 2.11. Integrated evaluation model (Gebauer and Scharl 1999; Scharl et al. 2000)

The triangular markers on the left-hand side of each object depict the effects that an investment in infrastructure (i.e., increasing the "*costs and quality of infrastructure*" parameter) is expected to have on the model's other elements. In most cases, infrastructure investments are offset by drastically reduced costs of standard operations and – due to the increased flexibility – less need for the handling of exceptional operations. On the output side, the customer-delivered value is pushed to a higher level by increasing the quality of existing products and services, and by providing additional utility not available via traditional channels.

The model depicted in Figure 2.11 reveals a fundamental trade-off between long-term and short-term efficiency. It supports the assumption that there is an optimal degree of integration – i.e., a balance between complete automation and maximum flexibility with no structuring at all. The model demonstrates the challenge for process design to find the optimal ratio between infrastructure expenses and running costs, simultaneously assessing standard situations, changing requirements, and possible exceptions. Besides the general innovation strategy of a company, a variety of factors have an impact on the decision's optimality, such as the size of a company, its organizational structure, or the specific business ecosystem it belongs to (↪ Section 2.1.2: Electronic Business Ecosystems).

The investment in infrastructure increases the total costs (input) and as such tends to lower a transaction's overall efficiency. This effect is offset in two ways: by lowering the cost of standard operations, and by achieving a higher customer-delivered value (output). If the level of output remains constant, the amortization of the investment in infrastructure can be achieved through lower costs of day-to-day operations, either by lowering the expenses for standard operations, or by increasing the range of situations that can be handled with the system. Web information systems, for example, allow customers to submit orders electronically instead of talking to a customer representative, or ordering via traditional mail.

The impact on overall efficiency is positive in cases where the overall cost savings offset the initial investment in infrastructure over the period that the system is utilized. In cases where the effect on overall costs (infrastructure-related costs plus changes in operation costs) is positive or zero, overall efficiency can still be improved through a sufficiently high increase in customer-delivered value. "Not only do buyers incur lower costs even after considering more product offerings, they also benefit from being able to identify and purchase products that better match their needs" (Bakos 1998, 39). Frequently, increasing customer-delivered value is regarded as more important than mere cost savings. Emerging technologies such as Web information systems allow the development, definition, and management of customer relationships in ways that were not feasible before.

2.3.4   Electronic Customer Relations

Online retailing is among the most active commercial applications of Web information systems (Segev et al. 1995, 7). Consequently, integrated marketing concepts for online retailing are becoming key issues in a world of increasingly dynamic and global business environments. Companies see an urgent need to focus their business activities on customer preferences in order to be able to respond instantly to constantly changing demands. Simultaneously, as demonstrated in the last section, overall cost and process efficiency impose stringent limits on many investment decisions (Brancheau et al. 1996; Gebauer and Scharl 1999).

Abstract marketing instruments, however, cannot generally be applied to the virtual economy's different industries without taking into account the specific features of these heterogeneous segments. The strong specialization of academic research and practice in formulating, analyzing, and implementing tailored marketing strategies for Web information systems was a direct result from that insight. In conformity with its core competencies and available resources, every organization needs specialized approaches for analyzing and addressing active and potential customers effectively (Haller 1997, 28f.). Traditional mass markets represent a constellation that is rare to find in electronic environments. Thus alternative strategies to specifically address particular (groups of) users are required. According to the granularity of the targeted segments, three approaches are distinguished in the following section: market segmentation, personalization, and customization.

2.3.4.1 *Customizing Corporate Communication*

"The environment in which business operates is far more turbulent, chaotic, and rapidly changing than ever before. Those big, beautiful mass markets are being shattered into fragments and splinter groups. Customers in every niche are less tolerant, less forgiving, less loyal" (Naumann 1994, 15). The selective *segmentation* of markets, therefore, has high priority for both academic research and industry practice. It enables retailers to counteract the increasing fragmentation of consumer markets, which is partially responsible for the success and popularity of direct-access media such as the World Wide Web (Wilde 1992, 792). The demand for responsiveness and organizational flexibility often results in efforts to hastily equip these direct-access media with adaptive components.

Many attempts at mere *personalization*, such as rudimentary mass mailings that only adjust the customer's name, actually represent the antithesis of customization, superficially occurring at the user interface level. This shortcoming is visualized in Figure 2.12, where the radial axis represents real or pretended product differentiation. Some companies try to make their offerings seem tailored to the users' requirements (dotted circles and black area that symbolizes the company's communications strategy). Their core products, however, remain identical. Real *customization* based on specific user requirements, on the other hand, not only penetrates the product itself, its packaging, and its online representation but also includes the entire organization in its efforts to establish an open and informed dialog with its customers (Kelly 1994, 81f.).

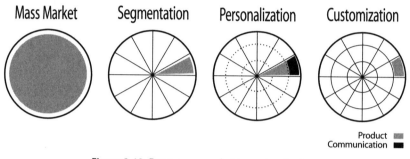

Figure 2.12. From mass market to customization

The degree of adaptivity regularly affects a project's appeal to the customer. The granularity, relevancy, timeliness, completeness, accuracy, and accessibility of the underlying database determine the scope of potential applications (Giannoccaro et al. 1999, 116). Evaluating these attributes, analysts can assess the level of inference and adaptivity theoretically supported by the data (Pyle 1999, 131). Three levels of data granularity are distinguished on a conceptual level: detailed data, aggregate data, and aggregate data with sampled detailed data. While for most mass marketing exercises aggregate data usually suffice (Kelly 1994, 34), detailed data are a key requirement for effective merchandizing cues and customized solutions. Merchandizing cues such as cross-selling, up-selling, promotions, or recommendations present and group products to motivate purchases (Lee et al. 1999; Lee and Podlaseck 2000). *Cross-selling*, for instance, requires a detailed account of a customer's current transaction and past activities. References between the observed interests and an organization's online offerings are established in order to recommend items related to the customer's product choice (e.g., book recommendations, accessories for mobile phones, batteries needed to operate a specific electronic device, and so forth). Similarly, *up-selling* recommends more expensive items of higher quality as an alternative to the customer's product choice.

However, in almost all cases there is a point of diminishing marginal returns when increasing the granularity provides little additional benefit. Completely accurate information, for example, is rarely required in a business context. Quantitative and qualitative characteristics of the database determine the degree of freedom for the information provider, the ability to generate customer value, and the overall economic potential of every single project relying on this pivotal source of information (Moody and Walsh 1999, 502).

Sustainable economic success can only be achieved by maximizing the perceived long-term value delivered to the customer (↪ Section 2.3.2: Redefining the Customer-Delivered Value). Such an organizational reorientation of markets requires tailored solutions at a cost level comparable to that of mass marketing. Adaptive Web applications provide such solutions. They help to identify the key attributes of specific customer segments for each of the company's online products and select the best promotional strategy to reach these segments. By building and targeting unique market segments, identifying the attributes of high-value customers, and effectively managing customer relationships, strong barriers to market entry are created for potential competitors. The extensive databases that drive adaptive Web applications facilitate cross- and up-selling on a large scale. By reducing total cost they increase the degree of freedom for price policy (Reiß and Beck 1995, 63; Mena 1999, 19). By querying these databases, analysts are able to test and determine which marketing activities have the greatest impact and may lead to brand switching. Those effects represent compelling evidence that the micro-segmentation of markets will result in significant competitive advantage, enhancing an organization's ability to gain new customers and retain existing ones.

2.3.4.2 Gathering and Representing Customer Information

The convergence of information retrieval and usage as far as adaptive marketing systems are concerned make the usual distinction between market research and market management obsolete. Nevertheless, isolated and sequential approaches are still quite common in practice. Seen as a closed loop that consists of conceptual design, pre-test, stimulus, customer response, and performance analysis, adaptive systems contribute to a more realistic, dynamic user model (↪ Section 5.4: User Modeling) and a more efficient allocation of an organization's limited marketing resources.

Due to the immaterial, non-tangible, and transitory nature of many Web offerings, and due to the fact that production and consumption take place synchronously, the value of product-oriented market research in the traditional sense is drastically reduced. The focus on products is replaced by an in-depth analysis of customers and target groups including their personal needs, preferences, and expectations. The regular gathering of stimulus-response data provides essential feedback for product design and for the strategic or operative decisions of the sales department (Hüttner 1997, 433). The integration with existing information for creating dynamic user models in conformity with observable real-world patterns helps the information provider to map and classify the customer's behavior, describe its geographic and temporal distribution, and accurately predict future behavior (Link and Hildebrand 1995, 47; Jaspersen 1997, 393; Zukerman et al. 1999, 275ff.). The organization's capacity to accumulate and leverage this information effectively becomes a key source of competitive differentiation.

Web developers, however, have to deal with a fundamental lack of faith between businesses and their potential online customers. The resulting fear of consumers to divulge personal information represents a formidable barrier to the commercial use of Web information systems (Hoffman et al. 1999, 80). Every information provider, therefore, has to create enough perceived individual utility to influence positively the user's willingness to provide personal data.

Legitimate objections regarding user privacy were the main reason behind the development of standardized description and transfer models for user profiles such as the *Open Profiling Standard (OPS)*,[20] the *Platform for Privacy Preferences (P3P)*,[21] or Novell's *digitalme* technology.[22] The World Wide Web Consortium's P3P project provides a framework for disclosing customer information during online interactions. By allowing users to specify what kind of personal information they are willing to divulge to whom and under what conditions, P3P applications support tailored relationships with specific Web information systems (Reagle and Cranor 1999, 48). Users can delegate decisions to their computer agent whenever they wish, infer about corporate privacy policies, and reconcile their preferences with these policies (Lee and Speyer 1999). They do not have to re-type or keep track of information that is stored locally in a user repository. Service providers also benefit by receiving the required information in a consistent and pre-structured way (Reagle and Cranor 1999, 49f.). OPS and P3P are somewhat similar, but the specific focus of each technology is different. While OPS deals with secure transport and control of user data, P3P concentrates on the management of online identity, addressing ques-

---

[20] http://developer.netscape.com/ops/ops.html
http://www.w3.org/TR/NOTE-OPS-FrameWork.html
[21] http://www.w3.org/P3P/
[22] http://www.digitalme.com/
http://www.novell.com/corp/cio/cioapr99.html

tions of not only *"where do you want to go?"* but also *"who do you want to be?"* (Psoinos and Smithson 1999, 14). It enables the expression of privacy practices and preferences, and allows services to offer multiple proposals (preferably on first contact), which enumerate the data elements the application wishes to collect. A P3P proposal also explains how each data element will be handled, whether it will be shared with other organizations, and whether it will be used in an identifiable manner. An extension mechanism of HTTP 1.1 transports the information, using a combination of *XML (eXtensible Markup Language)*[23] and *RDF (Resource Description Framework)*[24] to capture its syntax, structure, and semantics (↪ Section 6.1: Content-Based Information Agents).

Dubbed *"digitalme"*, Novell's digital identity technology for creating personalized Internet services has similar intentions and will transfer the point of control from a remote system into the hands of the end-user accessing that system. The system builds on the Novell Directory Services (NDS) as a tool to manage a user's digital identity, including both transfer of personal information and authentication (Psoinos and Smithson 1999, 16).

---

[23] http://www.w3.org/xml/
[24] http://www.w3.org/rdf/

3 A Static World

In the first stage of the evolution model (↪ Section 2.2.1), the purpose of the World Wide Web is the exchange of documents in heterogeneous environments. It is intended to be a pool of human knowledge, which allows collaborators in remote sites to "share their ideas and all aspects of a common project" (Berners-Lee et al. 1994, 76). Stand-alone servers deliver hypermedia compound documents to be displayed by the customer's browser. Information flows unidirectionally from the server to the client, since user feedback is disregarded in this early stage of Web development (↪ Figure 3.1). Hence most Web development activities are restricted to comparatively simple authoring tasks.

Nevertheless, the necessary design efforts for such Web sites can be quite substantial in scale and require a planned, organized, and structured approach. Such methods have been suggested in a number of publications (Isakowitz et al. 1995; Nanard and Nanard 1995; Bichler and Nusser 1996b; Scharl 1998a); Bauer and Scharl present classifications of existing academic and commercial methodologies (Scharl 1997b, 58ff.; Bauer 1998b). Due to a lack of (formal) feedback channels, the redesign of deployed systems that belong to stage one usually requires substantial effort.

Stage	Feedback Model	Enabling Technologies	Stage Description
1	D ⟶	*HTML, Plug-Ins*	**HTTP server delivers static hypermedia compound documents. Client displays them.**

D ... Design ——— Explicit Feedback
A ... Analysis ---- Implicit Feedback
N ... Negotiation

Figure 3.1. Characteristics of static Web information systems (Stage 1)

The development of the system follows the rather simplistic model depicted in Figure 3.2, which consists of only two phases: design and implementation. A corresponding modeling method such as the Extended World Wide Web Design Technique (eW3DT) is usually chosen to support both phases (↪ Section 4.2.4). Optimally, visual development tools such as Microsoft's *FrontPage*, Adobe's *PageMill,* Macromedia's *Dreamweaver*, or the *WebDesigner* in the case of eW3DT allow the interactive construction of conceptual design models.

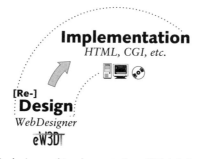

Figure 3.2. Static design and implementation of Web information systems

Aarseth's seven-dimensional framework of textual communication (↪ Section 1.4.5.2: Mapping Textons to Scriptons) is used to describe the hypertextual characteristics pertaining to this and the following stages (Aarseth 1994, 61f.; Aarseth 1998, 62ff.). Aarseth distinguishes seven attributes that characterize traversal functions of textual communication: (1) *Dynamics:* the number of textons can either remain fixed (intratextonic dynamics) or may vary as well (textonic dynamics); (2) *Determinability:* a text is determinant if the adjacent scriptons of every scripton are always the same; (3) *Transiency:* if the mere passing of the user's time causes scriptons to appear, an electronic document is called transient; (4) *Perspective:* texts with a personal perspective require the user to play a strategic role in the (virtual) world described by them; (5) *Access:* this attribute distinguishes random from controlled access; (6) *Linking:* documents may be organized by explicit links, conditional links, or no links at all; (7) *User function:* interpretative, explorative, configurative, and textonic.

The *semantics* attribute has been added as an additional dimension. In this way, a multidimensional descriptive space is built, the number of dimensions being given by the number of binary or multiple oppositions listed in Figure 3.3.[25]

---

[25] Terms in brackets signify hypertextual attributes that are principally not characteristic of this stage of Web evolution. Nevertheless, innovators and early adopters occasionally implement corresponding mechanisms by leveraging existing technologies.

Both individual Web information systems and their categories find a specific place in this space in the same way in which any point in the Euclidean space can be characterized by its numerical coordinates (Marcus 1997, 36).

Determinability	Transiency	Perspective	Access
☒ Determinable	☒ (Transient)	☐ Personal	☒ Random
☐ Indeterminable	☒ Intransient	☒ Impersonal	☐ Controlled

Dynamics	Linking	Semantics	User Function
☒ No (Static)	☒ Explicit	☒ Limited	☒ Explorative
☐ Intratextonic	☐ Conditional	☐ Supported	☐ Configurative
☐ Textonic	☐ None	☐ Required	☒ Interpretative
			☐ Textonic

Figure 3.3. Hypertextual attributes of static Web information systems

The traversal functions of static Web applications are determinable, that is, the adjacent scriptons of every presented document do not change. Typically, they are also intransient, as the mere passing of the user's time does not cause other scriptons to appear. Obviously, there are a number of exceptions. Server push and document redirection are the most popular examples of transient traversal functions within static applications. A personal perspective of the traversal function would require users to play a strategic role in the virtual world generated by the Web information system. The majority of commercial implementations, therefore, can be regarded as impersonal textual communication, independent of their technical sophistication. Users of static systems usually have unrestricted (random) and explicit access to the complete set of published documents. Arbitrary paths are not common in this early stage of Web development. Static Web information systems, by definition, do not support intratextonic dynamics (changing content of scriptons, but fixed number of textons) or textonic dynamics (changing content of scriptons and variable number of textons). Methods for expressing and processing semantic information are also limited, due to HTML's inflexibility and missing mechanisms to structure documents semantically. Despite these shortcomings, creative designers have found ways to work around some of these inherent limitations by using proprietary tags or software tools to extract content from ordinary, non-structured pages (Glushko et al. 1999, 106).

The customer's active role is restricted to reflecting about the meaning of the document (interpretative function) and deciding which path to take next (explorative function). With the progressive commercialization of the Internet and the integration of additional layout options, companies increasingly try to determine the exact design of their documents based on strategic marketing considerations and to maintain a consistent corporate identity. Nevertheless, every user is able to specify the general appearance of documents by setting standard browser preferences, which represents a rather low level of adaptability. Since choosing browser preferences only refers to basic issues of layout and presentation, these activities do not qualify as configurative user functions.

4 The Emergence of Interactivity

The planned and structured analysis of user feedback starts to change the underlying communication model. Arguably, every hypertext system which acts as an interactive form of communication must contain some kind of (low-level) information feedback loop as defined in Section 1.2: Ergodic Literature (Aarseth 1998, 19). The distinction between the first two stages, however, is based on the processing of application-oriented (high-level) feedback. Depending on the sub-model (Stages 2a-2c), the analytical process covers methods for gathering implicit and/or explicit feedback (↪ Figure 4.1; compare with Figure 2.6 on page 44). Empirical studies document the surprising fact that many Web information systems still belong to stage one. Small and medium-sized enterprises in particular do not gather user feedback in an organized way. A content analysis of the interactive features of 110 commercial Web information systems, for example, reveals that only a third of the systems allowed for feedback via e-mail, direct orders, online surveys, or toll-free numbers (Ha and James 1998, 457ff.; Bucy et al. 1999).

Stage	Feedback Model	Enabling Technologies	Stage Description
2c	D ⟶ ⟵----- A	*Technologies from 2a & 2b*	**Integrated data gathering for interactive applications and transaction processing.**
2b	D ⟶ ⟵----- A	*HTTP Log Files, XML, Cookie Data*	**Analysis of the discourse between a company and its customers based on implicit feedback.**
2a	D ⟶ ⟵ A	*CGI, Perl, Java, Active Server Pages*	**HTML-forms; database and application interfaces on both server and client side.**

D ... Design   —— Explicit Feedback
A ... Analysis   ---- Implicit Feedback
N ... Negotiation

Figure 4.1. Characteristics of dynamic Web information systems (Stage 2)

4.1 OVERVIEW

Explicit user feedback is easily obtained by means of questionnaires implemented via HTML forms or applets. The design of such questionnaires is critical to ensure their acceptance. Established fields such as demand-oriented market research or empirical social research, together with the corresponding statistical methods, provide a sound background for utilizing the acquired information.

Gathering, reporting, and visualizing implicit feedback usually requires more sophisticated approaches (Scharl and Bauer 1998). Therefore, it is still underutilized in many commercial applications, despite the availability of an extensive array of suitable software solutions (Malchow and Thomsen 1997). The lack of methods for the structured analysis of explicit and implicit feedback channels represents a serious shortcoming of prevalent methodologies for Web development.

4.1.1 Development Process

The emergence of interactivity as delineated above requires an extended development process, introducing formal feedback on the basis of usage patterns and its subsequent analysis – e.g., the sequence of HTTP requests of individual users and its visualization. Every unique navigational event leaves a tangible trace, the *clickstream*, which is one of the most important implicit sources. This record of a user's movements in a particular Web information system is stored in the transfer-log file of the HTTP server and can be used as a transcript of discourse (Sullivan 1997; Jasper et al. 1998). *WebMapper*, a Java-based prototype for visualizing individual and aggregated user clickstreams, interprets HTTP server log file data and matches the results to the meta-model of the extended World Wide Web Design Technique (↪ Section 4.4: Usage: Visualizing Topology and Access Patterns). The initial prototype is promising, albeit still simplistic, especially as far as the graphical user interface is concerned. Nevertheless, even at this early stage it is a concrete response to open questions about how to represent and visualize the access patterns of Web users. From the information provider's perspective, the examination of traffic patterns across documents can identify "dead space" within a Web information system, prioritize new content development according to user requirements, and improve the system's general accessibility and navigability (Sullivan 1997).

Considering the emergent character of modern organizations, the value of continually gathering, extracting, and analyzing structural Web data complements regular observations of user activities. The automated approach to Web analysis presented in Section 4.5 is suitable for benchmarking, longitudinal studies, and cross-sectional comparisons. It helps Web developers to chart the industry's evolution and compare the performance of their own system with those of competing organizations. The integration of explicit feedback, behavioral impressions, and structural Web data results in the closed feedback cycle of Figure 4.2, which is used to structure the main part of this chapter (↪ Sections 4.2 to 4.5). Most available Web development tools, however, do not provide continuity from one phase to the next throughout the cycle. In contrast to traditional CASE tools (Kendall and Kendall 1999, 14), many of them fail to integrate the various activities effectively. This represents a serious shortcoming, since the modeling languages and tools employed should be consistent with an organization's development methodology.

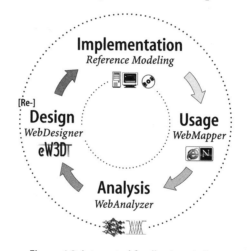

Figure 4.2. Integrated feedback cycle for
developing dynamic Web information systems

Systematically leveraging acquired feedback relies heavily not only on the visualization of data, but on sophisticated data mining capabilities, maintenance mechanisms to ensure consistency of the underlying databases, and statistical methods to aggregate available information and derive significant correlations between modifications to the system and user satisfaction. The existence of correlations between these variables does not necessarily denote causality, but nevertheless may suffice to guide subsequent development efforts.

4.1.2 Database Connectivity

Static Web information systems provide no mechanisms for user authentication, interactive dialogs, or the processing of transactions. As a consequence, little is known about the users themselves. Information about potential customers frequently remains incomplete and does not reflect economic reality. Therefore, more sophisticated markup languages such as XML, database connectivity, certification services, and application interfaces for integrated transaction processing gain popularity in stage two, overcoming the poor performance and functional limitations of applications based solely on a loosely connected set of documents. The connection between one hypertext front-end and the underlying database architecture is established either via the server by means of the *Common Gateway Interface (CGI)* and *Application Programming Interfaces (API)*, or via the client with technologies such as *Active X* or *Java-Applets* (Sommer and Zoller 1999). At the same time, the popularity of scripting languages for providing process control increases, again for both the server (e.g., *Perl, Python, server-side JavaScript, Active Server Pages*, etc.) and the client (e.g., *JavaScript* or *VBScript*). Currently, the *Practical Extraction and Report Language (Perl)* is the most popular interpreted language for programming CGI-based applications. More sophisticated transaction servers and packaged application toolkits streamline the development process, but require a substantial investment and often result in a long-term dependency on a specific supplier. Popular examples are Netscape's *ECXpert*, Open Market's *LiveCommerce*, Microsoft's *Site Server Commerce Edition*, or IBM's *Net.Commerce* (Jutla et al. 1999a, 72).

4.1.3 Presentational versus Semantic Markup Languages

The syntax of HTML is designed for simple hypertext representations. Although it has been extended with frames, tables, and other more advanced formatting constructs, it remains optimized for the document rendering requirements of early Web applications. As a consequence, HTML provides rich facilities for display, but no standard way to manage meta-data. The move from the *Hypertext Markup Language (HTML)* to the *eXtensible Markup Language (XML)*, an ISO compliant subset of the *Standard Generalized Markup Language (SGML)* that allows an easier definition of specialized markup languages, is likely to affect the customizability of Web documents significantly (Baeza-Yates and Ribeiro-Neto 1999, 154; Vasudevan and Palmer 1999). SGML, an international standard published in 1986 (ISO 8879: *Information Processing – Text and Office Systems*), is a complex meta-language formalism that allows the definition of descriptive markup languages for the purpose of electronic information encoding and interchange. Promoted by the International SGML Users' Group,[26] it was designed "to be formal

---

[26] http://www.isgmlug.org/isgmlug.htm

enough to allow proofs of document validity, structured enough to handle complex documents, and extensible enough to support management of large information repositories" (Werthner and Klein 1998, 79).

XML addresses the engineering complexity of SGML and the rigidity of fixed HTML tags. HTML as a *presentational markup language* imposes a lowest common denominator for document rendering and inextricably mixes presentation and representation (content and structure). As a *semantic markup language* founded on SGML, XML is extensible, validatable by external modules, and allows the definition of self-documenting tags (Ginsburg 1998). Its technique for specifying syntactical constraints is similar to Chomsky's generative meta-grammar to represent natural languages or the *Extended Backus-Naur Form (EBNF)* to describe computer languages (Chomsky 1986; Chomsky 1991; Renear 1997, 113; Noyes and Baber 1999, 98). XML forces the separation of presentation and representation by storing the definitions for non-standardized tags in a separate Document Type Definition (DTD) file. A DTD is the formal specification for documents of a given type, describing their constituting elements, required and optional attributes, and the exact order in which they have to appear. The structures constituting a document can be nested to arbitrary depth (Abiteboul et al. 2000, 28).

XML documents are usually presented with the *eXtensible Style Language (XSL)*, the HTML-based *Cascading Style Sheets (CSS)*, or the more complex, SGML-based *Document Style and Semantics Specification Language (DSSSL)*. Other than CSS, which can only present data in its original format, XSL includes mechanisms to transform, rearrange, and dynamically render XML documents.

Being interpretable by both human operators and computers, XML documents provide an incremental path to flexible business process automation. The two most prominent efforts to standardize industry-specific XML schemas and their definition are *XML.org*, hosted by the *Organization for the Advancement of Structured Information Standards (Oasis)*, and Microsoft's *BizTalk*.[27] XML's human readability is a significant advantage in comparison with distributed software component models such as the Object Management Group's *Common Object Request Broker Architecture (CORBA)*,[28] Microsoft's *Distributed Common Object Model (DCOM)*,[29] or Sun Microsystem's *JavaBeans Component Architecture*.[30] These models allow applications to communicate with

---

[27] http://www.xml.org/
    http://www.biztalk.org/
[28] http://www.omg.org/
[29] http://www.microsoft.com/NTServer/appservice/techdetails/prodarch/DCOM
[30] http://java.sun.com/beans/

one another, no matter where they are located or who designed them originally. They specify how systems from different vendors can inter-operate. However, just as HTML is a markup language for presenta-tional purposes, distributed software component models are standards for automated data processing, meant to convey information among programs with practically no concession to human readability (Fournier 1998, 382ff.; Glushko et al. 1999, 109).

The flexibility introduced by XML and multiple DTDs is not limited to business processes. It also impacts on the design and functionality of Web clients. XML supports annotations, facilitates the personalization of user interfaces, and provides at least a partial solution to the preva-lent problem of display device diversity. Compare, for example, the *Annotate!* system of Ginsburg and Kambil, which dynamically couples documents with XML annotations (↪ Section 5.5.1; (Ginsburg and Kambil 1999)). By increasing their overall semantics, this process adds value to publicly accessible Web information systems. Content-based text encoding strategies (↪ Section 1.1: Formal Definitions of Text) based on XML facilitate the generation of specialized views and support advanced link-level navigation. In this way, changes to structured XML documents can easily be synchronized among their components or with referring documents (Nguyen and Schmidt 1999, 95).

4.1.4 Traversal Functions

With the important exception of mechanisms to structure documents semantically, the hypertextual attributes of dynamic Web information systems resemble those of the first stage (↪ Figure 4.3). The mentioned popularity of scripting languages, however, facilitates the design of transient traversal functions and controlled access structures (e.g., for guiding the user through a questionnaire). Occasionally, conditional linking on a very basic level is incorporated on the basis of the explicitly acquired data.

Determinability	Transiency	Perspective	Access
☒ Determinable	☒ (Transient)	☐ Personal	☒ Random
☐ Indeterminable	☒ Intransient	☒ Impersonal	☒ (Controlled)

Dynamics	Linking	Semantics	User Function
☒ No (Static)	☒ Explicit	☐ Limited	☒ Explorative
☐ Intratextonic	☒ (Conditional)	☒ Supported	☐ Configurative
☐ Textonic	☐ None	☐ Required	☒ Interpretative
			☐ Textonic

Figure 4.3. Hypertextual attributes of dynamic Web information systems

4.2   DESIGN: THE CURRENT STATE OF WEB ENGINEERING

Being familiar and generally trusted, the generic term *engineering* is frequently and optimistically used to signify an orderly development in a new field (e.g., software engineering, knowledge engineering, or document engineering). In the context of the World Wide Web, it denotes a systematic, disciplined, quantifiable application of scientific knowledge (i.e., methods, tools, and technical concepts) to development, deployment, operation, and maintenance of Web information systems that meet a particular set of technical, economic, and social objectives (Deshpande et al. 1999; IEEE 1999b; Lowe and Hall 1999, 15; Murugesan et al. 1999).

The following section presents a number of general considerations regarding information complexity and its influence on the decision-making process. Visual techniques are identified that can amplify cognition and lessen the impact of information overload, which belongs to the characteristic features of Web-based environments. Many of these visual techniques support cooperative efforts to integrate Web site management, content production, and interface design (Section 4.2.2). In line with the definition of Web engineering stated above, Section 4.2.3 delineates and compares existing methods, tools, and technical concepts for the analysis and design of Web-based applications. This review sets the stage for introducing the Extended World Wide Web Design Technique (eW3DT) in Section 4.2.4 and subsequently applying its document-oriented modeling language to an electronic shopping mall in Section 4.2.5.

4.2.1   Processing and Visualizing Complex Information

"The deluge of Web pages has generated dystopian commentaries on the tragedy of the flood of information. It has also produced utopian visions of harnessing the same flood for constructive purposes" (Shneiderman 1997a, 5; also compare with Turban and Aronson 1998, 725). Empirical studies show that decision-makers indeed seek more information than can optimally be processed – i.e., the perceived value of information continues to increase beyond the point of information overload (Moody and Walsh 1999, 505). Complex managerial decisions with numerous and frequently contradictory information sources, alternative approaches to finding adequate solutions, and rather uncertain outcomes provide a high cognitive load. Pooling several experts may help, but often is restricted by the mounting coordination and communication overheads of larger workgroups (Turban and Aronson 1998, 10). When people are faced with moderately contradictory information regarding a certain problem, their information-seeking process will continue. Confrontations with high levels of discrepancy or complexity of the problem to be solved will tend to cut off this process and cause people to fall back on stereotypical behavior (Ozanne et al. 1992, 452ff.; Timmermans 1993, 95ff.; Allen 1996, 95ff.).

A high level of actual or perceived risk results in increased information seeking (Brown and Prentice 1987, 371ff.) and is associated with the chronic problem of filtering and processing large amounts of information in order to speed up the decision-making process. The highly dynamic environment and the cognitive demand of multidimensional problems place internal and external pressure on decision-makers. As comprehension degrades rapidly in such situations, overly complex environments negatively impact the efficiency of decision processes (Meyer 1997). As their capacity for processing information has some physical, biological, psychological, logical, and semiotic limitations, analysts need to reduce the multidimensional problem space to a manageable personal conceptual framework to cope with the complexities involved (Meyer and Grundei 1995; Meyer 1996; Marcus 1997, 37).

Fortunately, the human ability to perceive and process visual information is highly sophisticated. Spatial representations and cognitive processes allow people to visualize problems of high complexity, manipulate elements in the multidimensional problem space, and construct novel solutions (Mahling 1994, 42). "The ubiquity of visual metaphors in describing cognitive processes hints at a nexus of relationships between what we see and what we think" (Card et al. 1999, 1). As a consequence, the visualization of data remains a crucial factor for designing, analyzing, and using Web information systems. The interweaving of interior mental action and external perception (and manipulation) is no accident. On the contrary, it has profound effects on people's ability to assimilate and process information. Historically, the progress of human civilization is closely linked to the sequence of inventions regarding visual artifacts such as writing, mathematics, maps, printing, diagrams, and visual computing. Visual artifacts regularly employ techniques for depicting quantities such as *direct labels* (numerically labeled grids of statistical graphics), *encodings* (color scales), and *self-representing scales* (objects of known size appearing in an image; (Tufte 1997, 13)). Card et al. describe a number of ways in which combinations of these visual techniques can amplify cognition (Card et al. 1999, 16ff.):

- Increasing the processing and memory resources available to users:
  - The human moving gaze system is part of an active process in which head, eye, and attention are employed to make optimal use of the limited channel capacity. It partitions that capacity in order

to combine high spatial resolution and wide aperture in sensing visual environments (*high-bandwidth hierarchical interaction*).

- Some attributes of visualizations can be processed in parallel compared to text, which is usually accessed sequentially (*parallel perceptual processing*).
- Visualizations can expand the working memory available for solving a problem (*expanded working memory*).
- Some visualizations store massive amounts of information in a compact and quickly accessible form – e.g., distorted maps as discussed in Section 5.5.4: Meta-Level Adaptation (*expanded storage of information, high data density*).

- Reducing the search for information: visualizations often group related concepts together, reducing the necessary efforts for locating a particular piece of information. Moreover, the clustering of data objects can avoid the need for explicit symbolic labels (*locality of processing, spatially indexed addressing*).

- Enhancing the detection of patterns:
  - Recognizing information represented by a visualization tends to be easier for the user than recalling that information from her memory (*replacement of recall by recognition*).
  - Visualizations simplify and organize information, supplying a higher-level order with aggregated forms of information through abstraction and selective omission (*abstractions and aggregation*) – compare, for example, the tightly-coupled view presented in Section 5.5.4: Meta-Level Adaptation.
  - Visualizations can be constructed to enhance value patterns, structural relationship patterns, and trend patterns (*visual schemata for organization: value, relationship, trend*) – e.g., by time (average viewing times of documents), by predefined categories (user groups), or according to the system's inherent hierarchy (directed graph).

- Some cognitive inferences done symbolically can be recoded into inferences done with simple perceptual operations (*transfer of processes from cognitive to perceptual system*). Visualizations can support a large number of perceptual inferences that are extremely easy for humans, even in complex and specialized cases.

- Using perceptual attention mechanisms for monitoring: visualizations allow for the simultaneous monitoring of a large number of potential events if the display is organized so that these stand out by appearance or motion (*perceptual monitoring*).

- Encoding and representing information interactively: unlike static diagrams, visualizations allow exploration of a space of parameter values (*manipulable medium*). Interactive animations, for instance, fundamentally change the process of understanding data. The per-

ceptual phenomenon of object constancy enables the user to maintain context when using appropriate intermediate views to change
the perspective of information-rich diagrams (Robertson et al. 1991,
190ff.; Lamping and Rao 1996, 46). Without animation, the user
would take considerable time to re-assimilate the relationships
within substructures (*graphical computations*).

4.2.2   Cooperative Web Development

Developing Web information systems is a multidisciplinary activity that
usually involves the joint efforts of several departments and a team of
professionals with various skills, interests, and motivations. Project
management has to coordinate a broad spectrum of expertise and focus
the efforts of marketing managers, brand managers, account managers,
site analysts, marketing editors, content managers, content producers,
content editors, production engineers, system administrators, server
engineers, application developers, user interface designers, graphic
artists, and documentation managers (Mena 1999; Noyes and Baber
1999, xi). The ability to successfully assimilate and exploit advanced
Web technologies ahead of the industry curve requires a set of both
technical and managerial skills. As many employees lack hybrid competencies and specialize in one of these areas, they often fail to understand each other's objectives and processes (Winograd 1997, 159; Jutla
et al. 1999a, 74).

Without any explicit acknowledgement, computing professionals no
longer belong to a privileged minority mediating between advanced
information technology and the general populace, as advances in end-
user computing and interface design take their toll. This contrasts with
nearly 40 years of information systems' evolution, when the field pos-
sessed an exclusive and almost mystic aura even as it continued to
spawn different specializations (Deshpande et al. 1999). For this reason
the extended World Wide Web Design Technique (eW3DT) has been
developed as an alternative to technical modeling languages of little
descriptive power. Many researchers in Web development and visualization have recognized the split between explanatory (e.g., documenting
information system; ↪ Section 4.2.4: The Extended World Wide Web
Design Technique) and exploratory goals such as providing efficient
user interfaces (↪ Section 5.5.4: Meta-Level Adaptation; (Munzner
1998, 18)). eW3DT proves equally relevant for both types of goals. It
represents a context-providing electronic design space as defined by
Rheinfrank et al., a conceptual meeting ground for supporting the activities associated with bringing innovative Web-based applications to
life (Rheinfrank et al. 1994, 85). Placing its primary emphasis on con-

sumer-to-business transactions, the document-oriented modeling framework is intended to remove existing communication barriers between academic research, information system departments, top-level management, and functional units as depicted in Figure 4.4 (Scharl 1998b, 252; Scharl 1999b, 212). eW3DT represents a possible answer to the limitation of human information processing in short-term memory, which requires diagrams to be kept simple, multiple page displays to be consolidated, and window-motion frequency to be reduced (Shneiderman 1997b, 75; Bucy et al. 1999).

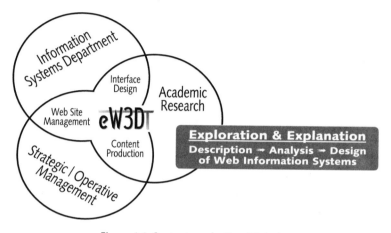

Figure 4.4. Content production, Web site
management, and interface design with eW3DT

One of the main challenges of modeling and developing hypertext applications derives from the strong interdependency between presentation (user interface) and representation (explicit structuring) of published information. Many meta-models and design methodologies for Web information systems lack the necessary object types for modeling this interdependency and are only suited to highly structured segments. To serve as an efficient interface to users with heterogeneous knowledge and expectations, visual representations of hypertext architectures intended for the general public have to include the essential information in an illustrative and comprehensible way. Optimally, the same visual language should be used for content production, Web site management, and interface design. In this way, the required training time allotted for codes, mnemonics, and sequences of actions can be reduced (Shneiderman 1997b, 75; Bucy et al. 1999).

4.2.3 Review of Existing Design Methodologies

Guiding innovative design on a conceptual level includes attempts to create novel technological solutions "based on an analytical perspective with a specific orientation towards the existing detail of practical action" (Button and Dourish 1996). Methodologies represent comprehensive, multiple-step approaches to providing this guidance during the development of (Web) information systems (Hoffer et al. 1999, 10). By no means can achieving this objective be considered a straightforward task. While technical restrictions play a pivotal role, the following approaches focus on conceptual aspects and the modeling of content, hypertext structure, navigational support, and hypertext presentation. Very general concepts like the *Corporate Web Site Development Methodology* (Chen et al. 1999) are not included as they only mirror the conventional systems analysis and design approach, frequently referred to as the *waterfall model* or *systems development life-cycle* (↪ Section 2.1.1: Alternative Life-Cycle Economies). Stressing the importance of site measurement and ongoing evolution, Buchanan and Lukaszewski present a slightly more advanced methodology, the *Web Site Life-Cycle* (Buchanan and Lukaszewski 1997, 4ff.).

Approaches of a more technical nature that focus on the World Wide Web and its hypertextual features comprise the widely accepted *Relationship Management Methodology (RMM)*, the *Web Site Design Method (WSDM)*, the *Object-Oriented Hypermedia Design Model (OOHDM)*, the *Relationship Navigation Analysis (RNA)*, *Araneus*, *LifeWeb*, or recent XML-based work such as the *Extensible Web Modeling Framework* (Balasubramanian et al. 1995; Isakowitz et al. 1995; Schwabe and Rossi 1995; Schwabe et al. 1996; De Troyer and Leune 1998; Gnaho and Larcher 1999; Mecca et al. 1999; Nguyen and Schmidt 1999; Sommer and Zoller 1999; Klapsing and Neumann 2000; Yoo and Bieber 2000). Lowe and Hall provide an in-depth comparison of these methodologies. Many of them are especially suited for highly structured, database-driven information domains (Lowe and Hall 1999, 477ff.) and succeed traditional hypermedia design techniques such as the Hypertext Design Model (HDM | HDM2), which themselves are under constant development (Garzotto et al. 1993; Garzotto et al. 1995; Garzotto et al. 1996). Well-known semantic data models, based on either entity relations or object-oriented approaches, are extended by providing additional components for hypertext structure, navigation, and presentation. Most methodologies specify a number of design steps for clustering entities and attributes, developing consistent navigational structures, and defining layout features of the user interface (Sommer and Zoller 1999).

The *paradox of systems design* states that the "introduction of technology designed to support 'large-scale' activities while fundamentally transforming the 'small-scale' detail of action can systematically undermine exactly the detailed features of working practice through which the 'large-scale' activity is, in fact, accomplished. It points, fundamentally, to the interdependence of minute practice and grand accomplishment" (Button and Dourish 1996). Due to the limitations found in many existing design concepts and as a possible answer to this paradox of systems design, Bichler and Nusser developed the *World Wide Web Design Technique (W3DT)*. Simultaneously, they implemented a working prototype of a software tool called *WebDesigner*,[31] which supports the graphical, interactive design of complex Web information systems from a user's perspective (Bichler and Nusser 1996a).

Development environments have to provide efficient methods and tools for document management and to deal with the increased complexity of the hypertext author's tasks. Even though site maps generated with modeling tools such as *WebArchitect, SchemaText,* Microsoft's *FrontPage,* Adobe's *GoLive,* or Macromedia's *Dreamweaver,* to name a few, provide similar "authoring-in-the-large" functionalities (Schwabe and Rossi 1995; Freisler and Kesseler 1997), they lack the semantic richness of (e)W3DT.[32] Most available products, for example, do not address responsibilities for content production, system implementation, or regular maintenance. In contrast to the database-oriented concepts mentioned above, W3DT was built from scratch to support the requirements of unstructured, hierarchical systems and to visualize them from a recipient's perspective. Utilizing practical experiences in developing Web information systems (Hansen and Scharl 1998, 994), the graphical notation of the design tool was further refined and used to analyze a number of deployed applications. With special regard to reference modeling of commercial applications, the *Extended World Wide Web Design Technique (eW3DT)* was developed (Scharl 1997b, 63ff.; Scharl 1998a).

Hypertext is more, not less, hierarchical than most paper-based texts, but enables advanced users to easily move up and down the hierarchy (Aarseth 1998, 174). Nevertheless, there still is a conspicuous lack of non-redundant, readable meta-models for Web information systems that do not ignore the hierarchical, recipient-oriented structure of current systems. Complementary to approaches that primarily focus on

---

[31] http://wwwi.wu-wien.ac.at/w3dt/
[32] http://www.schema.de/sitehtml/site-e/
http://www.microsoft.com/frontpage/
http://www.adobe.com/products/golive/
http://www.macromedia.com/software/dreamweaver/

technical issues, eW3DT is intended to drive structural design and to streamline the decision processes necessary for implementing complex applications. As far as database-centric hypermedia applications are concerned, there is no adequate substitute for relational or object-oriented approaches such as the *Unified Modeling Language (UML)*. In this sense, eW3DT is not intended to replace modeling techniques like UML, RMM, or HDM but to act as a complementary, visual, and hierarchically structured communication tool between researchers, system analysts, and management responsible for the decision to implement Web information systems. Section 4.3 describes the integration of conceptual and technical models during the implementation phase.

4.2.4   The Extended World Wide Web Design Technique

With the continuing introduction of new technologies, strategic management decisions have to consider innovation as a crucial parameter, particularly as far as information and communication technologies are concerned. Innovation substantially reduces the practical value of traditional communication models. A hierarchical description format is one of the prerequisites for overcoming the restrictions imposed by these traditional models. Hierarchical description formats facilitate an in-depth analysis of Web information systems and the formulation of conceptual design guidelines. Conceptual, user-centric modeling of Web information systems allows standardized visual communication between academic research, management, and Web developers. *User-centric* approaches direct the data, its organization, the retrieval mechanisms, and the interfaces toward enabling users to satisfy specific information needs or to solve specific problems (Allen 1996, 16). By contrast, *data-centric* and *technology-centric* approaches design data structures and user interfaces around the available data or the underlying technology (Hoffer et al. 1999, 14), which stringently dictates how information can be arranged for access and retrieval (↪ Section 2.2.2: Diffusion of Web Technology).

This section presents the object types of eW3DT, which are then applied to the (deductive) design of an electronic shopping mall in Section 4.2.5 and to the (inductive) visualization of customer access patterns in Section 4.4. The availability of distinct document object types makes it easier for content providers to talk about their work, express their ideas, and specify operational requirements. Following these specifications, developers can use eW3DT objects to rapidly and cost-effectively generate and visualize ideas for further evaluation (Rheinfrank et al. 1994, 85).

Diagrams relying on eW3DT are a user-centric combination of structural and process diagrams (Lohse et al. 1994), which requires an explicit explanation of symbols. This explanation (= notation) will be presented in the following paragraphs. Every eW3DT data object type represents a special variation of a standard symbolic element depicted in Figure 4.5 and is equivalent to an atomistic unit of the *Dexter Hypertext Reference Model* (Halasz and Schwartz 1994). Together with an (optional) differentiation by color, the sub-symbol (S) on the right-hand side of the object name signals the basic type of the information object. The hierarchical level where the document in question can usually be found within a hypertext application is specified in the bottom left field (x). The second digit (y) describes optional sub-components. An interaction, implemented as part of the homepage, for example, would receive the value 1.1.

Figure 4.5. Standard symbolic element of eW3DT

The hierarchical structure of most Web information systems resembles a directed graph, or digraph – i.e., a tree with additional cross-references between some of its nodes (Mladenic 1998, 68). Formally defined, a *directed graph* consists of a non-empty finite set of *vertices* (= hypertext documents) and a finite family of ordered pairs of elements called *arcs* (= links). A *walk* is a finite sequence of arcs, in which any two consecutive arcs are adjacent or identical. A walk in which all the arcs are distinct is referred to as a *trail*. If, in addition, all the vertices are distinct, then the trail becomes a *path* (Wilson 1996, 26f.; Abiteboul et al. 2000, 24f.). Visualizations of directed graphs and of the different types of user movements between their vertices are often employed to provide advanced supplemental navigational systems (↪ Section 5.5.4: Meta-Level Adaptation). These representations may pose some difficult algorithmical problems. Card et al., for example, suggest "not to try it at all, but rather to transform the generalized graph into a tree and mark it in some way to indicate discrepancies" (Card et al. 1999, 189). Breadth-first traversal of the graph is an efficient way to convert it into a tree. When several paths lead to a certain node, the shortest one is chosen to determine (x). The means for marking the remaining "discrepancies" (additional cross-references) are introduced in Section 4.2.4.2: Diagram Structuring.

As a precondition for pursuing a partial globalization strategy, eW3DT distinguishes technical from content-specific responsibilities for designing, implementing, and maintaining Web information systems. Two abbreviations next to the hierarchical level refer to functional units responsible for content (CT) and technical implementation (TI). In the bottom right field, one to three "☆"-symbols represent the maintenance intensity of information objects. Initial efforts to design, produce, and publish documents are not considered. Not surprisingly, the possibility to leverage existing databases influences this value substantially. In the following discussion, the data object types will be referred to as information object types, the objects themselves as information objects or documents. To visualize this distinction, the names of information object types are marked with <...>, those of information objects with {...}.

Independent of iconic similarity and real equivalence to a given object (hypertext compound document), every information object type defines a general profile for describing the characteristic attributes of this object. Each of these profiles corresponds to a set of abstractions commonly found in Web information systems. The attributes assign information on structural position, maintenance intensity, and organizational integration to the modeling constructs. Figure 4.6 categorizes the object types of eW3DT into the three functional segments *information, navigation*, and *structure*. With the help of these elements, which are described in sections 4.2.4.1 to 4.2.4.3, hierarchical information spaces of variable complexity can be visualized. It is of no importance whether the models based on these visualizations are intended for a real organization (customized model) or for an industry-specific analysis (reference model). The distinction between reference and customized models in the context of developing Web information systems will be explained in Section 4.3.

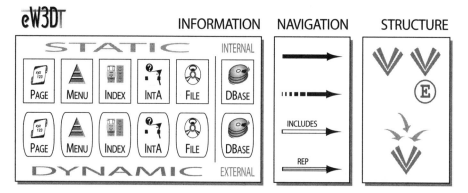

Figure 4.6. Object types of eW3DT, categorized into the functional segments *information, navigation,* and *structure*

4.2.4.1 Information Object Types

With the exception of <DBase>, there are information object types for both static and dynamically generated documents (the dotted line in Figure 4.5 signifies dynamic objects). In the case of <DBase>, internal and external data structures are distinguished since the content structure itself is inherently dynamic – a fact which does not require explicit visualization. Structural variability is the relevant characteristic to separate static from dynamic information objects. If the structure is changing, the dynamic process becomes part of the architecture, independent of its technical realization. Even if information objects are automatically generated out of database queries, their inherent character might be of a static nature.

- *<Page>*. This object type is used to model standard hypertext documents, which usually represent the logical end of a hierarchical tree. As mentioned above, the internal structure of a <Page> is not supported by the eW3DT meta-model.
- *<Menu>*. Alternative navigational paths and access mechanisms belong to the object type <Menu>. Objects of this type are usually found at higher hierarchical levels of Web information systems. They are strongly influenced by considerations regarding the content's optimal depth versus breadth ratio. The impact of the hierarchical tree's branching factor (↳ Section 5.5.4.2: View Types) on the system's usability is one of the most discussed issues in the literature (Shneiderman 1997a, 24; Hochheiser and Shneiderman 1999, 1). It represents a trade-off between the limited number of links that can be embedded in a document of limited resolution and the desire for a flat hierarchical structure to minimize the number of required navigational steps to access a certain piece of information. Hence every Web developer should bear in mind recommendations with regard to a limited number of unrelated elements appearing in a single document. Being able to build and represent complex structures does not imply that the user absorbs them in the intended way. As a consequence, hypermedia access structures like the {Electronic Shopping Mall} depicted in Figure 4.10 have to find a balance between horizontal and vertical integration density.
- *<Index>*. In contrast to menus, an <Index> contains a complete enumeration of links, for example a company's staff or a list of available products. Especially for statically implemented <Index> documents, maintenance is vital (and time-consuming) since links pointing to missing, inactive, or irrelevant sources substantially reduce the perceived quality of Web information systems (↳ Section 4.5.4: Validating Manual Evaluations of the LSE/Novell Survey).

- *<Interaction>*. This category includes various interactive elements, mainly characterized by their content and layout structure. Since eW3DT provides a conceptual meta-model, technical details referring to the implementation of the <Interaction> are of only secondary importance.

- *<File>*. Electronic software distribution or the transmission of application-specific data blocks requires secure and efficient mechanisms to transfer files of various formats and sizes from the content provider to individual users in a platform-independent way. These mechanisms are visualized with the object type <File>.

- *<DBase>*. Due to an ever increasing demand for up-to-date and consistent information, it seems justified to expect many of the organization's internal databases to be connected to increasingly complex Web applications over a relatively short period. Atomicity, consistency, isolation, and durability of database transactions must be enforced in distributed Web environments (Jutla et al. 1999b, 480). Economically, however, it is not feasible and definitely not in compliance with the basic assumptions behind a reference model to deal explicitly with all these databases. Any attempt to do so would result in a redundant remodeling of existing internal structures – a substantial effort in light of the heterogeneous character of corporate database architectures. With eW3DT, only user inputs that lead to the creation of new database entries or to the update of stored information are taken into consideration. The reserved symbol for these user inputs is the eW3DT object type <DBase>, which is available in two different representations: internal and external (dotted line in Figure 4.7).

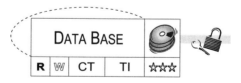

Figure 4.7. eW3DT object type <DBase>

While internal <DBase> objects refer to various corporate databases, the external ones include cooperative databases, databases held by other institutions, or supplemental external information sources. To distinguish them from hyperlinks (arrows), associations between database symbols and the corresponding documents are visualized by shaded connections (bars). If the object is marked with a lock, security mechanisms have to be implemented due to the sensitivity of the information provided. Technical details are only of secondary relevance for conceptual modeling. Thus eW3DT does not provide any attributes to distinguish different protocols such as the Secure Sockets Layer (SSL),[33] the Secure Hypertext Transfer Protocol (S-HTTP),[34] Secure Multipurpose Internet Mail Extensions (S/MIME),[35] Secure Electronic Transactions (SET),[36] or between the network or application layers at which they are targeted. The [R]ead and [W]rite attributes indicate the user's right to access individual entries, while the star symbols on the bottom right corner of the object indicate recommended update intervals, similar to the maintenance intensity of documents. "☆" is used for static permanent data, "☆☆" for occasionally updated entries (e.g., user profiles, marketing information, or compiled Web statistics), and "☆☆☆" for highly volatile transaction records (e.g., payment data, shopping lists, or log files that record user access patterns).

4.2.4.2 Diagram Structuring

With regard to the increasingly complex content and the variety of navigational elements, a Web information system's complete structure cannot be shown in just one single diagram (↪ Section 5.5.4.3: View Transformations). Since it causes an unnecessary loss of information, the object type <Diagram> of W3DT – predecessor of eW3DT – was eliminated. The required reduction in complexity is now achieved by hierarchical diagram structuring with the <Primary Structuring Element>, which is shown in the center of Figure 4.8. The information object type as well as additional attributes of the corresponding document located in the lower-level diagram are already part of the upper-level diagram, thus increasing the clarity and usefulness of the graphical representation.

Figure 4.8. Object types for diagram structuring

<External Links> are used to depict hyperlinks to external information sources that are not under the organization's direct control – for example, to Web sites of other companies, standardization committees, or governmental organizations. The object type <Multiple Sources>

---

[33] http://home.netscape.com/security/techbriefs/ssl.html
[34] http://www.terisa.com/shttp/index.html
      http://www.spyrus.com/content/products/ssl/tlsgold/terisafaq.html
[35] http://www.rsa.com/rsalabs/faq/html/5-1-1.html
[36] http://www.setco.org/

plays a vital part in reducing redundancy within the diagrams and may be found where multidimensional selections offer access to large amounts of data. Multiple destinations frequently emerge from the implementation of an <Index>. They are represented by the dynamic version of the navigational object type <Representative Link>, which will be introduced in the next section.

4.2.4.3 Navigation Design

The development of Web information systems and the navigation within their hypertextual structures are non-linear, non-sequential activities that require an appropriate visual (symbolic) representation. Navigation design has to counteract the reduction of coherence in Web-based applications, which arises due to an inadequate consideration of the specific linguistic features of hypertext environments. eW3DT comprises four distinct types of visual association: static, dynamic, representative, and horizontal links (↪ Figure 4.9):

- *<Static Links>* are implemented permanently; only structural redesigns of Web information systems require an adaptation.
- *<Dynamic Links>* refer to customized, automatically generated documents.
- *<Representative Links>* as a sub-type of the <Dynamic Link> point to different versions of static information that are delivered depending on the existence of certain conditions, or responding to specific user behavior. As mentioned previously, multiple destinations within Web information systems are also modeled via <Representative Links>.
- *<Horizontal Links>* do not show the characteristics of a hyperlink but enable designers to deal with heterogeneous documents (so-called *composites*, using the terminology of the *Dexter Hypertext Reference Model*; (Halasz and Schwartz 1994)). Besides, they are an effective way to model Web information systems that make use of frames.

Figure 4.9. Navigational object types

To increase flexibility and reduce the number of necessary object types, a dedicated symbol for bi-directional links does not exist in eW3DT. Bi-directional access structures may always be constructed using a combination of uni-directional navigational object types. In addition to that, cross-links and references to higher hierarchical levels are not part of standard eW3DT diagrams for reasons of readability. Interactive modeling tools relying on eW3DT, however, should support the dynamic presentation of the entire graph structure via location probes (↪ Section 5.5.4.3: View Transformations). If users move the mouse pointer over an information object *(brushing)*, the complete set of links originating from and leading to the object under consideration are temporarily displayed (Terveen et al. 1999, 90).

4.2.5 Application of eW3DT (Electronic Shopping Mall)

Four phases can be distinguished when market participants plan to exchange information and commodities: information, negotiation, settlement, and after-sales (↪ Section 2.3: Electronic Market Transactions). To demonstrate the semantic relationships between the eW3DT information object types described in the previous sections, the reference solution of Figure 4.10 visualizes standard components of an electronic retailing application that support these core phases of electronic market transactions – compare with the hierarchical tree and outline of Figure 5.9 (page 224). After-sales and transaction analysis are disregarded in this simplified example. The following abbreviations denote the functional units responsible for content and technical implementation: mall administration (MA), marketing department of one particular company (MKT), information systems department of mall (ISM), and the company's information systems department (ISC).

In the first phase, customers identify and evaluate their needs and possible sources to fulfill them. After accessing one of the {Company Storefronts} belonging to the {Electronic Shopping Mall}, the user is provided with a general {Company Profile}. After optional identification of the customer (explicit via forms or implicit via cookies), the stored {Customer Profile} can be accessed and updated. Existing customers may track the status of past orders – a function that is often supported by Web information systems of courier services such as *Fedex* or *UPS*.[37] New customers have the option to create a record by providing personal information such as name, mailing address, or credit card data. However, this is normally not required until they actually place an order.

At the same time, a number of {Product Families} are introduced. Having identified his general requirements by selecting a certain category, the customer can choose more specifically between a number of {Product Variations}. The product in question is represented by the description {Product X}. Optionally, {Technical Details} can be accessed

---

[37] http://www.fedex.com/
http://www.ups.com/

for further information. At any point during the transaction, items can be added to and removed from a temporary market basket, which also indicates product availability and the expected time of delivery. The information derived from such a {Shopping Cart} represents an important source of implicit feedback, even if the customer ultimately chooses not to place an order.

Subsequently, prospective customers and sellers negotiate the terms of the intended transaction by jointly identifying possible solutions with the goal of reaching a consensus, usually in the form of a contract. Should the {Negotiation Process} turn out to be successful for both parties, the customer is able to place an online order immediately by filling out the {Order form}. Naturally, every order is archived in the {Customer Profile} to provide for adaptive product recommendations, tailored marketing efforts, or secondary statistical analyses.

The contract is executed and goods and financial compensation are exchanged according to the conditions stipulated in the preceding negotiation phase. If the customer correctly enters all the necessary specifications, a separate market transaction is triggered between the seller and a financial clearing institution. The customer has no way of directly accessing the result of internal processes such as credit checks or supplier contact transactions. Therefore, eW3DT as a document-oriented modeling technique disregards these sub-transactions.

As soon as a form of payment is agreed upon and verified by the seller, the database entries {Accounting}, {Inventory}, and {Customer Profile} are updated and a {Confirmation of Order} can be sent immediately, either by e-mail or directly via a dynamic document. The whole transaction is completed with the physical distribution of the product. In the case of immaterial goods, the actual delivery of the product is executed without delay. Pioneered by companies such as *Digital Delivery, GLOBEtrotter, Reciprocal,* or *ReleaseNow.com,*[38] electronic software distribution (a customized <File> sent to the buyer) eliminates the need for physical distribution.

---

[38] http://www.digitaldelivery.com/
http://www.globetrotter.com/
http://www.reciprocal.com/
http://www.releasenow.com/

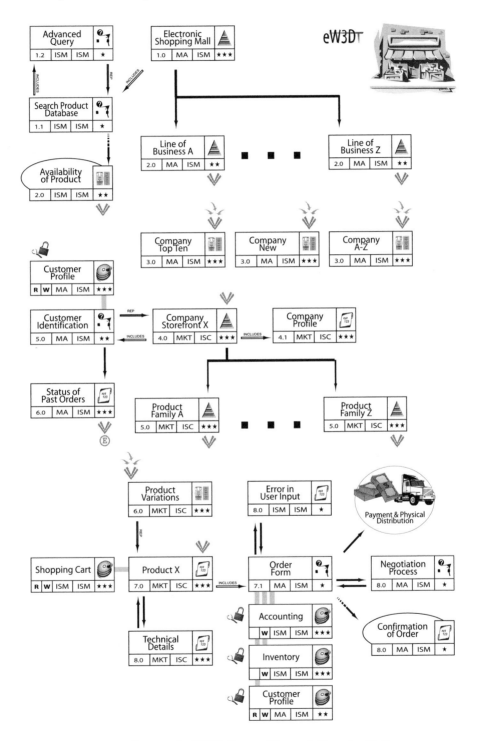

Figure 4.10. eW3DT-diagram {Electronic Shopping Mall}

4.3 IMPLEMENTATION: INDUSTRY-SPECIFIC REFERENCE MODELS

Practitioners frequently ignore the beneficial role of methodologies to both the quality of Web information systems and the economics of the development process (Chatzoglou 1997, 269f.). For any of the older, less knowledge-intensive technologies, knowledge could easily be trans-ferred from one organization to another (Nambisan and Wang 1999, 98). With the continuing evolution of the World Wide Web (↪ Section 2.2: A Brief History of Web Adaptivity), however, experience has shown that there is a growing need to structure and formalize this process (Hansen 1995, 128).

4.3.1 Definition and Overview

For deployed applications, implementation represents a straightforward and fully automated process. Integrated system components generate the system's predefined structure and content dynamically, without any need for direct human intervention. More effort is required in the initial development phase – compare with the internal (r)evolution of Section 2.1: Darwinian versus Technological Evolution (Figure 2.1). Guidelines and specifications for this phase are usually presented as *reference models*. A reference model is a normative concept that relies on expert industry knowledge or successful prior implementations. It represents an abstraction of a typical company, its functional units, or its (Web) Information Systems. The use of the term "reference model" will be restricted to industry-specific approaches throughout this book. This excludes similar concepts like process reference models (organizational guidelines for implementing new systems), or software reference mod-els that mirror the structure of standard applications at a higher level of abstraction (Scheruhn 1996, 116f.; Bauer and Glasson 1998, 471ff.).

4.3.2 Deducing Customized and Technical Models

Results of research activities formulated in industry-oriented reference models may be used by any organization to build up new systems from scratch, or to extend and adapt existing ones. The reference model stipulates guidelines for deducing *customized models* (= company-specific implementation models), streamlining the implementation of complex Web applications at reduced costs (Scharl 1997a, 287). Cus-tomized models apply general recommendations to the strategic plans and situational parameters of a specific company. They provide the conceptual basis for both the organization's strategic decisions and the required *technical models* for implementing the system (↪ Figure 4.11). The meta-model of *Extended World Wide Web Design Technique (eW3DT)* provides a framework for the construction of both reference and customized models during the development process of commercial Web information systems (Scharl 1997b, 63ff.). Note the difference in the level of abstraction (in decreasing order) between meta-models such as eW3DT, reference models, and customized models (Hars 1994). Provided that the chosen meta-model is relevant for the real-world object system under consideration (= Web information system), the developer can ensure *syntactic correctness* by properly applying the meta-model's notational rules. The second parameter, *semantic correctness,* is achieved by selecting appropriate object types, accurately specifying their attributes, and representing the object system's structure in a complete and undistorted way.

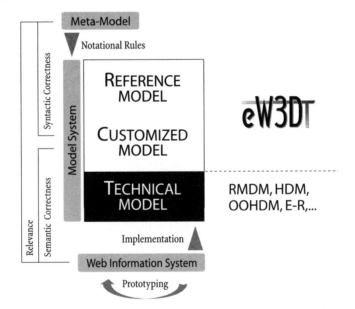

Figure 4.11. Relationships between reference, customized, and technical models for developing Web information systems

In a second deductive step, the customized eW3DT model is extended by and integrated with appropriate technical models to specify the underlying database architecture and prepare the system's physical implementation. Available meta-models for this extension include the Relationship Management Data Model (RMDM), the Hypertext Design Model (HDM), the Object-oriented Hypertext Design Model (OOHDM), or the wide range of options based on relational or object-oriented data models.

4.3.3   Removing Communication Barriers

More than any other form of text, hypertext is "irreducibly plural, suggested in its etymology (from the Latin *texere*, 'to weave'), which points
to its entwined (textile), or combinatory state, the interlacing of its materials" (Sutherland 1997, 4). Reference models support this plurality
and the cooperation between academic institutions, business partners,
and departments within a company. Provided that there are generic
similarities between two related industries, Bauer and Glasson conclude
that reference modeling may serve as a technology transfer mechanism
not only within but also across industries (Scheruhn 1996, 112ff.; Bauer
and Glasson 1998, 484). Reference models are adapted and improved in
line with the specific requirements of a particular business sector, different from the business sector at which the original model was aimed.

Designers of Web information systems have to envision new concepts, and embody those concepts as artifacts such as textual descriptions, two- or three-dimensional diagrams, structural models, and
working prototypes. Understanding how designers currently use artifacts and how those artifacts relate to their shared knowledge assumptions is one of the key aspects of user-centered design as introduced in
Section 2.2.2: Diffusion of Web Technology (Olson and Olson 1991, 79).
When the referenced concepts become increasingly defined, more formal description formats are required (Rheinfrank et al. 1994, 80). "One
of the major issues facing designers of communication systems concerns helping one person or group understand others and create and
maintain common ground" (Gay and Lentini 1995). The eW3DT meta-
model provides such common ground. It serves as a common symbolic
language that is clearly understandable for management and easy to
handle for technical experts and authors of reference models.

Modeling languages geared towards the World Wide Web should
support structured and unstructured information. By providing an
agreed semantics for the conceptual data and navigational model,
eW3DT is aimed at reducing the communication gap between domain
experts and system professionals (Hemingway 1999, 276). It serves as an
interpretative guideline for people with heterogeneous technical expertise and professional responsibilities. Traditionally, there is a contro-
versy between two positions emphasizing the primacy of either technological or social aspects of information systems design. A more realistic
perspective, often described as *"emergent"*, *"reinforcement politics"*, or
"structurational" (Jones 1999, 288), acknowledges the interplay of both
factors, thereby transcending the traditional polarities (↪ Section 5.2:
Classic Loop of Adaptation). Similar approaches are common in the
linguistic tradition, emphasizing the dialectical relationship between

texts and society. "Texts are socioculturally shaped but they also constitute society and culture, in ways which may be transformative as well as reproductive" (Fairclough 1995, 34). On the one hand, Web information systems influence the process of people's work, comparable to any "traditional" computer system (Chen and Rada 1996). On the other hand, they represent a subcategory of electronic texts that are embedded in a set of complex social relations (↪ Section 1.1: Formal Definitions of Text). The success of their implementation depends on the specific social context into which they are placed. As with every evolving technology, Web content and functionality are constructed socially in the sense that they are shaped by the interests and assumptions of particular social groups (Snyder 1996, 122). Shared meanings and knowledge of the user's skills, therefore, are vital for the design of Web information systems (Crabtree et al. 1998; Hemingway 1999, 284). Ethnomethodological fieldwork investigations,[39] for example, may be used to guide design by revealing the temporal organization of activities and interactions normally not captured by other methods (Button and Dourish 1996).

In summary, reference models help developers to avoid structural inconsistencies and mistakes. They facilitate the exchange and dissemination of information by replacing intuitive with semi-structured communication. Organizations can improve the overall quality of their systems, usually at low cost vis-à-vis acquiring the necessary know-how from external consultants. However, inductive approaches that process empirical data to generate, refine, and test hypotheses concerning industry-specific success factors of Web information systems remain vital since standard software metrics frequently fail to evaluate the structure of hypertext systems adequately (↪ Section 4.5.4: Validating Manual Evaluations of the LSE/Novell Survey). Currently, no valid theory exists "to assess formally whether a conceptual model of a hypertext is clear to readers. The only feasible alternative is testing the hypertext in as real a situation as possible" (Nanard and Nanard 1995).

---

[39] Rather than being a unitary method, ethnography can be thought of as a collection of techniques for gathering and organizing field materials. Ethnomethodology as an interpretative approach to sociology frequently draws upon ethnographic materials. It traces its philosophical heritage directly back to phenomenology (Gray 1993, 15f.; Fairclough 1995, 21; Button and Dourish 1996).

4.4   USAGE: VISUALIZING TOPOLOGY AND ACCESS PATTERNS

The World Wide Web is the largest repository of structured, semi-structured, and unstructured data. Its dynamic nature and the variety of data types it holds challenge analysts on both the conceptual and technological level. At a time when many traditional indicators are losing their relevance for examining communication patterns, a vast number of new indicators is becoming available. These emerging indicators need to be processed further and presented adequately if they are to be usefully applied in building corporate strategies (Paltridge 1999, 328). The following sections focus on the set of indicators available by identifying patterns within the vast amount of information available from the Web server's daily activities.

4.4.1   Categories of Perceptualization

Representing a subcategory of *perceptualization*, visualization is an advanced form of high-bandwidth communication that transcends domain-specific and technological boundaries (De Fanti et al. 1989, 15). As vision represents the sense with by far the highest bandwidth, less popular subcategories such as *sonification* or *tactilization* will be disregarded throughout this book, despite their obvious potential for future applications.

Originally, the power of visualization techniques was applied to science and physical spaces in rather diverse disciplines such as molecular modeling, medical imaging, mathematics, meteorology, astrophysics, fluid dynamics, and so forth *(scientific visualization)*. These disciplines provide data that are inherently graphical in nature, characterized by implicit spatial relationships (De Fanti et al. 1989, 17ff.; Leung and Apperley 1994, 127). More general approaches that do not necessarily rely on physical properties to provide an organizing structure are referred to as *information visualization* (Robertson et al. 1991, 189). Information visualization maps non-spatial abstractions from diverse areas such as business (Wright 1998, 39), education, or information technology. It relies on interactive, computer-supported representations of abstract data to amplify cognition (Card et al. 1999, 7). The resulting displays should induce the viewer to think about the substance rather than about methodology. They should avoid distorting what the data have to say, coherently present many numbers in a small space, and encourage the eye to compare different pieces of data (Tufte 1983, 13). From a procedural perspective, information visualization can be defined as "a set of mapping from some base data set, in some idiosyncratic representation through possibly intermediary representations to some analytic abstraction appropriate for insight or communication and then into a visualization representation suitable for visual analysis and communication with the user" (Chi et al. 1998, 402).

4.4.2 Observing and Visualizing Human Behavior

Behavioral observations and pattern recognition belong to the oldest processes of human endeavor. Our hairy ancestors relied on their ability to recognize patterns in the behaviors of their predators and prey (Mena 1999, 41). With the advent of technology, more advanced methods of gathering (e.g., light barriers, video cameras, or satellites for remote sensing) and representing (e.g., structured verbal descriptions, frequency distributions, or topographic maps) increasingly complex information have been developed. While the following paragraphs focus on the representational aspect, the consecutive Section 4.4.3 presents methods to gather and store behavioral data in Web-based environments.

From a theoretical perspective based on the level of abstraction, topographic maps can be regarded as a merged set of trails (Wexelblat 1999). Similar to Michel de Certau's *Wandersmänner*, online customers represent a collective and virtual presence hovering above a hypertext's topology. The operation of walking can be traced on city maps in such a way as to transcribe people's paths (here well-trodden, there very faint) and their trajectories (going this way and not that). But these curves only refer to the "absence of what has passed by. Surveys of routes miss what was: the act itself of passing by" (De Certeau 1983, 97; Rosello 1994, 136). Nevertheless, observing real-world human behavior is a rather common activity. Figure 4.12 shows two examples of cumulative visualizations that are not directly related to information systems. The diagram on the left visualizes the results of observational customer tracking typical for traditional retailing outlets (Becker 1973, 208). The diagram on the right displays real-time monitoring of the traffic situation in the urban area of Los Angeles. In its original representation, the map is color-coded according to the current average speed of vehicles with green for 35 miles per hour and above, yellow for 20 to 35 miles per hour, red for less than 20 miles, and white for no data available.

As shown in Figure 4.12, aggregation is one of the primary techniques for constructing quantitative models to describe real-world behavior. The human perception, for instance, often aggregates similar things into categories and then treats them as equivalent (Holland 1995, 10f.). Correspondingly, the cumulative human behavior when accessing published documents or performing transactions is of increasing interest to Web analysts. Monitoring city traffic represents a good analogy. Common attributes of intelligent transportation systems such as motor vehicle speeds, parking turnover, or average trip lengths (Payne 2000) are replaced by attributes available via HTTP transfer-log files. Attention usually centers on the type of items requested, the frequency of requests, and the hyperlink topology (Chi et al. 1998, 402).

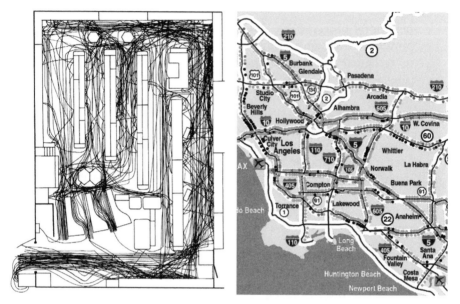

Figure 4.12. Monitoring and cumulative visualization of
real-world human behavior (Becker 1973, 208) [40]

4.4.3 Units of Analysis

In addition to the transfer-log (or access-log) and the error-log, two other logs are commonly recorded: the referrer log and the user agent log. Basic transfer-logs are usually generated in accordance with the *Common Log Format*.[41] In most cases, however, a combined, or extended, log format is chosen that integrates the information provided by the referrer and user agent logs into the transfer-log. Such combined log files typically contain the following parameters (Stout 1997, 17ff.):

- User's IP address *(client host)*, computing platform, and the name and version number of the browser used to make the request *(user agent)*.

- HTTP request type *(get, post, head)* and protocol version.

---

[40] http://traffic.maxwell.com/la/

[41] http://www.w3.org/Daemon/User/Config/Logging.html

- URLs of the requested file and of the referring document (the URL of the document that the user's browser was displaying immediately before it accessed the current page).

- Status code indicating the success or failure of the transaction (*2xx* for success, *3xx* for redirect, *4xx* for failure, and *5xx* for server error status codes).

- Transfer volume (number of bytes transferred).

- Exact date and time of access including offset from Greenwich Mean Time *(timestamp)*.

- Username (but not the password) that the reader enters to access password-protected documents *(authuser field)*; an additional entry, the *RFC 931 field*, is almost never used and originally was intended for authentication purposes.

The user's IP address can be employed to derive valuable information. Domain name, organizational affiliation, and approximate geographical location can be determined directly via the *Internet Domain Name Service (DNS)*. Indirectly, utilities functionally equivalent to the UNIX command *"whois"* query DNS servers to provide additional data. One caveat to this information is that it often lacks reliable references to a server's geographical location. For general domains such as .com, .edu, or .org that do not provide a country code, the running of a traceroute to the Web server can solve this problem (Paltridge 1999, 335). Figure 4.13 shows the output of the UNIX command *"traceroute"* for the World Wide Web Consortium's HTTP server. It reveals that the server is physically located at the *Massachusetts Institute of Technology (MIT)* in Boston, USA.

```
server> traceroute www.w3.org
traceroute to www.w3.org (18.29.1.23), 30 hops max, 40 byte packets
1 atlas-8.wu-wien.ac.at (137.208.8.2) 2 ms 1 ms 1 ms
2 perseus-sn19.wu-wien.ac.at (137.208.19.9) 2 ms 1 ms 2 ms
3 atm2-0-0-6001.cc03-wien.AT.EU.net (193.83.66.225) 4 ms 4 ms 4 ms
4 feth3-0-0.cc01-wien.AT.EU.net (193.154.145.11) 5 ms 5 ms 4 ms
5 Wie-ar02.AT.EU.net (134.222.161.2) 6 ms 6 ms 5 ms
6 Ffm-nr04.DE.EU.net (134.222.229.29) 26 ms 24 ms 25 ms
7 Ledn-cr01.NL.EU.net (134.222.229.153) 43 ms 48 ms 38 ms
8 Nyk-cr02.NY.US.EU.net (134.222.228.22) 120 ms 121 ms 119 ms
...
17 h3-0.cambridge2-br2.bbnplanet.net (4.0.1.202) 201 ms 194 ms 194 ms
18 ihtfp.mit.edu (192.233.33.3) 184 ms 188 ms 187 ms
19 B24-RTR-FDDI.MIT.EDU (18.168.0.14) 194 ms 193 ms 187 ms
20 RADOLE.LCS.MIT.EDU (18.201.1.3) 191 ms 199 ms 188 ms
21 anacreon.lcs.mit.edu (18.24.10.1) 192 ms 188 ms 207 ms
22 slow2.w3.org (18.29.1.23) 199 ms * 187 ms
```

Figure 4.13. Traceroute to the HTTP server of the World Wide Web Consortium[42]

---

[42] http://www.w3.org/

Every access to a Web server's resources counts as a *hit*. One hit represents one file retrieved from the server. Hits have been widely criticized, as their weakness as a valid measure of Web traffic is quite evident. They measure how close a server is to reaching its capacity, but are less useful in determining how many people are accessing the server. Since hits include all units of content sent by the server when a particular document is accessed (images, text, sound files, applets, frames, and so forth), they are inherently non-comparable across Web information systems (Novak and Hoffman 1997). The terms *request* or *qualified hit* describe hits that successfully retrieve content from the server, thus excluding less relevant information recorded in a transfer-log file such as error messages (Jasper et al. 1998). While qualified hits provide a better idea of traffic volume, they do not provide an accurate assessment of the actual number of users.

Visits can be identified by summarizing a certain number of raw *hits* on the transfer-log such as a set of documents and their embedded objects. The ability to clearly define a visit as a series of consecutive requests from a single user depends upon whether this user can be uniquely identified. If identification via cookies or registered user names is not possible, heuristics such as the popular 15-minute or 30-minute timeouts must be used to approximate the number of visits (Amor 1999, 170). The identification of visits is required to obtain some of the most informative and interesting parameters. Table 4.1 lists derivable variables for both hits and visits. Unfortunately, multi-user systems or irregular access patterns (e.g., users that perform other activities in the meantime) reduce the validity of *visits* as a measure of Web traffic.

Table 4.1. Available statistics from raw transfer-log hits versus visits

Raw Transfer-Log Hits	Visits
Total requests	Total visits
Total bytes transferred	Average number of requests per visit
Requests for each page and object	Average duration of visit
Most requested documents	Visits per (a) organization, (b) organization type, (c) country, (d) geographic region
Most requested documents by directory	Top entry and exit pages
Most requested files	Top referring pages
Top submitted forms and scripts	Top page durations
Average number of requests per (a) day, (b) hour, (c) weekdays vs. weekend	Average number of visits per (a) day, (b) hour, (c) weekdays vs. weekend

Several additional limitations have to be kept in mind. The routing of Web traffic via proxy servers is the most severe one in that it limits the interpretability of log files in two fundamental ways:

- If users access Web documents already stored on intermediary proxy servers, no entries in the log file of the actual server will be created.

- If a substantial number of hits originate from a proxy server, it is basically impossible to determine if they represent one very interested user or multiple individuals who just "hit and run" (Sullivan 1997).

Due to client-side caching, the recording of backtracking operations is equally impossible. Only unique navigational events are recognized. Moreover, long visits comprising many entries for a given visitor can represent both a deeply satisfied and a hopelessly lost user (Sullivan 1997; Hochheiser and Shneiderman 1999, 16).

Also existing entries in the log file do not guarantee that the user has comprehended or even read the transferred information. Only a more detailed analysis of the clickstream can increase the validity of the observation. If time-based metrics are available and valid, information providers can compare the actual viewing time with the average viewing time or with the minimal amount of time considered necessary for comprehending the information. But deriving time-based metrics is often problematic, since offline browsers and similar automated user agents can effectively mask reader interaction. They can make it appear as if users were uninterested, skimming rapidly from document to document. In truth, they were interested enough to pre-program the exact sequence of documents to be fetched (Sullivan 1997).

4.4.4 Tool Support

Operating systems like UNIX provide basic mechanisms to analyze user behavior manually (Sullivan 1997). The *grep* command, for instance, processes a file and prints out only those lines of the file that have a certain interesting property for the user. Similarly, numerous freeware or public domain tools for various platforms are available.[43] Nevertheless, most organizations tend to purchase commercial software pack-

---

[43] http://columba.its.uu.se/Software/Analyzers/
http://serverwatch.internet.com/dtanalysis.html
http://tucows.cyberspacehq.com/lognt.html
http://www.mela.de/Unix/log.html
http://www.nisto.com/mac/tool/logs.html
http://www.stars.com/Vlib/Software/Statistics.html

ages for the vital task of monitoring user behavior and analyzing HTTP log file data. Table 4.2 lists a number of popular examples (Busch 1997, 75ff.; Malchow and Thomsen 1997, 57ff.; Novak and Hoffman 1997; Stout 1997, 105ff.).

Table 4.2. Commercial Web-tracking software packages

Product	Company	URL
ARIA	Macromedia	http://www.macromedia.com/
Bazaar Analyzer	Aquas	http://www.bazaarsuite.com/
Enterprise Reporter	WebManage Technologies	http://www.webmanage.com/
GuestTrack	GuestTrack	http://www.guesttrack.com/
I/PRO	Engage Technologies	http://www.ipro.com/
Insight, Hit List	Accrue Software	http://www.accrue.com/
Log Analyzer	WebTrends	http://www.webtrends.com/
net.Analysis	Net.Genesis	http://www.netgen.com/
NetTracker	Sane Solutions	http://www.sane.com/
SurfReport	Netrics.com	http://netrics.com/
Whirl	Interlogue	http://www.interlogue.com/

The impressive number of available reports and filters cloaks the fact that most of these tools only provide descriptive statistics and static representations embedded in various reports including tables, histograms, or pie charts. The reports are usually generated either directly in HTML or in a file format compatible with popular word processing software. They lack interactive facilities, often obscure information detail, and do not consider additional information contained in the system's topology (Lee and Podlaseck 2000).

In contrast, a modified version of the eW3DT meta-model provides a visual framework for analyzing access patterns of online customers. *WebMapper*, a prototypical, platform-independent Java implementation of eW3DT (Bauer and Scharl 1999a; Scharl 1999a) enhances the limited, statistically oriented representations of commercially available Web-tracking software with a map-like view similar to customer tracking in traditional retailing outlets (Becker 1973). Such an interactive usage map, which is shown in the right-hand diagram of Figure 4.15, provides an interesting complement by showing sequence at a higher level, exposing the kinds of experiences that users can gain from Web information systems. Wexelblat denotes two main application areas for such an overview (Hemingway 1999, 285; Wexelblat 1999):

- Guidance of new users via interfaces that enable the semantics and assumptions of the underlying data model to be readily inferred (↪ Section 5.5.4: Meta-Level Adaptation).

- Web development, where the experience that users are having is compared with the designer's model(s) of how the Web information system would be experienced.

Creating the directed graph that is typical for most Web information systems can be done with two basic strategies. The first one, which is currently pursued by *WebMapper*, follows existing links of deployed applications. This breadth-first traversal transforms the graph into a tree by placing nodes as closely to the root as possible (Chi et al. 1998, 404). For yet unpublished material still lacking links, indexes, or annotations, the underlying directory and file structure can be utilized (Nation et al. 1997). Tapping the small amount of domain-specific knowledge hidden in the link structure usually improves the visualization's readability. URLs, for example, often encode the deliberately chosen directory structure on the Web server (Munzner 1998, 19).

WebMapper helps companies running commercial Web information systems in their efforts to map and classify individual and aggregated customer behavior. It enables them to predict future trends, to advertise more effectively, and to maximize the customer-delivered value of electronic transactions (↪ Section 2.3.2: Redefining the Customer-Delivered Value). In its early stages, the prototype exclusively focuses on visualizing user clickstreams by processing server-generated HTTP log files. The structure of the site's hierarchical document tree is generated automatically from the hyperlinks that are found within published HTML documents. This link information represents an enormous but often-neglected amount of latent human annotation (↪ Section 5.5.1; (Chakrabarti et al. 1999, 60)).

As already specified in Section 4.2.4, every information object type of eW3DT defines a general profile for describing the characteristic attributes of Web documents. With regard to the application domain of *WebMapper*, however, the rectangular symbols incorporate a different set of attributes compared to the eW3DT design meta-model (↪ Figure 4.14). The symbol's color does not refer to different document types any more, but to the cumulative frequency of their access.

Figure 4.14. Standard symbolic elements of eW3DT (left) and WebMapper (right)

Both color and line-width coding are employed to convey additional information about the users' actual behavior. While the color and shading of objects represent their actual number of HTTP requests during a certain period (N_Hits), the width and style of connecting links between the documents represent the frequency with which these links were followed by customers. Although default values are recommended by the system, the user has full control over both parameters by specifying threshold values. In addition to the visual cues, the field (Avg_VTime) displays numerically the average viewing time of documents in seconds. Detailed information about the object in question is accessible via the (Info) button (e.g., a list of host names / IP addresses of the most important visitors, aggregated number of entries and exits in a particular time interval, and so forth). Being part of the user interface, the two arrow symbols in the bottom right corner do not represent attributes of the object but provide the analyst with the option to move between lower-level and upper-level diagrams (↪ Section 5.5.4.3: View Transformations).

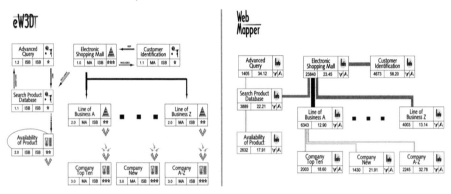

Figure 4.15. eW3DT diagram (left) and cumulative visualization of user access patterns (right) within the electronic shopping mall

4.5 ANALYSIS: GATHERING, EXTRACTING, AND PROCESSING OF MULTIDIMENSIONAL WEB DATA

The analytical phase of the evolutionary Web development cycle represents an inductive business process that extracts actionable and meaningful patterns, profiles, and trends by sifting through product, financial, customer, and Web site data (Mena 1999, 39). This chapter delineates the design of such a business process for analyzing and evaluating business-to-consumer Web information systems.

As already pointed out in Section 2.1: Darwinian versus Technological Evolution, Web analysis must be continuous under emergent assumptions. Analytic activities are no longer captured within the early stages of a system's life-cycle, but represent an ongoing part of system maintenance. Cyclical planning becomes obsolete. Analysis, operation, and maintenance activities become parallel but mutually dependent processes. Instead of obtaining individual maintenance requests, analyzing their feasibility, and eventually transforming them into changes (Hoffer et al. 1999, 806f.), the results of the ongoing analysis continuously trigger and guide maintenance activities (Accrue 1999, 5; Truex et al. 1999, 121).

4.5.1 Overview and Analytical Objectives

"When you can measure what you are speaking about and express it in numbers, you know something about it, but when you cannot measure it your knowledge is of a meager and unsatisfactory kind" (Lord Kelvin, in: (Moody and Walsh 1999, 496)). *Exploratory data analysis* involves a wide variety of single- and multi-variate statistical techniques to search for underlying systemic relationships between variables (Godehardt 1990, 13). In the context of competitive intelligence, the demarcation between exploratory data analysis and the more application-oriented concept of *data mining* is becoming somewhat difficult to discern from any but a philosophical perspective. Activities such as association, classification, clustering, estimation, optimization, segmentation, sequencing, prediction, or visualization that today come under the umbrella of the term data mining have been used for many years (Turban and Aronson 1998, 128; Mena 1999, 5). The two fields share much of their methodology and are both concerned with the inductive discovery and visualization of patterns and non-obvious relationships between data elements that might be useful in a particular business context (Kleinberg et al. 1998, 311; Pyle 1999, 486f.).

This chapter introduces a flexible analysis and evaluation framework of publicly accessible hypertext structures. Software tools are employed to capture and measure the characteristics of commercial Web information systems, determine their specific importance, and store them in a central database. Judged against human evaluation, automated approaches are more efficient at handling dynamically changing Web data and immune to inter- and intra-personal variances. Thus the regular sampling of thousands of systems becomes feasible compared to samples limited to tens or hundreds in previous efforts (Selz and Schubert 1997, 46ff.; Bucy et al. 1999; Witherspoon 1999).[44] Naturally, these advantages come at the expense of sacrificing a number of non-quantifiable, recipient-dependent attributes.

---

[44] http://www.excite.com/

The methods introduced facilitate automated data gathering, complement each other, and are suitable for both longitudinal studies and cross-sectional comparisons. As such they provide important feedback for constructing reference models (↪ Section 4.3), optimizing the allocation of marketing resources, or improving customer support. Implementing the methods does not require privileged access to computing or communication resources beyond those available to regular Web users. Due to their flexible nature, the analytical techniques cover a wide range of problem formulations, independent of the investigated system's level of technical sophistication. Only a few operations need to be adapted to specific situational parameters – e.g., word stemming, which requires a language-specific list of lemmas (↪ Section 4.5.8.4: Lemmatization).

Analysts have to be cognizant of the attributes of things to be able to evaluate and group them (Tesch 1990, 135). Accordingly, both the methodology and the software prototype introduced in this book imply the definition of measurable, operational criteria. These criteria are then investigated and pre-processed for each site separately. The methodology's potential applications can be categorized into four groups:

- *Snapshot analysis.* Analyzing single sites, business sectors, or the World Wide Web as a whole at a given time allows the assessment of descriptive parameters such as ratios, means, or variances. Samples are benchmarked and automatically clustered on the basis of automatically derived data on a Web site's structure and content (↪ Section 4.5.2.3: Integrative Analysis of Content and Form). Section 4.5.5, for example, classifies Web information systems of the information technology industry.

- *Cross-sectional analysis.* Comparative studies such as those presented in Section 4.5.6 help to structure the data according to company size, business sector, geographical region, high-level domain, experience with electronic transactions, and so forth. They provide companies with a pivotal source of information for maximizing their customer-delivered value (↪ Section 2.3.2). From an academic point of view, the discerning of similarities helps to refine the discriminative power of established categories (Tesch 1990, 96). The tool's commercial utility is the indications it gives toward early adoption of electronic commerce by particular sectors of an economy. Business users understand better how the rest of the World Wide Web relates to their own system and those of their competitors (Paltridge 1999, 338). They can assess alternative investment opportunities on the basis of reliable benchmark data about the differences and the relative performance of their information architectures. Benchmarks indicating weaknesses should trigger and guide the redevelopment and optimization of deployed applications.

- *Longitudinal analysis.* Particular sites or representative samples of certain business sectors are documented and analyzed over a longer period of time, that is, a series of snapshot analyses is conducted on the same sample. Trends, cyclical variations, turning points, and marginal changes are monitored for specific industries or arbitrary subcategories. The resulting indicators describe complex developments that can hardly be observed and quantified in traditional ways. Nevertheless, both industry and academic research urgently require such temporal data, which will be presented in Section 4.5.7.

- *Test of specific hypotheses.* Empirical data permits the direct verification of assumptions regarding the diffusion of particular Internet technologies, implementation strategies of certain organizations, or trends within particular business sectors.

4.5.2 Manual versus Automated Evaluation

Generally, manual and automated approaches to analyzing and evaluating online resources have to be distinguished (Bauer et al. 1999b, 54ff.). In most cases, manual evaluation of Web information systems relies on the judgements of individual analysts on the basis of a list of weighted attributes. Many of these attributes tend to be approximations for which exact data cannot be measured (Buchanan and Lukaszewski 1997, 81). Even if a group of experts is involved, the evaluation takes place with varying degrees of subjectivity regarding the process itself and the captured data structures. In addition to that, the highly dynamic nature of the World Wide Web requires rapid collection of data, limiting manual approaches to consider little beyond the introductory homepage (McMillan 1999b). The more specific the measure, the greater the need to revise manual methods prior to each evaluation cycle. Thus a high level of detail is inconsistent with the objectives of longitudinal studies and necessitates automated alternatives to acquire empirical data. Scalability, speed, consistency, rigorous structure, and abundance of data are assured if the processes of gathering and extracting information are handled by software tools.

4.5.2.1 Previous Web Evaluation Projects

Documented approaches to evaluate Web information systems can be found in many areas, which will be introduced in the following sections. They are intended to check everything from the basic questions of spelling, syntactical correctness and browser compatibility of HTML code to problems of higher complexity such as benchmarking server performance, rating content, evaluating representational quality, or assessing the application's overall business value.

Awards and Independent Rankings

With the commercialization of the World Wide Web, awards and independent rankings gained in popularity – e.g., Point Communications' Top 5% of All Websites Award, Magellan 4 Star Sites, Lycos Top 5%, WWW Associates Top Ten, and so forth. The evaluation process relies on either some sort of selection panel or public voting. More sophisticated approaches such as *SurveySite*[45] employ client-side applications to continuously capture user opinions and consumer perceptions.

Content Determination

Semantic labels, a subcategory of annotations (↪ Section 5.5.1), appear to be the most promising technology in this area, especially with regard to semantic markup languages like XML. The World Wide Web Consortium's *Platform for Internet Content Selection (PICS)*, for example, enables meta-data to be associated with Internet content. Originally designed to help control what children access on the Internet, its mechanisms can be employed for a variety of applications (Weinberg 1997, 453ff.).[46] Semantic labels enhance information retrieval and avoid undesired content. Search engines and hierarchical directories like Yahoo![47] represent classical examples of Web classification and content determination. Various criteria are employed including subject and geographical area. Occasionally, the perceived value of such collections is further improved by adding detailed reviews of indexed systems. Many independent tools for analyzing Web content such as Trivium's *UMAP* are conceptualized as overlays to search engines (Paltridge 1999, 336).[48] Therefore, their use is restricted to queries, lists of documents that are generated in response to these queries, and the identification of semantically related terms. In most cases it is not possible to interrogate the underlying database directly.

Quality Assessment

Simple checklists and guidelines such as Parker's *Web Site Impression Sheet* or the benchmarking metrics of Misic and Kelsey have been developed to allow even inexperienced users to assess the quality and reliability of various Internet resources (Parker 1997, 67ff.; Katerattana-

---

[45] http://www.surveysite.com/
[46] http://www.w3.org/PICS/
[47] http://www.yahoo.com/
[48] http://www.trivium.fr/
http://www.umap.com/

kul and Siau 1999, 279f.; Misic and Johnson 1999, 387).[49] More sophisticated approaches, which combine manual and automated gathering of
required data, face rigid limitations regarding objectivity and feasible
sample sizes. The *Web Site Quality Evaluation Method (QEM)* proposed
by Olsina et al., for example, uses the hierarchical system of attributes
listed in Table 4.3 to assess the artifact quality of academic Web information systems (Olsina et al. 1999).

Table 4.3. Domain-dependent variables for manual and
semi-automated data gathering (adapted from Olsina et al. 1999)

Functionality	Usability	Efficiency
❖ **Searching and Retrieving Issues**	❖ **Global Site Understandability**	❖ **Performance**
▪ Web-site Search Mechanisms	▪ Global Organization Scheme	▪ Static Page Size
- Scoped Search (People | Course | Academic Unit)	- Site Map	❖ **Accessibility**
- Global Search	- Table of Content	▪ Information Accessibility
▪ Retrieve Mechanisms	- Alphabetical Index	- Support for text-only version
- Level of Retrieving Customization	▪ Quality of Labeling System	- Image Title
- Level of Retrieving Feedback	▪ Student-oriented Guided Tour	- Global Readability
❖ **Navigation and Browsing Issues**	▪ Image Map (Campus/Buildings)	▪ Window Accessibility
▪ Navigability	❖ **On-line Feedback and Help Features**	- # Pages regarding frames
- Indicator of Path	▪ Quality of Help Features	- Non-frame Version
- Label of Current Position	- Explanatory Help	**Site Reliability**
- Average of Links per Page	- Search Help	❖ **Link Errors**
▪ Navigational Control Objects	▪ Web Site Last Update Indicator	▪ Dangling Links
- Contextual Controls Permanence	- Global	▪ Invalid Links
- Contextual Controls Stability	- Scoped (per sub-site or page)	▪ Unimplemented Links
- Vertical Scrolling	▪ Addresses Directory	❖ **Miscellaneous Errors or Drawbacks**
- Horizontal Scrolling	- E-mail Directory	▪ Deficiencies or Absent Features due to Different Browsers
▪ Navigational Prediction	- Phone-Fax Directory	▪ Deficiencies or Unexpected Results (e.g. non-trapped search errors, frame problems, etc.) independent of browsers
- Link Title (link with explanatory help)	- Post mail Directory	
- Quality of Link Phrase	▪ FAQ Feature	
❖ **Student-oriented Domain Features**	▪ Online Feedback	▪ Dead-end Web Nodes
▪ Content Relevancy	- Questionnaire Feature	▪ Destination Nodes (unexpectedly) under Construction
- Academic Unit Information (Index | Sub-sites)	- Guest Book	
- Enrollment Information (Entry Requirement Information, Form Fill, Download)	- Comments	
	❖ **Interface and Aesthetic Features**	
- Degree Information (Index, Description, Course Offering)	▪ Cohesiveness by Grouping Main Control Objects	
- Course Description (Syllabus, Comments, Scheduling)	▪ Presentation Permanence and Stability of Main Controls	
- Student Services Information (Index, Healthcare, Sport, Scholarship, Housing, Culture)	- Direct Controls Permanence	
	- Indirect Controls Permanence	
	- Stability	
- Academic Infrastructure Information (Laboratory, Library, Research Results)	▪ Style Issues	
	- Link Color Style Uniformity	
▪ Online Services	- Global Style Uniformity	
- Grade/Fees online Information	- Global Style Guide	
- Web Service	▪ Aesthetic Preference	
- FTP Service	❖ **Miscellaneous Features**	
- Newsgroup Service	▪ Foreign Language Support	
	▪ What's New Feature	
	▪ Screen Resolution Indicator	

Even though the abundance of data impresses at first sight, too many
variables pose some subtle problems of a computational nature, as the
predictive power of statistical algorithms and methods based on neural
networks tends to suffer from multidimensional input vectors of such

---

[49] http://www.unc.edu/~elliott/evaluate.html

high complexity. Regularly, the desired generalization can better be achieved using only a few but highly relevant features of the sample to be analyzed. The domain-dependency of Olsina et al.'s quality requirement tree further limits the potential scope of its application. More general tools such as the W3C's *HTML Validation Service*[50] help Web developers to assess the quality of their work and are frequently integrated into the underlying design architecture. Similar publicly available tools such as the *Web Site Garage,*[51] *Fritz-Service,*[52] or *Bobby*[53] deliver multi-dimensional ratings for the investigated Web information systems.

Server and Application Benchmarks

Server and application benchmarks measure and compare technical system performance with varying loads of data under either normal operating conditions *(performance testing)* or extreme conditions that strain the systems well beyond their limits *(stress testing)*. Several academic and commercial efforts aim at providing standardized methods to estimate technical parameters such as system response times under various loads, throughput, or scalability (Fournier 1998, 412ff.). Web information systems should be able to handle peak periods as well as slower times efficiently, and allow additional capacity to be added quickly and easily (Broadvision 2000). With special regard to electronic commerce applications, Jutla et al. introduce *WebEC*, which specifies a complex buying transaction (Jutla et al. 1999a, 73; Jutla et al. 1999b, 491). This buying transaction consists of a set of nested processes that perform credit checks, user authentication, and product availability searches. Related efforts include the *SPECweb99* server benchmark from the Standard Performance Evaluation Corporation,[54] Mindcraft's *WebStone*,[55] the Benchmark Factory's *Internet Module*,[56] or *TPC-W*, a transactional Web benchmark from the Transaction Processing Performance Council (TPC).[57]

---

[50] http://validator.w3.org/
[51] http://www.websitegarage.com/
[52] http://www.fritz-service.com/
[53] http://www.cast.org/bobby/
[54] http://www.specbench.org/osg/web99/
[55] http://www.mindcraft.com/benchmarks/webstone/
[56] http://www.benchmarkfactory.com/
[57] http://www.tpc.org/

Business Value Assessment

For commercial scenarios, this last category proves most important. Selz and Schubert propose a specific Web assessment model to identify and evaluate successful commercial applications (Selz and Schubert 1997, 46ff.). While the resulting model offers a detailed analysis of these solutions, the time-consuming method requires access to company information frequently not available. The *E-Audit* methodology used for the *"1999 Worldwide Web 100 Survey"* and the *"Web 2000 Growth Report"* of the London School of Economics (LSE) represents a more pragmatic approach (Psoinos and Smithson 1999, 44; Grover and Evans 2000, 7; Smithson 2000, 8). The authors of the LSE/Novell survey audited 100 Web information systems across eight business sectors. Mimicking all the stages of real online transactions, the business transaction cycle is divided into seven dimensions, which are then assessed separately: *Company information, advertising & promotion, product information, order, settlement, after-sales service, ease of use & innovation.* While most participants of the first survey were drawn from the 1998 Fortune 500 global rankings, the "Web 2000 Growth Report" used the international growth lists of *Deloitte Consulting/Braxton Associates.*

4.5.2.2 Web Classification Frameworks

Several frameworks for classifying Web information systems, both formal and informal, have been introduced previously. The majority of these efforts are driven by scholarly desire for typology, viewed not only as an intellectual tool for organizing data segments but also as a significant research result. While recapitulating the extensive literature on manual evaluation and addressing methodological strengths and weaknesses of the various surveys are clearly beyond the scope of this book, the following summary of their findings is useful to direct the search for alternatives on a conceptual level. Many of the manual approaches have a strong foundation in advertising and are utilized as guidelines for strategic decision-making and for defining the marketing goals of online businesses. Hoffman et al., for example, identify six distinct categories of commercial Web information systems based on a functional typology (Hoffman et al. 1997; Bauer and Scharl 1999b, 761): online storefront, Internet presence, content site, electronic mall, incentive site, and search agent. *Online storefronts* offer direct sales, electronic catalogs, and substantial customer support. An *Internet presence* can take the form of flat ads (single documents), image sites (emotional consumer appeal), or detailed information sites. *Content sites* are characterized by their funding model, which can be fee-based, sponsored by a third party, or indirectly funded by advertising. *Electronic malls* typi-cally feature a collection of online storefronts. *Incentive sites* make ef-fective use of the specific technical opportunities of the Web for adver-tising purposes. Members of the last category, *search agents,* identify other sites of presumed interest to the user.

Hansen presents a general commercial classification with similar in-tentions, but a mutually exclusive typology (Hansen 1996a). It com-prises two dimensions, content and interactivity, and defines five dis-tinct types of Web information system in the context of these dimen-sions: *electronic business card, advertainment, electronic brochure, electronic catalog,* and *Web-service.* Similar industry-specific classifica-tion schemes have been applied in the retail banking sector for building reference models (Bauer 1998a), observation of industry evolution (Mahler and Göbel 1996), and commercial Web site analysis (Booz-Allen 1999; Psoinos and Smithson 1999; Smithson 2000). Those frame-works provide a rich background to Web site evaluation, but do not directly address the selection of appropriate parameters for automated approaches. Most manual classification frameworks lack a clear and consistent distinction between identified categories, since many of these approaches are based more on anecdotal than empirical evidence.

Specifying appropriate variables is the first step toward an evaluation framework founded on empirical evidence (in contrast to conceptual frameworks). Considering technical feasibility, the four information categories of Table 4.4, which are characterized by varying degrees of measurability, evolved from reviewing previous approaches and ex-ploratory case studies. The methodology introduced in Section 4.5.3 depends on these categories.

Table 4.4. Domain-independent variables for automated data gathering

Category	Variable	Category	Variable
Content	# Documents [total]	Navigation	# Frames [total]
	Kilobytes downloaded [total | text only]		# Internal Links [total | distinct | broken]
	# File Types [distinct extensions]		# External Links [total | distinct]
	# Images [total | distinct]		# Anchors [total | distinct]
Interactivity	# Forms [total | distinct | fields]		# Links to Anchors [within | between documents]
	# Scripts [total]		# SSL Links [total | distinct]
	# Java Applets [total | distinct]	Textual	# Words [types / tokens / ratio]
	# MailTo-Links [total | distinct]		Average Length [words | sentences | documents]

4.5.2.3 Integrative Analysis of Content and Form

When analyzing media environments like the World Wide Web, content and form represent two complementary dimensions. While content consists of the textual and visual components of Web information systems, form refers to the packaging of that information and its representation. A growing body of media research documents that many effects of media messages such as increased attention, arousal, memory, or linking are the product of an interaction between content and form (Lang 1990, 275ff.; Reeves and Nass 1996; Bucy et al. 1999). By combining these two dimensions, the following analytical categories can be derived:

- Form-based, structural methods determine and classify formal features of Web information systems (↪ Section 4.5.3.3: Structural Parameters).
- Content-based methods provide a detailed account of textual patterns and their dynamic development (↪ Sections 4.5.3.4: Textual Parameters and 4.5.8: Exploratory Textual Analysis).
- Visual methods cover both dimensions, content and form. They help explore and explain the complex information spaces typical of the World Wide Web by documenting deployed information systems (↪ Section 4.2.4: The Extended World Wide Web Design Technique), and by providing efficient user interface representations (↪ Section 5.5.4: Meta-Level Adaptation).

McMillan compares 16 studies that apply content analysis techniques to the World Wide Web (McMillan 1999b). The context units of these studies cover a broad range, including personal homepages (Bates and Lu 1997, 331ff.), commercial Web information systems (Ho 1997; Ha and James 1998, 457ff.), and organizational Web applications in general (Aikat 1995). Some of these studies focus particularly on the systems' functionality and interactive features (Frazer and McMillan 1999). However, a number of prevalent shortcomings can be identified, particularly as far as sampling and intra-/intercoder reliability are concerned. Manual coding is the cumbersome process of tagging text segments with information about the category of the organizing system in which it belongs – or several categories if the segment is relevant to more than one (Tesch 1990, 121). The automation of this process promises to overcome problems such as coder fatigue, misapplication of coding rules, or missing browser standardization (Potter and Levine-Donnerstein 1996; Potter 1999).

The World Wide Web is characterized by large, non-homogeneous, distributed, and dynamically changing text domains with several tens or hundreds of thousands of features. A potentially infinite number of documents often originates from irrelevant, redundant, or misleading sources (Mladenic 1998, 5). Therefore, it seems inevitable to focus on automated approaches to analyzing the observable elements of deployed systems. To date, much of the analysis about Web content and form has been qualitative in nature or proprietary to industry and therefore only partially released (Bucy et al. 1999). To overcome the methodological limitations of subjective impressions, anecdotal evidence, or convenience samples, automated systems need to be introduced to complement qualitative methods. *Automated data gathering* is an essential prerequisite for obtaining training samples of appropriate size. *Automated coding* removes subjective interpretations and many of the questionable aspects of manual coding from the analytical process. It renders the problems of time-consuming and expensive coder training or intra- and intercoder reliability obsolete, as the process does not involve human coders who could disagree on particular attribute values. Automated approaches also tend to increase a project's overall reliability, understood as the degree to which three basic criteria are met (Krippendorf 1980, 130ff.; Potter and Levine-Donnerstein 1999): *Stability* (process and its results are invariant or unchanging over time), *reproducibility* (process can be recreated under varying circumstances), and *accuracy* (process functionally conforms to a known standard and yields what it is designed to yield).

4.5.3 Methodology

The evaluation framework intends to provide a concrete response to open questions about how to capture and analyze Web content, its structure, and its dynamic change (Scharl and Bauer 1999, 534ff.; Bauer and Scharl 2000, 31ff.). In contrast to approaches that concentrate on the homepage or certain segments of Web information systems (Bucy et al. 1999), the methodology described in this chapter deals with complete sites, following their hierarchical structure until a limit of ten megabytes of textual data is reached. The analytical process is broken down into five clearly defined phases as shown in Figure 4.16:

a) *Select business sector(s)*. Available resources and the analytical objectives (↪ Section 4.5.1) usually predetermine the number of business sectors to be included.

b) *Data gathering*. Any empirical study needs to systematically select representative elements of a population, a process that is usually referred to as *sampling*. It is assumed that analyzing the sample will reveal useful information about the population as a whole (Kendall and Kendall 1999, 79ff.). For longitudinal studies, appropriate intervals for repeatedly gathering the data have to be specified. During the process of data gathering, the analyst generates mirrors of the selected Web information systems in regular intervals and archives the retrieved data for future reference.

c) *Data extraction.* It is essential to determine relevant variables, attributes, and associated data items to be collected or described. If irrelevant data is gathered, valuable resources are wasted in its collection, storage, and analysis. A prototype based on a set of Perl scripts, *WebAnalyzer,* extracts structural information and related attributes from the archived data and produces a numeric record (vector) for each system (↪ Section 4.5.3.3: Structural Parameters). By deleting markup information and concatenating the mirrored documents, it also provides the complete content information for the textual analysis by means of a single ASCII file. Using the *WordSmith* tool set, additional statistics are then derived from this file to complement the structural information (↪ Section 4.5.3.4: Textual Parameters).

d) *Pre-processing.* The process of integrating structural and textual data is described in Section 4.5.3.5. Ratios are computed to reduce redundancy and derive more intuitive parameters, resulting in a vector of 27 dimensions for each of the cases.

e) *Application.* Statistical clustering and testing, non-supervised and supervised neural networks, exploratory textual analysis, and correspondence analysis are then applied to validate manual assessments, analyze and compare industries, and conduct longitudinal studies.

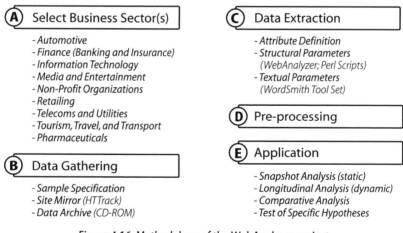

(A) Select Business Sector(s)
- *Automotive*
- *Finance (Banking and Insurance)*
- *Information Technology*
- *Media and Entertainment*
- *Non-Profit Organizations*
- *Retailing*
- *Telecoms and Utilities*
- *Tourism, Travel, and Transport*
- *Pharmaceuticals*

(B) Data Gathering
- *Sample Specification*
- *Site Mirror (HTTrack)*
- *Data Archive (CD-ROM)*

(C) Data Extraction
- *Attribute Definition*
- *Structural Parameters*
  (WebAnalyzer; Perl Scripts)
- *Textual Parameters*
  (WordSmith Tool Set)

(D) Pre-processing

(E) Application
- *Snapshot Analysis (static)*
- *Longitudinal Analysis (dynamic)*
- *Comparative Analysis*
- *Test of Specific Hypotheses*

Figure 4.16. Methodology of the WebAnalyzer project

Each of the five phases has clearly defined input and output interfacing with both the user and adjacent phases. In reality, the individual sub-processes can be executed rather independently from each other. Follow-up projects, therefore, may choose to implement a different component without affecting the other phases. Especially in the application phase, different analytical techniques may be employed in accordance with the specific requirements of certain domains and problem formulations.

While some of the chosen methods have been tried before, they have only been tried in isolation. The following sections introduce a suite of analytical techniques that can be combined flexibly to tackle a wide spectrum of problems. The first study, which is presented in Section 4.5.4, aims at identifying variables that influence the perceived quality of Web information systems. Using the structural and textual parameters of Section 4.5.3.5 as predictors, it intends to determine the reproducibility of qualitative rankings based on expert judgements. The first study is followed by a classification of the information technology sector in Section 4.5.5, which concentrates on the most current data from November 1999. Section 4.5.6 compares the four different sectors and relates them to the general sample of the LSE/Novell survey. It is followed by a separate longitudinal study to uncover variations associated with certain variables and to assess the significance of observed trends (Section 4.5.7). The exploratory textual analysis of Section 4.5.8 integrates all the analytical objectives stated in Section 4.5.1. It presents static snapshots of the textual content in the form of lemmatized word lists, identifies characteristic keywords by comparing specific word lists with a general reference corpus, analyses trends in the coverage of certain topics, and uses concordances and collocation tables to investigate the contextual meaning of certain expressions. Finally, lexical tables are processed and visualized by means of correspondence analysis and hierarchical cluster analysis.

4.5.3.1 Sampling Process

Considering the expansion rate and dynamic nature of the World Wide Web, it can be a daunting task to choose an expressive sample. There are a number of ways to identify categories of Web information systems and to draw samples of a given category – e.g., manual selection, search engines such as *Hotbot*[58] or *Altavista*,[59] hierarchical directories like *Yahoo!*,[60] domain-specific link collections such as the *Web Digest for Marketers*[61] or *Fortune 500*,[62] as well as various offline sources. Considering the specifics of each business sector, combinations of these methods

---

[58] http://www.hotbot.com/
[59] http://www.altavista.com/
[60] http://www.yahoo.com/
[61] http://www.wdfm.com/
[62] http://www.fortune.com/fortune/fortune500/

were used to compile the samples. According to *AltaVista*, the English language share of the World Wide Web in 1999 was 78%. Restricting the survey to commercial domains with links to secure servers, even 96% of the accessible documents were authored in English, followed by Japanese, German, French, Spanish, and Portuguese (Paltridge 1999, 334). An analysis of the distribution of native speakers reveals that 54% of the online population spoke English as of February 2000, followed by Japanese (7.1%), Spanish (6.2%), Chinese (5.4%), and German (5.0%).[63] Considering the dominance of the English language regarding both information providers and users, Web information systems that publish information in other languages were excluded from the sampling process for reasons of comparability.

For the analyses presented in Sections 4.5.4 to 4.5.8, a combination of purposive and stratified sampling was chosen. *Purposive samples* are based on expert judgements and pre-specified criteria. *Stratification* identifies sub-populations, or strata, and then selects objects for sampling within these sub-populations. Publicly available Web content was sampled repeatedly over time (05/99, 07/99, and 11/99). The combined sample of these three archives comprises 418 Web information systems. 156 of these cases represent the sample chosen by the *"1999 Worldwide Web 100 Survey"*, published by the London School of Economics (LSE) in cooperation with Novell (Psoinos and Smithson 1999, 44). Even though the LSE/Novell sample covers a broad range of business sectors, additional samples were specified to cover four particular sectors in more detail:

- *Information technology (n = 82)*. The sample was derived from the 1999 edition of the Fortune 500. Using the custom search option, 30 companies from the categories *Computers & Office Equipment*, *Computer Software*, and *Computer Peripherals* were ranked according to a combined measure of revenues, profits, and market value.

- *Travel and tourism (n = 41)*. The sample of companies operating in the travel and tourism sector was derived from a ranking of travel agencies compiled quarterly by *Gomez Advisers*,[64] a Massachusetts-based provider of electronic commerce data. It was extended by the *"airlines"* and *"hotels, casinos, resorts"* categories of the *1998 Global 500* and *1999 Fortune 500*.[65] In addition, destination-based systems such as *TIScover*[66] were added to cover the entire range of market participants (Werthner et al. 2000).

---

[63] http://www.euromktg.com/globstats/
[64] http://www.webtravelnews.com/226.htm
http://www.gomez.com/
[65] http://www.fortune.com/fortune/
[66] http://www.tiscover.com/

- *Retail banking (n = 57).* Thirty entries of international banks were randomly selected from Yahoo!,[67] excluding non-English sites, those that were not accessible, and rudimentary systems with less than one megabyte of publicly accessible textual information ("electronic business cards"). Midsize organizations with their headquarters in the Unites States represent the majority of the sample.

- *Environmental non-profit (n = 82).* Besides the availability of an English version, criteria that guided the sampling process were the site's registration within the .org domain and an international orientation, thus excluding Web information systems that primarily focus on regional projects or particular countries. To achieve a good representation, a number of different meta-indices were used to compile the sample.[68] The indices themselves and mere collections of environmentally relevant links without substantial content were not included. Query interfaces to bibliographic, full-text, or factual databases were excluded as well.

Table 4.5. List of organizations representing the information technology, travel and tourism, retail banking, and environmental non-profit sectors

Organization	URL		URL	Organization
INFORMATION TECHNOLOGY				
Adaptec	www.adaptec.com		www.informix.com	Informix
Pitney Bowes	www.pitneybowes.com		www.dg.com	Data General
Cadence Design Systems	www.cadence.com		www.microsoft.com	Microsoft
Compuware	www.compuware.com		www.dell.com	Dell Computer
Computer Associates Intl.	www.cai.com		www.gateway2000.com	Gateway 2000
Compaq Computer	www.compaq.com		www.imation.com	Imation
IBM	www.ibm.com		www.iomega.com	Iomega
Silicon Graphics	www.sgi.com		www.lexmark.com	Lexmark International
Hewlett-Packard	www.hp.com		www.quantum.com	Quantum
PeopleSoft	www.peoplesoft.com		www.seagate.com	Seagate Technology
Apple Computer	www.apple.com		www.wdc.com	Western Digital
EMC	www.emc.com		www.stortek.com	StorageTek
Novell	www.novell.com		www.ncr.com	NCR
Oracle	www.oracle.com		www.sun.com	Sun Microsystems
Sybase	www.sybase.com			
TRAVEL AND TOURISM				
Air France	www.airfrance.com		www.mirageresorts.com	Mirage Resorts
Airlines of the Web	flyaow.com		www.nwa.com	Northwest Airlines
Atevo	www.atevo.com		www.priceline.com	Priceline
BizTravel	www.biztravel.com		www.sabre.com	Sabre
British Airways	www.britishairways.com		www.tiscover.com	TIScover
Delta Air Lines	www.delta-air.com		www.travelscape.com	TravelScape
Expedia	expedia.com		www.trip.com	Trip.com
Internet Travel Network	www.itn.net		www.uniglobe.com	Uniglobe Travel Online
Japan Airlines Company	www.japanair.com		www.ual.com	United Airlines
Lufthansa	www.lufthansa.com		www.worldres.com	WorldRes
Marriott	www.marriott.com			

---

[67] http://dir.yahoo.com/Business_and_Economy/Companies/Financial_Services/
[68] http://www.wiwi.hu-berlin.de/~guenther/eis_book.html
http://www.webdirectory.com/General_Environmental_Interest/
http://dir.yahoo.com/Society_and_Culture/Environment_and_Nature/

Organization	URL	URL	Organization
RETAIL BANKING			
Cole Taylor Bank	www.ctbnk.com	www.charternational.com	Charter National Bank
York Federal	www.yorkfed.com	www.bankwi.com	State Bank of Howards Grove
Charter National Bank	www.charternationalbank.com	www.liberty-bank.com	Liberty Bank
Marine Midland Bank	www.marinemidland.com	www.bnkwest.com	Bank of the West
Omaha State Bank	www.omahastate.com	www.riggsbank.com	Riggs National Bank
Rayne State Bank	www.bankonnet.com	vermontnationalbank.com	Vermont National Bank
North Dallas Bank & Trust	www.ndbt.com	www.republicbank.com	Republic Bank & Trust Comp.
Carrollton Bank	www.carrolltonbank.com	www.dgb.com	Deposit Guaranty Nat'l Bank
Elgin Financial Center SB	www.elginfc.com	www.fcbmilton.com	First Community Bank
Southern Deposit Bank	www.sdb.abcbank.com	www.columbank.com	Columbia Bank The
Owensboro National Bank	www.onb.abcbank.com	www.milfordbank.com	Milford Bank The
British Bank / Middle East	www.britishbank.com	www.cpbi.com	Central Pacific Bank
First National Bank & Trust	www.fnb-tc.com	www.firstvirginia.com	First Virginia Banks
Farmers & Merchants Bank	www.fmmarinette.com	franklinsavings.com	Franklin Savings
Belmont National Bank	www.belmontbank.com	www.cavalrybanking.com	Cavalry Banking
ENVIRONMENTAL NON-PROFIT			
Sea Shepherd	www.seashepherd.org	www.ran.org/intro.html	Rainforest Action Network
Earthwatch Institute	www.earthwatch.org	www.conservation.org	Conservation International
Environmental Def. Fund	www.edf.org	www.wilderness.org	Wilderness Society
Int'l Rivers Network	www.irn.org	www.earthisland.org	Earth Island Institute
Sierra Club	www.sierraclub.org	www.iucn.org	World Conservation Union
EnviroLink	www.envirolink.org	www.greenpeace.org	Greenpeace International
Comm.f. Env. Cooperation	www.cec.org/english	www.tnc.org	Nature Conservancy
Nat'l Res. Defense Council	www.nrdc.org	www.unep.org	UN Environment Program
World Resources Institute	www.wri.org	www.panda.org	World Wide Fund For Nature
Comm. Constr. Tomorrow	www.cfact.org	www.2020vision.org	20/20 Vision
Action Resource Center	www.arcweb.org	www.earthpledge.org	Earth Pledge Foundation
State of the World Forum	www.worldforum.org	www.earthsummitwatch.org	Earth Summit Watch
EcoNet	www.igc.org/igc/econet	www.eli.org	Environmental Law Institute
Friends of the Earth	www.foe.org	www.worldwatch.org	World Watch Institute

4.5.3.2 Mirroring and Archiving Web Data

Archiving and documenting data for future reference and secondary analyses deserve high priority when investigating an expansive and dynamic medium like the World Wide Web. Both content and structure of Web information systems have to be captured. For the project described in this chapter, the offline browser HTTrack,[69] available for various Windows and UNIX platforms, was used to mirror the data. For the Web information systems contained in the sample, a short descriptor (usually the organization's name), the publicly accessible URL, and a local sub-directory for the mirror had to be specified. Upon successful completion of the mirroring process, the retrieved files including event-log and error-log were stored on CD-ROMs for further processing. Table 4.6 lists the options that were chosen for HTTrack's command line interface.

---

[69] http://httrack.free.fr/

Table 4.6. HTTrack command line options

Option	Description
p1	Save only HTML files
R5	Use relative links
c10	Number of multiple connections (10)
I0	Do not make an index
C0	Use no cache
M10485760	Maximum overall size in bytes to download
m100000,100000	Maximum file length for non-HTML and HTML files

Currently, deployed systems vary in size considerably, from small brochures to huge collections of knowledge spanning 100,000 documents and more. Most of them also grow explosively within the time span of longitudinal studies. The limitation to a maximum of ten megabytes of textual data (excluding graphics and other multimedia files) helps to compare systems of heterogeneous size. The specific information found in hierarchical levels below that limit does not belong to the primary user interface and thus can be disregarded for most analytical problem formulations. Furthermore, restricting the mirror size is the only way to effectively manage available local storage space.

The experienced load time of Web documents substantially influences the user's attention and their perceived quality. "Users tend to become annoyed when a page takes longer than 20 seconds to load. This means it is best to limit the total of the file sizes associated with a page, including graphics, to a maximum of 30-45 kilobytes to assure reasonable performance for most users" (IEEE 1999a). Nevertheless, time-dependent load characteristics (in contrast to content and structure) are not taken into account as they change dynamically and depend on numerous external factors. It is virtually impossible to automatically determine the actual bottleneck in the case of delayed transmission.

4.5.3.3 Structural Parameters

WebAnalyzer is currently available as a prototypical set of Perl-5 scripts in a Linux environment. The scripts recursively parse all (S)HTML files in the sub-directories of the archived sites for markup tags. All tags related to the variables of Table 4.4 result in an update of the record for this particular case. The input and output of *WebAnalyzer* are managed through comma-delimited text files, a file format that ensures interoperability with most applications. The only exception is the textual content, which is written to one single text file for further processing with the *WordSmith* tool set (↪ Section 4.5.8: Exploratory Textual

Analysis). Naturally, the size of this file can never reach or exceed the limit of ten megabytes, as all the tags and scripts of the original set of HTML files have to be removed. As a rule of thumb, ten megabytes of HTML code result in about three to five megabytes of plain text.

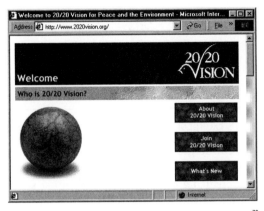

Figure 4.17. Web information system of 20/20 Vision[70]

Figure 4.17 shows a screenshot of the homepage of *20/20 Vision,* an environmental activism organization with its headquarters in Washington, DC. Figure 4.18 presents part of the corresponding HTML code. *WebAnalyzer* parses this code and searches for markup tags to establish the values for the predefined parameters. The variables *total number of images* and *distinct number of images,* for example, are derived from the occurrences and attributes of the <IMG>-tag (highlighted in Figure 4.18). Each occurrence of the tag increments the *"total number of images",* while the second variable is only increased when an image is referenced for the first time. The graphical resource's *Uniform Resource Locator (URL)* in the SRC-attribute of the <IMG>-tag serves as a good indicator for computing this value. Similarly, the number of links is calculated by counting the <A>-tags (also highlighted in Figure 4.18). A more detailed analysis of the referenced resource location enables the program to distinguish relative, absolute, and external links.

```
<HTML><HEAD>

...

<TITLE>Welcome to 20/20 Vision for Peace and the Environment</TITLE>
</HEAD><BODY BGCOLOR="#ffffff">
<IMG SRC="pictures/welcomebanner.gif" WIDTH="464" HEIGHT="85"
ALIGN="BOTTOM" NATURALSIZEFLAG="3">
<BR><IMG SRC="pictures/whois.gif" WIDTH="464" HEIGHT="27"
ALIGN="BOTTOM" NATURALSIZEFLAG="3"><BR>
```

---

[70] http://www.2020vision.org/

```
<TABLE border=0 width=464><TR>
<TD align=left><IMG SRC="pictures/globe.gif">
<TD align=right><A href="about2020.html">
<IMG SRC="pictures/about2020.gif"></A><BR><BR>
<A href="https://secure.intr.net/2020vision/secure/join2020.html">
<IMG SRC="pictures/join2020.gif"></A><BR><BR>
<A href="whatsnew.html"> <IMG SRC="pictures/whatsnew.gif"></A>
</TD></TR></TABLE><BR>
<IMG SRC="pictures/grassdemoc.gif" WIDTH="464" HEIGHT="27"
ALIGN="BOTTOM" NATURALSIZEFLAG="3"><BR>
...
</BODY></HTML>
```

Figure 4.18. Excerpt of the HTML source code for the homepage of 20/20 Vision

After executing the script, a comma-delimited text file (.csv) is generated. Embedded in this file, the data are represented as a case by attribute matrix, ensuring compatibility with most statistical software packages. For each of the sites included in the sample, the following 22 attributes are recorded (listed in alphabetical order):

- *Anchor.* The absolute number of anchors, which is identified through the <A NAME="…">-tag in the HTML code.

- *Applet.* The absolute number of hyperlink references to Java applets (i.e., their class files) or other applets that make use of the <Applet>-tag.

- *Applet_d.* The number of the site's *distinct* Java applets, as determined through the reference to its class file. Each class file results in one count.

- *Email.* The absolute number of direct links to e-mail addresses. In HTML syntax, these links are referenced through the specification of "mailto:" (service). The specification is followed by the actual e-mail address, referenced as <A HREF="mailto:…"> … </A>.

- *Email_d.* In contrast to the *Email* parameter, this variable establishes how many *distinct* e-mail addresses are accessible.

- *FileExt.* The number of *distinct* media types as indicated by their characteristic file extensions. Multiple files with a certain extension such as ".htm" only result in one count. The occurrence of ".html" files on the same site, however, leads to a separate count.

- *Form_d.* The number of mirrored forms. Every occurrence of the <Form>-tag is counted. Hypothetically, one HTML file could therefore result in more than one count for this variable.

- *FormField.* This variable measures the number of embedded form fields, which are created by the <Input …>-tag.

- *Frame.* The number of occurrences of the <Frameset>-tag is counted as a proxy for the intensity of frame use on the Web site.

- *Image.* The absolute number of images referenced in the mirrored set of documents. Every <Img>-tag produces one count, regardless of the physical location of the corresponding file.

- *Image_d.* The number of *distinct* image references. While the *Image* variable disregards the image source, this variable counts multiple references to the same image file only once.

- *KB_Text.* The size of the automatically generated text file in number of kilobytes. Since uncompressed ASCII representation is used, multiplying this value by 1,024 approximates the number of re-trieved letters.

- *KB_Total.* This attribute denotes the retrieved information's abso-lute number of kilobytes. Images are not taken into account. Values and their interpretability are limited by specifying a download maximum of ten megabytes in the mirroring tool's list of parame-ters. Naturally, many of the investigated sites are substantially larger than this arbitrary limit.

- *LinkAnchor.* The absolute number of (internal) hyperlinks to an-chors. This type of link can be used to structure the current docu-ment or establish semantic connections to anchors of other docu-ments. Both cases are measured by this variable.

- *LinkAnchor_w.* In contrast to *LinkAnchor*, this variable does only count the hyperlinks to anchors *within* the same document. Hyper-links to anchors of other documents are ignored.

- *LinkExt.* The absolute number of external links, counting each refer-ence to an external resource through a <A HREF="...">-tag. An external link is defined as an absolute reference to a resource located at a host other than the current one. Links utilizing both HTTP and FTP protocols are counted.

- *LinkExt_d.* The number of *distinct* external links. External links to the same resource are only counted once.

- *LinkInt.* The absolute number of internal links. Each reference to an internal link through a <A HREF="...">-tag counts as one link. An internal link is defined as a relative or absolute reference to a re-source that belongs to the current host. Both HTTP and FTP links are taken into consideration.

- *LinkInt_b.* The number of links that have been found to be *broken*, that is, not accessible at the time of mirroring. The variable is com-puted through the evaluation of the HTTrack error-log file, which provides an enumerative list of broken connections.

- *LinkInt_d.* The number of *distinct* internal links. In contrast to the *LinkInt* variable, internal links to the same resource are only counted once.

- *PageCount.* The actual number of mirrored HTML files. There is no fixed upper limit of documents, since the mirroring stops when ten megabytes of HTML code are reached.

- *Script.* The absolute number of occurrences of the <Script>-tag. This not only covers JavaScript (ECMAScript), but also other scripting languages such as VBScript or JScript that make use of this tag (ECMA 1999).[71] Small scripts that are invoked without the <Script>-tag are disregarded by this variable.

4.5.3.4 Textual Parameters

Based on the textual output of *WebAnalyzer*, the *WordSmith* tool set is used to derive additional attribute values for each case. As a by-product of compiling word lists (↪ Section 4.5.8.3), *WordSmith* generates a number of descriptive statistics, from which the following parameters were chosen:

- *Word (total number of tokens).* *Tokens* represent the number of all running words encountered as *WordSmith* processes the text file. A word is counted as a string of valid letters with a separator at each end.

- *Word_d (total number of types).* *Types* are the *distinct* words stored as the tool first processed the text; they represent the system's complete vocabulary. A Web site containing one million running words might only comprise 50,000 distinct occurrences. Different inflections of the same lemma such as *swim, swimming, swam,* or *swims* are counted separately (↪ Section 4.5.8.4: Lemmatization).

- *Alength_Wrd.* Average length of words, measured in letters.

- *Alength_Snt.* Average length of sentences, measured in words.

- *Alength_Doc.* Average length of documents, measured in words.

- *Type token ratio (TTR).* This parameter is a syntactical index that divides the number of distinct words V by the total number of words T (Titscher et al. 1998, 80f.). It has a value between zero for empty input files and one for files in which each word occurs only once. High values indicate texts with a heterogeneous vocabulary. Unfortunately, the type token ratio varies widely in accordance with the

---

[71] http://www.jsworld.com/
http://www.vbscripts.com/
http://www.webstandards.org/ecma.html
http://msdn.microsoft.com/scripting/

length of the original text. Therefore, Lebart et al. suggest the use of the Simpson's index (Lebart et al. 1998, 168). The latter represents the number of pairs of occurrences of the same word divided by the total number of pairs of occurrences and is computed according to the following equation:

$$D = \frac{\sum_r r(r-1) \cdot V_r}{T(T-1)}$$

where T is the total number of occurrences and V_r the number of distinct words appearing exactly r times in the text. While V has an upper limit for any given language, T is unlimited by definition. Being less dependent on the length of the text, the Simpson's index, therefore, provides more reliable results. Another possibility is the use of a *standardized type token ratio (TTR_s)*, which is computed every n words as the software processes the text file. *WordSmith* uses a default value of $n = 1,000$. The ratio is calculated for the first 1,000 words, then recalculated for the next 1,000, and so forth. A running average is computed, resulting in an average type token ratio based on consecutive 1,000-word chunks of text.

4.5.3.5 Combining and Pre-Processing the Extracted Parameters

Similar to the computation of the type token ratio as described above, several script-generated variables also require pre-processing, since their absolute values are of limited descriptive power. In addition, some statistical methods can have extreme problems with particular data representations (Pyle 1999, 356). Therefore, pre-processing should eliminate latent redundancy from the set of attributes. Suffixes signify the type of pre-processing or provide additional information on the attribute: "_d" stands for distinct occurrences, "_r" for variables expressed relative to the total number of documents, "_b" for between-document anchors, and "_w" for within-document anchors.

- **TextRatio.** The size of the automatically generated text file is not measured in absolute kilobytes *(KB_text)*, but relative to the total number of kilobytes.

$$TextRatio = \frac{KB\_text}{KB\_total}$$

- **LinkAnchor_br.** In addition to *LinkAnchor_w* for intra-document links, this variable measures the number of hyperlinks to anchors of different documents, relative to the total number of documents.

$$LinkAnchor\_br = \frac{LinkAnchor - LinkAnchor\_w}{PageCount}$$

- **LinkIntRatio, LinkExtRatio.** The total number of internal links is replaced by the ratio of distinct links, relative to the number of total links. The same process is applied to external links.

$$LinkIntRatio = \frac{LinkInt\_d}{LinkInt} \qquad LinkExtRatio = \frac{LinkExt\_d}{LinkExt}$$

- **FieldRatio.** The total number of fields can be misleading. Thus, the average number of fields per form is used, a better indicator for the system's interactivity and the amount of explicit information that is gathered.

$$FieldRatio = \frac{Field}{Form}$$

- **AppletRatio, ImageRatio, EmailRatio, FormRatio.** Absolute numbers of linked applets, images, e-mail addresses, and forms are replaced by their relative numbers, dividing distinct by total occurrences.

$$Var_x Ratio = \frac{Var_x\_d}{Var_x}$$

- **Anchor_r, LinkAnchor_wr, LinkInt_dr, LinkExt_dr, Form_dr, Image_dr, Script_r.** The script-generated variables are recomputed relative to the number of mirrored documents.

$$Var_x\_r = \frac{Var_x}{PageCount}$$

As their intrinsic information has already been leveraged during pre-processing, a number of the original (script-generated) parameters do not require a separate representation and can be eliminated from the input vector. The revised input vector consists of 27 variables. Table 4.7 lists these variables, thereby summarizing the attribute values of the whole sample (n = 418).

Table 4.7. Descriptive statistics for the variables after pre-processing

Variable	Min	Max	Mean	StdDev	Skewness	Kurtosis
Alength_Doc	59.84	1999.75	424.05	241.58	2.29	9.86
Alength_Snt	3.22	83.59	25.36	7.43	2.81	18.06
Alength_Wrd	1.76	6.33	5.10	.49	-3.68	20.56
Anchor_r	.00	5.84	.74	.85	2.65	9.33
Applet_d	.00	16.00	.74	1.79	5.08	33.64
AppletRatio	.00	1.00	.18	.33	1.59	1.09
Email_d	.00	816.00	55.93	98.26	4.34	24.51
EmailRatio	.00	1.00	.40	.29	.42	-.74
FieldRatio	.00	52.17	8.25	8.25	2.76	10.36
FileExt	1.00	28.00	6.15	4.55	1.53	2.88
Form_d	.00	195.00	15.43	21.72	4.85	30.57
FormRatio	.00	1.00	.33	.32	.85	-.49
Frame	.00	2823.00	77.38	249.31	7.18	62.61
Image_dr	.05	5.71	1.25	.86	1.72	4.53
ImageRatio	.01	.64	.14	.12	1.50	2.63
KByte	90.00	17210.00	8196.12	4822.07	-.36	-1.44
LinkAnchor_br	.00	6.30	.39	.80	4.61	25.23
LinkAnchor_wr	.00	12.71	.62	1.02	5.81	53.46
LinkExt_dr	.00	9.51	.63	1.12	5.39	34.94
LinkExtRatio	.01	1.00	.44	.24	.30	-.58
LinkInt_b	.00	343.00	34.68	52.64	2.58	7.88
LinkInt_dr	.22	18.87	2.25	1.81	3.80	24.62
LinkIntRatio	.02	.81	.23	.14	1.28	2.11
Script_r	.00	17.65	.74	1.71	6.25	50.23
TextRatio	.07	.71	.27	.13	1.04	.61
TTR_s	6.54	66.53	37.17	6.90	-1.33	5.51
Word_d	557.00	42838.00	12857.53	8894.23	1.10	.88

Frequently, hidden relationships between variables are of particular interest to the analyst. It is often necessary to assess the appropriateness of a specific set of variables for a statistical method. Some algorithms such as multiple linear regression, for example, can have extreme problems with certain representations of collinear variables that carry nearly identical information (Pyle 1999, 356). As no collinearity problems were detected during the analysis described in Section 4.5.4, no further modifications were necessary.

Dendrograms (cluster trees) are helpful to better understand the nature of the data being captured. Based on a hierarchical cluster analysis (↪ Section 4.5.5.4), they effectively visualize similarities within a set of variables (or cases) and their impact on cluster agglomeration. Instead of the *squared Euclidean distance*, which is normally used for clustering cases, the *Pearson correlation* was used for measuring the distance between the variables depicted in Figure 4.19. For joining the variables, the *between-groups linkage* method was chosen. Some of the obvious related parameters are *(TextRatio, ALength_Doc), (Word_d, FileExt, KByte),* or *(Anchor_r, LinkAnchor_wr).* By contrast, the variables *ALength_Snt, Script_r, EmailRatio,* and *Frame* are comparably independent of each other and of the rest of the vector. Another method to investigate linear combinations of variables is *principal components analysis* (Bortz 1999, 500ff.; SPSS 1999, 319ff.). However, applying this method to the same set of 27 variables revealed that only a comparably high number of factors would account for a substantial proportion of variability. For explaining 80 (90) percent of the variance, a total of 14 (18) factors were required. The lowest communalities were identified for the variables *Script_r* (0.414), *LinkInt_b* (0.509), *Alength_Snt* (0.515), and *EMail_d* (0.517).

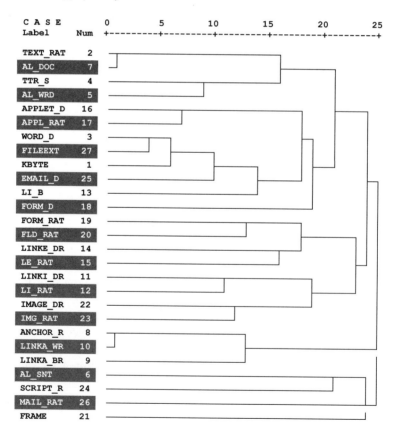

Figure 4.19. Dendrogram of the pre-processed set of variables

4.5.4   Validating Manual Evaluations of the LSE/Novell Survey

The overall goal of benchmarking is to discover the "best practices" within an industry and to find ways to embed these practices into one's own operations (Misic and Johnson 1999, 383). As a long-term strategy, manual classification and benchmarking suffer from the shortcomings of being extremely labor-intensive and essentially subjective in nature. Therefore, the most obvious application of quantitative methods to analyze Web information systems is to validate and complement prior studies based on expert judgements. As this process is founded on the results of manual assessment, the inherent restrictions of expert judgements still have to be kept in mind. Naturally, subjective influences during the manual evaluation process cannot be emulated based on empirical data. Thus the scope of the study, which will be introduced in Section 4.5.4.2 after a short introduction to the concept of artificial neural networks, is restricted to the identification of variables that significantly influence the perceived quality of Web information systems in the LSE/Novell survey (Psoinos and Smithson 1999, 44).

4.5.4.1   Introduction to Neural Networks

The application of the evaluation framework as described above requires a combination of quantitative methods such as K-Means and hierarchical clustering, statistical testing of hypotheses, and neural networks. Both supervised and unsupervised neural components were used as an alternative to statistical algorithms. Neural networks represent a family of models for quantitative data analysis, rather than a single technique (Turban and Aronson 1998, 666ff.). They are composed of a large number of processing elements (= neurons) that are linked via weighted connections. Learning typically occurs by example through exposure to a set of correct input-output data, where the training algorithm iteratively adjusts the connection weights. These connection weights associatively store the knowledge necessary to solve specific problems. Neural networks as universal approximators work very well for discovering regularities within a complex set of patterns, where the volume of the data is very great, the non-linear relationships between variables are only vaguely understood, or the relationships are difficult to describe with conventional approaches. Due to the inherent redundancy of their computational architecture, neural networks are fault tolerant in the face of environmental or internal degradation – i.e., background noise, missing data, or "damage" to a local portion of the network (Silipo 1999, 217). Thus they provide a promising analytical alternative to statistical techniques, which are often limited by strict assumptions of normality, linearity, or variable independence. Nevertheless, they are equally affected by the selection of independent input variables, their appropriate representation, and by the size of the training sample used for optimization.

If target output values are known for all the input patterns of the training set, *supervised neural networks* can be employed. They are typically organized in layers, each of them comprising a number of interconnected nodes. Learning rules such as *backpropagation* modify the weights of the connections according to the input patterns that they are presented with. The backpropagation algorithm, independently reinvented many times, performs a gradient descent within the solution's vector space along the steepest vector of the error surface (Mena 1999, 88ff.; Silipo 1999, 228ff.). Once a neural network is trained to a satisfactory level, it may be used as an analytical tool on other data. This process effectively segments state space with remarkable flexibility (Kratzer 1990, 146; Poddig 1992, 261). Frequently, decision processes of neural networks remain opaque and cannot be translated into meaningful symbolic knowledge. Therefore, hybrid approaches have become increasingly popular. They combine the adaptive features of supervised neural networks with the modeling flexibility and transparency of fuzzy logic (Berthold 1999, 269ff.). This section describes such a hybrid system and compares its results with those of two linear regression models.

If the task of neural learning is to discover regularities within the environment without specified output patterns or supervising structures, the corresponding learning process is called *non-supervised* or *self-organizing* (Masters 1993, 327ff.; Inform 1997, 160). The most popular algorithm geared toward non-supervised learning is the Kohonen network, named after its inventor, Teuvo Kohonen. Following early approaches, which successfully identified phonemes from continuous speech (Kohonen 1988, 11ff.; Kohonen 1997), the Kohonen self-organizing map has been used for diverse purposes (Chen et al. 1998, 75f.). The Kohonen algorithm effectively projects the original data onto a sub-space of (usually) two dimensions, such that similar data are placed close to one another. This representation is referred to as a *topographical map* or *feature map*, which denotes a two-dimensional array of neurons fully connected with the input vector, but without lateral connections (Silipo 1999, 253). The within-industry classification of Section 4.5.5 employs Kohonen networks and compares their results with those of K-Means and hierarchical clustering.

4.5.4.2 Test Design

The original data file consisted of 154 cases, which originated from two separate mirrors (07/99, 11/99). Using two separate mirrors, the impact of random influences on the results were lessened – i.e., temporary technical difficulties encountered during the mirroring process. From the 154 cases, two different samples were created by random selection: the training sample (n = 136) and an independent test sample (n = 18) to validate the results. Considering the sufficient number of cases, computationally more expensive resampling techniques such as cross-validation or bootstrapping were not applied (Feelders 1999, 55ff.). A multiple regression analysis was conducted on the training sample in order to evaluate how well the manual assessment conforms to the empirical data gathered by *WebAnalyzer*. The initial predictors were the 27 variables derived from pre-processing the output of the Perl script, while the criterion variable was the organization's overall score in the LSE/Novell survey. With stepwise regression the number of predictors was reduced to 6 (REG6) and 12 (REG12). The graphs of Figure 4.20 depict the standard error of the estimate, the F value, and the adjusted multiple correlation coefficient $(R^2_{adj.})$ as a function of the number of regressors included in the equation. Both linear combinations were significantly related to the criterion variable, with $F(6,129) = 10.599$, $p = 0.001$ and $F(12,123) = 8.650$, $p = 0.001$, respectively. The sample multiple correlation coefficients for 6 (12) predictors were 0.58 (0.68), indicating that approximately 33% (46%) of the score's variance in the sample can be accounted for by the linear combinations of predictors.

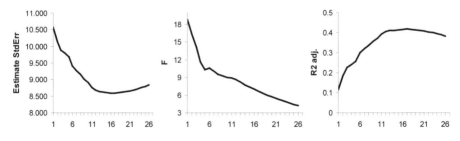

Figure 4.20. Standard error, F value, and adjusted multiple correlation coefficient

Table 4.8 presents the regression coefficients for REG6, which are significant at the 0.05 level. The standardized type token ratio *(TTR_s)* is the only predictor of this model with a positive impact on the estimated score of a Web site ($\beta = 0.325$). Alternative regression models with a higher number of predictors also reported a positive but less significant impact for other variables such as distinct internal links, anchors per page, image ratio, or distinct file extensions. The most powerful predictor in negative terms is the number of broken links *(LinkInt_b)*, which apparently reduces the perceived quality of Web information systems when evaluated manually ($\beta = -0.316$).

Table 4.8. Coefficients of the regression model comprising six predictors

Predictor	B	StdErr	Beta	t	Sig.
(Constant)	66.117	6.446	0	10.257	.000
LinkInt_b	-8.945E-02	.021	-.316	-4.336	.000
LinkAnchor_br	-8.659	2.355	-.276	-3.677	.000
FormRatio	-6.895	2.857	-.190	-2.413	.017
LinkExtRatio	-9.252	3.477	-.213	-2.661	.009
TTR_S	.471	.136	.325	3.455	.001
ALength_Wrd	-4.528	1.534	-.273	-2.952	.004

The two linear combinations were then compared to the output of a neuro-fuzzy model (FUZ6). For implementing the system, the neuro-fuzzy shell *FuzzyTech 5.01* was used (Inform 1997). To avoid arbitrary rule addition and deletion, FuzzyTech employs a method referred to as *Fuzzy Associative Map (FAM) inference,* where each rule is assigned a *degree of support (DoS)* representing the individual importance of the rule. Based on the same six predictors that were used for the smaller regression model, a corresponding input vector for the neuro-fuzzy shell was generated.

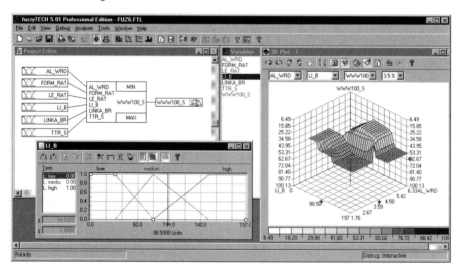

Figure 4.21. User interface of FuzzyTech 5.01 displaying the FUZ6-model, the membership functions of the linguistic variable LinkInt_b, and a three-dimensional surface plot

For most of the linguistic variables, including the LSE/Novell score, three membership functions were defined. To represent the form and external link ratios adequately, two membership functions sufficed. For defuzzification, the *Center-of-Maximum Method (CoM)* was chosen, which computes the crisp output as a weighted average of the term membership maxima. By means of supervised learning via backpropagation, the neural component then adapted the 972 rules of the fully connected inference structure by setting their DoS values. Synchronously, the linguistic variables' membership functions were optimized. Figure 4.21 displays the FUZ6-model with the corresponding variable list, the membership functions of LinkInt_b after completion of the training, and a three-dimensional plot of the transfer surface for the LSE/Novell Score and two input variables (LinkInt_b, ALength_Wrd).

4.5.4.3 Results

Table 4.9 lists the Pearson correlation coefficients between the three models and the original score of the LSE/Novell survey. All four variables were significantly correlated at the 0.01 level (two-tailed). FUZ6 showed the highest correlation with the original score ($r = 0.899$), compared to $r = 0.575$ for REG6 and $r = 0.677$ for REG12.

Table 4.9. Correlation coefficients for the training sample between the survey's score, the two linear combinations, and the neuro-fuzzy model

	SCORE	REG6	REG12	FUZ6
SCORE	1.000	.575**	.677**	.899**
REG6	.575**	1.000	.849**	.617**
REG12	.677**	.849**	1.000	.701**
FUZ6	.899**	.617**	.701**	1.000

** Correlation is significant at the 0.01 level (two-tailed).

For regression functions, the *mean squared error* is a natural measure of prediction error. The mean squared error for REG6 (REG12) was 84.04 (68.04), with a standard deviation of 8.93 (8.27). FUZ6 outperformed both regression models with a mean of 24.65 (SD = 4.43). The scatterplots in Figure 4.22 visualize these results. They facilitate the evaluation of the identified relationships by contrasting the estimates of each of the three models with the LSE/Novell score. The data points' higher density in the right-hand figure shows the superiority of the FUZ6 model vis-à-vis both regression models.

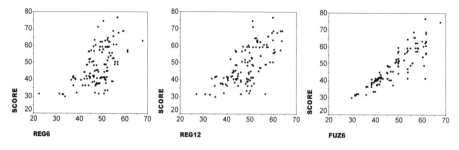

Figure 4.22. Scatterplots for the training sample, contrasting the survey's
score with the estimates of REG6, REG12, and FUZ6

As the assumptions of one-way analysis of variance (normal distribution for each of the populations, variance homogeneity) were violated, a Kruskal-Wallis test was conducted to evaluate these differences
on the basis of the models' squared residuals. The test indicated highly
significant differences at the 0.001 level, $\chi^2(2,N=408) = 70.995$. Follow-
up tests (Mann-Whitney U) were conducted to evaluate the pairwise
differences among the three groups. While there was no significant
difference between REG6 and REG12, FUZ6 performed significantly
better at the 0.01 level. Despite this good result, it should be kept in
mind that the true error of predictive models is usually much higher,
especially in the case of very flexible methods such as neural networks.
As the data available usually do not exhaustively describe the often
complex relationships between input and output variables, the ultimate
test of the derived models is their ability to successfully classify observations that are not part of the initial training sample (Walczak and
Sincich 1999, 11). Table 4.10 lists the Pearson correlation coefficients
between the three models and the LSE/Novell score for the test sample
(n = 18). As expected, the coefficients were distinctively lower than for
the training sample. FUZ6 again showed the highest correlation with the
original score (r = 0.634), compared to r = 0.498 for REG6 and r = 0.618
for REG12.

Table 4.10. Correlation coefficients for the test sample

	SCORE	REG6	REG12	FUZ6
SCORE	1.000	.498[*]	.618[**]	.634[**]
REG6	.498[*]	1.000	.881[**]	.649[**]
REG12	.618[**]	.881[**]	1.000	.768[**]
FUZ6	.634[**]	.649[**]	.768[**]	1.000

* (*) Correlation is significant at the 0.01(0.05) level; two-tailed.*

The mean squared error for REG6 (REG12) was 103.12 (96.00), with a
standard deviation of 36.05 (43.49). FUZ6 outperformed both regression
models with a mean of 91.95 (SD = 47.41). Again, a Kruskal-Wallis test

was conducted to evaluate the differences. In contrast to the training sample, the test did not reveal any significant differences between the error distributions, $\chi^2(2,N=54) = 0.648$, $p = 0.723$. To summarize the results, Figure 4.23 contrasts the absolute residuals of REG6, REG12, and FUZ6 for the training and test sample.

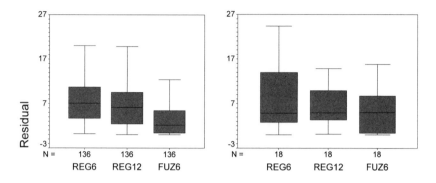

Figure 4.23. Boxplots of the absolute residuals for the training sample (left; n=136) and the test sample (right; n=18)

4.5.4.4 Discussion

The study aimed to identify variables that influence the perceived quality of Web information systems. The coefficients of the regression model based on six predictors (↪ Table 4.8) suggest that high values for the standardized type token ratio *(TTR_s)*, which serves as an indicator of the richness of the information system's vocabulary, are generally related to Web information systems of high quality. A *LinkInt_b* coefficient of $\beta = -0.316$ suggests that organizations should undertake efforts to minimize the number of broken links. This result is quite surprising, as the problem of outdated links and their negative impact on the system's perceived quality have been well known and documented since the World Wide Web's early days. Many integrated Web development tools generate the whole link structure on the fly. In these cases, no broken links at all should be expected. Referring to the complete sample comprising 154 cases, only 18 systems (= 11.7%) achieved this desired result. Most development environments that do not automatically generate the link structure at least support the detection and correction of broken connections. For the same task, separate software packages are available as an alternative to integrated development tools. These packages primarily target developers of small and medium-sized systems (Benbow 1998, 249). Allowing for network failures or temporary problems beyond the control of the host, it is nonetheless astounding to discover up to 197 broken internal links (mean = 31.8; SD = 42.0) in the upper hierarchical levels of Web information systems that are maintained by multinational corporations of the information technology sector (↪ Figure 4.24).

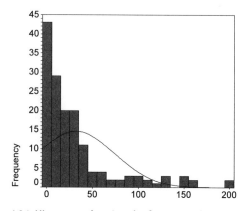

Figure 4.24. Histogram showing the frequency distribution of the number of broken links (LinkInt_b) among the LSE/Novell sample

A second goal of this study was to investigate the potential of quantitative methods to mirror existing rankings of Web information systems based on qualitative expert judgements. Such rankings are labor-intensive and essentially subjective in nature. Although it exceeded initial expectations, the presented study provided only a partial explanation for the LSE/Novell score. This raises the question of whether it would be worthwhile to extend or revise the set of predictors in order to achieve a more accurate result, especially with regard to content-related variables. It is unlikely that such a strategy would succeed. With the inclusion of additional variables into the input vector, the statistical requirements regarding sample size become very difficult to meet. The same holds true for neural components, which would require more instances to reduce the risk of over-fitting. The problem with small sample sizes and a high number of attributes is that the analysis tool might learn the specific pattern in each instance and take those specific patterns as predictive. Instead of generalizing, the neural network learns the particular instance configurations, which is particularizing rather than generalizing (Feelders 1999, 56; Pyle 1999, 395; Silipo 1999, 235f.).

Besides these methodological objections, it remains questionable if qualitative rankings can be fully explained by technical parameters at all. Expert judgements always include subjective components and variables that are impossible to measure precisely. This does not mean that qualitative benchmarking of Web sites is superior, as many organizations would like to eliminate the subjective influences this study was unable to capture, or at least separate them from the conclusions derived from empirical evidence. The most promising approach, therefore, is to integrate both quantitative and qualitative methods. In this way, the strengths of both approaches can mutually reinforce each other (Kelle 1995, 15). On the one hand, specific expert assessments can be included in the set of predictors. On the other hand, qualitative rankings can be based not only on response time, overall visual impression, or perceived quality of the navigational system, but also on detailed empirical data about the system's structure and content. The opportunity to automate the data gathering process and to substantiate adhoc expert judgements is invaluable for assessing dynamic media environments such as the World Wide Web.

4.5.5 Snapshot Analysis (Classification)

Cluster analysis is a generic name for a series of multivariate statistical techniques that proved to be effective in explorative studies for identifying data agglomerations (Godehardt 1990, 29). Cluster analysis systematically partitions state space into separate areas that contain data points sharing a common feature. The aim is to maximize the degree of similarity between the members of a group and to minimize the degree of similarity between different groups (Bortz 1999, 547; Pyle 1999, 491). The most popular methods can be grouped into two major families, partitioning (direct) and hierarchical clustering methods. While hierarchical algorithms allow the analyst to obtain a hierarchy of groups partially nested in one another, direct methods such as the K-Means algorithm produce only simple segments of the population under analysis and are therefore better adapted to large data sets. Connectionist approaches such as unsupervised neural networks are another promising alternative. The Kohonen competitive learning algorithm, for instance, has well documented similarities with conventional statistical techniques (Ueda and Nakano 1994, 1211ff).

K-Means, hierarchical clustering, and a Kohonen network will be used in the following to classify Web information systems of the information technology sector. The classification will be performed with respect to the same 27 pre-processed variables that were used as predictors in the preceding chapter. Thus the raw data comprise a set of real vectors of dimension 27, all of which have numeric, non-negative entries. The attribute values are very heterogeneous, with maximum values ranging from less than one to more than 40,000 (↳ Table 4.7). This variability requires the transformation of the original values into standardized, normally distributed values for each variable. Without this normalization, the clustering algorithm would be heavily biased by variables with higher values.

4.5.5.1 Partitioning Clustering

By its very nature, the information technology industry lends itself more readily to the adoption of electronic business models than other sectors. According to the LSE/Novell survey (Psoinos and Smithson 1999, 10f.), the information technology sector takes the lead in both offering accurate product information and providing customer service online. Fourteen out of fifteen surveyed companies allowed customers to ask questions in their own words and receive customized answers from the corporate Web information system. Nevertheless, there is substantial room for improvement as far as online ordering, settlement, and overall usability are concerned.

The sample of companies in the information technology industry as listed in Table 4.11 was derived from the 1999 edition of the Fortune 500.[72] Using the custom search option, 30 companies from the categories *Computers & Office Equipment*, *Computer Software*, and *Computer Peripherals* were ranked according to a combined measure of revenues, profits, and market value. From these 30 organizations, only one had to be eliminated from the sample as the mirroring tool *HTTrack* had problems retrieving its complete site (*Xerox*).[73] Table 4.11 lists the remaining 29 companies, together with their URL and the results of both statistical K-Means clustering with N cluster centers (KM-N) and the Kohonen network (KOH). For implementing Kohonen networks, a wide variety of freeware, shareware, and commercial tools for different platforms is available.[74] The information technology sample was clustered with the *Pittnet* shell, developed by Carnahan and Smith (Carnahan and Smith 1997).[75] With an adaptive learning rate between 0.01 and 1.0 and a maximum number of 20 clusters, the program needed approximately 500 iterations to accomplish the task.

The entries of Table 4.11 are sorted according to the K-Means result based on eight cluster centers (KM-8). Additionally, the last row provides the average distance from the cluster centers, which is usually negatively correlated to the specified number of clusters.

---

[72] http://www.pathfinder.com/fortune/fortune500/
[73] http://www.xerox.com/
[74] http://www.it.uom.gr/pdp/DigitalLib/Neural/Neu_soft.htm
[75] http://www.pitt.edu/~aesmith/

Table 4.11. Clustered sample of information technology companies (n=29)

Organization	URL	KM-4	KM-5	KM-6	KM-7	KM-8	KOH
Adaptec	www.adaptec.com	A	A	A	A	A	A
Pitney Bowes	www.pitneybowes.com	B	D	B	B	B	F
Cadence Design Systems	www.cadence.com	B	C	D	C	C	C
Compuware	www.compuware.com	C	C	F	C	C	C
Computer Assoc. Intl.	www.cai.com	B	C	D	C	C	E
Compaq Computer	www.compaq.com	C	B	F	D	D	D
IBM	www.ibm.com	C	B	F	F	D	E
Silicon Graphics	www.sgi.com	C	B	F	D	D	D
Hewlett-Packard	www.hp.com	C	B	F	D	D	D
PeopleSoft	www.peoplesoft.com	B	C	D	F	E	E
Apple Computer	www.apple.com	C	C	F	D	E	D
EMC	www.emc.com	B	C	B	B	E	E
Novell	www.novell.com	C	C	D	F	E	C
Oracle	www.oracle.com	C	B	F	F	E	E
Sybase	www.sybase.com	B	C	F	F	E	E
Informix	www.informix.com	B	C	F	C	E	E
Data General	www.dg.com	B	D	D	F	E	F
Microsoft	www.microsoft.com	B	C	D	F	E	E
Dell Computer	www.dell.com	B	D	D	F	F	F
Gateway 2000	www.gateway2000.com	B	D	D	F	F	F
Imation	www.imation.com	B	C	D	F	F	F
Iomega	www.iomega.com	B	E	D	F	F	F
Lexmark International	www.lexmark.com	B	D	D	F	F	F
Quantum	www.quantum.com	B	D	D	F	F	F
Seagate Technology	www.seagate.com	B	D	D	F	F	F
Western Digital	www.wdc.com	B	C	D	F	F	D
StorageTek	www.stortek.com	B	E	D	F	F	F
NCR	www.ncr.com	D	E	E	G	G	B
Sun Microsystems	www.sun.com	C	B	C	E	H	E
Distance (Mean)		4.11	3.96	3.73	3.56	3.27	--

There are no completely satisfactory methods for determining the optimal number of population clusters for any type of cluster analysis (Doux et al. 1997, 360; Bortz 1999, 553). The K-Means algorithm implemented in SPSS, for example, is an iterative process that requires the user to specify the number of desired clusters in advance. After creating an initial configuration, the cases are moved between clusters until it becomes impossible to improve the result (Taylor 1999, 121). If the purpose of clustering is dissection, that is, to summarize the data without trying to uncover real clusters, it usually suffices to look at the average distance of the cluster centers. Although the distance values are stated in Table 4.11, a graphical representation helps determine the optimal number of clusters. Figure 4.25 plots the mean Euclidean distance from the cluster centers as a function of the specified number of clusters (compare Meffert 1992, 277). There are two noticeable bends in the curve at KM-4 with an average Euclidean distance of 4.11 and at KM-8 with a distance of 3.27. This observation suggests that a further increase in the number of clusters would only result in a moderate increase in precision (KM-4), or even cause an increase of the average distance (KM-8).

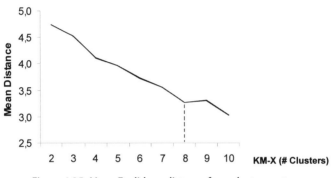

Figure 4.25. Mean Euclidean distance from cluster centers

4.5.5.2 Results

For the following analysis, the model with eight cluster centers (KM-8) was chosen. Intuitively interpreting the nature of more groups would become increasingly difficult, especially for a sample that comprises only 29 organizations. Interpretation as a mental overlay on our perceptions tends to be more content-oriented and domain-specific than automated evaluations. It relates the results of the clustering to meaningful properties of the application domain. At first sight, it is often problematic to extrapolate a meaning for each of the groupings after clusters have been discovered. Thus a detailed analysis of the underlying attribute values is absolutely necessary for a valid interpretation. Such an analysis is presented in Table 4.12, which compares the average attribute values for each of the eight clusters, all standardized to z scores (the numerals in the heading denote the number of cases assigned to each cluster).

Table 4.12. Attribute means of the final cluster centers

Variable	A (1)	B (1)	C (3)	D (4)	E (9)	F (9)	G (1)	H (1)
Alength_Doc	-0.12	-1.00	0.42	-0.90	0.39	-0.15	1.37	-0.05
Alength_Snt	0.86	-1.83	-0.36	1.41	0.02	-0.32	-0.48	-0.38
Alength_Wrd	-2.18	0.05	0.77	-0.01	0.58	-0.70	0.19	0.71
Anchor_r	4.11	0.63	-0.47	-0.60	-0.02	-0.20	1.49	-0.40
Applet_d	-0.10	-0.43	-0.10	1.38	-0.32	-0.32	-0.43	1.54
AppletRatio	0.72	-0.59	0.06	1.45	-0.30	-0.30	-0.59	-0.17
Email_d	-0.56	-0.69	2.31	-0.26	0.16	-0.60	-0.88	0.20
EmailRatio	-0.69	-1.59	-0.81	0.25	0.20	0.06	1.25	0.15
FieldRatio	0.22	-0.77	1.21	0.02	-0.40	0.27	-1.12	-0.90
FileExt	-0.33	-0.33	0.65	0.72	-0.15	-0.33	-0.75	0.93
Form_d	0.22	0.27	-0.29	0.21	-0.15	-0.39	-0.58	4.90
FormRatio	3.24	-0.23	0.30	0.17	-0.22	-0.22	-0.75	0.12
Frame	-0.49	4.50	-0.32	-0.03	-0.08	-0.14	-0.49	-0.49
Image_dr	-0.74	-1.16	-0.61	0.76	0.26	-0.30	1.20	-0.13
ImageRatio	-0.84	0.13	-0.07	0.07	0.32	-0.66	3.62	0.06
Jscript_r	0.69	-0.73	-0.68	0.17	-0.06	0.36	-0.71	-0.66
KByte	-0.05	-2.00	0.32	0.17	0.38	-0.15	-3.32	1.71
LinkAnchor_br	1.48	1.27	-0.54	-0.60	0.08	-0.42	2.76	1.59
LinkAnchor_wr	4.40	-0.64	-0.40	-0.43	-0.01	-0.23	0.77	0.50
LinkExt_dr	1.47	-1.34	-0.87	0.57	0.18	-0.36	2.02	-0.25
LinkExtRatio	-0.40	-0.35	0.40	0.24	0.53	-0.54	-0.90	-0.41
LinkInt_b	-0.53	-0.62	0.49	-0.31	-0.11	0.21	0.15	-0.19
LinkInt_dr	1.22	-1.47	-0.74	0.51	0.02	-0.33	-0.02	3.23
LinkIntRatio	-0.04	-0.11	0.48	1.09	0.11	-0.82	-0.42	1.09
TextRatio	-0.90	0.32	1.52	-0.62	0.14	-0.54	1.97	0.07
TTR_s	-1.96	0.32	1.00	-0.04	0.56	-0.64	-0.87	0.41
Word_d	-0.72	-0.70	1.55	0.20	0.50	-0.81	-1.46	0.27

Although they provide a detailed account of the clustering results, it is quite difficult to interpret the absolute values for the cluster centers in Table 4.12. Besides, there is no indication of the extent to which certain variables contributed to the clustering. The highest difference (the "bandwidth") in terms of distance between the identified groups is a first estimate of a variable's discriminative power. A one-way analysis of variance provides another, more reliable criterion to assess a parameter's relative importance by computing F values for each of the variables. These values help identify variables that drive the clustering and those that differ little across the clusters. However, the F tests should be used only for descriptive purposes. The observed significance levels are not valid and thus cannot be traditionally interpreted as tests of the hypothesis that the cluster means are equal. When plotted in decreasing order, the distribution of F values signifies the relative importance of certain variables in the clustering process. As shown in Figure 4.26, one of the variables (*Form_d;* F = 51.73) had a particularly high impact on the result.

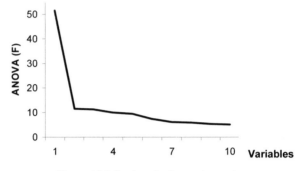

Figure 4.26. F values in decreasing order

More effective representations, therefore, rank the variables in decreasing order according to their F values. In addition to that, Table 4.13 replaces the absolute values with a set of symbols (++, +, -, --) that are easier to interpret (compare with Meffert 1992, 208).

Table 4.13. Ranked attribute means of the cluster centers

Variable	A	B	C	D	E	F	G	H	MIN	MAX	DIFF	F
Form_d	+	+	-	+	-	-	--	++	-0.58	4.90	5.49	51.73
LinkAnchor_wr	++	--	-	-		-	+	+	-0.64	4.40	5.04	11.63
Anchor_r	++	+	-	--		-	+	-	-0.60	4.11	4.71	11.34
Frame	--	++	-			-	-	-	-0.49	4.50	4.99	9.95
Email_d	-	-	++		+	-	--	+	-0.88	2.31	3.18	9.57
KByte		--	+	+	+	-	--	++	-3.32	1.71	5.04	7.39
Word_d	-	-	++	+	+	-	--	+	-1.46	1.55	3.01	6.10
ImageRatio	--			+	-	++			-0.84	3.62	4.46	6.03
LinkAnchor_br	+	+	--	--		-	++	+	-0.60	2.76	3.36	5.36
LinkInt_dr	+	--	-	+		-		++	-1.47	3.23	4.69	5.13
TextRatio	--	+	++	-	+	-	++		-0.90	1.97	2.87	4.06
TTR_s	--	+	++		+	-	-	+	-1.96	1.00	2.97	3.23

4.5.5.3 Discussion

From Table 4.11 it can be seen that clusters A (Adaptec), B (Pitney Bowes), G (NCR), and H (Sun Microsystems) each contain only one case. There are a number of typical features that differentiate these companies from the rest of the sample. Adaptec, for example, is characterized by the lack of frames but a very high number of anchors and within-document links associated with these anchors (Anchor_r, LinkAnchor_wr). This indicates a very granular document structure. The average document published on Adaptec's Web site comprises 5.8 anchors and 6.2 anchorlinks. On the negative side, the amount of textual information provided is limited (TextRatio) and reflects a very uniform vocabulary (TTR_s). Pitney Bowes follows the opposite strategy with many frames and few internal links (Frame, LinkInt_dr, LinkAnchor_w). For Pitney Bowes, 141 frame tags could be identified, nearly twice as many as for any other site. Even though they define scores of anchors, it is surprising that they do not effectively leverage them for within-document navigation (on average, 1.7 anchors per document but only 0.1 within-document links per page were identified). NCR evidently tries to increase the appeal of its system by embedding numerous images but offers practically no interactive features (low values for Form_d, Script_r, Applet_d, and Email_d), which is rather uncommon for the information technology sector. In contrast, Sun Microsystems runs a very sophisticated Web information system, providing a granular navigational system and a high level of interactivity via forms and applets.

Cluster C (Computer Associates, Compuware, and Cadence Design Systems) comprises companies that focus on integrated electronic commerce solutions and related consulting services. It is therefore not surprising that this cluster features the richest vocabulary and a multitude of distinct e-mail addresses. In terms of their navigational structure, however, Web applications of cluster C clearly lack the granularity of other systems such as those of Sun Microsystems or Adaptec.

With Compaq, Hewlett-Packard, IBM, and Silicon Graphics, cluster D represents a group of "big players" that target a very broad market spectrum by offering everything from hardware to software to integrated solutions. The diversity of products and services results in a high percentage of textual information and a diversified vocabulary.

Large software companies dominate cluster E, which includes major vendors of data base management systems (Oracle, Informix, Sybase), operating systems (Microsoft, Apple), network management software (Novell), and individual solutions (Peoplesoft). EMC and Data general, the two remaining companies of cluster E, merged in the fourth quarter of 1999. The formerly independent organizations focus on high-end servers and storage systems for mainframe and mid-range environments (Lelii and McCright 1999; DiCarlo 2000). The retail-oriented cluster F includes Dell and Gateway, which both pioneered the direct sale of computer systems and peripheral components. Practically all the sample's manufacturers of peripheral and storage devices also belong to this group (Imation, Iomega, Lexmark, Quantum, Seagate, StorageTek, and Western Digital).

With 18 companies grouped together, clusters E and F represent nearly two thirds of the information technology sample. Generally, a slight superiority of the software cluster can be observed. The uniform distribution of attribute values is a good indication for the homogeneity of the whole sector. This is not surprising, as the development and implementation of Web-related technologies represent the core business activities of many of these companies. From a technical perspective, it can be assumed that their Web sites document the state of the art and that none of them can afford to risk their reputation by deploying poorly designed Web information systems.

4.5.5.4 Hierarchical Clustering

The underlying principle of hierarchical agglomeration is simple for a set of n elements. First, the two elements that are closest to one another are agglomerated, constituting a new element for the second iteration with $n-1$ elements. Once elements are joined, they remain together until the final iteration. The last, $(n-1)^{th}$ iteration groups together the whole set of elements into one large cluster equivalent to the original data set (Lebart et al. 1998, 83; Taylor 1999, 119). The closeness of elements is computed according to a certain distance measure. For interval data, SPSS provides *Euclidean distance, squared Euclidean distance, cosine, Pearson correlation, Chebychev, block, Minkowski*, and customized measures (SPSS 1999, 294).

These clustering steps can be displayed in a dendrogram (cluster tree), which represents the nodes (= groupings created at each iteration) and clusters (= set of terminal elements corresponding to a node) as an indexed hierarchical tree with the clusters partially nested in one another. A dendrogram is an efficient way to visualize detected similarities within the sample of Web sites (Bortz 1999, 554). Both K-Means cluster analysis and the Kohonen network separated Adaptec, Pitney Bowes, NCR, and Sun Microsystems from the rest of the sample. The dendrogram in Figure 4.27, which is founded on Ward's method and the sites' squared Euclidean distance, confirms this result by agglomerating these cases with the other groups at a very high hierarchical level in the classification tree. The letters preceding the company names in the left-hand column of Figure 4.27 signify the result obtained by K-Means clustering with eight cluster centers. The homogeneity of the who. sector mentioned above and the resulting uniform distribution of at tribute values are responsible for the fact that the results of the different methods (K-Means, hierarchical clustering, Kohonen network) do not exactly match with regard to the remaining sites. In terms of interpretability and congruence with the structure of the business sector, the K-Means result with eight cluster centers offers the most plausible segmentation.

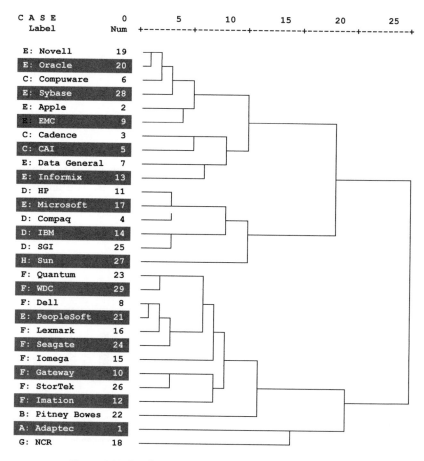

Figure 4.27. Dendrogram of the information technology sector

4.5.6 Cross-Sectional Analysis

After the preceding section introduced the characteristics of one particular industry (information technology), this section compares the sectors with each other and with the LSE/Novell sample. It structures data chronologically (05/99, 07/99, and 11/99; for 05/99, data are ..y available for the information technology and non-profit sectors) ..nd compares them according to the business sector from which they originate. As the assumptions of one-way analysis of variance (normal distribution for each of the populations, variance homogeneity) were violated, a non-parametric Kruskal-Wallis test was conducted for each of the presented variables to evaluate the sectoral differences. A separate effect size index was computed (η^2) to assess the proportion of variability in the ranked dependent variable accounted for by the sector variable. The commercial value of such an analysis is the indications it might give toward the general evolution of technologies and their adoption by particular sectors of the economy. Based on these indications, alternative plans to redevelop and optimize deployed applications can be evaluated.

4.5.6.1 Structure and Navigation

In section 4.5.4, the number of broken internal links has been identified as the most important, negatively correlated parameter to approximate the perceived quality of Web information systems. The left-hand boxplot of Figure 4.28 compares this parameter across the five populations.

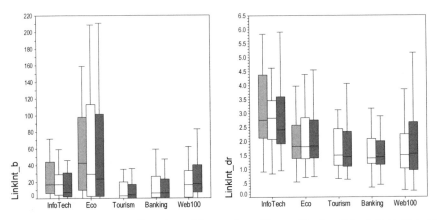

Figure 4.28. Clustered boxplots of the number of internal broken links (left; LinkInt_b) and the average number of distinct internal links per page (right; LinkInt_dr)

The Kruskal-Wallis test was significant, $\chi^2(4,N=418) = 27.297$, p = 0.001. The proportion of variability in the ranked dependent variable accounted for by sectoral differences was 6.5%. Follow-up tests (Mann-Whitney U) were conducted to evaluate the pairwise differences among the five sectors. The significance values of Table 4.14 document the results of these tests.

Table 4.14. Significance levels of the Mann-Whitney U tests for LinkInt_b

	InfoTech	Eco	Tourism	Banking	Web100
InfoTech	---	.009**	.005**	.058	.457
Eco	.009**	---	.000**	.000**	.014*
Tourism	.005**	.000**	---	.300	.001**
Banking	.058	.000**	.300	---	.009**
Web100	.457	.014*	.001**	.009**	---

*** (*) Correlation is significant at the 0.01(0.05) level; two-tailed.*

Applications deployed by travel and tourism companies have a very consistent link structure, which partially explains their good ranking by the LSE/Novell survey. The travel and tourism sector finished clearly ahead of the other industries. Within this sector, airlines belong to the economically strongest and technologically most advanced players (Werthner and Klein 1998, 44). Germany's national airline, *Lufthansa*,[76] for example, was the overall winner of the LSE/Novell survey. The travel and tourism industry tends to be more service focused than other industries, which explains why the support for the transaction phases *agreement* and *settlement* is particularly well implemented (Psoinos and Smithson 1999, 39).

In terms of the number of broken links encountered, the non-profit sector differs significantly from each of the other groups. Evidently, non-profit organizations find it very difficult to maintain a consistent link structure. The significantly lower budget of these organizations for Web development may explain this shortcoming. More surprisingly, information technology companies rank second along this dimension. Similar to the non-profit organizations, they were able to reduce the number of broken links substantially but this still does not clarify such an unexpected result. Only the right-hand diagram of Figure 4.28 puts this observation into context. The Kruskal-Wallis test for the number of distinct internal links per page (LinkInt_dr) was also highly significant, $\chi^2(4,N=418) = 47.840$, p = 0.001. The proportion of variability in the ranked dependent variable accounted for by sectoral differences was 11.5%, a stronger relationship compared to LinkInt_b. Again, follow-up tests (Mann-Whitney U) were conducted to evaluate pairwise differences among the five sectors. Information technology companies differ significantly from all the other populations (p = 0.001). They embed the highest number of links within their documents, a fact that is neglected in the left-hand diagram but should be considered when interpreting the number of broken links per page. For the remaining populations, significant differences were only reported for the non-profit sector,

---

[76] http://www.lufthansa.com/

ɹ is characterized by a higher average number of internal links per ɟe than both the retail banking sector (p = 0.010) and the LSE/Novell ɹmple (p = .023).

ɟ.2 Interface Representation

The previous section captured important characteristics of the applications' navigational system. The following analysis is more concerned with their visual and interactive features. It is based on two parameters, the number of distinct images per page (Image_dr) and the number of scripts per page (Script_r). For the variable Image_dr, the corresponding Kruskal-Wallis was significant, $\chi^2(4,N=418) = 32.665$, p = 0.001. The proportion of variability in the ranked dependent variable accounted for by the group variable was 7.8%, a relatively weak relationship. The results of the Mann-Whitney U follow-up tests are summarized in Table 4.15.

Table 4.15. Significance levels of the Mann-Whitney U tests for Image_dr

	InfoTech	Eco	Tourism	Banking	Web100
InfoTech	---	.000**	.023*	.011*	.983
Eco	.000**	---	.629	.113	.000**
Tourism	.023*	.629	---	.592	.012*
Banking	.011*	.113	.592	---	.004**
Web100	.983	.000**	.012*	.004**	---

** (*) Correlation is significant at the 0.01(0.05) level; two-tailed.

The left-hand diagram of Figure 4.29 demonstrates that the LSE/Novell sample and the information technology sector take the lead in terms of visual information per page. The similarity of these two sectors (p = .983) and the clear, statistically significant separation from the other populations are reflected in the values of Table 4.15. At first sight, visual differences in the interface representation may not be obvious when accessing some of these sites. Clickable maps or other advanced graphical representations, for example, often consist of more than one file and thus may have a strongly positive but unnoticed influence on this attribute value.

The other boxplot of Figure 4.29, *Script_r,* compares the number of occurrences of the <Script>-tag per page. This includes ECMAScript (JavaScript), VBScript, JScript, and other languages that make use of this tag. While some applications use scripts to provide real interactivity, others only tap their potential for special effects and to trigger navigational events such as opening new windows or automatic backtracking. Scripts that add real value to an application's functionality are often embedded in forms and thus avoid the <Script>-tag altogether. These scripts were not considered during the data extraction process, which has to be kept in mind when interpreting the right-hand diagram of Figure 4.29.

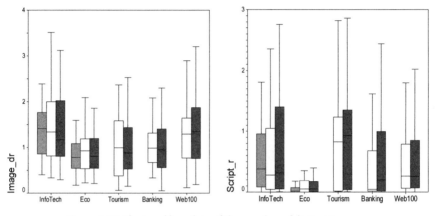

Figure 4.29. Clustered boxplots of the number of distinct images per page (left; Image_dr) and the number of scripting elements per page (right; Script_r)

The Kruskal-Wallis for Script_d was significant, $\chi^2(4,N=418)$ = 32.665, p = 0.001, with the group variable accounting for 10.9% of the dependent parameter's variability. The results of the Mann-Whitney U follow-up tests in Table 4.16 underline the observed differences. The non-profit sector has a significantly lower number of scripts per page than the other populations (p = 0.001), another factor that suggests budget restrictions for Web development and a focus on content to inform the public. At the 0.05 level, a higher number of scripts for the information technology sector compared to retail banking could be confirmed as well. The exclusion of form-embedded scripts mentioned above presumably inhibits more significant differences for this particular variable.

Table 4.16. Significance levels of the Mann-Whitney U tests for Script_r

	InfoTech	Eco	Tourism	Banking	Web100
InfoTech	---	.000**	.701	.049*	.375
Eco	.000**	---	.000**	.006**	.000**
Tourism	.701	.000**	---	.111	.190
Banking	.049*	.006**	.111	---	.127
Web100	.375	.000**	.190	.127	---

** (*) Correlation is significant at the 0.01(0.05) level; two-tailed.

4.5.6.3 Content and Strategy

The left-hand diagram of Figure 4.30 visualizes the standardized type token ratio, a linguistic indicator for the quality of a text in terms of the richness of its vocabulary. The non-profit sector ranks very highly in this comparison, followed by the information technology and tourism industries. Naturally, the type token ratio is positively influenced by the topical diversity addressed by a system. The variety of current ecological concerns and heterogeneity of resulting activities represent rich sources of information for environmentally oriented non-profit organizations. Similarly, the rapid introduction and increasing complexity of (Web) technologies result in a higher TTR_s for information technology companies. At the other end of the scale, the very low TTR_s values of the banking sector suggest a narrow spectrum of topics and – in some cases – poorly designed Web information systems that rely more on embedding images than on publishing value-adding information. Even for large international banks, the LSE/Novell survey identified serious technical problems, especially as far as their functionality for supporting the phases agreement and settlement are concerned (Psoinos and Smithson 1999, 11). Thus it had to be expected that small and midsize organizations of this industry are plagued by similar shortcomings.

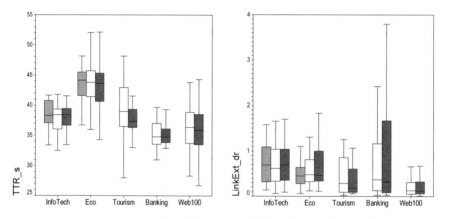

Figure 4.30. Clustered boxplots of the standardized type token ratio (left; TTR_s) and the number of distinct external links per page (right; LinkExt_dr)

The Kruskal-Wallis for TTR_s was significant, $\chi^2(4, N=418) = 149.248$, $p = 0.001$. The sector variable accounts for 35.8% of the dependent parameter's variability, the highest value among all parameters considered in the cross-sectional analysis. Accordingly, the Mann-Whitney U follow-up tests showed highly significant results. With the exception of the relationship between information technology and tourism companies, which seem to be quite comparable regarding the sophistication of their systems' vocabulary (p = 0.966), highly significant differences at the 0.01 level were reported for most of the sector combinations. Only pairing the banking sector with the LSE/Novell sample resulted in a less apparent result, significant only at the 0.05 level (p = 0.021).

Topical variety encourages organizations to embed more external links in their Web information system. Non-profit organizations, for instance, often leverage third party reports to underline the legitimacy and objectivity of their claims. Most of them regard information as a powerful tool of social and environmental change. Both the volume and the quality of environmental information available in digital form has increased rapidly in recent years (Günther 1998, 144). In their efforts to inform their audience and raise public awareness, non-profit organizations regularly provide access to involved government agencies, to academic departments that compiled reports about a particular issue, or to articles published in newspapers and magazines.

Similarly, many external links of information technology companies result from collaborations between manufacturers and standardization committees, from providing access to favorable newspaper articles about the company or its products, or from presenting successfully implemented solutions. Using more than one domain name for presenting information distorts the statistics regarding external links, as intra-organizational links are mistakenly counted as external ones. This poses a serious problem for the automated analysis of such systems, as it is basically impossible for the mirroring tool to distinguish intra- from inter-organizational links. Multiple domain names can result from mergers and acquisitions, which are very common in the information technology sector, from special events such as symposia or sponsored conferences, or from providing separate domain names for particular products and technologies. In the case of IBM, for example, detailed information about their latest software technologies is distributed via their *alphaWorks* initiative.[77] Their domino server family, which is marketed by its subsidiary Lotus Development, is also presented under a separate domain name.[78]

The strategy of many companies of the travel and tourism sector is to provide all the necessary information themselves. Referring prospects to promotional material offered directly by the destination's tourist office or local businesses could easily distract these users and induce them to leave the site permanently. Due to their dependence on electronic bookings, most of them are therefore reluctant to provide links to the offerings of other organizations. Consequently, verbose descriptions

---

[77] http://www.ibm.com/
http://www.alphaworks.ibm.com/
[78] http://www.lotus.com/domino/

of particular holiday destinations and high type token ratios are characteristic of many travel and tourism applications, differentiating them from domains with a narrow spectrum such as electronic retail banking.

The Kruskal-Wallis for LinkExt_dr was significant, $\chi^2(4,N=418) = 102.394$, $p = 0.001$. Similar to TTR_s, a strong relationship to the sector variable was reported, accounting for 24.6% of the dependent parameter's variability. Mann-Whitney U follow-up tests showed highly significant results, particularly for the low values of the LSE/Novell sample ($\hookrightarrow$ Table 4.17).

Table 4.17. Significance levels of the Mann-Whitney U tests for LinkExt_dr

	InfoTech	Eco	Tourism	Banking	Web100
InfoTech	---	.063	.000**	.030*	.000**
Eco	.063	---	.003**	.114	.000**
Tourism	.000**	.003**	---	.370	.011*
Banking	.030*	.114	.370	---	.000**
Web100	.000**	.000**	.011*	.000**	---

** (*) Correlation is significant at the 0.01(0.05) level; two-tailed.

4.5.7 Longitudinal Analysis

Longitudinal approaches help the analyst chart the evolution of Web information systems, investigate the interaction between structure and content, and ascertain what time-related variations might be present. The longitudinal partitions of the last section were obtained by sampling Web content at three points in time (05/99, 07/99, and 11/99). This section presents a more focused approach by specifically comparing the two archives of July and November 1999.

From the total sample, 169 sites were successfully mirrored and processed twice and thus qualified for a repeated-measures study. Based on these 169 cases, a *paired-sample t test* was conducted to evaluate whether any of the variables showed a significant change between July and November 1999. At the 0.05 level, the results indicated that this was the case for only three variables: LinkInt_dr, ImageRatio, and Script_r. The highest significance was observed for the Script_r parameter. With a mean value of 0.80 scripts per page (SD = 1.82), the use of scripting languages obviously enjoyed increasing popularity (M7 = 0.67, SD = 1.71; t (168) = -2.608, p = 0.010). Over the period of four months, the average number of distinct internal links per page rose as well, from 2.08 (SD = 1.49) to 2.30 (SD = 2.19) links per document. Both the increasing overall number of documents and the higher granularity of navigational systems contribute to this effect. The ImageRatio, however, declined from 0.15 (SD = 0.12) to 0.14 (SD = 0.11). This movement expresses an increased visual redundancy due to the reuse of graphical data such as company logos, brand names, bullet symbols, and so forth.

Table 4.18 lists the complete set of variables, sorted in decreasing order of the change's significance. For 05/99, 07/99, and 11/99, the attribute's mean values are listed (M5, M7, M11; it is not valid to directly compare M5 since only the information technology and non-profit sectors are included in the first longitudinal partition). The remaining columns show the relative change in percent between 07/99 and 11/97 (Diff %), the Pearson correlation coefficient (P), the t value, and the significance of the change.

Table 4.18. Longitudinal data for 05/99 (n = 52), 07/99 (n = 169), and 11/99 (n = 169)

Variable	[M5]	M7	M11	Diff %	P	t	Sig.
Script_r	.42	.66	.80	21.21	.919	-2.608	.010
LinkInt_dr	2.56	2.08	2.30	10.58	.858	-2.425	.016
ImageRatio	.13	.15	.14	-6.67	.848	2.275	.024
FieldRatio	7.62	8.91	8.27	-7.18	.879	1.925	.056
LinkExt_dr	.65	.59	.66	11.86	.910	-1.728	.086
TextRatio	.35	.26	.26	0.00	.933	1.591	.114
FileExt	9.98	5.75	5.49	-4.52	.852	1.572	.118
EmailRatio	.38	.40	.42	5.00	.909	-1.540	.125
Frame	32.29	72.76	90.12	23.86	.916	-1.461	.146
TTR_s	40.74	37.11	36.72	-1.05	.847	1.270	.206
Anchor_r	.81	.74	.76	2.70	.944	-.903	.368
FormRatio	.31	.35	.33	-5.71	.895	.895	.372
LinkInt_b	51.98	32.31	33.37	3.28	.924	-.692	.490
LinkRatio	.24	.22	.22	0.00	.917	.665	.507
Email_d	108.96	48.66	50.17	3.10	.915	-.523	.602
LinkAnchor_wr	.63	.62	.60	-3.23	.787	.487	.627
ALength_Wrd	5.22	5.09	5.10	0.20	.953	-.416	.678
LinkExtRatio	.45	.45	.45	0.00	.937	-.398	.691
ALength_Snt	24.00	25.25	25.44	0.75	.501	-.315	.753
Image_dr	1.06	1.27	1.27	0.00	.924	-.290	.772
LinkAnchor_br	.45	.40	.39	-2.50	.711	.266	.791
Applet_d	1.19	.68	.67	-1.47	.931	.249	.803
Word_d	18076	12312	12363	0.41	.893	-.167	.867
Form_d	17.08	14.92	14.76	-1.07	.748	.126	.900
ALength_Doc	528	414	415	0.24	.902	-.115	.909
AppletRatio	.22	.18	.18	0.00	.773	.018	.986
KByte	10201	7915	7914	-0.01	.900	.007	.995

4.5.8   Exploratory Textual Analysis

From a theoretical perspective, there are many different approaches to analyzing the textual content of Web information systems. Textual analysis has grown out of the meeting of a variety of disciplines including linguistics, discourse analysis, statistics, computer science, and socio-economic survey analysis (Lebart et al. 1998, 5ff.). The textual analysis of Web documents is founded on three theoretical concepts: syntax, semantics, and pragmatics, neglecting other established linguistic fields such as phonetics, lexicology, or morphology (Fairclough 1995, 57; Yule 1996, 4). *Syntax* refers to the structure of symbols and investigates relationships between linguistic forms – e.g., words or lemmas in sentences. *Semantics* is the study of the relationships between linguistic forms and the users of those forms. It tries to uncover the real meaning of symbols – i.e., words if encoded in language. *Pragmatics* is the study of contextual meaning concerned with the interpretation and usage of symbols, with associations between utterances, and with the specific circumstances of communicating. It investigates the relationship between a sign, its source, and its respondent – i.e., people's intended meanings, their assumptions, or their purposes and goals (Ackoff and Emery 1972, 169). Following a quantitative approach to analyzing Web information systems, pragmatic parameters are practically impossible to capture in consistent and objective ways and thus will be disregarded in the following. Instead, the emphasis will be on the center of Figure 4.31, "text as data", studying language as a prerequisite of communication by discovering and visualizing regularities in textual data. More precisely, the communicated content (= *content analysis*) is analyzed rather than the process of communicating itself (= *discourse or conversation analysis*). In contrast to discursive situations, texts in general and Web information systems in particular provide less contextual meaning as they are divorced from an individual's subjective interpretation (Raudaskoski 1997, 535).

The analysis relies entirely upon textual raw data. Different from many traditional methodologies, the highly domain-independent approach does not require any preconceptions about the existence or nature of certain dependencies or categories. In the light of modern communication theory, however, the suggestion to conduct research that is largely descriptive in nature can be distressing. Potter addresses the legitimacy of such an approach by looking at the history of social scientific investigation of the media and by contrasting the characteristics of different media in the light of this history (Potter 1999). The study of traditional media like television, for example, has moved beyond the point where further descriptions of content are needed. Research in that

area now focuses on building theories concerning the connections between corporate influences on production and the final content, or between the content and audience effects. In the case of the World Wide
Web, the situation is utterly different: "We have no real idea what Web
content consists of, and it is arguably important ... to obtain that
knowledge before we chase after the content trying to superimpose
theories upon it" (Potter 1999).

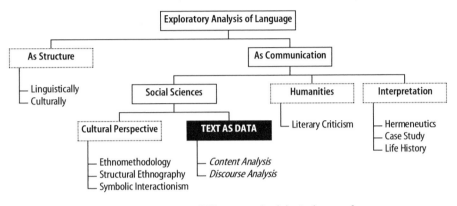

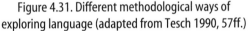

Figure 4.31. Different methodological ways of
exploring language (adapted from Tesch 1990, 57ff.)

Figure 4.32 illustrates the scope of exploring the textual dimension of
Web information systems with special emphasis upon exploratory textual data analysis. Automatic indexing and frequency computations
ignore information of a semantic or syntactic nature that is usually
available to any reader – e.g., synonyms (two strings that have identical
meaning), homonyms (one string that has more than one meaning), or
the particular order of words within a text (Lebart et al. 1998, 113).
However, it is important to keep in mind that even this reduced set of
textual data not only comprises the textual material itself but also
abundant linguistic meta-data. Words with rich semantic meaning are
often allocated several pages in encyclopedic dictionaries; even comparably insignificant function words require several rows. For Web information systems, external references are available as well: genres,
authors, responsible departments, hierarchical position, type of document, or the date of publication.

With its roots in modern information retrieval, *text summarization* is
a closely related field. It helps users to digest information by extracting
information content from partially structured text and presenting the
most relevant aspects in a manner sensitive to their needs. Text summarization involves three phases: analysis (building the representation),
refinement (condensing the input by selecting salient information), and
synthesis (rendering the summary representation in natural language).

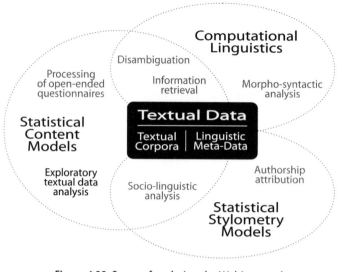

Figure 4.32. Scope of exploring the Web's textual
dimension (adapted from Lebart et al. 1998, 10ff.)

The purpose of summaries can be *indicative* to alert users as to what the source is about, *informative* to stand in place of the source, or *evaluative* to offer a critique of the source (Mani and Bloedorn 1999, 35f.). While there are certain similarities, especially as far as the evaluative approach is concerned, four main characteristics distinguish exploratory textual analysis as presented in this section from text summarization and from information retrieval in general:

- Instead of recommending or processing single documents, large collections of documents (= Web information systems) are the primary unit of analysis.

- The concept of comprehension occupies a central position in most research on information retrieval and text summarization. Many projects acknowledge the value of sound content theories. By contrast, comprehension is virtually foreign to textual statistics (Lebart et al. 1998, 8; Chandrasekaran et al. 1999, 21).

- While text summarization focuses on optimizing the information access of users, the primary target groups of exploratory textual analysis are corporate clients such as Web developers, marketing managers, or business analysts.

- The output of the synthesis phase consists of statistical representations. There is no need to condense the original document's content using natural language.

4.5.8.1 Types of Content

No human editor can cover the full extent of information available, and the limits of aggregate judgements have already been discussed in Section 4.5.2. Thus textual analysis, which indicates major areas of economic and social content, should be regarded as a key component of any empirically founded Web evaluation framework. The words most commonly used, for example, reveal popular products and services, the relative importance of sales and marketing terms, well-known geographic names, and clusters of editorial activity such as major political events, financial news, or reports on natural disasters (Paltridge 1999, 336).

The *WebAnalyzer* architecture fulfills the need for descriptive content analyses of Web information systems. But what is the nature of the content to be analyzed? To answer this question, Potter and Levine-Donnerstein distinguish manifest from latent content (Potter and Levine-Donnerstein 1999):

- *Manifest content* consists of discrete textual elements and is easily observable (e.g., the length of a text, its characteristic sequence of words, the occurrences of a particular word, and so forth).
- *Latent content* shifts the focus to the meaning underlying the surface elements of a text. Latent content, obviously, is a very broad term and comprises two subcategories:
  - *Pattern content* identifies objective patterns across the content's textual elements and the connections between them, and
  - *Projective content* requires readers to access their pre-existing mental schema and focuses on their judgements and subjective interpretations of the perceived textual meaning. "It is true that a language is a code which pairs phonetic and semantic representations of sentences. However, there is a gap between the semantic representations of sentences and the thoughts actually communicated by utterances. This gap is filled not by more coding, but by inference" (Sperber and Wilson 1986; in: Ulmer 1994, 346).

Qualitative Web analysis can be understood as a hermeneutic process (Burbules and Callister 1996), inevitably open-ended and indeterminate as novel information continually changes the way the analyst understands familiar structures, thereby creating novel information (= *hermeneutic circle*). This implies that both interface structure and textual content must be read *and* interpreted to clarify their intended and perceived meaning (Gray 1993, 16). As only manifest content is processed, comprehension and interpretation of textual meaning and related linguistic or cultural aspects play a marginal role in the remainder of this book.

4.5.8.2 Common Methods for Describing and Analyzing Textual Data

Cyclic Web analysis is concurrent with data collection, evolving together with the body of material it seeks to investigate. The latter is segmented into relevant and meaningful units (*"de-contextualization"*), separating relevant portions of data but always maintaining the connection to the whole document. These units – e.g., words or lemmas – are categorized according to an organizing system that is predominantly derived from the data themselves (*"re-contextualization"*). The final goal is the emergence of a larger, consolidated picture regarding the high-level patterns and fundamental structural properties of the system under consideration.

Manipulating textual data during analysis is an eclectic activity. It can be argued that there might not even exist an optimal method of doing textual analysis. "There is no one correct way of drawing a face, either. No two artists will produce exactly the same drawing of someone's features. If they are skillful and competent, we will nevertheless recognize the same person in their renditions. 'Pictures' of an experience, social phenomenon, or culture don't have to look exactly alike to be valid" (Tesch 1990, 305). Thus the following chapters do not seek to prescribe a "right" way of analyzing this type of material but rather acknowledge the plurality of available approaches. They enlarge the developer's assortment of methods and tools and help her select the most appropriate strategy for a particular organization.

Cross-tabulations, contingency tables (lexical tables), principal axis methods (principal components analysis, factor analysis, correspondence analysis), and clustering algorithms are among the most common methods used for describing and analyzing textual data. Software for automated content analysis covers a broad spectrum of applications. While some of the tools are only intended for coding responses to open-ended questions, others process content of a more general nature. Naturally, most of the tools that come with built-in dictionaries are restricted to a certain language. General content analysis packages such as *Word-Smith,*[79] *Intext/TextQuest,*[80] *TextPack,*[81] or *WordStat,*[82] to mention a few, do not have built-in repositories but allow analysts to create their own dictionaries (compare with Weitzman and Miles 1995, 338f.). For the project described in this chapter, the *WordSmith* tool set was chosen.[83] It supports three types of analysis:

---

[79] http://www.liv.ac.uk/~ms2928/
[80] http://www.intext.de/
[81] http://www.zuma-mannheim.de/software/en/textpack/
[82] http://www.simstat.com/wordstat.htm
[83] http://www.oup.co.uk/isbn/0-19-459283-9

- *Word List Generation,* which produces a list of all the words in a text, set out in alphabetical or frequency order (↪ Section 4.5.8.3).
- *Keyword Analysis,* which detects words of unusual high frequency vis-à-vis a reference corpus (↪ Section 4.5.8.5).
- *Concordance Analysis,* which displays any word or phrase in its immediate context and enables the analyst to search for occurrences of a particular phrase in the text (↪ Section 4.5.8.6).

4.5.8.3 Word List Generation

The first step of any lexical analysis is the conversion of a stream of characters (= the original text) into a stream of coding units. *Coding units* represent the smallest segments to be analyzed, sometimes also referred to as items, incidents, meaning units, or analysis units. The *context unit* is the body of material surrounding the coding unit, in the case of Web information systems an organization's hierarchical structure of published documents (Tesch 1990, 116; Titscher et al. 1998, 78; Baeza-Yates and Ribeiro-Neto 1999, 165; McMillan 1999b; Terveen et al. 1999, 70).

Coding Units

In contrast to process-oriented investigations (e.g., discourse analysis) that focus on conversational units like utterances or speaking turns (Tesch 1990, 104), coding units for content-oriented approaches are usually identified on the basis of their graphical form. These textual pieces of information are often referred to as strings or tokens and belong to one of the following categories (Aarseth 1994, 60; Pearce and Miller 1997, 111):

- Syntagms (= sequences of words):
  - Whole paragraphs,
  - Sentences,
  - Repeated segments.
- Lexemes (= single words or lemmas).
- Graphemes (= sequences of consecutive characters in a document, for example parts of a word like syllables or letters; the term *n-gram* is used for partial character sequences of length *n*):
  - Prefixes,
  - Suffixes, or
  - Infixes.

There is some evidence in information retrieval research for the limited value of additional (meta-) information in very large text domains (Mladenic 1998, 6). Therefore, using single words or lemmas as coding units is the most popular approach to building statistical content models of those domains (structural features of the information space are covered by the other components of *WebAnalyzer*, described in Section 4.5.3.3).

Conversion, Segmentation, and Identification

The first requirement for any quantitative approach to textual analysis is that the text to be analyzed has to be *converted* into an adequate, machine-readable representation. In comparison to the time-consuming process of scanning printed material, this seems to be a straightforward process in the case of Web information systems. However, a number of transformations are needed prior to any statistical analysis. First, the HTML documents have to be converted into plain text. This step has already been described in Section 4.5.3.3: Structural Parameters.

In the second step, it is necessary to *segment* the derived textual chain into minimal units, removing coding ambiguities such as punctuation marks, the case of letters, hyphens, or points occurring within abbreviations. A series of non-delimiters whose bounds at both ends are delimiters is referred to as an occurrence. To obtain an automatic segmentation of a text into occurrences of graphical forms, a subset of characters must be specified as delimiting characters. Most regular texts contain paralinguistic items such as word delimiters (blanks), sequence delimiters (weak punctuation marks), and sentence separators (strong punctuation marks). All other characters contained in the text are then considered to be non-delimiting characters. Two or more identical series of non-delimiters constitute two or more occurrences of the same word (Lebart et al. 1998, 22f.). Frequently, numeric coding is employed to identify words to be used during calculations in a more memory-efficient way.

The third step, *identification*, groups identical units together by counting the number of their occurrences – i.e., a word list is created ("inventory of words"). This exhaustive index regularly uses decreasing frequency of occurrence as the primary sorting criterion and lexicographic order as secondary criterion. If frequency order is selected, the most popular words are displayed at the top of the list. Figure 4.33 depicts such a frequency-ordered word list, which was compiled on the basis of *Travelscape's* Web site as of November 1999 (part of the travel and tourism sample).[84] The following settings were used to generate the

---

[84] http://www.travelscape.com/

word list: plain text (English), numbers not included, word length of 3-20 letters, no minimum and maximum frequencies, clustering and case sensitivity deactivated, type token basis of 1000 words, and no filtering of tags.

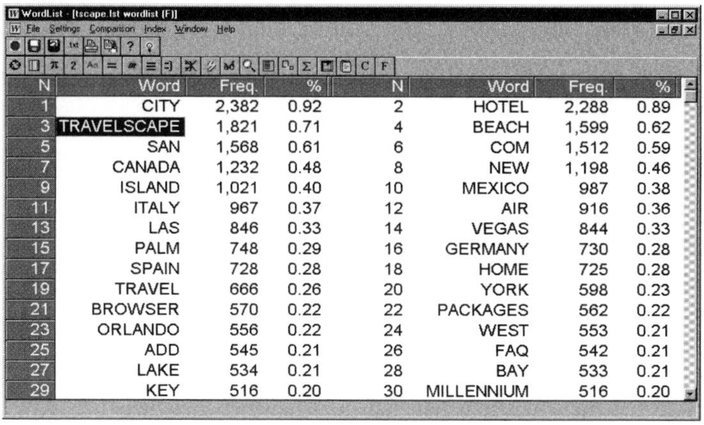

N	Word	Freq.	%	N	Word	Freq.	%
1	CITY	2,382	0.92	2	HOTEL	2,288	0.89
3	TRAVELSCAPE	1,821	0.71	4	BEACH	1,599	0.62
5	SAN	1,568	0.61	6	COM	1,512	0.59
7	CANADA	1,232	0.48	8	NEW	1,198	0.46
9	ISLAND	1,021	0.40	10	MEXICO	987	0.38
11	ITALY	967	0.37	12	AIR	916	0.36
13	LAS	846	0.33	14	VEGAS	844	0.33
15	PALM	748	0.29	16	GERMANY	730	0.28
17	SPAIN	728	0.28	18	HOME	725	0.28
19	TRAVEL	666	0.26	20	YORK	598	0.23
21	BROWSER	570	0.22	22	PACKAGES	562	0.22
23	ORLANDO	556	0.22	24	WEST	553	0.21
25	ADD	545	0.21	26	FAQ	542	0.21
27	LAKE	534	0.21	28	BAY	533	0.21
29	KEY	516	0.20	30	MILLENNIUM	516	0.20

Figure 4.33. Word list of Travelscape (11/99)

Further Processing

In sharp contrast to stylometry, content-oriented statistical analyses regard function words as less relevant statistical units. The nature of large texts like those contained in Web information systems generally limits the role of these words. Lebart et al. compare them to noise that is introduced into the signal – i.e., the document's primary content (Lebart et al. 1998, 124). After text segmentation and identification of occurrences, two simple techniques are therefore applied to obtain a list of semantically meaningful terms: requiring a minimum word length and specifying enumerative stop lists.

Short words comprising less than a certain number of letters can usually be deleted without any considerable impact on the result. For the current example, all words with a length of less than three letters were eliminated from the output. Similar applications also prune infrequent and very frequent words (Lebart et al. 1998, 116; Mladenic 1998, 26; Crimmins and Smeaton 1999, 58). *Stop lists* are lists of words not to be included in the analysis. Function words such as articles, prepositions, or conjunctions are natural candidates for a stop list (Baeza-Yates and Ribeiro-Neto 1999, 167). Figure 4.33 was computed after eliminating the following terms: *the, and, for, with, that, are, this, from, all, can, will, its, have, has, other, not, about, one, also, which, may, these, any, than, was, you, your, our, more, their, they, when, how, based, first, only, such, through, into, over, what, most, end.*

Word list representations can be modified and extended in various ways. Figure 4.34, for example, shows a word list that is not limited to the Web information system of Travelscape but represents the whole travel and tourism sector as of November 1999 (n=21). Instead of using single words as coding units, word clusters comprising three words each are listed in decreasing order of frequency.

N	Word	Freq.	%	N	Word	Freq.	%
1	AIRLINES OF THE	8,052	0.16	2	ALL RIGHTS RESERVED	6,528	0.13
3	ABOUT TO LEAVE	2,402	0.05	4	TO VIEW AN	2,393	0.05
5	CONTINUE OR RETURN	2,392	0.05	6	AN EXTERNAL RESOURCE	2,389	0.05
7	CLICK HERE FOR	1,967	0.04	8	TERMS OF USE	1,745	0.03
9	FOR MORE INFORMATION	1,322	0.03	10	DELTA AIR LINES	1,058	0.02
11	FREQUENT FLYER CENTER	1,054	0.02	12	TERMS AND CONDITIONS	1,024	0.02
13	ARE SUBJECT TO	982	0.02	14	SIGN UP FOR	951	0.02
15	THE UNITED STATES	932	0.02	16	A FREETRAVEL NEWSLETTER	876	0.02
17	COPYRIGHT AND PRIVACY	865	0.02	18	PLACES TO GO	831	0.02
19	SALT LAKE CITY	770	0.02	20	HOLIDAY SPECIAL OFFERS	767	0.02
21	MY TRAVEL DEALS	756	0.02	22	NEW YORK CITY	734	0.01
23	RENT A CAR	729	0.01	24	TEXT-ONLY VERSION	679	0.01
25	IN ADDITION TO	675	0.01	26	DO NOT INCLUDE	646	0.01
27	PRIVACY AND SECURITY	624	0.01	28	PROFESSIONAL TRAVEL AGENT	624	0.01
29	IN THE WORLD	615	0.01	30	ARE PER PERSON	555	0.01
31	BASED ON DOUBLE	555	0.01	32	E-MAIL US	555	0.01

Figure 4.34. Clustered word list of the travel and tourism sector (n=21; 11/99)

4.5.8.4 Lemmatization

On top of frequency thresholds, word length limits, and stop lists, rule-based algorithms can be used to group together words arising from different inflections of one lemma (*word-stemming, lemmatization;* a *stem* is the portion of a word which is left after removal of its prefixes and suffixes). Plurals, gerund forms, and past tense suffixes are syntactical variations that complicate the process of analyzing textual data. This problem can be partially overcome by lemmatizing a text, which puts verb forms into the infinitive, nouns into the singular, and removes elisions (Lebart et al. 1998, 23). Lemmatization usually reduces the number of occurrences of the lemmatized corpus as compared to the initial text – with the exception of contracted graphical forms like "cannot" (Lebart et al. 1998, 42). More sophisticated approaches for eliminating ambiguities[85] concerning the syntactic function or semantic na-

---

[85] A sign (X) is denotatively *ambiguous* if (a) the sender intends X to denote (Y), (b) X is an efficient denoter of something other than Y for the receiver, and (c) the receiver intends to respond to the denotation intended by the sender (Ackoff and Emery 1972, 172).

ture of occurrences require grammatical analysis of the sentence structures. While being indispensable for socio-linguistic or morphosyntactic studies, such methods seem of limited value for analyzing Web content.

Figure 4.35 depicts the changes to *Travelscape's* word list of Figure 4.33 after its lemmatization. The frequency of particular occurrences and, consequently, the rank order of the list have changed considerably. For compiling this example and for the keyword analysis in Section 4.5.8.5, a lemma list compiled by Someya containing 40,569 tokens in 14,762 lemma groups was imported into *WordSmith* (Someya 1998).

N	Word	Freq.	%	Lemmas	N	Word	Freq.	%	Lemmas
1	CITY	2,666	1.03	cities(284)	2	HOTEL	2,449	0.95	hotels(161)
3	TRAVELSCAPE	1,821	0.71		4	BEACH	1,623	0.63	beaches(24)
5	SAN	1,568	0.61		6	COM	1,512	0.59	
7	CANADA	1,232	0.48		8	NEW	1,200	0.47	newest(2)
9	ISLAND	1,048	0.41	islands(27)	10	MEXICO	987	0.38	
11	ITALY	967	0.37		12	AIR	916	0.36	
13	LAS	846	0.33		14	VEGAS	844	0.33	
15	LAKE	783	0.30	lakes(249)	16	PALM	751	0.29	palms(3)
17	GERMANY	730	0.28		18	HOME	728	0.28	homes(3)
19	SPAIN	728	0.28		20	TRAVEL	669	0.26	travels(3)
21	PACKAGE	646	0.25	packages(562),packaged(2)	22	YORK	598	0.23	
23	BROWSER	582	0.23	browsers(12)	24	ORLANDO	556	0.22	
25	WEST	553	0.21		26	ADD	548	0.21	adding(3)
27	FAQ	542	0.21		28	BAY	533	0.21	
29	KEY	531	0.21	keys(15)	30	SPRING	518	0.20	springs(516)
31	MILLENNIUM	516	0.20		32	HILL	514	0.20	hills(265)

Figure 4.35. Lemmatized word list of Travelscape (11/99)

While the vocabulary of a text consists of the entire set of distinct occurrences, its size (or length) is determined by the total number of occurrences. When occurrences are added to a text, its vocabulary tends to grow at a decreasing rate, which tends to be lower for the lemmatized corpus as compared to the initial text. Both lemmatizing texts and applying a frequency threshold for words considerably reduce the size of the vocabulary by grouping words of similar meaning together and discarding occurrences that only appear once (hapaxes) or rarely used expressions. The patterns obtained are more significant and the accuracy of statistical tests is increased (Lebart et al. 1998, 104).

4.5.8.5 Keyword Analysis

In this section, keywords are utilized to characterize Web information systems and compare them by organization or business sector. The purpose of keyword analysis is to locate and identify characteristic words in a given text (= sample). The frequency of words in the text is compared with their frequency in a reference set of words usually taken from a larger corpus of text. Thus at least two word lists are needed to conduct a keyword analysis.

For each word occurring in the sample, the program computes and cross-tabulates the frequency of that particular word and the total number of words in both the sample and the reference corpus. Any word which is found to be outstanding in its frequency in comparison with the reference corpus is considered characteristic. The key words are then presented in order of significance. To compute the significance, *WordSmith* provides two statistical tests: Dunning's *log likelihood test* and the classic chi-square test of significance with Yates' correction for a 2 x 2 table. Dunning's test was chosen because it gives a better estimate of significance, especially when contrasting long texts or a whole genre against the reference corpus (Dunning 1993, 61ff.).

The examples presented in the following are based on lemmatized word lists for each organization, for each sector, and for the whole sample (n = 480). The results are highly significant at the 0.01 level. Contrasting the word lists of particular sectors to the average frequency distribution of the whole sample required considerable resources in terms of memory and computational speed. Consuming more than 930 megabytes in standard ASCII representation, the reference corpus comprises approximately 575,000 distinct terms (types), resulting in a total of more than 153 million words (tokens) with an average length of 5 letters. These words constitute 6.6 million sentences with an average sentence length of 23 words.

Table 4.19 shows the typical output of the program, sorted in decreasing order of the frequency score (= the "keyness" of a particular word). The additional columns list the word's absolute and relative frequency in both the sample (environmentally oriented non-profit organizations) and the reference corpus.

Table 4.19. List of keywords, absolute and relative frequencies, and frequency scores

Keyword	Freq. (s)	% (s)	Freq. (r)	% (r)	Freq. Score
ENVIRONMENTAL	163,128	0.32	175,673	0.11	86,304
FOREST	104,621	0.21	106,576	0.07	60,014
WATER	94,819	0.19	106,147	0.07	47,192
CONSERVATION	67,063	0.13	68,956	0.05	37,944
ACTION	84,272	0.17	102,110	0.07	36,726
SPECIES	62,318	0.12	63,395	0.04	35,800
RIVER	65,848	0.13	70,186	0.05	35,342
PROJECT	97,032	0.19	130,586	0.09	34,646
LAND	64,943	0.13	72,450	0.05	32,490
NATIONAL	82,572	0.16	115,637	0.08	27,106

On the basis of this information, a between-industry comparison was performed. Table 4.20 lists the keywords and transformed frequency scores for the non-profit, information technology, travel and tourism, and retail banking sectors. Naturally, various function words or terms of other languages (e.g., in the case of applications that offer multilingual documents) had to be eliminated.

Table 4.20. Keywords for each sector and corresponding frequency scores

Non-Profit	FSc	InfoTech	FSc	Tourism	FSc	Banking	FSc
ENVIRONMENTAL	8.63	SERVER	11.04	AIRLINE	14.62	BANK	16.44
FOREST	6.00	PRODUCT	10.49	TRAVEL	12.44	RETIREMENT	15.11
WATER	4.72	SYSTEM	10.48	HOTEL	11.29	RATE	11.19
CONSERVATION	3.79	DATA	10.17	DOCUMENT	8.39	INCOME	10.74
ACTION	3.67	SOLUTION	9.31	FLIGHT	7.63	HELP	9.94
SPECIES	3.58	APPLICATION	9.27	RESERVATION	6.83	BALANCE	8.64
RIVER	3.53	SOFTWARE	9.11	CITY	6.38	ANNUAL	7.50
PROJECT	3.46	SUPPORT	7.76	CRUISE	5.65	ACCOUNT	6.24
LAND	3.25	STORAGE	7.11	NORTHWEST	5.23	TAX	5.78
NATIONAL	2.71	DRIVE	7.05	HILTON	4.74	LOAN	5.36
DAM	2.68	DESIGN	5.95	MARRIOTT	4.63	CONTRIBUTION	5.31
UNEP	2.28	ENTERPRISE	5.88	NIGHT	4.52	SAVINGS	5.20
GOVERNMENT	2.27	TECHNOLOGY	5.82	AIRPORT	3.86	INVESTMENT	4.49
NATURAL	2.27	ORACLE	5.45	AIR	3.82	ROTH	3.98
WASTE	2.07	CUSTOMER	5.09	FARE	3.81	TAXABLE	3.98
GREENPEACE	1.99	NOVELL	4.42	TRAVELSCAPE	3.62	BRANCH	3.83
PROTECT	1.98	EMC	4.35	ROOM	3.44	DEFER	3.59
STATE	1.93	COMPUTER	4.34	VACATION	3.32	RETURN	3.16
CLIMATE	1.92	USER	4.32	MILE	3.16	DEPOSIT	3.00
POPULATION	1.91	WINDOW	4.19	BEACH	2.96	MORTGAGE	2.84
AREA	1.90	CADENCE	3.96	TICKET	2.91	CALCULATOR	2.38
SUSTAINABLE	1.89	DATABASE	3.92	DOUBLECLICK	2.51	SPOUSE	2.36
FISH	1.85	HP	3.85	SAN	2.29	AVERAGE	2.15
EARTH	1.84	INFORMATION	3.84	RESORT	2.28	CHECK	2.09
WILDLIFE	1.83	PERFORMANCE	3.74	SABRE	2.27	PENSION	2.06
HABITAT	1.80	BUSINESS	3.61	DELTA	2.26	FUND	1.91
POLLUTION	1.80	DISK	3.51	DESTINATION	2.24	PAYMENT	1.66
PUBLIC	1.80	MICROSOFT	3.36	NWA	2.19	INTEREST	1.59
RAINFOREST	1.77	SYBASE	3.33	WORLDPERKS	2.11	ATM	1.59
NATION	1.77	INFORMIX	3.31	WORLDWEB	2.08	TRUST	1.46

FSc = Frequency score in 10,000s

Relying on the same method of identifying characteristic terms, a within-industry analysis was conducted. Table 4.20 lists the keywords of four environmental non-profit organizations: World Wildlife Fund, World Resources Institute, Greenpeace, and Sierra Club. To improve the results' validity, the general reference corpus was replaced by a reduced, sector-specific reference corpus comprising the data of the non-profit sample (about 300 megabytes with 235,000 types and more than 50 million tokens). Therefore, the terms listed in Table 4.20 can be regarded as characteristic for one particular organization and are not biased by terms that may be typical for non-profit organizations in general.

Table 4.21. Keywords and corresponding scores for the World Wildlife Fund (WWF), the World Resources Institute (WRI), Greenpeace, and the Sierra Club

WWF	FSc	WRI	FSc	Greenpeace	FSc	Sierra Club	FSc
WWF	7.64	WRI	3.69	GREENPEACE	9.75	SIERRA	7.53
FOREST	0.85	RESOURCE	1.49	NUCLEAR	2.68	CLUB	7.47
RHINO	0.82	BIODIVERSITY	1.42	GREENBASE	2.52	TRIP	2.74
PANDA	0.54	FOREST	1.29	PLUTONIUM	0.95	OUTING	2.71
TIGER	0.37	CLIMATE	1.02	PVC	0.89	HIKE	0.81
CONSERVATION	0.25	WORLD	0.82	HEADLINE	0.86	SAN	0.81
ELEPHANT	0.23	INSTITUTE	0.78	SHIP	0.84	TRAIL	0.77
RHINOCEROS	0.22	BUSINESS	0.76	WASTE	0.81	LEADER	0.74
CLIMATE	0.21	FRONTIER	0.73	GENETICALLY	0.75	SPRAWL	0.71
LOCATION	0.21	DEVELOP	0.63	TREATY	0.68	PLANET	0.63
WWFNET	0.19	POLICY	0.60	BAN	0.65	FLOOR	0.53
GORILLA	0.18	CHANGE	0.53	MAIZE	0.65	FRANCISCO	0.53
WHALE	0.14	EMISSION	0.51	RADIOACTIVE	0.64	LODGE	0.48
DANUBE	0.14	COUNTRY	0.51	SHIPMENT	0.52	TELEPHONE	0.45
CERTIFICATION	0.14	CARBON	0.45	TEST	0.50	PARTICIPANT	0.36
CONGO	0.14	WASHINGTON	0.44	CLIMATE	0.50	PEAK	0.35
HORN	0.14	PERCENT	0.44	TOY	0.48	MUIR	0.32
FISHERY	0.13	ENERGY	0.44	VESSEL	0.42	CAMP	0.28
MEDITERRANEAN	0.12	GLOBAL	0.41	PACIFIC	0.42	YOSEMITE	0.25
NATURE	0.12	INDICATOR	0.38	SPAR	0.40	TRANSPORT	0.24

FSc = Frequency score in 10,000s

Keyword analysis can also be applied to longitudinal data. For that purpose, an organization's Web information system has to be repeatedly mirrored and archived. For compiling the examples in Table 4.22, the systems of the World Resources Institute (WRI) and Greenpeace were sampled in May, July, and November 1999. Integrating the data from the three operations resulted in two separate reference files. The reference corpus for the World Resources Institute (Greenpeace) comprises 17.0 (16.6) megabytes and 2.6 (2.7) million tokens on the basis of 24,700 (41,500) types. Table 4.22 lists keywords with a significantly higher frequency in November 1999 compared to their average frequency for that particular organization. Querying the search engine of the World Resources Institute for these ten words, a number of articles on *"exploring sustainable communities"* were displayed, including two recent case studies on Detroit and Jakarta (WRI 1999a; WRI 1999b), and an article contrasting both cities (WRI 1999c).[86] This focused coverage serves as a good explanation for the exceptional frequency score. In the case of Greenpeace, the emphasis on polyvinyl chloride (PVC) and its use for manufacturing children toys is quite obvious (Greenpeace 1999b). The toxicity and potential leaching of plasticizers (phthalate esters in most cases) especially have been subject of growing concern.

Table 4.22. Keywords, absolute frequency and frequency
score for the World Resources Institute (WRI) and Greenpeace (11/1999)

WRI	Frequency	FSc	Greenpeace	Frequency	FSc
CITY	919	123.0	GREENBASE	4,093	552.3
IMPLICATIONS	132	83.3	TOY	1,094	322.8
DETROIT	136	67.7	HEADLINE	1,869	225.0
PLATFORM	86	46.4	NEWS	2,026	180.3
RESIDENT	223	44.1	GLOBAL	2,795	150.3
FACULTY	204	43.2	SOFT	437	126.9
JAKARTA	145	32.2	CHILD	330	67.0
COFFEE	101	30.4	PVC	1,219	66.4
NITROGEN	162	30.4	WHALE	574	63.9
COMMUNITY	1,212	26.4	PHTHALATES	203	58.8

FSc = Frequency score

Besides its obvious value for analyzing and comparing the textual content of Web information systems, the discriminative potential of keyword analysis can also be leveraged for information retrieval tasks of a more general nature. Most search engines, for example, rely on document-oriented metrics for determining if and how precisely a given document matches the user's query. Current implementations ignore the organization's level of expertise in a certain area. To find technical documentation about a product, however, its manufacturer tends to be a more reliable source of accurate information than an article in a daily newspaper, no matter how often the name of the product appears in one particular document. Combining document-oriented metrics with site-

---

[86] http://www.igc.org/wri/enved/

oriented parameters such as the "keyness" of a term would not only consider its significance for the organization as a whole but also eradicate the common practice of misleadingly attracting non-interested users by hiding a list of popular but irrelevant search terms within a document.

4.5.8.6 Concordance Analysis and Collocation

The term *sign* can be defined as "anything that is a potential producer of a response to something other than itself" (Ackoff and Emery 1972, 161). The terms *"sign"* and *"medium"* are interrelated in complex ways. On the one hand, the sign represents the medium between our consciousness and the world, from which it was originally drawn. On the other hand, the medium is the foundation of the sign itself (Walther 1997, 79). Semiotics is the study of sign processes and systems in nature and culture. As such it treats textual analysis as a key component of cultural media research (Uzilevsky 1994, 1f.; Fairclough 1995, 24). Generally speaking, it tries to give a comprehensive account of potential meaning structures, (written) language being only one of them (Raudaskoski 1997, 536; Titscher et al. 1998, 38). The study of concordances seeks to discover the range of meaning a particular word expresses in the context of Web information systems and is especially valuable for comparative purposes (Tesch 1990, 80).

To semiotics, as for linguistics, texts are chains of signs, and therefore linear by definition (Aarseth 1994, 80; Aarseth 1998, 26). If the textual chain is reduced to a succession of disconnected units, much of the content of the text resulting from the relative positioning of words, their possible juxtapositions, or co-occurrences is neglected (Lebart et al. 1998, 2). Therefore, concordances are used to enrich basic word representations and systematically examine the immediate context of occurrences, including both implicit and explicit local coherence relations (see below). A concordance is produced by searching and rearranging specific target words and their immediate contexts[87] within a text, congregating occurrences of a given word along with a fixed-length fragment of their immediate context (Tesch 1990, 80; Lebart et al. 1998, 32). Concordance displays such as those presented in Figure 4.36 are the basic data set on top of which more sophisticated representations such as word clusters, dispersion plots, or collocation displays can be generated (see below).

---

[87] The linguistic material accompanying certain expressions (= its linguistic environment) is also referred to as *co-text*, distinguishing it from *context* as its physical environment (Yule 1996, 21).

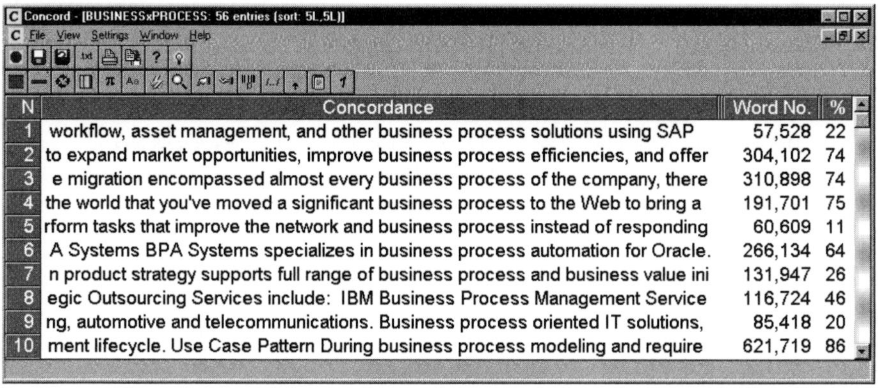

Figure 4.36. Concordance display of the term "business process"

Cohesion and coherence represent the constitutive attributes of textual material. While cohesion describes syntactical interconnections between textual elements, the term coherence refers to their semantics and logical structures (Titscher et al. 1998, 40). Generally speaking three types of local coherence relations are distinguished: elaboration, extension, and enhancement (Fairclough 1995, 121; Halliday 1998, 202ff.). Optionally, they are signalled by markers of cohesion such as conjunctions or sentence-linking adverbials. In elaboration, one clause elaborates on another by describing it, rewording it, exemplifying it, or clarifying it. In extension, the meaning of clauses is extended by either straight addition (*"and"*, *"moreover"*), comparison (*"but"*, *"yet"*, *"however"*) or variation (*"or"*, *"alternatively"*). Clauses are enhanced by other, qualifying clauses in terms of time, place, cause, or condition. Word clusters effectively identify cohesion by revealing patterns of repeated phraseology in the list of concordances. In contrast to basic concordance listings, they present information at an agglomerated level, which makes it easier to generalize from their results. Table 4.23 contrasts ten frequent word clusters of Sun Microsystems, IBM, and Apple Computer that contain the keyword "java". While Sun Microsystems emphasize the technological foundations, applications, and development resources, IBM and Apple Computer naturally focus on their own products based on Java – e.g., *Visual Age for Java* or *QuickTime for Java*.[88]

---

[88] http://www.ibm.com/software/ad/vajava/
http://www.apple.com/quicktime/qtjava/

Table 4.23. Word clusters ('java') for Sun Microsystems, IBM, and Apple Computer

Sun Microsystems	Freq.	IBM	Freq.	Apple Computer	Freq.
The Java platform	107	Java developer kits	10	QuickTime for Java	20
Java programming language	90	Java-based trademarks	9	Runtime for Java	19
Java Web server	63	VisualAge for Java	9	Java virtual machine	10
Java development kit	54	Java technology edition	8	Written in Java	6
Java runtime environment	53	Product support Java	8	Java games hardware	4
Card™ Java compiler	48	Java servlets and	7	Java-based network	4
Web server Java	48	Java virtual machine	6	Quicktime Java games	4
Java technology and	47	Java into Linux	4	And Java logos	3
Development kit JDK	46	Java server pages	4	Cornell uses Java	3
Blend java card™	42	Pouring Java into	4	Java logos™	3

Figure 4.37 depicts a dispersion plot that compares the occurrences of the term *"java"* among ten companies of the information technology sector. The plot shows the filename of the source text, the absolute number of words in the source text, the absolute number of occurrences of the term *"java"*, the number of occurrences per 1,000 words, and a graphical display that visualizes these occurrences. The length of this display reflects the original size of the text file. Not surprisingly, the number of occurrences of the term *"java"* is highest in the case of Sun Microsystems, the inventor of this technology (6.86 occurrences per 1,000 words). The other end of the spectrum represents Microsoft with only 0.07 occurrences per 1,000 words, as the company traditionally regards Java as a potential threat to its dominant position in the operating system market.

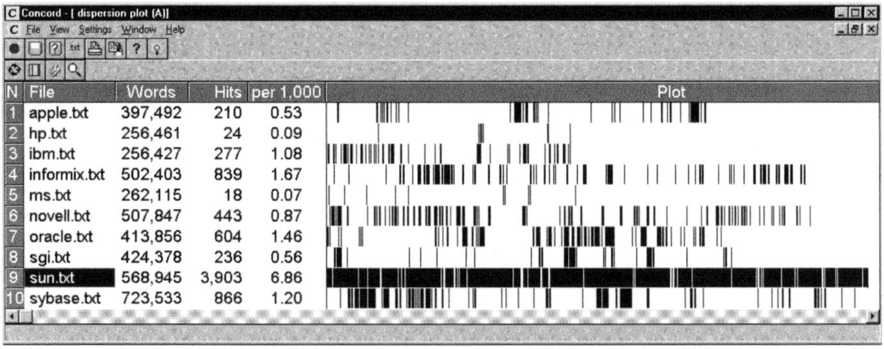

Figure 4.37. Dispersion plot to compare occurrences of the term "java" among ten companies of the information technology sector

Coherence collocates are associated with another word (e.g., *"java"* and *"applet")*. It is difficult to detect this type of collocate, as once the analyst starts looking beyond a horizon of about four or five words on either side, there is more noise than signal in the system. In contrast, *neighborhood collocates* are words that merely occur in the neighborhood of a particular term; they enable the analyst to identify characteristic lexical patterns. The collocation display in Table 4.24 shows neighborhood collocates of *"jini"* in decreasing frequency order (*Jini* is Sun's Java-based connection technology for building ad-hoc communities of autonomous devices that offer independent services).[89] Beside each word, the total number of times it co-occurred with the search word in the list of concordances is displayed, followed by a separate display for the total occurrences left and right of the term. The remaining columns show how many times the term appeared *n* words to the left and right of the term (bold and underlined numbers signal the highest frequency in a row). Obviously, values of the center column (*), which indicates the position of the search term, always have to be zero.

Table 4.24. Collocation display ('jini') for Sun Microsystems

WORD	TOTAL	LEFT	RIGHT	L5	L4	L3	L2	L1	*	R1	R2	R3	R4	R5
JINI	409	29	35	2	14	13	0	0	**345**	3	1	12	17	2
TECHNOLOGY	284	44	240	11	7	6	13	7	0	**151**	51	22	10	6
JAVA	62	57	5	16	5	8	**19**	9	0	0	3	1	0	1
CONNECTION	61	9	52	1	2	0	4	2	0	**28**	20	2	2	0
NETWORK	40	19	21	5	2	3	7	2	0	**10**	0	2	4	5
TECHNOLOGIES	32	4	28	2	1	1	0	0	0	**23**	0	0	0	5
SUN	27	7	20	3	3	1	0	0	0	5	**12**	0	3	0
COMMUNITY	24	11	13	3	3	0	3	2	0	**6**	1	0	**6**	0
SYSTEM	21	2	19	0	0	2	0	0	0	**9**	5	0	3	2
COMPUTING	18	9	9	0	1	**6**	2	0	0	0	4	3	0	2

4.5.8.7 Analysis of Contingency Tables

Even though we daily navigate through a perceptual world of three spatial dimensions and occasionally reason about higher-dimensional arenas with mathematical ease, the world portrayed on our information displays is caught up in their two-dimensionality. For centuries, therefore, the central issue in depicting information has been how to represent the multivariate complexity of real-world objects and processes on the endless flatlands of stone, canvas, paper and, recently, computer screens (Tufte 1983, 40; Tufte 1990, 12; Tufte 1997, 17). Distorted projections such as the display of multiple or complex axes represent visual

---

[89] http://www.sun.com/jini/
http://jini.org/

attempts to get beyond the fundamental limitation of two dimensions by subtly integrating additional attributes into the graphical architecture (↪ Section 5.5.4.3: View Transformations).

Orthogonal axis composition represents a powerful and ubiquitous technique for information visualization, unfortunately limited to three dimensions. However, the analyst usually has to encode multidimensional data comprising so many variables that an orthogonal visual structure is not sufficient (Card et al. 1999, 61). Subdividing a given problem or computationally reducing the dimensionality often leads to more effective results – i.e., results that are faster to interpret, convey more information, and lead to fewer interpretive problems (Bertin 1982, 26). Correspondence analysis is an example of this class of computational solutions, which represents the rows and columns of a contingency table in a joint plot. It belongs to the family of principal axes methods which themselves are largely based on linear algebra. Trying to uncover major structural traits, correspondence analysis identifies lower-dimensional sub-spaces that most accurately approximate the original distribution of data points. In such a series of nested sub-spaces of varying dimensionality, the two-dimensional one is computed most often as it is compatible with our standard communication devices (Lebart et al. 1998, 53).

Before correspondence analysis can be applied to textual material, it has to be transformed into an aggregated lexical table (= *two-way contingency table, incidence matrix*). Such a table is a powerful, two-dimensional knowledge representation that allows the comparison of different text categories such as Web genres, corporate Web information systems, or individual documents. A particular cell of a lexical table may contain frequency data, percentages, ratings, or heterogeneous sets of data (Phillips 1995). When analyzing textual data of Web information systems, a general cell f_{ij} of a lexical table with n rows and p columns contains the number of occurrences of a word (or lemma) in a particular text group. $f_{i.}$ designates the sum of the elements of row i, and $f_{.j}$ the sum of the elements of column j of this table. The profiles of a row or column are defined as follows ($i \in \{1,...n\}; j \in \{1,...p\}$):

$$p_i = \left(\frac{f_{ij}}{f_{i.}}\right) \qquad p_j = \left(\frac{f_{ij}}{f_{.j}}\right)$$

If two row- or column-points have identical or similar profiles, they appear in almost the same position on each of the principal axes. The chi-square distance (χ^2) is a weighted Euclidean distance that is based on the chi-squared test of association. It includes the reciprocal of a term's frequency as the weighting factor (Greenacre 1994, 11; Taylor 1999, 107). The chi-square distance is distributionally equivalent, which means that the distances among rows (or columns) remain the same when two columns (or rows) with identical profiles are merged (Lebart 1994, 164; Lebart et al. 1998, 53). The chi-square distances between two row points (left) and two column points (right) is given by the following equations:

$$d^2(i,i') = \sum_{j=1}^{p} \frac{1}{f_{.j}} \left(\frac{f_{ij}}{f_{i.}} - \frac{f_{i'j}}{f_{i'.}} \right)^2 \qquad d^2(j,j') = \sum_{i=1}^{n} \frac{1}{f_{i.}} \left(\frac{f_{ij}}{f_{.j}} - \frac{f_{ij'}}{f_{.j'}} \right)^2$$

For the following example, ten keywords characteristic of the non-profit sector were selected from Table 4.20. Their frequency was compared among a group of six environmental organizations: *Greenpeace (GRP), Sierra Club (SCL), World Resources Institute (WRI), World Wildlife Fund (WWF), World Watch Institute (WWI)*, and the *United Nations Environment Program (UNEP)*. Instead of having different diagrams for depicting the occurrences of keywords for each Web information system separately, a combined sub-space was used for the whole sample to facilitate the interpretation of results. The sub-space comprised every single document of the sample during the entire time range of the longitudinal study. Combining the retrieved data from the three available archives (05/99, 07/99, and 11/99), the total number of tokens for the six environmental organizations listed in Table 4.25 ranged from 0.8 to 3.3 million. Naturally, the number of absolute occurrences had to be corrected for these differences proportionally. Table 4.25 crosstabulates the corrected frequencies.

Table 4.25. Corrected keyword frequencies for six environmental organizations

Keyword	GRP	SCL	WRI	WWF	WWI	UNEP	Σ
CLIMATE	6943	588	9754	5523	5378	3993	*32180*
CONSERVATION	490	3646	5415	9195	1060	2878	*22683*
GOVERNMENT	5739	1561	4079	4396	5370	5357	*26503*
HABITAT	211	2630	1743	2174	1112	1458	*9328*
POLLUTION	1251	2029	4035	1538	2179	3595	*14627*
POPULATION	843	2294	4223	3886	7874	1826	*20946*
RAINFOREST	405	320	769	529	268	49	*2340*
WASTE	9390	3154	1267	436	2255	2870	*19372*
WATER	3417	6836	4085	3094	11656	6654	*35743*
WILDLIFE	501	2830	874	2937	312	661	*8114*
Σ	*29190*	*25887*	*36244*	*33709*	*37465*	*29341*	*191836*

On the basis of this lexical table, a correspondence analysis was conducted. The *ANACOR* and *CORRESPONDENCE* commands of SPSS were used to perform the underlying calculations. Alternatively, special purpose software is available from several sources (Van der Heijden et al. 1994, 110; Thioulouse et al. 1997, 77ff.). The result of the correspondence analysis is depicted in the biplot of Figure 4.38. The first dimension explains 47.1% of the total inertia, a measure of the spread of points that is calculated by dividing the total Pearson chi-square by the total sum. The first two dimensions together, which are depicted in the diagram, explain 72.6% of the variance – i.e., the relative frequency values that can be reconstructed from both dimensions can reproduce 72.6% of the total chi-square value. The remaining 27.4% of the inertia can only be explained by including the other three dimensions, which are not portrayed in the map (StatSoft 2000). Even though the necessary reduction in dimensionality cannot be obtained without a certain loss of information, these percentages are a rather conservative measure and often underestimate the representational quality (Lebart et al. 1998, 57).

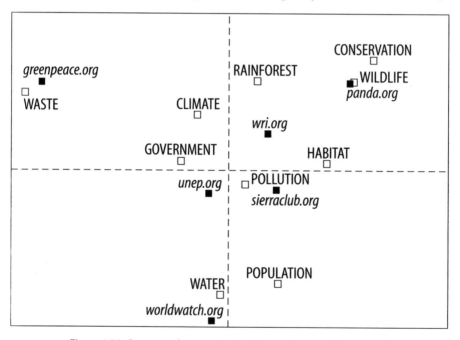

Figure 4.38. Correspondence analysis of the environmental non-profit sector

An examination of the contribution to the inertia of each row and column point helps in the interpre0tation of the two dimensions. Low values are typical for variables that resemble the average profile of the sample. These variables are usually located close to the diagram's origin – e.g., *"pollution"* in Figure 4.38. Terms related to wildlife and the protection of its habitats dominate the display's upper right corner. By projecting the six column variables on the horizontal axis it can be seen that this factor is dominated by *Greenpeace* (0.625) and the *World Wildlife Fund* (0.295). These organizations contributed most to the inertia of the horizontal dimension, together with the terms *"waste"* (0.495) and *"conservation"* (0.285). From the organizational perspective, the vertical dimension's inertia is largely determined by the *World Watch Institute* (0.605), the *World Wildlife Fund* (0.182), and *Greenpeace* (0.162). From the linguistic perspective, the model receives its vertical orientation mainly from the keywords *"water"* (0.396), *"conservation"* (0.196), and *"population"* (0.192).

It is often tempting but generally not permitted to interpret cross-proximities between row- and column-points (i.e., terms and organizations), because they originate from different initial spaces. Thus it would be misleading to overvalue such descriptive maps (Fricke 1990, 159; Blasius 1994, 29). Nevertheless, a joint interpretation of the row- and column-points with respect to the principal axes of the map is possible (Greenacre 1994, 21). As transition relationships link the coordinates of one point to those of all the points of the other space, the position of this single point may be interpreted with respect to the set of points of the other dimension.

The concurrent use of correspondence analysis and clustering methods provides more secure and robust conclusions. The configurations of points resulting from correspondence analysis often need further summarizing, which can often be achieved satisfactorily with the help of hierarchical cluster analysis. Distortions due to the sensitivity to outlying observations relative to the principal axes represent an additional rationale to use agglomerative cluster algorithms, which are "locally robust in the sense that the lower parts of the produced dendrograms are largely independent of possible outliers" (Lebart 1994, 163). However, when hierarchical cluster analysis is performed on the complete textual information of Web information systems, the high number of terminal elements complicates any global summarization. Thus the interpretation frequently focuses on the associations that appear at the two extremities of the dendrogram (Lebart et al. 1998, 92):

- Low-level clusters characterized by agglomerations of words with a very small index whose distribution profiles are similar in different parts of the Web information system (random co-occurrence, repeated segments, repeated words within a segment).
- High-level clusters, which usually comprise the main observed oppositions of the first principal plane (spanned by the first two principal axes).

Another way to avoid the problem of too many terminal elements is the use of keywords instead of a sample's complete text. Such an approach is presented in Figure 4.39, which hierarchically clusters the same terms that were already used for the correspondence analysis of Figure 4.38. The frequencies were z score standardized and grouped via Ward's method based on the squared Euclidean distance. Correctly, the distribution profiles of semantically related terms such as *(habitat, wildlife, rainforest)* or *(pollution, population)* were found to be very similar among the six organizations.

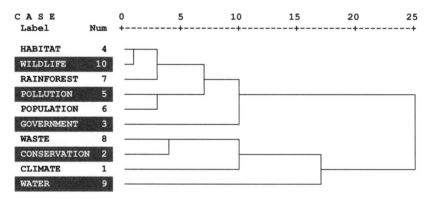

Figure 4.39. Hierarchical cluster analysis of environmental keywords

So far, the presented analyses of lexical tables have been restricted to static snapshots, based on either one particular archive or on aggregate values covering a certain period of time. By contrast, the following example addresses the impermanence of the World Wide Web's textual content (Mitra 1999). It focuses on the application of correspondence analysis for longitudinal studies and more specific problem formulations. Table 4.26 shows frequency distributions for a number of terms related to marine life, structured chronologically (05/99, 07/99, 11/99) and derived from the Web information systems of six non-profit organizations: *World Wildlife Fund (WWF), Greenpeace (GRP), Conservation International (CI), Nature Conservancy (TNC), Natural Resources Defense Council (NRDC),* and the *World Resources Institute (WRI).* As lemmatized word lists were used, both singular and plural forms of the terms are considered.

Table 4.26. Corrected keyword frequencies for marine life coverage

	ATLANTIC	CORAL	DOLPHIN	FISH	PACIFIC	SHRIMP	TURTLE	WHALE	Σ
May 1999									
WWF	99	106	54	555	88	37	66	328	1415
GRP	72	16	14	492	354	33	4	128	1117
CI	84	62	2	284	82	14	17	6	551
TNC	73	65	4	397	81	5	59	9	694
NRDC	76	18	2	306	43	31	36	110	629
WRI	18	138	4	205	53	4	4	6	436
July 1999									
WWF	64	86	59	434	75	33	56	298	1180
GRP	90	72	7	294	442	21	2	56	986
CI	91	67	3	267	93	12	119	5	658
TNC	77	64	4	398	83	6	66	7	707
NRDC	86	19	14	299	44	34	40	161	702
WRI	18	143	4	227	50	6	4	6	463
November 1999									
WWF	51	72	40	394	54	29	46	197	950
GRP	94	68	16	548	425	51	5	194	1406
CI	77	60	2	326	101	17	90	4	679
TNC	76	61	4	396	84	7	63	7	700
NRDC	85	19	14	297	44	34	40	165	704
WRI	10	132	4	204	48	6	4	6	417
Σ	1146	1116	231	5823	2152	10735	20325	39534	81330

On the basis of this lexical table, a second correspondence analysis was conducted to visualize the emergence and decay of topics of interest (= semantic "movements" over time). Müller-Schneider presents a similar approach that uses relative frequencies and supplementary variables – i.e., non-active variables that did not participate in the construction of the planes (Müller-Schneider 1994, 272ff.). Since the computation is executed separately for each one, it is not necessary for these illustrative elements to constitute a homogeneous set (Lebart et al. 1998, 60). In addition to supplementary variables, further modulations of the original display may include the identification and visualization of syntactic (adjectives, verbs, pronouns, etc.) or semantic categories such as words relating to a particular concept.

According to Müller-Schneider's approach, there are two alternative choices of reference frames: either using the first time point for showing changes forward in time or using the last time point for showing backward changes. To generate the display of Figure 4.40, no supplementary variables were needed. Instead, the whole table comprising three time points was used to directly calculate the corresponding sub-space. The

black markers visualize the data points as of November 1999, while the
grey ones indicate the development between May and November 1999.
Strong fluctuations are an indicator of dynamic sites and activistic organizations with a broad topical spectrum that often change their focus
in reaction to current events. The first dimension explains 40.9%of the
total inertia. The first two dimensions together, which are depicted in
the diagram, explain 73.7%. Clearly, the terms in Figure 4.40 are not
distributed randomly. While pelagic marine mammals occupy the far
left of the diagram, other life forms that are more closely connected to
coral reef ecosystems congregate in the bottom right corner. The *World
Wildlife Fund* (05/99: 0.141; 07/99: 0.164) and *Greenpeace* (07/99: 0.114)
contributed most to the inertia of the horizontal dimension, together
with the terms *"whale"* (0.575) and "pacific" (0.202). By projecting the
six column variables on the vertical dimension it can be seen that this
factor is largely determined by *Greenpeace* (05/99: 0.182, 07/99: 0.279,
11/99: 0.188) and the *World Resources Institute* (05/99: 0.54, 07/99: 0.62,
11/99: 0.54). The keywords with the most impact are *"pacific"* (0.550)
and *"coral"* (0.215).

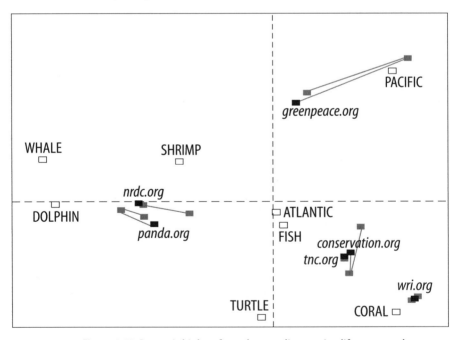

Figure 4.40. Dynamic biplot of trends regarding marine life coverage by
environmental non-profit organizations between May and November 1999

Querying a number of databases for press releases and newspaper
articles published in July 1999, reasons for the observable changes in the
Web information system of Greenpeace soon became obvious. Two

shipments of mixed oxide (446 kilograms of reprocessed uranium and plutonium fuel) heading for Japan left Europe on July 21st aboard two British-flagged vessels, the *"Pacific Pintail"* and the *"Pacific Teal"*.[90] Armed with 30mm naval guns, they were the first armed British merchant ships since World War II and faced protests at every stage of their controversial journey. On July 19th, a Dutch court had seized Greenpeace International's bank account at the request of *British Nuclear Fuels Ltd. (BNFL)*.[91] The company sought compensation for the delayed departure of one of the freighters. On the same day, the British government invoked the 1995 Merchant Shipping Act to ban the vessel *"MV Greenpeace"* from all United Kingdom waters, citing safety concerns (BBC 1999b; BBC 1999a; BBC 1999c; Greenpeace 1999a; Greenpeace 1999b). The dispersion plot of Figure 4.41 displays the occurrences of the term "pacific" between May and November 1999. In June, "pacific" accounted for 0.148% of total tokens, compared to 0.143% and 0.117% percent for November and May, respectively. Between May and July, the number of references to "pacific" increased considerably. After that, even though the percentage remained almost the same, the topic was replaced by other current issues and thus moved to lower hierarchical levels of the Web information system (symbolized by the arrow in Figure 4.41).

Figure 4.41. Dispersion plot of the term "pacific"
(http://www.greenpeace.org; 05-11/99)

As demonstrated above, correspondence analysis is an effective method that provides initial answers about the general patterns contained in textual Web data. Its easily interpretable displays facilitate the heuristic exploration of these patterns, without the need to specify a priori assumptions about the distribution that yielded the values in the matrix to be studied (Blasius 1994, 51; Van der Heijden et al. 1994). The method is based on a scientific orientation that emphasizes the importance of models that fit the data, rather than the rejection of hypotheses based on the lack of fit. Therefore, statistical significance tests are not usually applied to the results of a correspondence analysis. Although not based on an a-priori model itself, correspondence analysis is often a useful preliminary to a more structured multivariate modeling of categorical data (Phillips 1995; StatSoft 2000).

---

[90] http://www.tepco.co.jp/index-e.html
[91] http://www.bnfl.com/

5 Adaptive Solutions

As the World Wide Web continues to grow and expand, information redundancy becomes increasingly evident. Competitive advantage can only be achieved through creative information packaging or interactive features to distinguish an organization's efforts from those of its competitors. Keeping track of user interactions and reasoning about the user's intentions, adaptive solutions provide such a competitive advantage (Milosavljevic 1998, 27; Bucy et al. 1999). They avoid redundant repetition, facilitate navigation, and increase the overall perceived value of the information, goods, or services provided. But with more functionality added to the repertoire of deployed Web information systems, the complexity of their usage inevitably increases. Adaptive solutions promise to lessen the impact of this trade-off between functionality and ease of use (Psoinos and Smithson 1999, 8). With reduced barriers between productive data processing (transactions) and dispositive data processing like market analysis, Web-tracking, or data warehouses, the widespread consideration of dynamic user models[92] for customizing Web-based applications will become a necessity for every serious commercial project. In contrast to mobile agent technology, user modeling does not require a complete redesign of the underlying IS architecture.

Simple applications often rely on general-purpose documents that are written according to a wide audience model, or provide multiple documents for the users' anticipated needs (Milosavljevic and Ober-

---

[92] The terms *user profile* and *user model* are often used synonymously. If they are distinguished, a user model represents the more sophisticated approach, suggesting that available attributes are stored in a database using a consistent modeling language. In contrast, any collection of user data may be called a user profile, independent of formal considerations.

lander 1998). Delivering customized content, by contrast, aims at identifying profitable potential customers and presenting them with information specifically tailored to their individual preferences. While being motivated by a user-centered design perspective, a paradigm advocated by Norman and Draper (Norman and Draper 1986; Akoulchina and Ganascia 1997, 21), the question goes beyond the scope of Web interfaces or document presentation. Flexible software architectures and corresponding business models need to be developed to take advantage of adaptive system behavior. However, due to the heterogeneous character of customer profiles and market allocation mechanisms, it remains difficult to adequately support them using traditional system architectures. In the advanced scenario of stage three, user feedback is instantly being collected, processed, and integrated into the user model within the expected system response time. Adaptive technologies such as neural networks, genetic algorithms, natural language processing (Sampson 1976, 190ff.; Milosavljevic 1998, 26ff.), case-based reasoning (Maule 1997, 349f.; Finnie and Wittig 1998; Turban and Aronson 1998, 571ff.), or related soft computing approaches are used to leverage the knowledge contained in such user models. Although they require considerable resources in terms of memory and computational speed during initialization and training, most of these technologies perform well when it comes to applying the knowledge to a particular case. Incorporation of knowledge-based methods increases the functionality of deployed applications, independent of the complex infrastructure being necessary for the agent-mediated systems of stage four. Hybrid intelligent systems especially, which draw on the strengths and address the weaknesses of particular adaptive technologies, promise to revolutionize the structure of electronic markets (Medsker 1995, 227ff.).

Adaptive applications still use the same, slightly advanced network information infrastructure based on the Hypertext Transfer Protocol (HTTP). In order to enhance communication with dynamic responses generated on the fly, they need to be designed with a clear understanding of the appropriate parameters on which the intended adaptation effect should be based – e.g., characteristic attributes of the user and her tasks. These parameters are different from user to user and often vary for the same user over time (Brusilovsky 1998, 9). Their identification requires a detailed economic and socio-behavioral analysis as well as an assessment of whether it will be technically, economically, and operationally feasible to gather and use the required information on a large scale (Kendall and Kendall 1999, 57).

The concept of adaptivity is extended beyond visual design by building systems with parameterized functionality. Customized text and graphics, for example, may be attached to an existing directed graph of links (Brereton et al. 1998, 54). Parameterized functionality promotes the reuse of documents and link structures. Available attributes and preferences of registered users (= the extra-linguistic context; (Geldof 1997)) are stored in profile databases and can be incorporated into Web-based applications using simple rule-based constructs. Granting different access privileges according to the client's Internet domain, personally addressing customers with dynamically generated documents, or determining purchase conditions according to user category are typical scenarios that require sophisticated server-side database and application interfaces. However, this tighter integration of technology and business context may pose considerable knowledge barriers. These barriers are relatively straightforward to resolve as far as technology-related (hardware platform, operating system, security, and so forth) and project-related (resource requirements, process duration, leadership, or functional participation) issues are concerned. Especially in stages three and four, technology-related knowledge barriers are intensified by the fact that many of the available Web technologies are not yet mature. Application-related and organizational barriers are even more difficult to tackle. Organizations have to focus on the application's specific business objectives, clearly identify the purpose of new technologies, and assess the impact of new electronic business models on the current organizational structure (Nambisan and Wang 1999, 99).

5.1   SEPARATING PRODUCT AND PROCESS LIFE-CYCLES

The exchange of information between producers and audiences on the Internet can be grouped into three categories: (a) one-way asynchronous communication such as electronic mail, (b) two-way asynchronous communication such as electronic bulletin boards, and (c) two-way synchronous communication (compare with Morris and Ogan 1996). Due to technological advances the simple one-way communication of stage one and the asynchronous two-way communication of stage two are replaced by synchronous two-way communication between a company and its active and potential customers. Some of the commercially most promising activities on the World Wide Web involve synchronous two-way communication – e.g., auctions, individual negotiations, shopping cart applications, and so forth (Chen et al. 1999). Therefore, integrated tools for designing and analyzing Web information systems are a necessity in this stage ("A&D" in Figure 5.1; compare with Figure 2.6 on page 44). Web developers increasingly employ such development tools for the creation of real-time commercial applications. Immediate responsiveness, interactive visualization, and dynamic site management extend the functionality of prevalent modeling methods. Being responsible for generating hypertext documents and customizing their embedded link structures, such environments have to constantly incorporate new additions to the repository of Web technologies. Most of these additions are derived from research on artificial intelligence, data mining, (dynamic) user modeling, or advanced knowledge representation.

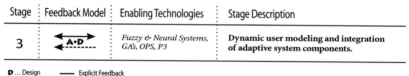

Stage	Feedback Model	Enabling Technologies	Stage Description
3	**◄──A•D──►** **◄┄┄┄┄┄**	*Fuzzy & Neural Systems, GA's, OPS, P3*	**Dynamic user modeling and integration of adaptive system components.**

D ... Design   ——— Explicit Feedback
A ... Analysis   ┄┄┄ Implicit Feedback
N ... Negotiation

Figure 5.1. Characteristics of adaptive Web information systems (Stage 3)

While not necessarily being visible to the ordinary Web user, the internal processes undergo a dramatic change, as the authoring of hypertext documents faces two important challenges (Kent and Neuss 1997, 83). In the case of manually created and edited documents, the author may inadvertently omit important information or meaningful semantic connections. Even if legacy data is available in the form of pre-HTML documents or other structured data, their conversion into hypertextual form requires enormous manual effort.

One of the key elements of customization, therefore, is the separation of product and process life-cycles (Kelly 1994, 86f.). Companies often assume incorrectly that process innovations are exclusively cost-oriented and product enhancements are intended solely to enhance differentiation (Porter 1998, 177). The integration of adaptive system components demonstrates that a change in process technology (= Web development) can be the key to differentiation. The process life-cycle becomes the primary element as depicted in Figure 5.2. The term *implementation* in this context denotes document presentation – i.e., the rendering of HTML or XML documents in contrast to specifying their structure or content. Based on a central user model (e.g., stereotype or domain overlay models), the Web information system is automatically generating and presenting the documents without human intervention (↳ Section 5.4). This process is depicted as a set of secondary (fully automated) development cycles in Figure 5.2 within the boundaries defined by the primary (manual or semi-automated) development process. Specifying the traversal function is becoming a system task, automatically mapping the topologically non-linear textons of the database to the scriptons presented to the user in a temporally linear sequence. One of the basic differences to the preceding stage is the higher frequency of this automated feedback cycle for providing instant response. The more quickly the data is captured, processed, and analyzed, the sooner system improvements can be suggested and implemented.

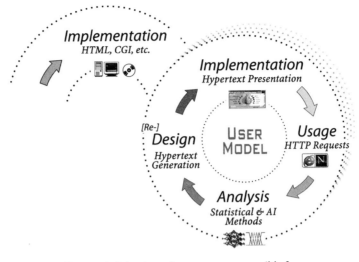

Figure 5.2. Adaptive sub-processes responsible for
document generation and presentation

A text is determinant if the adjacent scriptons of every scripton are
always the same (Höök et al. 1998, 144; Klein 1999, 34). In sharp contrast to the preceding stages, dynamic and indeterminable traversal
functions are the key characteristic of adaptive Web information systems (↪ Figure 5.3). Scriptons and their associative connections constantly appear, disappear, or evolve, creating a network of multiple
discursive sequences. The basic distinction between textonic and intratextonic dynamics is that the number of textons remains fixed in the
case of intratextonic dynamics. While both types are common for adaptive applications, textonic dynamics tend to dominate with an increased
level of technical sophistication. Controlled access and conditional
linking represent the norm rather than an exception, since the available
navigational options are customized as well. As far as the attributes
transience and perspective are concerned, adaptive systems do not differ much from static and dynamic approaches. The semantics attribute,
however, gains importance and is usually required for the more advanced functionality of adaptive systems (e.g., domain knowledge
stored in the user model).

    The indirect influence of the user's behavior on the traversal function
and the direct editing of the user model both add configurative power to
the explorative and interpretive function a user performs when accessing static or dynamic Web information systems. Nonetheless, the system has to ensure consistent document structures. From a linguistic
point of view, the stability of the traversal function is the key element
for ensuring consistency, which is obtained when the context is une-
quivocally defined at any given time and from any given perspective.

Consistency requires a deterministic system behavior in the case of perturbations – i.e., a stable relation between stimuli and response (Von Bertalanffy 1974, 18). The same input in the same context (or, more precisely, what the user perceives as being the same input in the same context) should always result in the same output.

Determinability	Transiency	Perspective	Access
☐ Determinable	☒ (Transient)	☐ Personal	☒ (Random)
☒ Indeterminable	☒ Intransient	☒ Impersonal	☒ Controlled

Dynamics	Linking	Semantics	User Function
☐ No (Static)	☒ (Explicit)	☐ Limited	☒ Explorative
☒ Intratextonic	☒ Conditional	☒ (Supported)	☒ Configurative
☒ Textonic	☐ None	☒ Required	☒ Interpretative
			☐ Textonic

Figure 5.3. Hypertextual attributes of adaptive Web information systems

5.2   CLASSIC LOOP OF ADAPTATION

Cyber is derived from *cybernetics*, the name of Norbert Wiener's science of "Control and communication in the animal and the machine" (Wiener 1961), again derived from the Greek *kybernêtês, steersman*. Emphasizing the spatial dimensions of computer-mediated environments, William Gibson coined the term *cyberspace* in his famous novel *Neuromancer* (Gibson 1984). The *cyber-* prefix has since come to be associated with many different dimensions of computer-mediated communication and experience (McMillan 1999a). In the context of this book, its textual dimension as described by Aarseth is most relevant: "A cybertext ... is a self-changing text, in which scriptons and traversal functions are controlled by an immanent cybernetic agent, either mechanical or human" (Aarseth 1994, 71f.). As a system-theoretical approach, cybernetics is focused on both living and inert systems that include intertwined cause-and-effect relationships, and information feedback loops for self-regulation (Boulanger 1969, 5; Von Glasersfeld 1992, 2; Murray 1997, 91f.). Although their underlying models are different (feedback circuit versus dynamic system of interactions), cybernetics and related approaches show several parallelisms with general system theory (Von Bertalanffy 1974, 15; Pask 1992, 13f.). While classical system theory places the primary emphasis on formal languages to provide structural internal descriptions (state variables and their interdependence), external descriptions assuming the system to be opaque to the outside world (= "black box") are usually more relevant in communications research.

The function of a system is to produce the outcomes that define its goals and objectives. Adaptive systems respond immediately to changes in their environmental or internal state that potentially reduce their efficiency in pursuing the goals that define their function. They do so by changing their own state or that of their environment in order to increase their efficiency with respect to their goals. An adaptive system, therefore, has the ability to "modify itself or its environment when either has changed to the system's disadvantage so as to regain at least some of its lost efficiency" (Ackoff 1974, 35). *Other-self adaptation* modifies the system (and not the environment) in response to external change. It is the most commonly considered mechanism because it was used by Charles R. Darwin to describe the dynamic behavior of biological species as systems (↪ Section 2.1: Darwinian versus Technological Evolution). Most adaptive Web presentation techniques as delineated in Section 5.5 (content-level, link-level, and meta-level adaptation) instantiate the concept of other-self adaptation.

Some authors argue that the process of developing Web applications of higher complexity starts to resemble traditional software development, which includes formal requirements analysis (Vassileva 1998, 211). They call for a detailed analysis of a hypertext document's ability to meet organizational needs, for structured design and implementation, and for follow-up testing regarding consistency and effectiveness (Brereton et al. 1998, 49ff.). By contrast, emergent systems thinking disregards most of these steps and assumes that considering day-to-day turmoil is central to determining system requirements, which are open-ended in nature, always in motion, unfrozen, and negotiable. Analysts, therefore, must come to terms with ambiguity. They have to accept new and evolving technologies, shifting and often contradictory organizational goals, and constantly increasing volumes of data (Accrue 1999; Truex et al. 1999, 120f.).

At the same time, user needs and the corresponding requirements are changing as well, even during requirement determination activities. Thus they cannot be fully defined up front (Jacobson et al. 1999, 8). Without adaptive components (= *mechanical cybernetic agents*), users might become frustrated and trapped by the system and its inherent limitations they are helping to shape. The diminishment of the formal user requirements goal relates to the obsolescence of initial large-scale systems analysis. It is replaced by a cybernetic feedback loop, consisting of gathering information about users and their behavior, storing this information in a user model, and subsequently leveraging it for adaptive systems on the basis of semantic domain models. In the following, three phases in the adaptation process are outlined in conformity with the feedback loop described above:

- Collecting information about the user (↪ Section 5.3),
- Processing the information to build, initialize, or update the user model (↪ Section 5.4), and
- Applying the user model to provide content-level, link-level, and meta-level adaptation (↪ Section 5.5).

It is important to keep in mind that biases and errors can be introduced in all three phases, even if the model itself is correct – e.g., by inappropriate acquisition mechanisms, by incorrect assumptions when deducing the user model, or by errors providing the adaptation itself (Brusilovsky 1998, 32).

5.3 COLLECTING INFORMATION ABOUT USERS

Despite technological and organizational changes, the real information needs of real customers provide a uniform purpose and guide for developing Web information systems. The role of customers, however, is getting transformed in the virtual marketplace. The emergence of the World Wide Web has eroded brand loyalty and altered the bargaining relationship between many industries and their buyers. Repetitive tasks are shifted to experienced customers than gain convenience through faster problem solutions. By tapping the flexibility of financial Web-based applications, for example, individual customers can act, if they choose to, as the analyst, the portfolio manager, or the broker (Dutta et al. 1997, 2; Werthner and Klein 1998, 41). The impact of this reallocation of tasks and accompanying technological changes on differentiation and switching costs, is instrumental in determining buyer power and individual behavior (Bakos 1991, 297; Porter 1998, 173). Potential customers access electronic product catalogs "with their finger poised on their mouse, ready to buy or click on should they not find what they are looking for – that is, should the content, wording, incentive, promotion, product, or service of a Web site not meet their preferences" (Mena 1999, 8).

The collection of information about customers and their interaction history is a necessary prerequisite for any form of relationship marketing, from face-to-face contact to globally distributed electronic media. A cornerstone and major obstacle of relationship marketing via the Internet is the availability (or lack) of user data. User needs, preferences, tasks, and actual behavior are vague variables that can be hard or even impossible to measure accurately (Stein et al. 1997, 90). Beyond that, user needs "may unfold rapidly in directions that are poorly understood by the users themselves" (Truex et al. 1999, 119). Users tend to opportunistically and unpredictably change their behavior over time. Despite these uncertainties, the potential benefits of customizing corporate communication justify intensified research efforts to operationalize this type of information.

Econometric, psychometric, and demographic data are the most likely categories of data that an organization would seek to include in the adaptive system's database. User demography (e.g., language, country, profession, and so forth) and behaviors of consumption, choice, attention, reaction, and learning are widely captured and logged – compare with, for example, the *Lifestyle Finder*, a system for user profile generation based on demographic data (Newhagen and Rafaeli 1996; Krulwich 1997, 37ff.). Fortunately, Web-based communication leaves tracks to an extent unmatched by that in any other context or medium. To supplement behavioral data, organizations transform external information sources (e.g., federal publications, addresses acquired from list brokers and publishing companies, customer information from credit reports, feedback from telemarketing efforts, and so forth), and embed interfaces to internal database systems into their data gathering process (historic data about customers, transactions, and distribution channels; see Table 5.1).

Table 5.1. Internal versus external sources of data (Kelly 1994, 32f.)

Internal data (System categories & examples)	External data (Data categories & examples)
FINANCIAL General ledger, accounts payable, accounts receivable, budget control, treasury management, cost accounting	COMPETITOR Products, services, pricing, sales promotion, mergers and takeovers
LOGISTICS Materials requirement planning, fleet transport, purchasing, distribution control	ECONOMIC Currency fluctuations, political indicators, interest rate movements, stock, bond prices, commodity prices
SALES Multiple service order systems for different products and services	INDUSTRY Technology trends, marketing trends, management science and trade information
PRODUCTION Production control, works order tracking, project tracking, quality control, computer integrated manufacturing	CREDIT Individual credit ratings and business viability assessments
PERSONNEL Personnel records, payroll, staff development	ECONOMETRIC Income groups and consumer behavior
BILLING Multiple billing systems for different products and services	SALES AND MARKETING Lists of prospective customers, psychometric consumer profiling, demographic data (age profiles, population densities, etc.)

5.3.1   Available Online Sources

User preferences and requirements must be discovered from scratch starting with their first visit. Organizations that operate Web information systems gather more information about economic and social activity than can be readily imagined. This capability raises the question of what can be inferred about the demand and supply curves of Web content. Exploring the structure of Web information systems in terms of different types of content, services, and patterns of communication reveals much about new ways of transacting electronic commerce (Paltridge 1999, 328). Consequently, a consistent framework including operational guidelines for assembling accurate profiles is needed. Customers, third parties, Web client data, or relevant network parameters constitute potential information sources. These information sources and their respective attributes are categorized in Table 5.2 (Bauer and Scharl 1999a). Various methods are available to obtain customer information. These (implicit or explicit) acquisition methods obviously depend on where the information originates. The actual creation of new and useful knowledge is closely related to the efficiency and the scope of the acquisition method being employed.

Table 5.2. Online sources of customer information (Bauer and Scharl 1999a)

Source			Acquisition Method	Information
I	Client/ Network (Implicit)	Network Information	Environment Variables, HTTP Log Files	e.g., Remote Host (Name), Browser, etc.
		Browser Support	Cookies, Java-Applets, Hidden CGI data	Visited Pages, Clickstream Analysis
II	User (Explicit)	Interactive	Online Forms, etc.	Questionnaires, etc.
		Records	Customer Database	All of the Above
III	Third Party (Explicit)		Network Infrastructure	Verified Network Information

Explicit channels of feedback imply an active role of the user, who can either be co-operative, indifferent, or obstructive regarding the intended purpose of gathering the information – compare with Höök et al.'s account of different plan recognition characteristics (Höök et al. 1998, 162). Common disadvantages of explicit methods are their limited reliability and the additional burden they place on the (inexperienced) user while accessing Web information systems (Vassileva 1998, 241). Therefore, analysts often corroborate and supplement explicitly obtained information by direct user observations. Most implicit methods such as automated field studies or log file analysis provide an appraisal of the system based on recorded transactions or other behavioral measures. They have the advantage of systematically assessing the users' actual performance with the system, rather than relying on their subjective views and often obstructive inputs (Noyes and Baber 1999, 119). This passive assessment is supplied without conscious effort, usually as a by-product of accessing Web information systems. Conversely, when a user stops to think about leaving a record, he is creating an active history element.

5.3.2 Explicit Acquisition Methods

A major shortcoming of many approaches to evaluate Web information systems is the neglect of user judgements regarding perceived quality, relevance, or usability (Allen 1996, 292). Explicit methods of data gathering such as questionnaires or relevance feedback try to overcome this limitation. They process information that is consciously provided by Web users, who usually agree to fill out questionnaires about themselves under certain circumstances. However, the quality of this feedback source remains disputable and companies rely on the willingness of Internet users to provide personal information. This information can either be acquired interactively (e.g., questionnaires submitted via electronic mail, online forms via CGI-scripting, or more sophisticated approaches), gathered from past records and offline user surveys, or derived from unsolicited user feedback. With regard to response time and ease of acquisition, interactive methods usually represent the preferred mode of gathering personal customer information.

Although controlled experimental studies are an important complement to observational analysis (↪ Section 5.3.3: Implicit Acquisition Methods), they are only suitable for narrow, predetermined issues and do not provide ongoing streams of data that are necessitated by the highly dynamic nature of the World Wide Web (Shneiderman 1997a, 28; Sullivan 1997). User questionnaires support a broader perspective, but their development can be an arduous and involved process. Designers of online questionnaires should also keep in mind that most information is cumulative in nature and should not be requested all in one session but only when it is needed for a transaction or immediately used to customize the system (Mena 1999, 38). From a methodological perspective, questionnaires raise the issues of self-selection and objectivity. Users are not always very reliable informants, even when they try to be objective and tell what they think is the truth (Hoffer et al. 1999, 252). They cannot be trusted to interpret and report their own activities reliably, especially in the case of non-standardized approaches that rely on open-ended questions and offer no proven incentive to tell the truth.

In addition to the methods mentioned above, rating the information contained in individual pages according to its perceived usefulness is employed to modify the underlying user model. This approach, known as *relevance feedback,* is one of the most widespread techniques for object grouping and linking in information retrieval research (Kaplan et al. 1998, 50; Melucci 1999, 91; Tu et al. 1999). The direct, manual editing of the underlying user model represents another explicit method and will be described in Section 5.4.2: Typology of the Extra-Linguistic Context *(collaborative* or *cooperative user modeling).*

5.3.3   Implicit Acquisition Methods

Most implicit methods are based on unobtrusive observations of online behavior without the user's assistance and without influencing her individual working style. In fact, many users might not even be aware of the information being transmitted (Beaumont 1998, 96). This is an important advantage over other types of observation as the mere presence of an observer may lead to behavioral modifications *(Hawthorne effect).* Similar modifications occur when people are placed in situations that are different from their normal setting (Hoffer et al. 1999, 253; Noyes and Baber 1999, 121). Therefore, it is important to collect the interaction history in a passive way so that inexperienced users are not constantly thrown out of the cognitive state necessary to satisfy their informational needs or get their tasks done (Wexelblat 1999). However, most implicit feedback channels are limited by their narrow bandwidth, that is, they do not offer any causal explanations for the observed activities (Beaumont 1998, 109; Boyle 1998, 81; Noyes and Baber 1999, 123). As long as they are not enriched by other sources of (explicit) information, they are therefore only suited for stereotype user models (↪ Section 5.4: User Modeling).

On a formal level, the interaction history – the accumulated record of the interactions of people with Web information systems – encompasses three categories of representation (Wexelblat 1999):

- *Sequences of actions* (relationships of documents and other elements on which people have acted, and the resulting structures).
- *Temporal collage* (direct representation of multiple states or the processes that produced them).
- *Recurrent opposed states* (contrast of the present state both with remembered past states and with the expected future state).

All three categories affect not only the object but also our perceptions of, and uses for, this particular object. Log file analysis of individual ("sequence of action") and aggregated ("temporal collage") clickstreams has to deal with a number of disadvantages, which might explain why most of this data is never examined. First of all, it does not provide meta-information (e.g., subject transcripts) to reveal the underlying "train of thought", which is common for qualitative discourse process tracing (Calway and Smith 1998, 44).

In addition to that, the semantics may be fuzzy as well. When trying to determine exactly the viewing time of documents, for example, it always remains unclear what the user is actually doing in this time. In the case of significant delays, there is no way of telling whether she is actually reading the text on the screen, wasting valuable time with backtracking (client-side caching effectively masks this activity), talking on the phone, or merely having a cup of coffee (Sullivan 1997; Kaplan et al. 1998, 56; Vassileva 1998, 241). Even if the access time is spent on inspecting a particular topic and attention can be assumed, reading about a concept does not automatically imply its comprehension. Comprehension depends on the material's legibility and readability – i.e., the detection and discrimination between individual characters and the transformation of these characters into meaningful units (Noyes and Baber 1999, 40). More valid approaches to determining the user's level of knowledge would have to include an explicit tutoring component that tries to generalize from various tests whether a particular topic has been really understood (Hohl et al. 1998, 138). Fortunately, the technical infrastructure of the World Wide Web tends to be more formalized than other discourse environments. Therefore, despite the restrictions mentioned above, a good approximation of the user's motivations can be inferred indirectly by observing her actual behavior.

Online customers use anonymous clients that communicate with the information provider's Web server via the stateless Hypertext Transfer Protocol (HTTP), which provides only little support for direct observation. There are millions of potential routes that users of complex Web information systems can (and do) take. Thus, reporting their actual paths is far from trivial. Without proper visualization, for example, the isolated statistical correlations lack the kind of relationship structure to deduce useful history (Wexelblat 1999).

Theoretically, various functions requested from browsers could be monitored, especially in controlled corporate Intranet environments – e.g., document scrolling, printing, sharing of directories, exchange of files, and so forth (Mladenic 1998, 100). In practice, implicit information for publicly available Web information systems is most often limited to detailed transaction log files. HTTP is an effective client-server design that allows instantaneous connections but a rather poor environment for electronic transactions. The limitations of the traditional "request-response" communication model negatively impact transaction-oriented applications. With explicit user authentication, persistent client state HTTP cookies, or more advanced mechanisms, transactions gain the continuity that is inherently absent in the protocol itself (Stout 1997, 80ff.; Netscape 1998). Following a user through a site is no longer a matter of interpreting IP addresses and visit times or manually logging visits to a database. Instead, user identity information can be collected directly through the log file or associated data sources and is instantly processed by integrated analysis tools such as those included in Microsoft's *Site Server Commerce Edition* or iPlanet's *MerchantXPert*.[93] Even if the user's IP address is assigned dynamically from an Internet service provider's reserved address pool using the *Dynamic Host Configuration Protocol (DHCP),* such a tool can link multiple sessions by retrieving cookies of prior visits (St. Laurent 1998, 326).

The value of data about Web usage patterns cannot be overemphasized. This explains why Web monitoring software such as *HitBox*[94] is frequently distributed for free, in return for continuous access to usage statistics. The commercially available tool *Alexa,*[95] another popular example, works as a browser add-on to provide traffic information on sites visited by users and to suggest links to related sites. In early 1999, *Amazon.com*[96] paid US-\$250 million in stock for the huge database on Web usage patterns compiled by this tool (Paltridge 1999, 330).

The power and sophistication of these tools cause a number of privacy concerns. Customer relationships in electronic environments are largely built on trust, a somewhat more tenuous link than a formal contract (Broadvision 2000). Due to the inherently insecure nature of the World Wide Web, customers who do not trust the information provider or do not see any immediate benefit might oppose mechanisms such as explicit authentication or client state HTTP cookies. The concept of traceable anonymity offers a potential solution (in contrast to untraceable anonymity, which denotes systems of even higher security where the author is simply not identifiable at all; current Web technology allows this form of anonymity by the rerouting of messages through a series of anonymous devices). Traceable anonymity provides a pseudo-identity that can be associated with the consumer only by a trusted third party, whose reputation is the key factor for the system's acceptance.[97] The pseudo-identity cannot be traced back by the Internet service provider. While sellers receive necessary information to com-

---

[93] http://www.microsoft.com/siteserver/commerce/
http://www.iplanet.com/products/ecommerce/
[94] http://www.hitbox.com/
[95] http://www.alexa.com/
[96] http://www.amazon.com/
[97] Being usually conceived as a multidimensional value, reputation can be defined as the amount of trust inspired by a particular organization in a specific setting or domain of interest (Zacharia et al. 1999).

plete the transaction, effectively ensuring authentication, certification, confirmation, payment, and non-repudiation, they have no way to find out about the consumer's real identity. Although traceable anonymity offers a comparably low level of security, it suffices for many commercial purposes (Froomkin 1996; Hoffman et al. 1999, 85).

5.4 USER MODELING

User models are explicitly represented collections of data about the user or a group of users that allow an adaptive Web information system to tailor its content, structure, and interface representation to the needs of the user(s). A set of user models should be central to the design process and substantially influences the basic functionality of every adaptive Web information system. Experimental results confirm that even a minimalist user modeling component can improve the subjective measure of user satisfaction at low cost and negligible commercial disruption (Strachan et al. 1997, 189f.).

User models are only required for applications belonging to stage three or four of the evolutionary framework presented in Section 2.2: A Brief History of Web Adaptivity. Figure 5.4 depicts the conceptual structure of a Web information system with an embedded user modeling component (Strachan et al. 1997, 192). Individual user profiles are typically stored in a separate database. Balancing occasionally conflicting requirements stipulated in the user and (system) task models, the inference engine customizes the application structure on the basis of the application model and immediately generates the Web documents requested by the user.

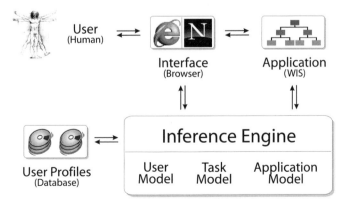

Figure 5.4. Web information system with embedded user modeling component (adapted from Strachan et al. 1997, 192)

To prevent the user from feeling a loss of control, many systems provide flexible means for user-initiated customization and correction of erroneous adaptations generated by the system (Hohl et al. 1998, 138). For example, users may be provided with a number of options and given the choice of setting up the application according to their own preferences. This direct approach relies on a publicly available tool to edit the user model (*"preferences page"*), either before accessing the Web information system or at any point during browsing. However, there is an inherent contradiction between this requirement and the general idea of adaptive hypertext systems (Höök et al. 1998, 144).

In the interest of maximizing the likelihood of consumer acceptance, user characteristics modeled by the system must be made transparent to and controllable by the user (Hohl et al. 1998, 127). This transparency, which gives the user a mostly abstract view of the internal workings of the system, lessens the inevitable negative ramifications of customization efforts for user privacy. At the same time, it represents an effective method against a potential problem of adaptive applications: the user could become disoriented and irritated just because of the tailored presentation – e.g., if the revisited text is unpredictably different each time she accesses it (Kay and Kummerfeld 1997, 66).

Thus the process of adaptation should neither comprise the system's central interface representations nor be implemented as a system task alone. Höök suggests splitting the user interface into a stable, unchangeable core component and a number of secondary adaptive interface components to support specific tasks (Höök et al. 1998, 144). Adaptation of the secondary components then has to be approached as a joint task of the system and the user, to be solved in interaction (Pollack et al. 1982, 358ff.; Höök et al. 1998, 143). Incremental customization, for example, requires techniques which allow the user to move up the "customization curve", gaining more adaptability and adaptivity at the cost of a (preferably minimal) increase in complexity (Bentley and Dourish 1995).

Even in the case of incremental customization, which is less obtrusive than other approaches, the data intended to enhance document composition and representation should not permeate the documents in an explicit form. Providing feedback and editing preferences are side activities and should not disturb the user's primary task (Brusilovsky 1998, 35). Introducing additional complexity and cognitive overheads would be counterproductive in the process of maximizing the individual user's expected utility, obscuring or even destroying the very information it was trying to augment.

5.4.1 Characteristics of User Models

User populations may be composed of individuals, groups, or a combination of both. Analyzing the information needs of such user populations including their hierarchical systems of goals and sub-goals, purposes, and objectives is highly context sensitive and does not always offer enough potential for generalization (Dillon and Watson 1996, 619f.). Fortunately, numerous methods of social science research and market research provide methodological guidelines. The most important characteristics of user models are the stored audience attributes. Demographic data such as gender, age, economic status, ethnic origin, educational background, professional experiences, and language belong to the primary audience attributes in media research (Shneiderman 1997a, 9). Not all of them are readily available in Web-based environments. Consequently, user models tend to focus on information about the "online lifestyle" of a particular user, comprising her identity, e-mail address, shopping choices, preferred methods of payment, subscription services, and so forth. If available, this information is complemented by psychographic data such as the user's general opinions and values, hobbies, and specific interests.

The *Values and Lifestyles (VALS)* project of the *Stanford Research Institute*, established in 1978, was one of the first consumer segmentation systems based on such lifestyle characteristics. It continues to be calibrated against today's consumer attitudes via the VALS survey, which is available online.[98] The VALS segmentation system defines eight mutually exclusive segments of adult consumers who have different attitudes and exhibit distinctive behavior and decision-making patterns: *Actualizers, Fulfilleds, Achievers, Experiencers, Believers, Strivers, Makers,* and *Strugglers.* The main dimensions of the typology are self-orientation and resources. The following example describes the profile of *Actualizers,* characterized by the highest resources among all groups: "Actualizers are successful, sophisticated, active … people with high self-esteem and abundant resources. They are interested in growth and seek to develop, explore, and express themselves in a variety of ways; sometimes guided by principle, and sometimes by a desire to have an effect, to make a change. Image is important to Actualizers, not as evidence of status or power but as an expression of their taste, independence, and character. Actualizers are among the established and emerging leaders in business and government, yet they continue to seek challenges. They have a wide range of interests, are concerned with social issues, and are open to change. Their lives are characterized by richness and diversity. Their possessions and recreation reflect a cultivated taste for the finer

---

[98] http://future.sri.com/VALS/

things in life" (SRI_Consulting 2000). A similar segmentation, *Internet Values and Lifestyles (iVALS)*, has been developed to enhance the quality of online environments for end users, content providers, and intermediaries. iVALS identifies the following clusters: *Wizards, Pioneers, Upstreamers, Socialites, Workers, Surfers, Mainstreamers, Sociables, Seekers,* and *Immigrants.* Mena states the following example of an iVALS profile, describing *Wizards,* the technologically most advanced group of Internet users (Mena 1999, 151f.): "Wizards are the most active and skilled Internet users. Computers are a key aspect of their lifestyles, and mastery of technology figures prominently in their identities. More than 80% of Wizards have been on the Internet for three or more years. Although Wizards report meeting many new people during their years online, it is likely that such friendships often stay virtual. That is, Wizards are not necessarily seeking to meet people in the traditional sense. Rather, their sociability appears as a byproduct to their heavy involvement in so many aspects of Net culture. ... Wizards are nearly all males ... with a median age under 30. Despite their age, many work as computer technicians, professors, middle managers, consultants, or industry analysts, and therefore earn a medium to high household income".

If no behavioral observations are available, such psychographic profiles represent an ideal foundation for initializing stereotype user models (↪ Section 5.4.2: Typology of the Extra-Linguistic Context) and as such can become critical to the successful tailoring of Web information systems to meet the individual expectations of particular user groups. Although many user models can function adequately with only a behavioral impression of the user (Ramscar et al. 1997, 429), it is nearly impossible to anticipate behavior in particular domains, especially in those that emphasize configurative and textonic user functions (↪ Section 1.2: Ergodic Literature). Thus it is often difficult to determine which (types of) elements have to be incorporated into the model and what level of abstraction should optimally be chosen. Considering the high variability of knowledge resources, abilities, styles, and preferences in any given user population or the observable diversity regarding cultural norms and regulatory jurisdictions, past attempts to include all these aspects in any realistic manner frequently failed. Not surprisingly, mounting evidence of many unsuccessful implementations caused a great deal of general scepticism about user models in the minds of some Web developers (Allen 1996, 42f.).

Therefore, a theoretical framework to guide user modeling is clearly needed to deal with rather heterogeneous collections of information categories, their sources, and the dominant acquisition methods. In addition to the audience attributes described above, the space of existing user models spans the following dimensions (Finin 1989, 411ff.; Beaumont 1998, 95f.; Wexelblat 1999):

- *Purpose.* The main reason for implementing user models is the provision of adaptive output to the user, including general help and advice. On the input side, user models help to obtain data from the user in a more consistent way and to better understand her information-seeking behavior.

- *Degree of specialization.* Many existing tools focus on personal historical data such as bookmarks for Web browsers or private annotations. The basic distinction refers to individual users versus classes of users. User information can be social (*"What has been done here?"*) or intimate to a particular individual (*"What has the user done?"*). Integrated solutions for defining and managing user models have to consider both categories (e.g., analysis of individual and aggregated user clickstreams). They also have to address the question of single identity versus multiple identities. The customer's demand for privacy and flexibility requires additional functionality to switch between multiple identities, encompassing sub-identities for personal, corporate, or anonymous Web access (Psoinos and Smithson 1999, 15).

- *Temporal extent.* This dimension describes the synchronicity continuum covered by a particular system. Messages transferred via the World Wide Web travel at unprecedented speed, but can also be consumed at unprecedented delays (Newhagen and Rafaeli 1996). The temporal extent is influenced by the transiency of Web information systems. If the mere passing of the user's time causes scriptons to appear (↪ Section 1.4.5.2: Mapping Textons to Scriptons), a document is called transient (Aarseth 1998, 63). Synchronous (real-time) transiency may apply to certain electronic transactions and requires instant user models to be updated on the fly. The next category, short-time user models, are built incrementally up after every login and only contain features of the current visit (Stein et al. 1997, 89). This distinguishes them from medium-term and long-term models.

- *Characteristics of change.* This dimension is closely related to a user model's temporal extent. While new data accumulates, domain concepts not used for a long time tend to slowly fade from the user's memory. This "fade function" consists of three independent components: obscuring (new data blocking the perception of old), losing (removing data), and disconnecting (losing the connection between the data and its present interpretation). One of the key benefits of user modeling and visualizing the dynamics of the resulting information space (↪ Section 5.5.4: Meta-Level Adaptation) is the ability to distinguish obscuring from loss, and the prevention of disconnection. Important domain concepts should be reiterated from time to time, balancing issues of redundancy, comprehensibility, and the user's assimilation rate. Planning these reiterations and maintaining a user model's overall validity, therefore, requires the integration of a theory of forgetting, where more recent information dominates and the value representing the state of knowledge regarding a domain concept is gradually reduced – as opposed to continuously incrementing this value with each interaction involving that particular concept (Hohl et al. 1998, 138; Milosavljevic and Oberlander 1998; Mladenic 1998, 100). In addition to that, different types of memory (iconic, short-term, factual, and procedural) and their heterogeneous characteristics regarding learning, storing, and forgetting information should be considered (Mahling 1994, 47).

- *Model acquisition and maintenance.* Many of the approaches embodied in research prototypes are far too complex to be of practical use in commercial applications. Even integrated approaches of simultaneously gathering implicit and explicit customer feedback have certain limits as far as the granularity of information is concerned. Among the concerns are the performance overheads inevitably incurred, time and expenses to build up and maintain the user modeling component, and often unproven advantages of the added functionality (Strachan et al. 1997, 189). Therefore, the lack of empirical studies is considered to be one of the major shortcomings of modern user modeling research (McTear 1993, 157ff.; Strachan et al. 1997, 189).

5.4.2 Typology of the Extra-Linguistic Context

If context is established as the collection of features that determine the desirable adaptation effect, its extra-linguistic parameters can be grouped along three dimensions (Geldof 1997). *General user characteristics* are usually stable across different interaction sessions and include parameters such as language preference, working practices, or the general and specific level of knowledge. *Situation-specific features* comprise time and place of use, hardware and software environment, weather conditions, and so forth. *Teleological features* evolve dynamically during a single interaction section and reflect the goals of the system and its users.

The application context determines the optimal degree of specialization. Incremental knowledge acquired from user observations and clickstream traces is often too fine-grained to be helpful for designing adaptive architectures (Stein et al. 1997, 89). Web applications have to aggregate real-world information about individual users to achieve generalizations and economies of scale. Alternatively, some of them rely on idealistic stereotype user models, which are usually based on the following user attributes:

- *Behavior and working practices.* Direct observation and other implicit methods yield abundant information about these situation-specific factors (↪ Section 5.3.3).

- *Level of knowledge.* Designers of adaptive systems should bear in mind that actual knowledge has less impact on the user's behavior than perceived knowledge (Allen 1996, 37). Customarily, three types of knowledge are distinguished:

  - *General knowledge.* This broad category is difficult to capture and depends on the user's education, background, and experiences.

  - *System-specific knowledge.* In-depth information about the objective realities in a subject domain includes the operational context, participants involved, objects and their relations, and so forth. These categories refer to the experience with a particular application (e.g., *naïve, novice, beginner, intermediate, skilled, expert*), which can be determined by clickstream analysis or other implicit forms of data gathering – also compare with Brusilovsky's remarks on adaptive dialog systems (Brusilovsky 1998, 32).

  - *Domain-specific knowledge.* Procedural, problem-solving knowledge prescribes how to complete various information tasks, both internal and external (Allen 1996, 36; Chandrasekaran et al. 1999, 24). It is closely connected with the (often overlapping) role of a user in a certain organization (Vassileva 1998, 214).

- *Personal interests and preferences* in both absolute terms and relative to the user's current hypertext location (node). As it is difficult to deduce this category of information automatically, most analysts favor explicit forms of data gathering such as questionnaires or relevance feedback.

- *Goals and Tasks.* For systems engineers, a *goal* is a non-operational objective to be achieved by the composite system (Web information system together with its environment). A *requirement* specifies how a goal should be accomplished by a proposed system (Gnaho and Larcher 1999). According to this terminology, goals or tasks in the context of user modeling may generally be defined as "states of affairs which the user wishes to achieve" (Beaumont 1998, 96). They are related to the context of the user's work rather than to the user as an individual, often varying between and sometimes even within single sessions. Thus they are the most changeable user feature, forming a highly dynamic hierarchy of informational and procedural processes that is often represented via probabilistic overlay models.

Task analysis can be seen as an attempt to "gain the abstract and objective neutrality of the software system for the activities that the interface must support" (Robinson 1990, 43; compare with Gray 1993, 127). This attempt includes the acquisition and modeling of specific user knowledge necessary for performing these activities (Noyes and Baber

1999, 127; Paternò 1999, 20). Neglecting the activities' requirements, adaptivity and the changes it occasions may lead to unpredictable, obscure, and inconsistent interfaces (Höök et al. 1998, 143). Task analysis determines what cognitive and social tasks users accomplish as they attempt to meet their information needs and how those tasks are performed, both individually and collectively. It results in a set of *task models*, which indicate all main activities and their possible temporal relationships. *Scenarios*, in contrast, indicate only one specific sequence of occurrences of such activities. A scenario is a statement of assumptions about the operating environment of a particular system at a given time. Such a narrative description, which often includes variables, procedures, and constraints for the modeling process, represents a common supportive technique for understanding application domains and eliciting task requirements (Turban and Aronson 1998, 51; Paternò 1999, 31f.). Seta et al. emphasize the role of task ontologies as static user models, analyzing the user's epistemological conceptual structure of problem solving (Seta et al. 1997, 207). The key to designing usable systems is to shift task ontology close to the domain activities of the user and to embody the functionality to bridge the gap between the user and the system. Drawing on methods of social science research, Allen suggests subordinating internal, device-dependent tasks to external, device-independent tasks to remove potential barriers to innovative systems design (Allen 1996).

5.4.3 Building and Initializing User Models

There are basically two approaches to building and initializing user models, which are usually referred to as *stereotype models* and *overlay domain models*. For building stereotype user models, several groups of users have to be identified. If a particular user fulfills a number of sufficient conditions, she is recognized as being member of the group (*stereotype activation*). Lack of these criteria causes the user to be removed from the stereotype either immediately or at certain intervals in order to improve system consistency (*stereotype deactivation*; (Beaumont 1998, 97; Ardissono and Goy 1999, 38)). Predefined user segments represent a very good starting point for formulating stereotype models – e.g., an organization's list of generic job titles (Strachan et al. 1997, 193). However, it is necessary to continuously observe the user's actual access strategies to improve the representation. This evolution based on subsequent interactions suggests the use of connectionist architectures such as neural networks or hybrid neuro-fuzzy systems to recognize behavioral patterns and reassign them to stereotypes dynamically (Allen 1996, 42; Hohl et al. 1998, 131).

Alternatively, an individual user's knowledge can be expressed by building a unique "overlay" of the underlying domain model, storing either binary or metric values for the user's estimated knowledge of domain entities. Therefore, overlay models require a structural model of the subject domain. They are usually represented as a semantic or hierarchical network of domain concepts that rely on a common ontology. The term *ontology*, in a general (philosophical) sense used for the study of the kinds of things that exist, refers to content theories about the sorts of objects, properties of objects, and relations between objects that are possible in a specified domain of knowledge. More specifically, it can signify two different concepts: as a *representation vocabulary*, an ontology provides potential terms for describing knowledge about this specific domain. It is not the vocabulary as such that qualifies as ontology, but the conceptualizations that the terms in the vocabulary are intended to capture. The term is also used to refer to the *body of knowledge* itself, which portrays the intrinsic conceptual structure of the domain. It is composed of two parts: a taxonomy (= ordered system of concepts) and a number of axioms (= established rules, principles, or laws) relating to that taxonomy (Seta et al. 1997, 208). Knowledge objects are clustered according to their similarities to make up classes, called *taxa*, organized in hierarchical structures, called *taxonomies*, which are often depicted as inverted tree-type diagrams. The *taxum* description is a synthesis of the common anatomy of its instances and characteristics of these instances (Tesch 1990, 106; Akoulchina and Ganascia 1997, 23). By including propositional attitudes, ontologies may represent not only simple facts but also beliefs, goals, hypotheses, and predictions about a domain (Chandrasekaran et al. 1999, 20ff.). For user models to be of practical value, they also have to support ontology-based inference. If the user knows all the refinements of a concept, for example, the system can conclude that the user is also familiar with the more general concept (Kay and Kummerfeld 1997, 55).

Web designers that favor semantic domain models let the system set the appropriate parameters for the users after their behavior has been recognized and classified (Allen 1996, 47). In this indirect scenario, it is usually a good idea to start with a questionnaire-based concept inventory, a short dialog with the user to initialize the system and build an initial model of existing background knowledge and level of expertise regarding the central conceptual foundations (Kay and Kummerfeld 1997, 49). Familiar patterns from previous experiences that we use to interpret new inputs are commonly referred to as *schemata*. Depending on their temporality, those pre-existing knowledge structures in memory are either called *frames* when describing fixed and static patterns, or *scripts* if some sort of event sequence is involved (Yule 1996, 85f.).

Stereotype user models may be used in combination with overlay models. Most user groups of Web applications are largely unknown from the start (Waern et al. 1999, 319). Thus it is rather difficult to initialize overlay models. Since setting attribute values after only a short interaction with new users is practically impossible, hybrid approaches are quite popular. They use stereotypes to classify new users and set the appropriate default values for the attribute clusters. As soon as direct observations allow a more fine-grained assessment, regular overlay models are used (Brusilovsky 1998, 10f.).

High-level user modeling operations allow new knowledge to be created dynamically. Accumulating individual preferences, for instance, is an efficient way to combine several individual user models and calculate a group model. Such a group model may serve as a template for initializing overlay domain models – e.g., for new members of a group who request a default profile (Brusilovsky 1998, 13).

5.5 ADAPTIVE WEB PRESENTATION TECHNIQUES

All texts and their electronically distributed variations are multimodally articulated, integrating language, spatial arrangements, visual elements, and other semiotic modes (Kress and Leeuwen 1998, 186f.). Users tend to have varying preferences regarding the multimodal access of electronic media (Höök et al. 1998, 155). While the number of alternatives provided by paper-based media is inherently limited (Newhagen and Rafaeli 1996), adaptive hypertext applications do not share this limitation. To support the users' preferences and capacities optimally, three categories of information and their interface representation are subject to customization (Scharl 2000a):

- *Content of documents* (↳ Section 5.5.2: Content-Level Adaptation).
- *Primary navigational system*, comprising links between and within these documents (↳ Section 5.5.3: Link-Level Adaptation).
- *Supplemental navigational systems;* e.g., index pages, trails, guided tours, or site maps (↳ Section 5.5.4: Meta-Level Adaptation).

Content-level adaptation is frequently used to tackle the problem of heterogeneous user knowledge. Summarizing, for instance, can be useful both as an introduction and to condense a series of previously presented scriptons. Link-level adaptation is used to provide navigation support and prevent users from following paths that are irrelevant with regard to their current goals (Brusilovsky 1997, 13). Supplemental navigational systems operate on the meta-level and generate overviews of the system as a whole. They enable users to verify their location, confirm the current context, or access their own interaction history.

Table 5.3 lists a number of adaptive presentation techniques and their applicability to the three categories described above. The question marks symbolize restrictions that have to be kept in mind when applying a particular technique: sorting of non-contextual links, for example, makes their order unstable and tends to decrease the system's usability (Brusilovsky 1998, 16). Although being designed for the benefit of the user, a constantly changing system can introduce confusion and decrease confidence (Vassileva 1998, 216). Sorting of indexes can be equally problematic, as their structure might be rendered obsolete by that operation. Hiding of contextual links can only be achieved via *stretchtext*, a technique that will be introduced in Section 5.5.2: Content-Level Adaptation.

Table 5.3. Adaptive content-, link-, and meta-level Web presentation techniques

Presentation Technique	Content	Primary Navigational system		Supplemental Navigational systems	
		Contextual Links	*Non-Contextual Links*	*Indexes*	*Local and Global Maps*
Summarizing	✓				
Sorting	✓		?	?	
Highlighting	✓	✓	✓	✓	✓
Hiding	✓	?	✓	✓	✓
Direct Guidance		✓	✓	✓	✓
Annotation	✓	✓	✓	✓	✓

The application of both highlighting and annotation is straightforward, independent of presentational category. Highlighting facilitates access of complex information spaces and potentially increases the application's interactivity – e.g., by raising curiosity, discussion, or comments from the user (Paternò 1999, 94). To acknowledge the importance of annotations as a powerful and most flexible presentation technique, the following Section 5.5.1 describes its conceptual foundations and areas of applicability. The other three techniques (sorting, hiding, and direct guidance) will be discussed in the succeeding chapters. These technologies do not contradict themselves but rather provide a variety of synergies when used in combination.

5.5.1 Annotations

Most scholarly articles and books exemplify explicit hypertextuality in non-electronic form by using a sequence of numeric symbols to denote the presence of footnotes, signaling the existence and location of subsidiary texts (explanations, citations, elaborations, and so forth) to the main document (Burbules and Callister 1996; Snyder 1996, 55f.). However, as far as printed material is concerned, the reader is rarely exclusively attracted by the footnotes and rarely "becomes fascinated with the non-linearity and incompleteness of such a collection of fragments, just as one does not give up a novel to start reading the phone directory" (Rosello 1994, 143). Annotations are quite similar to the concept of a footnote in traditional texts but are usually added by an author or, collaboratively, by a group of authors different from the producer of the main document. Common interface representations of annotations include various visual cues such as icons, highlighting, or color coding (↪ Section 5.5.4: Meta-Level Adaptation). These visual cues map attribute values to the visual representation and effortlessly differentiate between annotation and the annotated (Tufte 1990, 54). Textual additions are common as well, ranging from small floating text boxes, frequently using yellow windoids in homage to *3M's Post-It* notes (Nielsen 1995, 143), to separate documents that are syntactically independent of the main text.

Footnotes in printed material are usually presented together with the text (the note and text form one "visual gestalt"). Hypertext annotations are considered less intrusive because they are not shown unless the reader conciously activates them (Kolb 1994, 329; Nielsen 1995). Another distinction refers to the process of link-based reference, which can continue indefinitely in distributed hypertext systems. According to Aarseth (Aarseth 1998, 8), a footnoted text may be described as multicursal on the micro level and unicursal on the macro level (↪ Section 1.4: Web Information Systems). Writing in layers is therefore both possible and tolerable, and accessing these multidimensional structures is facilitated by graphical user interfaces (Snyder 1996, 16).

5.5.1.1 Historical Background

Already in the Middle Ages, many texts have attracted extensive commentaries in the form of annotations (e.g., biblical, legal, or medical documents). As far as traditional print media are concerned, annotations either remove obscurities or manifest external sources (Lamont 1997, 47). Although some traditional critics consider them oppressive and authoritarian, the extra functions of user participation provided by hypertext annotations are seen as liberating and empowering by most authors. "To turn from contemporary theoretical considerations of annotation to the electronic hypertext is to turn from a theology of guilt to a theology of liberation" (Lamont 1997, 54; Aarseth 1998, 163).

The bridging of the perceived gap between production and consumption of symbolic artifacts questions one of the most profound ideological divides in the social reality of modern Western society and therefore became highly contested ground. Many traditional thinkers feel cultural achievements to "be threatened with oblivion by the brave new world of technology" (Murray 1997, 276). Contradicting obsolete concepts of authorship decisively shaped by romantic theories of the solitary genius, hypertext annotations allow authors and readers to incrementally augment Web documents (Sutherland 1997, 14). They interactively create an ancillary structure that captures some aspect of the meaning of those documents. Declarative ancillary structures for this two-level model of hypertext include semantic nets, Petri nets, Bayesian nets, and clustering schemes (Mayfield 1997, 90; Kaplan et al. 1998, 49; Paternò 1999, 24ff.).

By allowing users to explore the multi-layered hierarchical space between creativity and passivity and to become secondary authors within the constraints laid down by the primary author, annotations draw attention to the fact that there have been previous readers (Liestøl 1994, 99; Aarseth 1998, 176). Historical documents, however, were often written under different economic, technological, and social circumstances. Actual, potential, and possible readers thus have to be distinguished when "marrying the daily knowledge of the past with the partial ignorance of the present" (Lamont 1997, 49). Similar concerns arise when addressing groups of readers with heterogeneous background and expertise.

5.5.1.2 Automated Document Annotation

In addition to adding commentaries manually, automated systems to annotate documents with information retrieved from search engines, databases, or newsgroups are useful in contextualizing the document to the reader's interest. The ubiquity of Web content and constraints regarding the capability and efficiency of the current Web infrastructure motivate the need for lightweight, efficient, non-intrusive (preferably transparent), platform-independent, and scaleable Web annotation systems that are usually founded on abstract intermediary architectures. With the exception of the initial configuration the user should be unaware of mediation by a proxy server and the fact that she is reading a personalized document.

Automated annotation architectures serve as paratextual expansion joints in the client-server connection. They customize communication on a per interaction basis, bringing down neither the client nor the provided service (Vasudevan and Palmer 1999). Even rather basic annotation mechanisms can facilitate hypertext navigation by improving link evaluation and decision processes. Campbell and Maglio, for example, conducted a series of experiments where they used small red, yellow, and green symbols ("traffic lights") added around the anchor text of each link to indicate its connection speed (Barrett et al. 1997, 79; Campbell and Maglio 1999, 311ff.). For each link embedded in the set of available documents, their proxy server maintains a periodically updated database of how long it takes to establish a connection. The algorithm for determining whether links are fast, medium, or slow adapts to the client's connectivity. It samples connection speeds over a period of time and models them as an exponential distribution. Connection speeds with an expected delay of less than 0.6 seconds are deemed green, yellow between 0.6 and 0.8 seconds, and red if expected to be greater than 0.8 seconds.

Figure 5.5 conceptualizes a more advanced annotation system architecture with the interceptor tapping into a client-server interaction, triggering the annotation process and invoking the composer to produce the annotated content. The annotation sets are retrieved from the annotation repository in accordance with the document, user model, and context. Vasudevan and Palmer separate stylistic, versioned and semantic composers (Vasudevan and Palmer 1999). While stylistic composers only locate the annotation sets, anchor them, and choose a customized presentation scheme to visually distinguish them from the document content, versioned composers take the versioning semantics of both the document and the annotation sets into account. The most sophisticated approach, semantic composing, does not rely exclusively on explicit authoring but allows knowledge-based processing on the basis of annotation micro-languages.

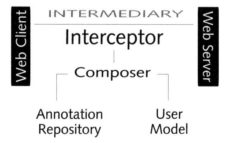

Figure 5.5. Annotation System Architecture (Vasudevan and Palmer 1999)

5.5.2 Content-Level Adaptation

A fundamental property of useful languages is the shared meaning of their tokens (Labrou et al. 1999, 45). The amount of interaction (= the number of tokens) employed to accomplish a particular goal is a pragmatic indicator of the relative distance between the participants. An exchange of ideas occurs most frequently between individuals who are alike. The more two individuals have in common, the fewer tokens they need to identify familiar things (Rogers 1995, 286; Yule 1996, 8). Consequently, the more Web information systems are able to learn about the user's behavior and preferences, the better they can adapt their traversal functions and representations. Sophisticated user models efficiently mediate the communication between an application and the user.

5.5.2.1 Deictic Expressions

Deictic expressions are just one example of how people manage to understand each other without having to repeat the full context of the conversation all the time. Deixis can be used to indicate extra-linguistic context (↪ Section 5.4.2) – e.g., people via personal deictic expressions like *"me"* or *"you"*, location via spatial deictic expressions like *"here"* or *"there"*, or time via temporal deictic expressions like *"now"* or *"then"*. Without detailed user models, domain representations, and interaction histories, this basic feature of our everyday language cannot be incorporated into Web documents. Another good example is the distinction between proximal *("this"*, *"here"*, *"now"*) and distal terms *("that"*, *"there"*, *"then"*), referring to the author's mental or physical context, which is also called the deictic center. Web technologies and their ability to manipulate location encourage the use of deictic projections, from both the author's and the user's perspective. Authors of hypertext documents are usually aware that the time and place of document production is different from the time and place of its consumption. Even the production itself is often spatially and temporally disjoined, particularly in the case of globally distributed hypertext projects (↪ Section 4.2.2: Cooperative Web Development). Deictic projections try to reduce the (perceived) importance of this temporal and spatial disjunction (Fairclough 1995, 36). Spatial deictic projections, for example, are common for messages left on telephone answering devices. *"I am not at home right now"* does not make sense without temporally projecting the term *"now"* to any time someone tries to call, which naturally is different from when the words actually were recorded (Yule 1996, 13). Similarly, personal homepages often refer to the author as if residing permanently in that virtual place.

5.5.2.2 Expressing Shared Meaning

When interacting with Web information systems, users generally appreciate the option to refer to previously mentioned or related entities via deictic expressions. This option can be implemented by keeping track of a *focus stack* (Höök et al. 1998, 156) where referents are stored together with a two-dimensional score indicating their proximity to the deictic center and their saliency for subsequent mention.

For global media like the World Wide Web, cultural disjunctions are quite common as well. Documents are produced in one part of the world, written in a particular language and influenced by the cultural environment of the author, which may be completely different from the reader's attitudes and values. Not surprisingly, this last category of disjunctions is much harder to overcome than the two preceding ones (spatial and temporal). A variety of methods has therefore been developed to express shared meaning and hence increase the usability of complex Web information systems. Nielsen classifies them into the following categories of content-based adaptation, which require or benefit from an accurate user model (Nielsen 1999):

- *Aggregation* produces a single unit that represents a collection of smaller ones, both within and across Web information systems.
- *Summarization* represents a large amount of data by a smaller amount – e.g., textual excerpts, thumbnails, or sample audio files.
- *Filtering* eliminates irrelevant information.
- *Elision* uses only a few examples for representing numerous comparable objects.

5.5.2.3 Techniques for Generating and Arranging Scriptons

Technically, the term content-level adaptation refers to all different forms of data embedded in Web documents. In practical terms, however, almost all prototypes and implemented systems concentrate on textual segments (= lexias), neglecting visual and audiovisual forms of data. A good indicator of the adaptation's granularity is the average length of these lexias – e.g., template-based versus full text generation (Geldof 1997). Scope for contextual variability is introduced by establishing an independent format for storing textons, and by incorporating a flexible mapping algorithm to provide various types of traversal functions (Knott et al. 1996, 151ff.). A large number of very short textons ensure maximum flexibility and potentially a very exact match between the presented sequence of scriptons and the user's actual needs. However, the required effort to maintain the database as well as the rule set significantly increases with the number of distinct elements. It is generally not easy to specify the optimal length of lexias for a specific application, which is to a large extent determined by the trade-off between granularity and maintenance intensity.

One of the simpler but nevertheless quite effective low-level techniques for content adaptation is conditional text (also referred to as *canning* or *conditionalization*), which requires the information to be divided into several chunks of data (Knott et al. 1996, 151ff.; Brusilovsky 1998, 20ff.). Each chunk is associated with a condition referring to individual user knowledge as represented in the user model. Only those chunks appropriate for the user's current domain knowledge are considered when generating the document. The granularity of this technique can range from node-level adaptivity (i.e., storing different variations of whole documents) to very fine-grained approaches based on sentences or even smaller linguistic units.

The term *stretchtext* denotes a higher-level technique. The idea is to present a requested page with all stretchtext extensions that are irrelevant to a particular user being collapsed. While reading the document, the user is able to collapse optional chunks of text and expand the corresponding terms whenever she desires. Applications of stretchtext can be categorized along two dimensions (Boyle 1998, 78):

- *Placement* of the text relative to the original, either at the beginning or the end of the scripton, embedded inside the scripton, or completely replacing it.
- *Granularity,* understood as the average length of lexias, usually based on graphical forms such as words, sentences, or paragraphs.

By activating and closing stretchtext extensions, the user creates summary and ellipsis (missing out repeated material or replacing it with a substitute word), by means of which the articulated discourse is shortened (Liestøl 1994, 94; Fairclough 1995, 122). One of the main advantages of stretchtext is that it lets both the user and the system adapt the content of documents, giving the user the possibility to "override" the system's recommendations. Similar concepts were already found in *Augment* and several early text editors at *Xerox PARC* (↪ Section 1.3: Hypertext and Hypermedia; (Nielsen 1995, 56)).

The most powerful content adaptation technique is based on frames and presentation rules where slots of a frame can contain several different explanations of the concept, links to other frames, or additional examples. Usually a subset of slots is presented in order of decreasing priority (Brusilovsky 1997, 16ff.; Turban and Aronson 1998, 542ff.). Research on natural language generation, which aims to produce coherent natural language text from an underlying representation of knowledge (Milosavljevic and Oberlander 1998), provides valuable insights for implementing such an advanced content adaptation technique. The generation process requires both text and discourse planning. While text planning comprises all the choices of what to say in the document, discourse planning determines the optimal sequence of scriptons in a coherent way. Ensuring coherence (= joint representation of related aspects) is a complex task and may be achieved by selecting a prepared discourse plan from an appropriate repository and instantiating this plan using textons from the knowledge base (Stein et al. 1997, 99; Milosavljevic 1998, 28).

5.5.3 Link-Level Adaptation

"The electronic age is the age of globally dispersed capitalist economies, of transnational corporations, of complexly mediated and hybridized cultural experiences, and, above all, of distance ... presented as proximity" (Sutherland 1997, 3). While urban planning and social anthropology use the terms proxemic and dystemic to describe the closeness relationship of people and spaces, Web user proximity can be regarded as a function of the actual distance and the cognitive distance between the person and the (virtual) space. As such it is concerned with the user's mental state and her perceived relationship to the history-rich objects.

The proximity of adaptive hypertext systems correlates with the quality of link-level adaptation techniques, which relies on how well the user's past experiences and knowledge are represented in the user model. Basic link-level adaptation techniques, which usually aim at decreasing the cognitive load *("hypertext syndrome")* caused by complex Web information systems (Gnaho and Larcher 1999), can be grouped into four categories:

- *Providing relevant starting points* in the information space (Vassileva 1998, 240), a feature that is particularly valuable for inexperienced users.
- *Influencing link perception.* Traditional applications either show a menu of destinations or open a separate window for each of the available destinations. Adaptive architectures, by contrast, automatically reduce the set of accessible destinations or choose one particular link. Once numeric interest values have been computed, it is relatively straightforward to transform that knowledge into interactive visualizations that consider the user's current interests with respect to their current location. In his paper on fisheye views, which belong to the category of distortion-oriented visualization techniques (↪ Section 5.5.4.3: View Transformations), Furnas proposes a formal *degree of interest* metric (Furnas 1981; Furnas 1986, 17f.). This metric enables adaptive systems to identify and display only those parts of the document tree that are of greatest relevance to a particular user. The degree of interest (DOI) in a is given by $DOI(a|.=b) = API(a) - D(a,b)$ where b is the current point of focus, $API(a)$ the *a priori importance* (= pre-assigned values to each point in the structure under consideration), and $D(a,b)$ the distance between point a and the current focus (Leung and Apperley 1994, 136). There are a number of mechanisms to convey and visualize the presumed relative importance of a document to the user. *Hiding* actually restricts browsing to smaller sub-spaces for inexperienced users. *Dimming* decreases the cognitive load as well, but leaves dimmed links still visible – and traversable, if required. *Highlighting* is the

most popular mechanism. Its attributes include boxing, blinking, color (hue, saturation, brightness), texture, and reverse video. As lateral and temporal masking negatively impact the other attributes, color coding remains the method of choice for most applications (Johnson and Shneiderman 1991, 289; Mahling 1994, 44f.; Ishai and Sagi 1995, 1772ff.); see for example the *Personal WebWatcher*, a prototype for customized browsing (Mladenic 1998, 11; Mladenic 1999, 53f.).[99] Using color for highlighting decreases search times if there is at least a chance of 50 percent that the highlighted element is the target. This quality is termed highlight validity, which can be increased by providing graphic link indicators for localizing relevant links (Campbell and Maglio 1999, 313).

- *Sorting* presents recommendations in the form of a sorted list of links and thereby transforms the complex problem of advice giving into the much simpler problem of rank ordering a list (Kaplan et al. 1998, 48). Occasionally, the non-stable order of links introduced by adaptive sorting may lead to incorrect mental maps, especially in the case of inexperienced users (Brusilovsky 1998, 17). To avoid confusion and optimize the interface representation, primary and recency effects should thus be taken into account when compiling such a list. The first and last words of a given list usually have the highest impact on the user's memory. Recall for the central words (or links) is worse because some never make it into short-term memory due to its limited capacity, or because some have already decayed from it. "Roughly seven (plus or minus two) words can be placed in short-term memory without exceeding its capacity. Left alone and unrehearsed, a single word will persists in some form for up to 18 seconds" (Mahling 1994, 48).

- *Annotating* (history-based versus user model-based) and semantic link labels, which can be regarded as a subcategory of annotations from a theoretical perspective (↪ Section 5.5.1).

The following paragraphs focus on the last category, annotations, and the importance of more advanced mechanisms for specifying semantic link labels within Web documents. Due to limitations in the current infrastructure of the World Wide Web, most applications lack mechanisms to show mutual dependencies and co-constitution among possible categories of thought (Kolb 1994, 332). Many systems do not provide links that allow the user to anticipate where the link will lead them, or to clearly distinguish them from other links located in the vicinity (Spool et al. 1998, 31). Semantic link labels address this problem of inexpressiveness (Mayfield 1997, 91) by conveying information about a link's purpose and destination, its relevance in the current context, its creator,

---

[99] http://www.cs.cmu.edu/afs/cs/project/theo-4/text-learning/www/pww/

or its date of creation. This information enables users to evaluate whether to follow a link without having to select it (Bieber 1997, 1ff.). By providing the user with meta-information about the relationships between documents, semantic link labels increase cohesion and help maintain context and orientation in non-linear Web presentations.

Current Web browsers only support history-based annotation, signaling whether a link has already been followed by the user. This is a very basic mechanism, not tapping the full potential of hypertextual navigation. It can easily be extended by including a more fine-grained link categorization. Labeling links according to their type, for example, might use the following categories:

a) *Intratextual links* within a document (related content marked by anchors, annotations, footnotes, citations, figures, etc.).
b) *Intertextual links* between documents of a particular Web information system.
c) *Intra-organizational links* to other systems of the same company.
d) *Inter-organizational links* to systems of other corporations within the same business ecosystem
e) *External links* to sources of information different from (a)-(d), which are located outside the corporation's business ecosystem.

Combining these categories with explicit annotations (e.g., numerically or via color coding) of the percentage of people who followed each of the links off the current page further increases the system's usability (Wexelblat 1999). Such a mechanism should also incorporate an adaptive component, considering only those links relevant to a user and computing percentages exclusively for this subset.

Trigg presents a rather elaborate taxonomy of 75 semantic link labels to distinguish between different forms of relationships between nodes (Trigg 1983). The taxonomy comprises both commentary link types, which are basically equivalent to the concept of annotations (↪ Section 5.5.1), and regular link types such as abstraction, example, formalization, application, rewrite, simplification, refutation, support, data, and so forth. Some applications do not adhere to a fixed set of link types but allow users to define their own types. Trigg mentions three reasons for not providing such a facility:

- *Explosion of link types.* Without restrictions, users would possibly flood the system with an unmanageably high number of new link types.
- *Reader confusion.* It seems unlikely that the name of a link type originally chosen by its creator would be sufficient to convey its meaning to future readers. This in turn could lead to misuse of the new link type by later critiques.

- *System confusion.* The semantics of some link types are partially understood by the system. Creators of new types would have to somehow define the type and its special features to the system.

5.5.4 Meta-Level Adaptation

Powell et al. distinguish three types of navigational support: textual, visual, and metaphorical (Powell et al. 1998, 162). Covering all three categories, this section will focus on *supplemental navigational systems*, in contrast to the primary navigational system comprising contextual and non-contextual links as discussed in the previous section. Supplemental navigational systems are used to locate and interpret a given item of information, providing full context by verifying the relation between different items and the virtual spaces surrounding them. They should include mechanisms to signify the user's current location and to retrace her individual steps. "As the navigator gets further and further from home, and especially if one hypertext is connected to another, he or she may sail out of protected waters and feel the full buffet of unmediated knowledge, but this should not happen by accident" (Lamont 1997, 61).

Supplemental navigational systems become more than mechanisms to navigate a virtual space; they become crucial textual elements themselves, replete with their own interpretive assumptions, emphases, and omissions (Burbules and Callister 1996). To support the different preferences, levels of technical knowledge, and cognitive styles of their users (Allen 1996, 40),[100] advanced Web applications usually employ a combination of the following supplemental navigational systems:

- *Site maps.* In contrast to manually designed representations of hypertext structures, automatically generated site maps are composed on the fly according to the system's topology and a set of pre-supplied layout rules (Andrews 1995, 90).
- *Site indexes* and *tables of contents* add a second-level structure (often alternatively referred to as *thesaurus, semantic net, domain knowledge,* or *index space*) on top of the basic document hypertext structure in order to provide more flexible and intelligent navigation (Mathé and Chen 1998, 173).

---

[100] "Cognition is the set of activities by which a person resolves differences between an internalized view of the environment and what actually exists in that environment" (Turban and Aronson 1998, 62). Thus the cognitive style is the subjective process through which a user perceives, organizes, and modifies information during the decision-making process.

- *Site indexes* are alphabetical lists of terms that are similar to the manually created index usually found at the back of books. Unlike tables of contents or site maps, they are not constrained by the site's hierarchy (Rosenfeld 1997). Compared to other supplemental navigational systems, they reference very granular bits of information. Their high number of entries and relatively flat hierarchical structure are two additional attributes that differentiate site indexes from tables of contents. They are capable of summarizing content, but usually fall short in presenting structural information adequately (Johnson and Shneiderman 1991, 285).

- Graphically enhanced tables of contents do not require the user to parse textual path information. Figure 5.6 shows a screenshot from the *WebToc* prototype.[101] This visualization tool automatically generates an expandable and contractible table of contents, indicating the number of elements in branches of the hierarchy as well as individual and cumulative sizes. Color mapping is used to represent file type (text, images, audio, and other); the length of the bars signifies their overall size (Nation et al. 1997).

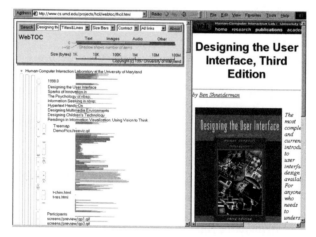

Figure 5.6. Graphically enriched table of contents for the
University of Maryland's Human-Computer Interaction Lab[102]

- *Direct guidance.* The tension between the content of a document as freely interpreted versus the content relevant for a specific situation (e.g., describing requirements and steps to complete a certain task) creates uncertainty. *Guided tours* in the sense of predefined *trails* as originally suggested by Vannevar Bush in 1945 (Bush 1945, 101ff.; Nielsen 1995, 247) provide a good example of presentational linearization. They try to overcome the uncertainty mentioned above by

---

[101] ftp://ftp.cs.umd.edu/pub/hcil/Demos/WebTOC/
[102] http://www.cs.umd.edu/hcil/

connecting to the next recommended step. They can be understood as virtual discourse that is produced by an absent author (Raudaskoski 1997, 535; Wenz 1997, 580).

- *Retrospective access* via
  - *Chronological* or *parameterized backtracking* to relate the current context to previously covered information. Nielsen provides a descriptive overview of conceptual backtracking models (Nielsen 1995, 249ff.).
  - *Topic* or *access histories* (Hohl et al. 1998, 123).
  - *Hierarchical bookmark lists* (also called *Hotlists* or *Favorites*) that enable users to tag elements perceived to be of long-term importance so that they can directly return to a particular document without having to remember and retrace the original pathway (Burbules and Callister 1996; Barrett et al. 1997, 75).
- *Search engines* and public *databases* that can be accessed by means of queries (full-text, via keywords, or based on personal conceptual descriptors) partially eliminate the need to pre-organize the information space in a hierarchical or alternatively structured way (Mathé and Chen 1998, 174). Query-based information retrieval is particularly useful when the user precisely knows the nature of the information she is seeking (Yang et al. 1999, 32).

5.5.4.1 Site Maps

Aarseth defines the textonomical version of topology as the study of ways in which the various sections of a text are connected, disregarding the physical properties of the transmission channel (Aarseth 1994, 60). In the case of print narratives, for example, the perception of spatial form occurs as readers work their way "through layers of narrative time, juxtaposed images, recurrent themes, multiple perspectives on events, and parallel lives" (Douglas 1994, 174). When readers access Web information systems, this process becomes more apparent. Hypertext systems represent semantic networks in themselves. Therefore, it is only natural to leverage the semantics that already exist in such networks (Kaplan et al. 1998, 48). A very intuitive way to tap the potential of such "hidden" semantics is the use of *site maps*, sometimes also referred to as *map windows*. In contrast to handcrafted representations of hypertext structures, automatically generated site maps are composed on the fly by the underlying system according to the system's topology and a set of pre-supplied layout rules (Andrews 1995, 90). The underlying semantic relationship between information objects (= documents) is mapped onto a spatial arrangement, associated with the domain-dependent semantic properties of various links.

Maps express quantities visually by location and areal extent (Tufte 1997, 14). For nautical navigation, for example, the map is the navigator's main representation of position. It stores enormous amounts of information about the earth's irregular features, naturally located near where they are needed for calculation (Card et al. 1999, 3f.). Twenty years of hypertext research indicates that maps, understood as explicit graphical representations of the node and link structure, significantly improve user performance. They are indispensable for helping users to get an in-depth understanding of the navigation space. These positive effects are further amplified if these visual representations are implemented in an interactive way (Beard and Walker 1990, 451ff.; Card et al. 1999, 8; Nielsen 1999, 67).

Augmenting the basic spatial substrate with marks and graphical properties to encode information is complicated, because it is easy for unwanted data to appear on the map. This "noise" makes it more difficult to understand and interpret the meaning of diagrams. Expressiveness and effectiveness, therefore, represent the main quality criteria for visualizations. A mapping is said to be *expressive* if the input information is exactly represented in the resulting visual structure, that is, all the information and only the information. It is more *effective* if it can be interpreted more accurately or quickly, conveys more distinctions (= navigational paths), leads to fewer navigational errors than some other mapping, and can be rendered in a cost-effective manner (Mackinlay 1986, 118ff.; Card et al. 1999, 23).

The following sections 5.5.4.2 and 5.5.4.3 introduce a number of basic view types and transformations commonly associated with them. Their layout simultaneously involves three signifying systems, all serving to structure the interface and present it as a coherent and meaningful whole (Kress and Leeuwen 1998, 188ff.):

- Specific *information values* are attached to the various zones of a document's visual space (↪ Figure 5.7). The further an item is placed from the gaze fixation, the less the likelihood that it will be identified correctly (Schiepers 1980; Noyes and Baber 1999, 40). Although the gaze fixation cannot be predetermined, elements presented in the center of a document suggest the nucleus of information to which all the other elements are in some sense subservient. Good examples of this effect are the circular algorithms for visualizing Web information systems that are presented in Section 5.5.4.2. Layout also polarizes left (given facts, common knowledge) and right (new or innovative content), as well as top (abstract concepts, the ideal) and bottom (factual data, the real).

- *Salience* denotes the varying degree to which the elements of a document attract the reader's attention. Salience has a considerable impact on navigation design. It can be influenced by a wide variety of means such as arrangement and perspective (placement in the foreground versus placement in the background), relative size, contrast, color, crispness, transparency, and so forth.

- *Framing* includes both connective devices (vectors between elements, repetitions of formal features, common symbols or color, etc.) and separating devices (framelines, empty spaces, discontinuities of color, etc.). It substantially determines the trajectory established on a document (*"reading path"*). Although it is impossible to automatically judge their aesthetic value, the occurrence of framing devices and their functionality can easily be measured, for example by counting the number of matching markup tags in the documents' HTML code (↪ Section 4.5.3.3: Structural Parameters).

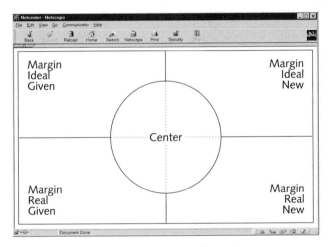

Figure 5.7. The dimensions of visual space
(adapted from Kress and Leeuwen 1998, 198)

5.5.4.2 View Types

Visualization envisions and embodies concepts as combinations of forms, textures, and colors (Rheinfrank et al. 1994, 78). From a purely technical point of view, visualization represents a simple, two-directional tool. It can be used for both making conceptual models operative and for formalizing information (Pitasi 1999). Taking social considerations into account, visualization has to respond to latent and expressed human needs, focusing on the specific environment and situational parameters of its application.

Hierarchical Data Structures

Effective Web development is heavily reliant upon the provision of means for eliciting and reconciling the semantics of non-technical users (Hemingway 1999, 284). Fortunately, a hierarchical model is already ingrained in the human brain to break down large sets of ideas into related categories. One of the first intellectual successes of infants, for instance, consists of mastering the task of distinguishing material objects according to rather basic attributes such as shape or color. They gradually learn to compare and to notice similarities and differences (Tesch 1990, 135). Cognitive scientists, however, disagree on the exact form of knowledge representation in human memory. Current models range from pictorially stored associations to complex propositional networks. Nevertheless, most experts agree on the information's structured and (where the domain permits it) hierarchical format (Collins and Loftus 1975, 407ff.; Mahling 1994, 49f.).

Since hierarchy represents an information artifact already familiar to every Web user, well-organized Web information systems most closely resemble this model (Rumpradit and Donnell 1999). Hierarchies are almost ubiquitous and represent a great way to indicate prominence (Robertson et al. 1991, 189; Rosenfeld 1997). Thus it is not a coincidence that many decision support systems use hierarchical data sets (trees) to organize and represent complex sets of data points. Commonly used visualizations of these data sets include two- or three-dimensional node-link diagrams, space-filling tree maps, or tables of contents (Kumar et al. 1997, 103). Given the option of representational dimensionality, a central question is which type of visualization to use (Card et al. 1999, 61). *One-dimensional* visual structures are typically used when space is at a premium. *Two-dimensional* structures are the most common. *Three-dimensional* structures are visually exciting, but are computationally intensive and have yet to prove their superiority in practical applications.

Node-Link Diagrams

Trees or directed graphs encode hierarchical data, typically visualized using connection (node-link diagrams, circular trees) or containment (tree maps, information slices). Whereas node positioning is irrelevant for the logical definition of a tree, it is important for its visualization. Unfortunately, large node-link diagrams acquire an extreme aspect ratio due to their exponential growth as expressed by the following equation to compute the number of nodes (n) in a fully populated hierarchy:

$$n = \sum_{i=1}^{d} b^{(i-1)}$$

where b represents the branching factor and d the level of depth. Figure 5.8 shows the truly remarkable dimensions of this growth, assuming squares with a side length of only 1.2 centimeters (drawn side by side) for calculating the drawing length of the last hierarchical level (Beaudoin et al. 1996, 87). The hypothetical 10x10 hierarchy would approximately cover the distance from Vienna (Austria) to the Hawaiian Archipelago.[103]

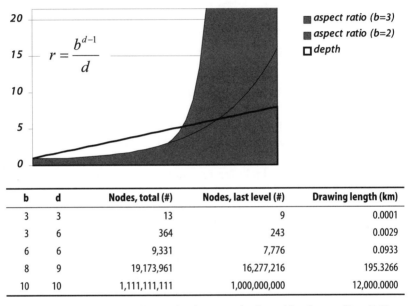

b	d	Nodes, total (#)	Nodes, last level (#)	Drawing length (km)
3	3	13	9	0.0001
3	6	364	243	0.0029
6	6	9,331	7,776	0.0933
8	9	19,173,961	16,277,216	195.3266
10	10	1,111,111,111	1,000,000,000	12,000.0000

Figure 5.8. Aspect ratios of hierarchical trees with a branching factor of b = {2,3}

As an inevitable result, these diagrams waste valuable screen space, especially when real names are used for identifying objects instead of acronyms and abbreviations. The same effect can be observed for outlines (Figure 5.9). Even a tree with a branching factor of only two, which is extremely unlikely for Web information systems, gets wider proportionally to $2^{(d-1)}$ and results in an aspect ratio of $2^{(d-1)}/d$ (Robertson et al. 1991, 190). Without effective view transformations and interactive control ($\hookrightarrow$ Section 5.5.4.3), static node-link diagrams of almost all but the most simple Web information systems come to resemble a straight line.

---

[103] http://www.indo.com/distance/

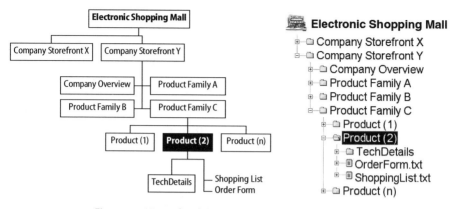

Figure 5.9. Hierarchical tree (left) and outline (right) representing
an electronic shopping mall's simple hierarchical structure

Circular Visualizations of Hierarchical Data

A potential solution that addresses the problem of extreme aspect ratios is the rendering of cone trees, wrapping hierarchical trees into two- or three-dimensional displays. They dramatically increase the number of nodes that can be included in a square-shaped aspect ratio (Card et al. 1999, 149f.). Parent nodes in such a tree are located at the apex of the cone, while their children are arranged around the cone's circular base. Generated by the *Astra SiteManager*,[104] the two-dimensional cone tree in the left part of Figure 5.10 visualizes publicly accessible nodes and links from the *University of California at Berkeley's* Web site (as of August 14, 1999; only the first three levels of the hierarchical structure are considered).[105] The recursive algorithm always uses the same circular layout, independent of an object's hierarchical position. The basic cone tree representation is often augmented with usage-based filtering, animated fisheye zooming, coalescing of distant nodes, texturing, or color-coded depth cueing (Carrière and Kazman 1995). Three-dimensional variations like the Euclidean cone tree depicted in the lower right corner of Figure 5.10 (Munzner and Buchard 1995) are visually impressive but necessarily occlude some of the tree's objects, particularly in the case of dense information spaces. This negative effect can be lessened by interactively adjusting the user's viewing angle and position, or by transparently shading the body of each cone (Robertson et al. 1991, 190; Chuah et al. 1995, 65; Hendley et al. 1995, 93ff.; Carpendale et al. 1997, 42).

---

[104] http://www.mercuryinteractive.com/products/astrasitemanager/
[105] http://www.berkeley.edu/

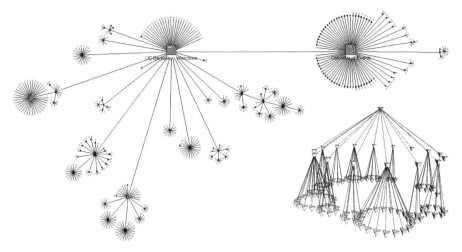

Figure 5.10. Two- and three-dimensional cone trees
(compare with the eW3DT diagram of Figure 4.10 on page 93)

Other (semi-)circular layouts for representing structural hypertext features are *disk trees* and *information slices*, which depict the hierarchical levels as successive circles of increasing radius with a common center at the root of the tree (Andrews 1998, 41; Chi et al. 1998, 404). Figure 5.11 contrasts both techniques, while Figure 5.14 on page 231 exemplifies the use of circular visualizations as components of overview diagrams.

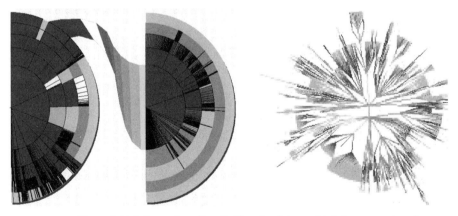

Figure 5.11. Information slices (left) and a disk tree (right) as examples of
(semi-)circular visualization of hierarchical data (Andrews 1998, 41; Andrews and
Heidegger 1998; Chi et al. 1998; Chi 1999b, 25)

Tree Maps

Unlike node-link diagrams, the concept of enclosure realized in tree maps by means of nested rectangles or in information slices by means of semicircular disks fills space rather than wasting it. Tree maps divide the space allocated for a node among its descendants according to certain numerically represented properties of the descendants. When the aspect ratio is held constant, both color and size of a rectangle can be used to compare particular target values. Thus it is relatively straightforward to realize adaptive presentations with the help of tree maps, as sections of the hierarchy relevant to the user's current tasks and goals can be allocated more display size dynamically (Johnson and Shneiderman 1991, 284). Unfortunately, tree maps tend to obscure the tree's hierarchical structure and provide no way of focusing without losing context (Lamping and Rao 1996, 37). Figure 5.12 compares a conceptual tree map representing the hierarchical structure already known from Figure 5.9 with a real-world example depicting more than 600 stocks of the New York Stock Exchange as of May 2, 2000.[106]

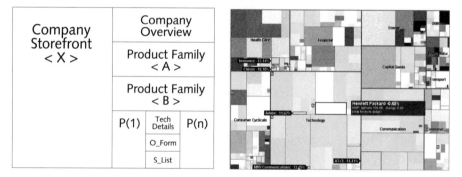

Figure 5.12. Conceptual versus real-world tree map

5.5.4.3 View Transformations

In almost all cases it is impossible to draw a diagram of the entire Web information system with its thousands of nodes and connecting links on a single computer screen. Therefore, view transformations that interactively modify and augment topographic maps on the basis of structural or semantic parameters (e.g., depth bound, color mapping, annotations, and so forth) are crucial for the map's usability. Card et al. distinguish three common transformations (Card et al. 1999, 31):

---

[106] http://www.smartmoney.com/marketmap/

- *Location probes* (also referred to as *brushing*) reveal the precise numerical or textual information for particular locations on the map on user demand – e.g., pop-up dialog windows that reveal document details as the mouse is dragged over the document's representation in the display (Johnson and Shneiderman 1991, 288; Wright 1995, 24). They are usually integrated with one of the other two categories, viewpoint controls or distortions.

- *Viewpoint controls* determine the number of details shown by zooming, panning, and clipping the visual representation. The spatially indexed data can be further enriched by adding landmarks to provide rapid access (Card et al. 1999, 16). While *geometric zooming* just provides a magnified version of the same graph, *semantic zooming* shows more details when approaching a particular area of the information structure. The main limitation of zooming is the lack of context as the details are magnified. To increase the number of variables per object shown for a given screen resolution, the absolute number of objects or the quality of their representation have to be reduced. To overcome this intrinsic limitation, designers either implement multiple views or employ rapid and easy to invoke zoom algorithms.

- *Distortions* (e.g., *fisheye views, hyperbolic trees,* or *perspective walls*) show the entire information space in a single site map. This feature makes them better suited for certain applications. Their hyperbolic transformations shrink the nodes of the tree far from the root, thus balancing the need for local detail and global context. For nautical navigation, compromised (distorted) projections of the round earth are also common. They enable graphical operations to be performed on the two-dimensional chart, with each type of projection sacrificing accuracy to support specific calculations (Card et al. 1999, 3f.).

5.5.4.4 Implications for Hypertext Navigation

Combining view types and transformations, two distinct approaches for providing visual site maps have become popular. The first one, *overview & detail*, integrates multiple views including at least one overview and one detailed view. The second one, *focus & context*, generates only one view that relies on distorted projections of the whole information space. In the latter case, the focal point can be either a particular node or simply a location in (eventually empty) space (Carpendale et al. 1997, 49). Figure 5.13 contrasts a file system's hyperbolic tree, generated by Inxight's interactive navigation tool *MagniFind*,[107] with a conceptual screen layout based on multiple views (compare with Figure 5.14). The

---

[107] http://www.inxight.com/demos/mf/

immediate access of full-screen versions of each view at any point during the interaction blends *space multiplexing* (showing overview and
detail displays at the same time in different parts of the screen) with
time multiplexing (showing the various displays one at a time). Such a
mechanism provides maximum flexibility and support of the user's
current tasks and individual navigation style (Card et al. 1999, 285).

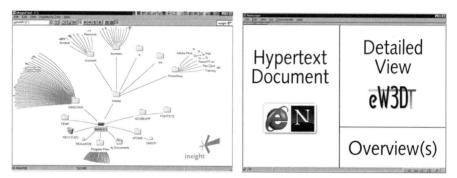

Figure 5.13. Focus & Context (left) versus Overview & Detail (right)

Overview and Detail

When defining graphical excellence, Tufte recommends graphical displays that reveal the data at several levels of detail. He identifies layering
and separation as the most powerful devices for reducing noise and
enriching the content of displays (Tufte 1983, 13; Tufte 1990, 53). Site
maps following this recommendation consist of two components that
visually stratify the hierarchical document structure. The context-
providing *overview* reduces search, allows the detection of global patterns, and aids the user in choosing the next node to visit. The *detailed
view* displays a magnified focus for the local neighborhood surrounding
the user's current location (Nielsen 1995, 3; Card et al. 1999, 285).

To aid users in remembering their location, interface designers
should provide some sort of "you are here" indicator as part of the
overview (also referred to as *viewports* or *panners*). This "meta-
navigation" may be realized in the form of control widgets to pan the
detailed view (e.g., sliders, buttons, or wire-frame boxes that can be
dragged around in the overview). Similarly, scrolling the detailed view
updates the position of the indicator in the overview. Hence, both views
are said to be tightly coupled (Kumar et al. 1997, 104). Such *tightly coupled views,* also referred to as *multiple coordinated views* or *linked
views,* provide rapid access and are simple to implement and understand. They are frequently complemented by additional zoom facilities
to adjust the level of detail. The coordination between the views is *com-*

mutative (bidirectional) and *transitive* (North and Shneiderman 1999). User actions in either visualization cause modifications in the other. If visualization A is coupled with B and B is coupled with C, then user actions in visualization A will produce modifications in both related displays.

The advantages and positive effects of tightly coupled interface components on user performance have been documented in several studies (Norman et al. 1986; Shneiderman et al. 1986; Chimera and Shneiderman 1994). The quality of such components is founded in several conceptual aspects (Ahlberg and Shneiderman 1994, 315f.):

- Continuous and synchronized display of the information space with rapid, incremental and reversible interactions among components. This requires smooth direct manipulation operations such as zooming, rotation, and translation, which are computationally more demanding but cognitively more comprehensible (Tweedie 1997, 376; Munzner 1998, 22; Card et al. 1999, 286).

- Constraints on permissible operations to prevent errors and preserve logical display propositions.

- Intuitive and consistent mechanisms to guide users, progressively refine parameters, and show details on demand – often in combination with location probes (↪ Section 5.5.4.3: View Transformations). Shneiderman, for example, recommends the following visual information seeking strategy: "Overview first, zoom and filter, then details-on-demand" (Shneiderman 1997a, 23).

Focus and Context

Overview & detail representations often entail disruptive shifts of attention to the overview window. Distorted views do not require such shifts. They follow a *focus & context* approach, providing great detail for those parts of the system in the vicinity of the user's current location of interest and gradually diminishing amounts of detail for remote parts of the information space. As the nodes' spatial positions and adjacency relationships often carry specific meaning, distorted views should not compromise them severely (Leung and Apperley 1994, 139; Carpendale et al. 1997, 42). Meta-navigation similar to the viewpoint control's wireframe box (e.g., direct manipulation by dragging a particular node to the center of the display) belongs to the common features of distorted views. It helps users perceive the larger, undistorted structure. To enable distortions, the information space has to satisfy two conditions (Furnas 1981; Nielsen 1995, 259f.): (a) the possibility to estimate the distance, either linear or structurally defined, between a given location and the user's current focus of interest, and (b) the existence of methods and tools to display the information at several levels of detail – e.g., variable resolution, highlighting, filtering, or selective aggregation (Card et al. 1999, 307f.).

Hyperbolic projections are very common for the *focus & context* approach. Hyperbolic space, on which the hierarchies are laid out, is infinite in extent, just like Euclidean space. In contrast to Euclidean space, however, the circumference of a circle (and thus the available space for representing data points) grows exponentially with its radius. Therefore, hierarchical structures that also expand exponentially with depth can be conveniently mapped onto the display, representing a finite portion of Euclidean space (Lamping and Rao 1996, 35f.; Munzner 1998, 20; Munzner 1999).

Distorted views face a number of drawbacks (Chuah et al. 1995, 69; Card et al. 1999, 31f.). Due to their geometrically complex transformations, they can be difficult to understand. Distant information may become so small that it cannot be perceived. For inexperienced users, the unlimited scope of most distortions may also be disconcerting, because a local action affects objects in the entire visualization in sometimes unpredictable ways (Herman et al. 1999). In distorted views based on hyperbolic geometry, for example, objects tend to get rotated during pure translations (Lamping and Rao 1996, 45).

Integration via Tightly Coupled Views

Many of the geometrically complex displays provide only limited node and link semantics or no semantics at all. As additional context information quickly overwhelms the available display space, most of them rely on color coding or location probes to provide that information. This limitation makes them suitable for interactive navigation, but renders them practically useless for documenting or presenting Web information systems. The following sections introduce a concept based on multiple views that integrates methods from both categories, *overview & detail* and *focus & context*. It draws on the strengths and addresses the weaknesses of available view types and transformations to provide site maps that satisfy all the fundamental principles of interactive user interface design as postulated by Shneiderman (Shneiderman 1997b, 74f.; Bucy et al. 1999): strive for consistency, enable frequent users to access shortcuts, offer informative and intuitive feedback, permit easy reversal of actions, support an internal locus of control, and reduce short-term memory load.

Two-dimensional browsers such as Netscape *Navigator* or Microsoft *Internet Explorer* do not take advantage of the underlying structure of the information space. Figure 5.14 resolves that limitation by applying the concept of tightly coupled views introduced above to the electronic product catalog of Compaq as of January 1999. Figure 5.13 on page 228 introduced a conceptual screen layout including an overview area, an eW3DT map as detailed view, and the actual hypertext document. Figure 5.14 represents an application of this conceptual layout that uses three types of overview diagrams: disk tree, three-dimensional cone tree, and tree map (the overviews have symbolic character and do *not* represent the actual example). Instead of providing three different types of overview diagram, the application of visual operators enables users to identify areas of current interest, visualize longitudinal patterns, or compare the structural features of several systems (Furnas 1981; Hasler et al. 1994, 325ff.; Levoy 1994, 139ff.; Chi 1999a; Chi 1999b, 25).

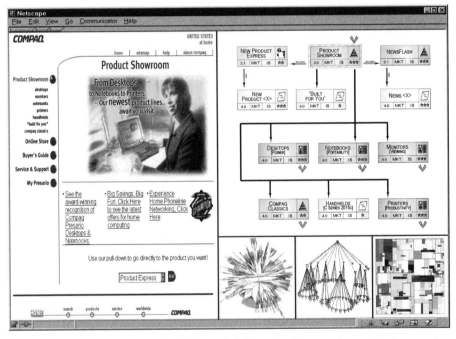

Figure 5.14. Example of tightly coupled views showing a rendered Web document, the corresponding eW3DT diagram, and three distinct overviews[108]

Each of the visualization techniques introduced in the previous sections such as the various types of hyperbolic projections, hierarchical trees, or outlines can be utilized for overview diagrams. Independent of the chosen method, the user should be able to select the arrangement of her preferred display techniques. Complementarily, a variety of adaptive presentation techniques is suitable to customize overview maps: highlighting, hiding, direct guidance, or annotation (↪ Section 5.5:

---

[108] http://www.compaq.com/showroom/

Adaptive Web Presentation Techniques). Instead of considering all existing links, for example, links originating from a particular document or links that are particularly relevant to a user's current goals can be derived from the user model.

For the detailed view, the extended World Wide Web Design Technique (eW3DT) of Section 4.2.4 is used. eW3DT maps of complex Web information systems as part of high-level graphical interfaces reduce the cognitive overhead caused by a lack of spatial and temporal context (Turoff et al. 1999). They represent an attempt to "build a visual interaction system that wastes the least amount of cognitive effort, thereby allowing users to direct the major part of their attention and cognitive processing power to the domain task" (Mahling 1994, 42). Site maps such as those depicted in Figure 5.14 can show not only where users are located at the moment but also where they have already been during the current or preceding visits (their "footprints"; compare with Section 4.4: Usage: Visualizing Topology and Access Patterns). Furthermore, comparing the user's own path with the paths taken by others represents a special type of collaborative filtering and provides reassurance when implemented as a supplemental navigational system (↪ Section 6.2: Collaborative Filtering). Another promising method is to highlight nodes in the site map that contain particularly relevant information. The two most common mechanisms are color coding to indicate a data value (e.g., closeness of the match regarding a full-text query) and contours to indicate a constant data value – e.g., visualizing iso-interest contours that connect nodes with the same hypothetical level of interest (Furnas 1981; Nielsen 1995, 232; Bryson et al. 1999, 85).

Generally speaking, successful visualizations consist of "complex ideas communicated with clarity, precision, and efficiency" (Tufte 1983, 51). However, it has been demonstrated above that no single layout algorithm will ever be entirely satisfactory and always produce the best results (Smith et al. 1997, 70). Web navigation frequently requires the user to make comparisons, or to look at some distant parts referenced from the current location. As Henry points out, good interface layout does not neglect the user's current region of interest (Henry and Hudson 1991, 55ff.; Henry 1992, 81ff.). Consequently, representational adaptivity and multiple simultaneous foci (e.g., interactively animated overview diagrams) are essential keys to the further improvement of the functionality of supplemental navigational systems.

6 Agent-Mediated Architectures

Ambitious efforts to automate and optimize electronic business-to-consumer transactions gradually transfer certain tasks to digital agents, the fourth and last stage of Web evolution as introduced in Section 2.2.1 (Glushko et al. 1999, 108). Modern information retrieval and research into complex negotiations pioneered the application of agent-mediated architectures (Maglio and Barrett 1997, 6ff.; Tu et al. 1999). By further increasing system flexibility, digital agents promise to radically change the inherent characteristics of doing business electronically.

Falchuk and Karmouch define a digital agent as "an autonomous software object that performs tedious and repetitive computer-based operations on behalf of a human user or another agent. If the agent can be serialized (prepared for transfer over a network in a way that lets its state be recovered) and if it migrates, it is a mobile agent" (Falchuk and Karmouch 1998, 31). Digital agents are characterized by a number of abilities, which can be grouped into six categories. These categories, delineated in Table 6.1, determine the agents' cooperative or competitive behavior (Schubert et al. 1998, 306; Turban and Aronson 1998, 723ff.; Werthner and Klein 1998, 117; Lange and Oshima 1999, 88; Singh 1999, 40).

Table 6.1. Characteristic attributes of digital agents

Ability	Description
Proactivity, Reactivity	Perceive environmental attributes, initiate processes, and react to internal or external events in a timely fashion.
Intentionality, Goal-orientedness	Accept high-level requests and actively choose appropriate methods for pursuing a certain goal. Digital agents are goal-seeking systems that can respond differently to one or more events in one or more different states. They can respond differently to a particular event in an unchanging environment until a particular state is reached. Production of this state is the goal of the system. Thus such a system has a choice of behavior (Ackoff 1974, 32f.).

Ability	Description
Adaptivity	Learn from past actions and adapt to environmental changes. Potential information sources include the observation of user actions, the analysis of user feedback, explicit user instructions, or multi-agent collaboration (Akoulchina and Ganascia 1997, 22).
Autonomy	Act in an independent manner without direct intervention by the principal. Digital agents must be able to alter their course or behavior when they meet obstacles to find ways around the impediment.
Interactivity	Communicate with each other, usually via an agent communication language (ACL). Some authors use the term multi-agent system to describe this attribute.
Mobility	Migrate between different environments (hardware platforms, operating systems, or applications). In contrast to their mobile counterparts, stationary agents are bound to the system on which they began execution.

Many definitions in the literature do not require an agent to be *interactive* or *mobile*. Thus these two orthogonal properties will not be generally assumed for the applications presented in this chapter. Prior to introducing the process of developing agent-mediated architectures in Section 6.4, the following sections present a functional categorization of digital agents into content-based information agents, collaborative filtering systems, and transaction agents (Brenner et al. 1998, 21ff.; Schubert et al. 1998; Scharl et al. 1999, 37ff.).

6.1 CONTENT-BASED INFORMATION AGENTS

Information agents are used for individualizing Internet-based communication. Similar to the adaptive Web information systems of stage three, they present each user with a personalized, intuitive interface that hides the more complex system and network architectures. Information agents typically store a user model together with the learning algorithm either on the client side for general Internet browsing, or on the server side for facilitating access to specific Web information systems. To update the user model, hybrid approaches that allow both manual editing and incremental learning in line with the user's interaction history are most common (↪ Section 5.4.2: Typology of the Extra-Linguistic Context). Filtering agents such as *All Direct Books, BargainFinder, Jango, MySimon, Dealpilot.com* (formerly known as *Acses*), or *Dealtime* represent a rather simple category of information agents.[109] They are most

---

[109] http://www.alldirect.com/
http://www.bargainfinder.com/
http://jango.excite.com/
http://www.mysimon.com/
http://www.dealpilot.com/
http://www.dealtime.com/

useful for information retrieval as an intermediary or gateway to one or more third-party information offerings. The difference between information retrieval and information filtering is that *ad hoc* retrieval requires active participation by the user (e.g., formulating full-text queries). It is usually focused on specific informational needs, whereas filtering is done continuously according to a user model and a predefined set of criteria (Nielsen 1995, 224; Baeza-Yates and Ribeiro-Neto 1999).

To allow advanced information retrieval and automated filtering, structured meta-data describing the content of Web-based applications is essential. By providing a data model of meta-data instances, the *Resource Description Framework (RDF)*[110] enables interoperability between Web information systems that exchange machine-understandable information. RDF and XML are complementary. Since RDF only superficially addresses many encoding issues, it typically leverages XML as an interchange syntax for the properties and relationships of Web objects (Cover 1998; Lassila 1998, 34). XML formally governs syntax only and thus needs RDF for defining what instances of meta-data mean, and for allowing digital agents to agree on a common meaning. RDF allows digital agents to share and exchange knowledge (agent to agent), communicate (agent to service or user), and to "understand" their environment. In this way, it facilitates resource discovery and permits the description of Web content and its semantic structure (Lassila 1998, 31; Flammia 1999, 21; Abiteboul et al. 2000, 47). Netscape's *"What's related"* feature implemented in *Communicator 4.06* and above, for example, was the first widely deployed application of RDF. It queries a remotely located and continually updated database of relationships between Web resources to generate a list of Web sites semantically related to the currently displayed document (Swick 1999, 25).

Advanced approaches that rely on meta-data descriptions imply higher degrees of autonomy. They automate repetitive tasks by accessing distributed information sources and deriving run-time navigational decisions based on what they find. NetCognition's *SiteAccelerator*, the content-based user interface agent *Letizia*, or its collaborative extension *Let's Browse* (↪ Section 6.2: Collaborative Filtering), for instance, assist and speed up Web browsing by tracking user behavior (Lieberman 1995; Lieberman 1997, 67ff.; Lieberman et al. 1999, 65ff.).[111] They attempt to anticipate items of interest by performing a concurrent, autonomous exploration of links from the user's current position. Sophisticated algorithms are employed to accurately predict a link's de-

---

[110] http://www.w3.org/rdf/
[111] http://www.netcognition.com/
http://lieber.www.media.mit.edu/people/lieber/Lieberary/Lieberary.html

gree of interest and the likelihood of its selection by the user. *Letizia* does not require any keyword input or explicit rating from the user. As users tend to perform depth-first searches, the agent is synchronously reading Web documents to perform a breadth-first search from the current location. Potentially interesting links are then suggested in a separate window (Mladenic 1998, 1; Mladenic 1999, 46). NetCognition's site acceleration technology does not recommend particular links but utilizes idle client-side bandwidth to retrieve predicted content and accelerate the visitor's overall browsing experience.

6.2 COLLABORATIVE FILTERING

Information systems support different types of spatiality and dimensionality. Therefore, most of them are capable of generating virtual environments within the user's mind (Ipsen 1997, 559; Wenz 1997, 582; Díaz and Melster 1999). Hypertexts and agent-mediated architectures are no exception, but strain our capacity for imagination. Since we are not acquainted with visualizing their specific form of spatiality, additional features are required to ease this situation. Besides navigation based on *spatial* relationships (above, below, outside) and *semantic* relationships (bigger, alike, faster) mapped to spatial concepts, Dourish and Chalmers propose a third category: *Social* navigation where movement from one object to another is provoked as an artifact of the activity of other users (Dourish and Chalmers 1994). In the case of Web information systems, the term refers to the usage of cues and information from others to locate required information and potentially to understand better the nature, context, and purpose of retrieved documents. Inexperienced users in particular might follow access paths of other users or retrieve documents because others have examined them before. In this way their course of action is highly authorized because it seems to be the kind of action that a "person like me" would do (Allen 1996, 64).

Collaborative filtering, the customization of information on the basis of clustering like-minded individuals, relies on the concept of social navigation. Most collaborative filtering systems are founded on subjective evaluations about the delivered content (= social knowledge). They synchronize, share, and communicate the subjective preferences of user groups by means of analogies, correlations, and other statistical methods in order to identify and recommend items of interest. This approach resembles a familiar real-world situation based on spatial relationships (Dourish and Chalmers 1994). The underlying assumption is that users will converge on satisfying solutions, showing a tendency to do things in groups and to identify with these groups even if no specific members of the group are present or known. The resulting agglomeration provides reassurance and is the basis for establishing authority and possibly authenticity (Wexelblat 1999).

In analogy to an attentive shop assistant, collaborative filtering systems observe customer habits and interests as they browse the product displays. To implement customization technologies on the server-side it is important to ask visitors to register online and provide basic information about their identity before access to protected parts of the Web information system is granted. Each individual's path is then monitored to infer conclusions about the rationale behind the behavior of the user. Frequent returns by the user result in a higher quality of the user model, improving the system's effectiveness with every additional attribute gathered. It takes several subsequent visits before the system can come up with meaningful recommendations for a visitor. A person's reaction to a delivered document is tracked either by explicit or by implicit ratings and is saved in the user model for later information delivery. For gathering explicit feedback, the system usually provides a means for users to vote on cognitive variables such as the perceived utility, quality, or usability of retrieved documents. They allow the user to express opinions about delivered recommendations directly by evaluating the content either numerically or on qualitative terms (e.g., poor, fair, average, good, and excellent). Implicit ratings are collected by observing which products customers look at, inquire about, or purchase. Collaborative filtering systems correlate one customer's ratings with those of others in order to identify patterns of preferences resembling those of that particular customer. Initiating a process of social learning, the interconnected systems combine the ratings of these like-minded individuals to recommend items of interest (Balabanovic and Yoav 1997, 66ff.; Mladenic 1999, 47).

Collaborative filtering is used typically for non-textual data and for recommending opinion-based content such as books or music to users with similar demographic or psychographic profiles. Pioneers in collaborative filtering technologies were *Firefly's CD Recommender System* (now a Microsoft subsidiary),[112] the University of Minnesota's *GroupLens* technology (commercialized by *NetPerception*),[113] and *Open Sesame's eGenie*[114] (Cohen 1998; Solutions 1999; Zacharia et al. 1999). Among the current limitations of these systems is the observable dominance of early ratings, as very few other users will bother reading a

---

[112] http://www.microsoft.com/PressPass/
[113] http://www.grouplens.org/
http://www.netperception.com/
[114] http://www.opensesame.com/

document once it has gathered a string of poor judgements. A second potential problem is the possibility of "rating wars" where people disqualify a document solely based on opportunistic personal motivations, without having read its content (Nielsen 1995, 239). Consequently, clustering like-minded individuals can only succeed if a critical mass of individual evaluations is available. Furthermore, if new information objects are added to the system, no evaluations are available for that particular object. A collaborative system must then solve the problem of an information object's relevancy for certain (groups of) users. By contrast, *content-based filtering* can suggest personalized content even if there is only one visitor. Hybrid approaches that integrate collaborative and content-based approaches, therefore, are the most popular for practical applications. Systems such as *OpenSesame* and *WiseWire* (acquired by *Allaire* and *Lycos,* respectively) apply such a hybrid approach.[115]

6.3 TRANSACTION AGENTS

Negotiation or transaction agents represent highly specialized programs that complement information agents to perform the negotiation and settlement phases of electronic transactions (↪ Section 2.3: Electronic Market Transactions). Negotiation processes between market participants are characterized by high degrees of unpredictability, complexity, and importance to organizations (Beam and Segev 1997, 263ff.; Schmid and Lindemann 1998, 193ff.).

In traditional markets the number of participants and the range of negotiated attributes has to be kept low, as the negotiation process is usually complex and time consuming (Brandtweiner and Scharl 1999a, 81ff.). Transaction agents increase efficiency and thus do not share these limitations. They meet in a virtual marketplace, which provides a negotiation protocol, determines the trading partners' valid actions, and sets the matchmaking rules. Highly sophisticated algorithms and communication architectures enable customers and suppliers to participate in such electronic marketplaces by setting strategies and endorsing their digital agents. Nevertheless, a number of challenges remain unanswered, which usually fall into one of the following categories (Wong et al. 1999, 99f.):

---

[115] http://www.opensesame.com/
http://www.wisewire.com/
http://www.allaire.com/
http://www.lycos.com/press/wisewire/release1.html

- *Deferred interaction.* Economically and technically most efficient frequency of reporting back to the principal and refining the agent's parameters.
- *Understanding.* Realistic and intuitive modeling of the principal's goals, intentions, and preferred negotiating style.
- *Flexibility.* Required degree of accommodation in dynamic and highly competitive markets.
- *Robustness.* Adequate protection of an agent's secrecy and integrity from other agents and from malicious or erroneous execution environments (Corradi et al. 1999, 519ff).

An early example of an agent-mediated transaction system is *Market Maker* (formerly known as *Kasbah*). *Market Maker* and *Tête-à-Tête (T@T)*, which help consumers match their needs with merchants' value-added offerings, are both ongoing research projects at the Software Agents Group of the *MIT Media Laboratory*. They are intended to help realize the fundamental transformation in the way people transact goods and services (Chavez and Maes 1996; Zacharia et al. 1999).[116] Table 6.2 provides a comparison of digital agent projects regarding their support of *product brokering, merchant brokering,* and *negotiation* as described in Section 2.3: Electronic Market Transactions.

Table 6.2. Transaction framework with
representative examples of agent mediation (Maes et al. 1999, 82)

Transaction Phase	Persona Logic	Firefly	Bargain Finder	Jango	Market Maker	Auction Bot	T@T
Product Brokering	✓	✓					✓
Merchant Brokering			✓	✓			✓
Negotiation (Agreement)					✓	✓	✓

Currently, the *Market Maker* system facilitates the trading of books, computer games, and various music media. The agents in the *Market Maker* project are not mobile but are executed on a dedicated server that represents the market environment. A user wanting to trade goods creates an agent, gives it some strategic direction, and sends the agent off into the virtual marketplace. *Market Maker* agents proactively seek out potential buyers or sellers and negotiate with them on their creator's behalf. Constraint-satisfaction engines built into the agent try to meet or optimize a number of user-specified criteria, such as a desired price, a highest (or lowest) acceptable price, and a date by which to

---

[116] http://agents.www.media.mit.edu/groups/agents/projects/

complete the transaction. In the *Market Maker* system, negotiation is straightforward, bilateral, and competitive. It provides buyers with three different negotiation strategies: anxious, cool-headed, and frugal (depending on the selected price raise function which can be specified as being linear, quadratic, or exponential; see left-hand screenshot of Figure 6.1).

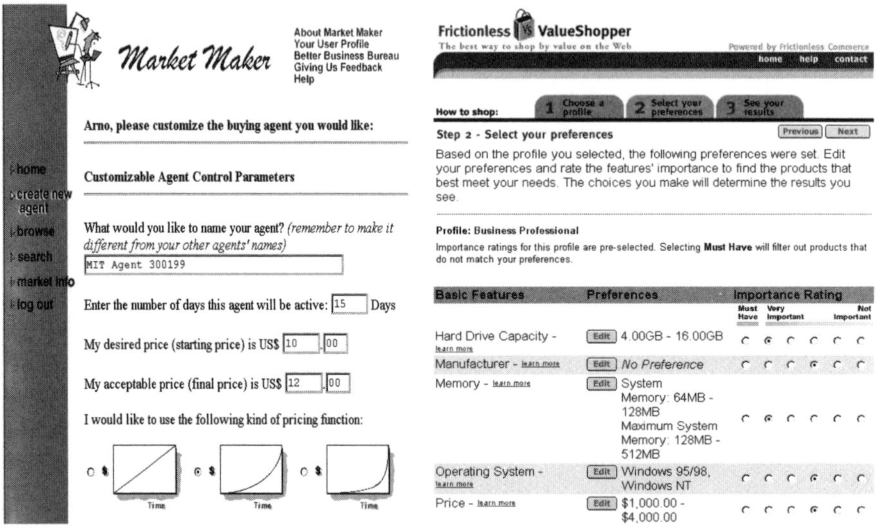

Figure 6.1. User interfaces for customizing the buying agents of
Market Maker (left) and Frictionless ValueShopper (right)

Negotiation mechanisms such as those provided by *Market Maker* may generally be defined as a computer-assisted form of decision-making "where two or more parties jointly search a space of possible solutions with the goal of reaching a consensus" (Rosenschein and Zlotkin 1994; Guttman et al. 1998). The parties first verbalize contradictory demands and then move towards agreement by either making certain concessions or searching for alternatives (Sierra et al. 1997, 17ff.). Although researchers in economics, game theory, and behavioral sciences have investigated negotiation processes for a long time, a solid and comprehensive theoretical framework is still missing. "Over forty years of intense theoretical research has failed to produce an adequate general, computational theory of bargaining and negotiation" (Gresik and Satterthwaite 1989). One of the basic findings of negotiation sciences is the lack of an optimal protocol for all possible negotiation situations. The application context determines the optimal mechanism, taking into account the participants' current needs, preferences, and goals. In line with these parameters, the optimal protocol is usually chosen based on criteria such as expected utility, cost, required resources, or available know-how. Consequently, different negotiation protocols are appropriate in different situations. Generic mediation services should therefore support a range of options (Wurman et al. 1998).

Currently, most transaction agents are only able to compare products by price. Innovative price negotiation models such as those pioneered by *Mercata* or *Accompany* are of obvious value in many situations.[117] They bundle purchase requests for the same goods to shift the bargaining relationship and negotiate discounts from the manufacturers. But more often than not, there is a need for more complex allocation schemes considering multiple attributes of a deal (Bakos 1998, 42; Bichler and Scharl 1999, 2f.). In traditional marketplaces products and services tend to be similar in functionality with the only difference between them being their price. In the case of customized (digital) products (Brandtweiner et al. 1998, 38f.), the retailer can negotiate an individual price with each customer. However, available technologies frequently do not adequately capture, locate, and display the full value of complex products and services (Miles et al. 2000, 142). A notable exception of that rule is the Frictionless *ValueShopper*, a commercial implementation of the value-based comparison shopping technologies of *Tête-à-Tête*.[118] Current corporate customers include, among others, *Lycos*, *Brodia*, *WebHelp*, and *Wingspan Bank*.[119] *ValueShopper* uses multidimensional matchmaking to rank individual merchant offerings by their overall value to the customer. While price may be an effective criterion for evaluating rather basic products such as books or CDs, consumers tend to consider a more sophisticated matrix of features when they are buying more complex items such as computers, consumer electronics, or financial services. Therefore, *Tête-à-Tête* and *ValueShopper* feature an advanced decision support environment, an intuitive graphical interface (↳ Figure 6.1), and an extensive database of merchant and customer comparison shopping information. Both products support bilateral argumentation via an exchange of XML-based proposals, critiques, and counter-proposals (Maes et al. 1999). Based on this exchange, shopping and sales agents cooperatively negotiate across multiple terms of a transaction, including prices, warranties, delivery times, service contracts, return policies, loan options, gift services, and so forth.

---

[117] http://www.mercata.com/
http://www.accompany.com/
[118] http://www.frictionless.com/
[119] http://shop.lycos.com/
http://www.brodia.com/
http://www.wingspanbank.com/
http://webhelp.com/frictionless/

6.4 DEVELOPING DIGITAL AGENTS

The enhanced functionality of autonomous or semi-autonomous agents negotiating with each other requires rethinking and rebuilding the World Wide Web's established communication models. Nevertheless, every innovation in this specific segment will have to provide backward-compatibility and inter-operability to enable seamless integration and incremental adoption (Lindemann and Runge 1998; Reagle and Cranor 1999, 54). Principal-agent relations replace the traditional client-server approach with agent software acting as client and server at the same time (Hansen and Tesar 1996). Digital agents consider the principal's preferences, employ predefined and standardized coordination mechanisms, and adapt autonomously to the situational requirements of their current tasks.

6.4.1 Agent Communication Models

The potential advantages of these features become most apparent in the implementation of complex negotiation mechanisms for commercial applications. The communication model dominating stage four, therefore, no longer refers to design or analysis but replaces these traditional concepts by the term negotiation as denoted by the letter "N" in the second column of Figure 6.2 (↳ Section 2.2.1: Stage Models for Describing Web Evolution).

Stage	Feedback Model	Enabling Technologies	Stage Description
4	N ◀┅┅┅▶	*ACL, KQML, KIF, Aglets, Odyssey, Concordia*	**Digital agents further increase flexibility; negotiations represent the cornerstone of electronic markets.**

D ... Design   ——— Explicit Feedback
A ... Analysis   ---- Implicit Feedback
N ... Negotiation

Figure 6.2. Characteristics of agent-mediated architectures (Stage 4)

To compare products or suppliers, express preferences, and specify needs, transaction agents have to interact and exchange both syntactic and semantic information with other local or remote agents. They usually communicate through asynchronous message-passing based on speech act theory. Speech acts are actions performed via utterances. The circumstances surrounding the utterance, including other utterances, are called speech events (Yule 1996, 47). For most computing scenarios (Yule 1996, 53f.; Singh 1999, 43), speech acts inform (*assertive*), request (*directive*), promise (*commissive*), give permission for another act (*permissive*), ban another act (*prohibitive*), cause events (*declarative*), or express emotions and evaluations (*expressive*).

The exchange of messages is established via an *agent communication language (ACL)*, which provides agents with a means of exchanging information and knowledge. Every ACL needs a vocabulary, an "inner language" (e.g., *Knowledge Interchange Format | KIF*),[120] and an "outer" language (e.g., *Knowledge Query and Manipulation Language | KQML*). Other popular examples of agent communication languages are the Foundation for Intelligent Physical Agents' *FIPA ACL*, France Télécom's *Arcol*, the *Formal Language for Business Communication (FLBC)*, or *Agent-0* (Labrou et al. 1999, 45ff.; Moore 1999b; Singh 1999, 41).[121]

KQML is a language and protocol for exchanging information and knowledge, which can be used for an application program to interact with an intelligent system or for two or more intelligent systems to share knowledge and solve problems cooperatively.[122] The following example of a simple KQML message uses lambda Prolog (Miller 1991, 497ff.)[123] as the content language to describe a query about the price of a share of stock *(Ballard Power Systems)* and the server's corresponding reply (compare Werthner and Klein 1998, 121; Labrou et al. 1999, 47):

(ask-one	*(tell*
:sender joe	*:sender stock-server*
:content (PRICE BLDP ?price)	*:content (PRICE BLDP 32 1/4)*
:receiver stock-server	*:receiver joe*
:reply-with bldp-stock	*:in-reply-to bldp-stock*
:language LPROLOG	*:language LPROLOG*
:ontology NASDAQ-TICKS)	*:ontology NASDAQ-TICKS)*

Since KQML lacks precise semantics it is applied in conjunction with KIF. The latter is a computer-oriented language for the interchange of knowledge among disparate programs. More precisely, it is a prefix version of first-order predicate calculus with extensions to support meta-operators and definitions (Labrou et al. 1999, 47). As such it includes declarative semantics – i.e., the meaning of expressions in the representation can be understood without referring to an interpreter to manipulate those expressions. KIF is logically comprehensive (i.e., it provides for the expression of arbitrary sentences in the first-order predicate calculus) and provides for meta-knowledge representation (knowledge about knowledge).

---

[120] http://www.csee.umbc.edu/kif/
[121] http://www.fipa.org/
http://www.francetelecom.fr/
http://www-personal.umich.edu/~samoore/research/flbc/
[122] http://www.cs.umbc.edu/kqml/
[123] http://www.cse.psu.edu/~dale/lProlog/

Negotiation processes between business entities are characterized by high degrees of unpredictability, complexity, and strategic importance to organizations (Beam and Segev 1997) and it can be assumed that a number of methods and tools for commercial utilization will be made available with the progress of agent communication languages. With their Java-based *Iconic Modeling Tool*, Falkuk and Karmouch present an early example where users can interactively model agents and their dynamic itineraries in a visual environment (Falchuk and Karmouch 1998, 31ff.). Novice users are able to create complex agents within minutes. However, as the architecture is layered from simple iconic representation down to a textual itinerary language, skilled users can bypass the higher-level interface and program directly in the itinerary language.

6.4.2 Traversal Functions of Agent-Mediated Architectures

It is difficult to identify the hypertextual attributes of agent-mediated architectures, since many of the unique features of digital agents can be realized via rather different presentational techniques. The personal perspective of the traversal function is probably the most important and distinctive characteristic. It is determined by the principal's tasks and goals, which result in a particular set of instructions for the agent. The specification of these instructions represents a permanent change in the semantic structure of the Web information system. In other words, the user (= principal) performs a textonic user function as well. After these initial efforts, she remains passive for a certain period of time (= negotiation phase). Transient traversal functions are common due to the proactive behavior of the agent and cause scriptons to appear, disappear, or evolve without human intervention. The remaining hypertextual dimensions of Figure 6.3 do not differ substantially from advanced adaptive Web information systems of the third stage.

Determinability	Transiency	Perspective	Access
☐ Determinable	☒ Transient	☒ Personal	☒ (Random)
☒ Indeterminable	☐ Intransient	☐ Impersonal	☒ Controlled

Dynamics	Linking	Semantics	User Function
☐ No (Static)	☒ (Explicit)	☐ Limited	☒ Explorative
☒ Intratextonic	☒ Conditional	☐ Supported	☒ Configurative
☒ Textonic	☐ None	☒ Required	☒ Interpretative
			☒ Textonic

Figure 6.3. Hypertextual attributes of agent-mediated architectures

6.4.3   Modeling Multilateral Interactions

"Architects have long understood the relationship between the structure of space and the interactions it can support, and much the same holds true of information structures" (Dourish and Chalmers 1994). Direct interaction of equal partners in an agent-driven communication network environment will bypass the "request-response" model predominant during the first three stages and the underlying protocol (HTTP). Agents generally act independently of specific platform or transport layers, constrained only by their execution environments (Lange and Oshima 1999, 88). The transformation of the client-server infrastructure into an agent-mediated environment with multilateral interactions between independent market participants requires the extension of prevalent modeling approaches to include Web development efforts by all market participants. Figure 6.4 incorporates the feedback loops for the development of two transaction agents interacting via a brokered electronic market. All market participants have to complete the same cycle of design, implementation, usage, and analysis for optimizing the agent's behavior.

The specification of a negotiation agent deals with similar challenges as the development of adaptive Web information systems, but additionally has to embody the principal's intentions and strategies. Besides, the implementation must address the complex infrastructural requirements of transaction agents. Because of the ubiquity of the Java virtual machine and advanced class-loading mechanisms (Wong et al. 1999, 93f.), tools for developing mobile agent systems are often released in the form of Java classes that support their implementation. Popular examples are IBM's *Aglets*,[124] General Magic's *Odyssey*[125] (the Java-based successor to *Telescript*), Mitsubishi Electric's *Concordia,* or Nortel Networks' *FIPA-OS* (Jamali et al. 1999, 44; Koblick 1999, 96f.; Tai and Kosaka 1999, 100f.; FIPA 2000, 2).[126]

---

[124] http://www.research.ibm.com/iagents/
[125] http://www.genmagic.com/
[126] http://www.meitca.com/hsl/projects/concordia/

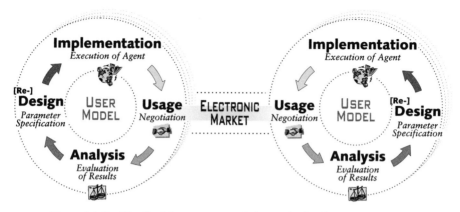

Figure 6.4. Dual feedback loops connected via standardized transaction environments

In the usage phase, agents show more activity compared to earlier stages of Web development, autonomously identifying negotiation partners in their specific transaction environment. It is the usage phase where the agents and their underlying development loops are tangent to each other, with their interaction facilitated by sophisticated electronic infrastructures. Following the usage phase, the principals evaluate the agent and critically review negotiation processes and their outcomes. The insights gained in this analysis phase are then incorporated into the design specifications of the next agent, pursuing a strategy of continuously fine-tuning and optimizing the set of agent parameters. Unfortunately, most of the development methodologies for digital agents are still in their infancy. There are practically no user-friendly tools with graphical interfaces that intuitively implement the underlying theory: "A large and ugly chasm still separates the world of formal theory and infrastructure from the world of practical nuts-and-bolts agent-system development" (Bradshaw et al. 1999, 62).

7 Conclusion and Outlook

Commercial organizations participating in electronic markets are no longer stable but have to adapt continuously to their rapidly shifting environment. Due to a poor understanding of user requirements and a lack of willingness to modify existing organizational structures, the full economic potential of electronic business models has not been realized up until now. With the ongoing introduction of new technologies, strategic management decisions have to consider innovation as a crucial parameter, particularly as far as information and communication technologies are concerned. Innovation threatens traditional business models, substantially reduces their practical value, and disrupts established market structures (Psoinos and Smithson 1999, 32). In such a dynamic and competitive environment, customizing Web information systems receives utmost attention from early adopters. Their efforts focus on gathering information about customers and competitors in their specific business ecosystem. Leveraging the acquired knowledge, Web developers should constantly question and refine the structure and content of their systems. Complex Web applications cannot be fully specified in advance. Like the organizations for which they are built, such information systems are subject to constant adjustment and adaptation (Truex et al. 1999, 123).

Thus, there is a need to radically rethink the process of developing Web-based applications, which requires a continuous and evolutionary perspective founded on iterative cycles of evaluation and refinement. Lengthy analysis, centralized design, and rigid process infrastructures are poor investments in volatile market environments. Considering the emergent character of modern organizations, the value of recurrently gathering, extracting, and analyzing both structural Web data and user requirements has been emphasized throughout this book. Detailed user data can be acquired either explicitly via methods such as question-naires or relevance feedback, or implicitly by observing the behavior of customers and analyzing their individual and aggregated clickstreams. Systematically leveraging the acquired feedback relies heavily not only on the visualization of data, but also on sophisticated data mining ca-pabilities and streamlined maintenance mechanisms. Pre-processed and stored in a user model, information about active and potential custom-ers is employed to tailor content, link structures, and interface repre-sentations.

Only a small amount of literature discusses the automated analysis and industry-wide comparison of Web information systems. This book partially fills the void by introducing a comprehensive suite of analyti-cal techniques that can be combined flexibly to address a broad spec-trum of problem formulations. Specific procedural recommendations referring to the status quo are "little more than a history lesson in past organizational states, and future requirements are abstractions of ob-scure user guesswork about future organizational states" (Truex et al. 1999, 120). This objection represents the primary reason why no strin-gent formal methodology has been developed. Strict procedural guide-lines are replaced by a set of advanced tools that need to be adapted to the organization's situational parameters. This set of tools covers a wide range of analytical objectives, from snapshot analyses to cross-sectional comparisons and longitudinal studies. Trends, cyclical variations, turning points, and marginal changes are monitored for specific indus-tries and structured according to company size, business sector, geo-graphical region, high-level domain, or experience with electronic transactions. These indicators represent a pivotal source of information for maximizing an organization's customer-delivered value. Businesses are able to understand better how the rest of the World Wide Web re-lates to their own system (Paltridge 1999, 338). They can assess alterna-tive investment opportunities on the basis of reliable benchmark data about the differences and the relative performance of their information architectures. Benchmarks indicating weaknesses should trigger and guide the redevelopment and optimization of deployed applications. Founded on the results of general benchmarking, specific hypotheses can be tested regarding the diffusion of particular Internet technologies, implementation strategies of certain organizations, or trends within particular business sectors.

The rapid evolution of electronic marketplaces is not only grounded on the World Wide Web's simple means for authoring documents and accessing its vast resources, but also in its effective support for multiple communication models. Most currently deployed systems rely on the exchange of information between client and server. Digital agent tech-nology, however, which is rapidly becoming a viable and exploitable alternative to the client-server concept, will have a significant impact on the shape and functionality of the World Wide Web (FIPA 2000, 1). At the same time, the increasing popularity of the *Resource Description Framework (RDF)* to convey meta-data and the use of semantic markup languages such as the *eXtensible Markup Language (XML)* for interchange encoding (W3C 2000) confirms the diminishing relative importance of semantically unstructured Web documents. Semantic markup languages ensure interoperability between Web information systems and allow digital agents to share and exchange knowledge. They substantially extend the possibilities of automated Web analysis. Analytical frameworks that leverage the meta-data contained in advanced transaction architectures enable analysts to answer questions of both quantitative and qualitative nature simultaneously.

Adding adaptivity to deployed applications purchases important leverage in volatile market environments, particularly given the wide range of users with heterogeneous needs and preferences. Adaptive Web information systems and agent-mediated architectures serve as excellent examples of the *expansion* stage of Moore's ecology-oriented framework, which has been presented in Section 2.1.2: Electronic Business Ecosystems. To develop and implement these new technologies successfully, cooperation as precondition of co-evolution is a necessity. Up until now, electronic business ecosystems have not reached the stages *authority* or *renewal*. Obviously, some companies are prospering very well and may be regarded as innovators or early adopters. Even though many ambitious efforts to dominate the market can be observed, there still is a lack of formal leadership, which suggests that the real battle for ecosystem leadership is yet to come.

8 References

Aarseth, E.J. (1994). "Nonlinearity and Literary Theory", *Hyper/Text/-Theory*. Ed. G.P. Landow. Baltimore: Johns Hopkins University Press: 51-86.

Aarseth, E.J. (1998). *Cybertext: Perspectives on Ergodic Literature*. Baltimore: Johns Hopkins University Press.

Abiteboul, S., Buneman, P. and Suciu, D. (2000). *Data on the Web: From Relations to Semistructured Data and XML*. San Francisco: Morgan Kaufmann.

Accrue (1999). *eBusiness Analysis and Accrue Insight White Paper*. White Paper, Fremont: Accrue Software. http://www.accrue.com/products/whiteprs.html.

Ackoff, R.L. (1974). "Towards a System of Systems Concepts", *System Analysis Techniques*. Eds. J.D. Couger and R.W. Knapp. New York: John Wiley & Sons: 27-38.

Ackoff, R.L. and Emery, F.E. (1972). *On Purposeful Systems*. Chicago: Aldine Atherton.

Ahlberg, C. and Shneiderman, B. (1994). "Visual Information Seeking: Tight Coupling of Dynamic Query Filters with Starfield Displays", *Conference on Human Factors in Computing Systems (CHI-94)*. Boston, USA: Association for Computing Machinery. 313-317.

Aikat, D. (1995). *Adventure In Cyberspace: Exploring the Information Content of the World Wide Web Pages on the Internet*. Doctoral Thesis, Athens: Ohio University.

Akoulchina, I. and Ganascia, J.-G. (1997). "SATELIT-Agent: An Adaptive Interface Based on Learning Interface Agents Technology", *6th International Conference on User Modeling (UM-97)*. Chia Laguna, Italy: Springer. 21-32.

Albrecht, K. (1993). *Total Quality Service: Das einzige, was zählt.* Düsseldorf: Econ.

Allen, B.L. (1996). *Information Tasks: Toward a User-Centered Approach to Information Systems.* San Diego: Academic Press.

Amor, D. (1999). *The E-business (R)evolution: Living and Working in an Interconnected World.* Upper Saddle River: Prentice Hall.

Andersen, P.B. (1990). *A Theory of Computer Semiotics: Semiotic Approaches to Construction and Assessment of Computer Systems.* Cambridge: Cambridge University Press.

Anderson, J.C. and Narus, J.A. (1998). "Business Marketing: Understand What Customers Value", *Harvard Business Review,* 76(6): 53-65.

Andrews, D.C. and Leventhal, N.S. (1993). *Fusion: Integrating IE, CASE, JAD: A Handbook for Reengineering the Systems Organization.* Englewood Cliffs: Prentice-Hall.

Andrews, K. (1995). "Visualizing Cyberspace: Information Visualization in the Harmony Internet Browser", *1st IEEE Symposium on Information Visualization (InfoVis-95).* Atlanta, USA: IEEE Computer Society: 90-96.

Andrews, K. (1998). "Visualizing Rich, Structured Hypermedia", *IEEE Computer Graphics and Applications,* 18(4): 40-42.

Andrews, K. and Heidegger, H. (1998). "Information Slices: Visualizing and Exploring Large Hierarchies using Cascading, Semi-Circular Discs", *4th IEEE Symposium on Information Visualization (InfoVis-98).* Research Triangle Park, USA: IEEE Computer Society.

Apter, M.J. (1969). "Models of Development", *Survey of Cybernetics: A Tribute to Dr. Norbert Wiener.* Ed. J. Rose. New York: Gordon and Breach: 187-208.

Ardissono, L. and Goy, A. (1999). "Tailoring the Interaction with Users in Electronic Shops", *7th International Conference on User Modeling.* Banff, Canada: Springer. 35-44.

Arthur, L.J. (1991). *Rapid Evolutionary Development.* New York: John Wiley & Sons.

Avison, D. and Fitzgerald, G. (1988). *Information Systems Development: Methodologies, Techniques and Tools.* Oxford: Blackwell.

Baeza-Yates, R. and Ribeiro-Neto, B. (1999). *Modern Information Retrieval.* Harlow: ACM Press Books.

Bakos, Y. (1991). "A Strategic Analysis of Electronic Marketplaces", *MIS Quarterly,* 15(3): 295-310.

Bakos, Y. (1998). "The Emerging Role of Electronic Marketplaces on the Internet", *Communications of the ACM,* 41(8): 35-42.

Balabanovic, M. and Yoav, S. (1997). "Fab: Content-Based, Collaborative Recommendation", *Communications of the ACM,* 40(3): 66-72.

Balasubramanian, V., Ma, B.M. and Yoo, Y. (1995). "A Systematic Approach to Designing a WWW Application", *Communications of the ACM,* 38(8): 47-48.

Barbatsis, G., Fegan, M. and Hansen, K. (1999). "The Performance of Cyberspace: An Exploration Into Computer-Mediated Reality", *Journal of Computer-Mediated Communication,* 5(1): http://www.ascusc.org/jcmc/.

Bardini, T. (1997). "Bridging the Gulfs: From Hypertext to Cyberspace", *Journal of Computer-Mediated Communication,* 3(2): http://www.ascusc.org/jcmc/.

Barrett, R., Maglio, P.P. and Kellem, D.C. (1997). "How to Personalize the Web", *ACM Conference on Human Factors in Computing Systems (CHI-97).* Atlanta, USA: ACM Press. 75-82.

Barthes, R. (1977). "The Death of the Author", *Image-Music-Text.* Ed. S. Heath. London: Fontana: 142-148.

Bates, M.J. and Lu, S. (1997). "An Exploratory Profile of Personal Home Pages: Content, Design, Metaphors", *Online and CDROM Review,* 21(6): 331-340.

Bauer, C. (1998a). *Internet und WWW für Banken: Inhalte, Infrastrukturen und Erfolgsstrategien.* Wiesbaden: Gabler.

Bauer, C. (1998b). "Using Reference Models to Develop WWW-Based Applications", *9th Annual Australasian Conference on Information Systems (ACIS-98).* Sydney, Australia: University of New South Wales. 14-25.

Bauer, C. and Glasson, B. (1998). "Extending the Concept of a Reference Model Across Industries", *IFIP WG 8.2 and 8.6 Joint Working Conference on Information Systems: Current Issues and Future Changes.* Helsinki, Finland: IFIP. 471-487.

Bauer, C., Glasson, B. and Scharl, A. (1999a). "Evolution of Web Information Systems: Exploring the Methodological Shift in the Context of Dynamic Business Ecosystems", *Doing Business on the Internet: Opportunities and Pitfalls.* Eds. C.T. Romm and F. Sudweeks. London: Springer. 53-64.

Bauer, C., Parkinson, A. and Scharl, A. (1999b). "Automated versus Manual Classification: A Multi-Methodological Set of Web Analysis Components", *10th Australasian Conference on Information Systems (ACIS-99).* Wellington, New Zealand: Victoria University of Wellington. 54-64.

Bauer, C. and Scharl, A. (1999a). "Acquisition and Symbolic Visualization of Aggregated Customer Information for Analyzing Web Information Systems", *32nd Hawaii International Conference on System Sciences (HICSS-32).* Maui, USA: IEEE Computer Society Press.

Bauer, C. and Scharl, A. (1999b). "A Classification Framework and Assessment Model for Automated Web Site Evaluation", *7th European Conference on Information Systems (ECIS-99).* Copenhagen, Denmark: Copenhagen Business School. 758-765.

Bauer, C. and Scharl, A. (2000). "Quantitative Evaluation of Web Site Content and Structure", *Internet Research: Networking Applications and Policy,* 10(1): 31-43.

BBC (1999a). British Nuclear Fuel Ships Armed. *BBC Online Network.* London. http://news.bbc.co.uk/.

BBC (1999b). Nuclear Exporter Freezes Greenpeace Cash. *BBC Online Network.* London. http://news.bbc.co.uk/.

BBC (1999c). Stormy Waters for Nuclear Shipments. *BBC Online Network.* London. http://news.bbc.co.uk/.

Beam, C. and Segev, A. (1996). *The Rise of Electronic Commerce: Contributions from Three Factors (= CMIT Working Paper 96-WP-1015).* Berkeley: Fisher Center for Management and Information Technology University of California.

Beam, C. and Segev, A. (1997). "Automated Negotiations: A Survey of the State of the Art", *Wirtschaftsinformatik,* 39(3): 263-268.

Beard, D.V. and Walker, J.Q. (1990). "Navigational Techniques to Improve the Display of Large Two-dimensional Spaces", *Behavior & Information Technology*, 9: 451-466.

Beaudoin, L., Parent, M.-A. and Vroomen, L.C. (1996). "Cheops: A Compact Explorer for Complex Hierarchies", *2nd IEEE Symposium on Information Visualization (InfoVis-96)*. San Francisco, USA: IEEE Computer Society. 87-92.

Beaumont, I.H. (1998). "User Modelling in the Interactive Anatomy Tutoring System ANATOM-TUTOR", *Adaptive Hypertext and Hypermedia*. Eds. P. Brusilovsky et al. Dordrecht: Kluwer Academic Publishers: 91-115.

Becker, W. (1973). *Beobachtungsverfahren in der demoskopischen Marktforschung*. Stuttgart: Ulmer.

Belady, L.A. and Lehman, M.M. (1976). "A Model of Large Program Development", *IBM System Journal*, 15(3): 225-252.

Belz, C. (1997). *Strategisches Direct Marketing: Vom sporadischen Direct Mail zum professionellen Database Management*. Vienna: Ueberreuter.

Benbow, M.P. (1998). "File not Found: The Problems of Changing URLs for the World Wide Web", *Internet Research: Networking Applications and Policy*, 8(3): 247-250.

Bentley, R. and Dourish, P. (1995). "Medium versus Mechanism: Supporting Collaboration through Customisation", *4th European Conference on Computer-Supported Cooperative Work (ECSCW-95)*. Stockholm, Sweden: Kluwer.

Berners-Lee, T., Cailliau, R., et al. (1994). "The World-Wide Web", *Communications of the ACM*, 37(8): 76-82.

Berthold, M. (1999). "Fuzzy Logic", *Intelligent Data Analysis: An Introduction*. Eds. M. Berthold and D.J. Hand. Berlin: Springer. 269-298.

Bertin, J. (1982). *Graphics and Graphic Information Processing*. Berlin: Walter De Gruyter.

Bichler, M. and Nusser, S. (1996a). "Modular Design of Complex Web-Applications with W3DT", *5th Workshop on Enabling Technologies: Infrastructure for Collaborative Enterprises (WETICE-96)*. Stanford, USA: IEEE Computer Society Press. 328-333.

Bichler, M. and Nusser, S. (1996b). "SHDT: The Structured Way of Developing WWW-Sites", *4th European Conference on Information Systems (ECIS-96)*. Lisbon, Portugal. 1093-1101.

Bichler, M. and Scharl, A. (1999). "Multi-dimensional Approaches to Automating Resource Allocation", *1st International Workshop for Transaction-based Electronic Commerce (IWTEC-99)*. Perth, Australia: Electronic Commerce Network, Curtin University of Technology. 1-8.

Bieber, M. (1997). "Enhancing Information Comprehension Through Hypertext", *Intelligent Hypertext: Advanced Techniques for the World Wide Web*. Eds. C. Nicholas and J. Mayfield. Berlin: Springer. 1-11.

Blasius, J. (1994). "Correspondence Analysis in Social Science Research", *Correspondence Analysis in the Social Sciences*. Eds. M. Greenacre and J. Blasius. London: Academic Press. 23-52.

Bolisani, E. (1999). "Communication Processes and Electronic Communication: A Framework for the Assessment", *7th European Conference on Information Systems (ECIS-99)*. Copenhagen, Denmark: Copenhagen Business School. 27-39.

Bolter, J.D. (1991). *Writing Space: The Computer, Hypertext, and the History of Writing*. Hillsdale: Lawrence Erlbaum Associated.

Bolter, J.D. and Grusin, R. (1999). *Remediation: Understanding New Media*. Cambridge: MIT Press.

Booz-Allen (1999). *Corporate Internet Banking: A Global Study of Potential*, Booz-Allen & Hamilton. http://www.bah.com/press/net_-corpbank.html.

Bordewijk, J.L. and van Kaam, B. (1986). "Towards a New Classification of Tele-Information Services", *InterMedia*, 14(1): 16-21.

Borges, J.L. (1981). "The Garden of the Forking Paths", *Labyrinths: Selected Stories and other Writings*. Eds. D.A. Yates and J.E. Irby. Harmondsworth: Penguin Books. 44-54.

Bortz, J. (1999). *Statistik für Sozialwissenschaftler*. Berlin: Springer.

Boulanger, G.R. (1969). "Prologue: What is Cybernetics?", *Survey of Cybernetics: A Tribute to Dr. Norbert Wiener*. Ed. J. Rose. New York: Gordon and Breach. 3-9.

Boyle, C. (1998). "Metadoc: An Adaptive Hypertext Reading System", *Adaptive Hypertext and Hypermedia*. Eds. P. Brusilovsky et al. Dordrecht: Kluwer Academic Publishers. 71-89.

Bradshaw, J.M., Greaves, M., et al. (1999). "Agents for the Masses?", *IEEE Intelligent Systems*, 14(2): 53-63.

Brancheau, J.C., Janz, B.D. and Wetherbe, J.C. (1996). "Key Issues in Information Systems Management: 1994-95 SIM Delphi Results", *MIS Quarterly*, 20(2): 225-242.

Brandtweiner, R., Loicht, H. and Scharl, A. (1998). "The Internet-induced Digitalization of Commodities (Products)", *Forum Ware*, 26(1): 37-40.

Brandtweiner, R. and Scharl, A. (1999a). "An Institutional Approach to Analyzing the Structure and Functionality of Brokered Electronic Markets", *International Journal of Electronic Commerce*, 3(3): 71-88.

Brandtweiner, R. and Scharl, A. (1999b). "Value Chain Transformation in the Retailing Sector", *Systémová Integrace (System Integration)*, 6(3): 7-14.

Brenner, W., Zarnekow, R. and Wittig, H. (1998). *Intelligente Softwareagenten: Grundlagen und Anwendungen*. Berlin: Springer.

Brereton, P., Budgen, D. and Hamilton, G. (1998). "Hypertext: The Next Maintenance Mountain", *Computer*, 31(12): 49-55.

Broadvision (2000). *Finding the 80-20 Solution*, Broadvision. http://-www.broadvision.com.

Brown, R.D. and Prentice, D.G. (1987). "Assessing Decision Making Risk and Information Needs in Evaluation", *Evaluation Review*, 11(3): 371-381.

Brusilovsky, P. (1997). "Efficient Techniques for Adaptive Hypermedia", *Intelligent Hypertext: Advanced Techniques for the World Wide Web*. Eds. C. Nicholas and J. Mayfield. Berlin: Springer. 12-30.

Brusilovsky, P. (1998). "Methods and Techniques of Adaptive Hypermedia", *Adaptive Hypertext and Hypermedia*. Eds. P. Brusilovsky et al. Dordrecht: Kluwer Academic Publishers. 1-43.

Bryson, S., Kenwright, D., et al. (1999). "Visually Exploring Gigabyte Data Sets in Real Time", *Communications of the ACM*, 42(8): 83-90.

Buchanan, R.W. and Lukaszewski, C. (1997). *Measuring the Impact of Your Web Site: Proven Yardsticks for Evaluating Customer Impact, Site Evolution, Revenue Growth, and Return on Investment*. New York: John Wiley & Sons.

Bucy, E.P., Lang, A., Potter, R.F. and Grabe, M.E. (1999). "Formal Features of Cyberspace: Relationships Between Web Page Complexity and Site Traffic", *49th Annual Conference of the International Communication Association (ICA-99)*. San Francisco, USA.

Burbules, N.C. and Callister, T.A. (1996). "Knowledge at the Crossroads: Alternative Futures of Hypertext Environments for Learning", *Educational Theory*, 46(1). 23-50.

Busch, D.D. (1997). "Count Your Blessings", *Internet World*, 8(6): 75-83.

Bush, V. (1945). "As We May Think", *The Atlantic Monthly*, 176(1): 101-108.

Button, G. and Dourish, P. (1996). "Technomethodology: Paradoxes and Possibilities", *ACM Conference on Human Factors in Computing Systems (CHI-96)*. Vancouver, Canada: Association for Computing Machinery. 19-26.

Calway, B.A. and Smith, R. (1998). "Discourse Strategies Model: A Proof-Of-Concept Research Design", *9th Annual Australasian Conference on Information Systems (ACIS-98)*. Sidney, Australia: University of New South Wales.

Campbell, C.S. and Maglio, P.P. (1999). "A Framework for Understanding Human Factors in Web-based Electronic Commerce", *International Journal of Human-Computer Studies*, 50(4): 309-327.

Card, S.K., Mackinlay, J.D. and Shneiderman, B. (1999). *Readings in Information Visualization: Using Vision to Think*. San Francisco: Morgan Kaufmann.

Carnahan, B. and Smith, A.E. (1997). *User's Guide to Pittnet Neural Network Educational Software*, Pittsburgh: University of Pittsburgh. http://www.pitt.edu/~aesmith/.

Carpendale, M.S.T., Cowperthwaite, D.J. and Fracchia, F.D. (1997). "Extending Distortion Viewing from 2D to 3D", *IEEE Computer Graphics and Applications*, 17(4): 42-51.

Carrière, J. and Kazman, R. (1995). "Interacting with Huge Hierarchies: Beyond Cone Trees", *1st IEEE Symposium on Information Visualization (InfoVis-95)*. Atlanta, USA: IEEE Computer Society. 74-81.

Caudill, E. (1997). *Darwinian Myths: The Legends and Misuses of a Theory*. Knoxville: University of Tennessee Press.

Chakrabarti, S., Dom, B.E., et al. (1999). "Mining the Web's Link Structure", *IEEE Computer*, 32(8): 60-67.

Chandrasekaran, B., Josephson, J.R. and Benjamins, R. (1999). "What Are Ontologies, and Why Do We Need Them?", *IEEE Intelligent Systems*, 14(1): 20-26.

Chatzoglou, P.D. (1997). "Use of Methodologies: An Empirical Analysis of their Impact on the Economics of the Development Process", *European Journal of Information Systems*, 6(4): 256-270.

Chavez, A. and Maes, P. (1996). "Kasbah: An Agent Marketplace for Buying and Selling Goods", *1st International Conference on the Practical Application of Intelligent Agents and Multi-Agent Technology (PAAM-96)*. London, UK: Practical Application Company. 75-90.

Chen, C. and Rada, R. (1996). "Modelling Situated Actions in Collaborative Hypertext Databases", *Journal of Computer-Mediated Communication*, 2(3): http://www.ascusc.org/jcmc/.

Chen, H., Nunamaker, J., Orwig, R. and Titkova, O. (1998). "Information Visualization for Collaborative Computing", *Computer*, 31(8): 75-82.

Chen, L.-d., Sherrell, L.B. and Hsu, C.-Y. (1999). "A Development Methodology for Corporate Web Sites", *First ICSE Workshop on Web Engineering (WebE-99)*. Los Angeles, USA: 19-28.

Chi, E.H., Pitkow, J., et al. (1998). "Visualizing the Evolution of Web Ecologies", *Conference on Human Factors in Computing Systems (CHI-98)*. Los Angeles, USA: Association for Computing Machinery. 400-407.

Chi, E.H. (1999a). *A Framework for Information Visualization Spreadsheets*. Doctoral Thesis, Minneapolis: University of Minnesota.

Chi, E.H. (1999b). "Web Analysis Visualization Spreadsheet", *Digital Library Workshop on Organizing Web Space (WOWS-99)*. Berkeley, USA: Association for Computing Machinery. 24-31.

Chimera, R. and Shneiderman, B., (1994). "An Exploratory Evaluation of Three Interfaces for Browsing Large Hierarchical Tables of Contents", *ACM Transactions on Information Systems*, 12(4): 383-406.

Choi, S.-Y., Stahl, D.O. and Whinston, A.B. (1997). *The Economics of Electronic Commerce*. Indianapolis: Macmillan.

Chomsky, N. (1986). "Barriers", *Linguistic Inquiry Monographs Series*. Cambridge: MIT Press. 13.

Chomsky, N. (1991). "Some Notes on Economy of Derivation and Representation", *Principles and Parameters in Comparative Grammar*. Ed. R. Freidin. Cambridge: MIT Press. 417-454.

Chuah, M.C., Roth, S.F., Mattis, J. and Kolojejchick, J. (1995). "SDM: Selective Dynamic Manipulation of Visualizations", *8th Annual Symposium on User Interface Software and Technology (UIST-95)*. Pittsburgh, USA: Association for Computing Machinery. 61-70.

Cleland, A.S. and Bruno, A.V. (1996). *The Market Value Process: Bridging Customer and Shareholder Value*. San Francisco: Jossey-Bass Publishers.

Clemons, E.K., Reddi, S.P. and Row, M.C. (1993). "The Impact of Information Technology on the Organization of Economic Activity: The "Move to the Middle" Hypothesis", *Journal of Management Information Systems*, 10(2): 9-35.

Cohen, J. (1998). "It's Nothing Personal", *The Industry Standard*, 07-12-1998.

Collins, A.M. and Loftus, E.F. (1975). "A Spreading Activation Theory of Semantic Processing", *Psychological Review*, 82: 407-428.

Conklin, J. (1987). "Hypertext: An Introduction and Survey", *IEEE Computer*, 20(9): 17-41.

Corradi, A., Cremonini, M., Montanari, R. and Stefanelli, C. (1999). "Mobile Agents Integrity for Electronic Commerce Applications", *Information Systems*, 24(6): 519-533.

Cover, R. (1998). *XML and Semantic Transparency*, Organization for the Advancement of Structured Information Standards (OASIS). http://www.oasis-open.org/cover/xmlAndSemantics.html.

Crabtree, A., Nichols, D.M., et al. (1998). *The Contribution of Ethnomethodologically-informed Ethnography to the Process of Designing Digital Libraries*, Lancaster: Lancaster University. http://www.comp.lancs.ac.uk/computing/research/cseg/projects/ariadne/docs/ethno.html.

Crimmins, F. and Smeaton, A.F. (1999). "TétraFusion: Information Discovery on the Internet", *IEEE Intelligent Systems*, 14(4): 55-62.

Crowston, K. and Williams, M. (1999). "The Effects on Linking on Genres of Web Documents", *32nd Hawaii International Conference on System Sciences (HICSS-32)*. Hawaii, USA: IEEE Computer Society Press.

Damsgaard, J. and Scheepers, R. (1999). "A Stage Model of Intranet Technology Implementation and Management", *7th European Conference on Information Systems (ECIS-99)*. Copenhagen, Denmark: Copenhagen Business School. 100-116.

Darwin, C. (1859). *The Origin of Species by Means of Natural Selection or the Preservation of Favoured Races in the Struggle for Life*. London: John Murray.

De Certeau, M. (1983). *The Practice of Everyday Life*. Berkeley: University of California Press.

De Fanti, T.A., Brown, M.D. and McCormick, B.H. (1989). "Visualization - Expanding Scientific and Engineering Research Opportunities", *IEEE Computer*, 22(8): 15-25.

De Troyer, O. and Leune, K. (1998). "WSDM: A User-Centered Design Method for Web Sites", *7th International World Wide Web Conference (WWW7)*. Brisbane, Australia: Elsevier. 85-94.

Deledalle, G. (1997). "Media between Balnibarbi and Plato's Cave", *Semiotics of the Media: State of the Art, Projects, and Perspectives*. Ed. W. Nöth. Berlin: Mouton de Gruyter. 49-60.

Demczynksi, S. (1969). "The Tools of the Cybernetic Revolution", *Survey of Cybernetics: A Tribute to Dr. Norbert Wiener*. Ed. J. Rose. New York: Gordon and Breach. 10-28.

Deshpande, Y., Hansen, S. and Murugesan, S. (1999). "Web Engineering: Beyond CS, IS and SE - An Evolutionary and Non-Engineering Perspective", *First ICSE Workshop on Web Engineering (WebE-99)*. Los Angeles, USA. 10-16.

Díaz, A. and Melster, R. (1999). "Designing Virtual WWW Environments: Flexible Design for Supporting Dynamic Behavior", *First ICSE Workshop on Web Engineering (WebE-99)*. Los Angeles, USA.

DiCarlo, L. (2000). *Tucci: More Acquisitions, Partnerships for EMC*: PC Week Online. http://www.zdnet.com/pcweek/.

Dillon, A. and Watson, C. (1996). "User Analysis in HCI: The Historical Lesson from Individual Differences Research", *International Journal of Human-Computer Studies*, 45(6): 619-637.

Dix, A.J., Finlay, J.E., Abowd, G.D. and Beale, R. (1998). *Human-Computer Interaction*. Hemel Hempstead: Prentice Hall.

Douglas, J.Y. (1994). "How Do I Stop This Thing? - Closure and Indeterminacy in Interactive Narratives", *Hyper/Text/Theory*. Ed. G.P. Landow. Baltimore: Johns Hopkins University Press. 159-188.

Dourish, P. and Chalmers, M. (1994). "Running out of Space: Models of Information Navigation", *Ninth Conference of the British Computer Society Human Computer Interaction Specialist Group*. Glasgow, Scotland: Cambridge University Press.

Doux, A.-C., Laurent, J.-P. and Nadal, J.-P. (1997). "Symbolic Data Analysis With the K-Means Algorithm for User Profiling", *6th International Conference on User Modeling (UM-97)*. Chia Laguna, Italy: Springer. 359-361.

Dunning, T. (1993). "Accurate Methods for the Statistics of Surprise and Coincidence", *Computational Linguistics*, 19(1): 61-74.

Dutta, S., Kwan, S. and Segev, A. (1997). *Transforming Business in the Marketspace: Strategic Marketing and Customer Relationships (= CMIT Working Paper)*. Berkeley: Fisher Center for Management and Information Technology University of California.

Earman, J. (1993). "Carnap, Kuhn, and the Philosophy of Scientific Methodology", *World Changes: Thomas Kuhn and the Nature of Science*. Ed. P. Horwich. Cambridge: MIT Press. 9-36.

ECMA (1999). *ECMAScript Language Specification*, Geneva: European Computer Manufacturers Association (ECMA). ftp://ftp.ecma.ch/-ecma-st/Ecma-262.pdf.

Economist (1995). Electric Metre. *The Economist*. http://www.economist.com/archive.

Eldredge, N. (1995). *Reinventing Darwin: The Great Evolutionary Debate*. London: Weidenfeld & Nicolson.

Engelbart, D.C. and English, W.K. (1968). "A Research Center for Augmenting Human Intellect", *Fall Joint Computer Conference (AFIPS-68)*. San Francisco, USA: 395-410.

Eriksen, L.B. and Ihlström, C. (2000). "Evolution of the Web News Genre - The Slow Move Beyond the Print Metaphor", *33rd Hawaii International Conference on System Sciences (HICSS-33)*. Hawaii, USA: IEEE Computer Society Press.

Fabian, A.C. (1998). "Introduction", *Evolution: Society, Science and the Universe*. Ed. A.C. Fabian. Cambridge: Cambridge University Press.

Fairclough, N. (1995). *Media Discourse*. London: Edward Arnold.

Falchuk, B. and Karmouch, A. (1998). "Visual Modeling for Agent-Based Applications", *Computer*, 31(12): 31-38.

Feelders, A.J. (1999). "Statistical Concepts", *Intelligent Data Analysis: An Introduction*. Eds. M. Berthold and D.J. Hand. Berlin: Springer. 15-66.

Fidler, R. (1997). *Mediamorphosis: Understanding New Media*. Thousand Oaks: Pine Forge Press.

Finin, T.W. (1989). "GUMS - A General User Modeling Shell", *User Models in Dialog Systems*. Eds. A. Kobsa and W. Wahlster. Berlin: Springer. 411-430.

Finnie, G. and Wittig, G. (1998). "Electronic Commerce via Personalised Virtual Electronic Catalogues", *2nd Annual Collaborative Electronic Commerce Technology and Research Conference (CollECTeR-98)*. Sydney, Australia: University of Wollongong. 6-14.

FIPA (2000). *Inform! The Newsletter for the Foundation of Intelligent Physical Agents,* Foundation of Intelligent Physical Agents. http://-www.fipa.org/.

Flammia, G. (1999). "The Skinny on Metadata", *IEEE Intelligent Systems,* 14(4): 20-22.

Fogel, D.B. (1997). "Evolutionary Computation: An Introduction, Some Current Applications, and Future Directions", *Brain-like Computing and Intelligent Information Systems*. Eds. S.-i. Amari and N. Kasabov. Singapore: Springer. 275-292.

Fournier, R. (1998). *A Methodology for Client/Server and Web Application Development*. Upper Saddle River: Yourdon Press.

Fowler, M. and Scott, K. (1997). *UML Distilled: Applying the Standard Object Modeling Language*. Reading: Addison-Wesley.

Frazer, C. and McMillan, S.J. (1999). "Sophistication on the World Wide Web: Evaluating Structure, Function, and Commercial Goals of Web Sites", *Advertising and Consumer Psychology Conference*. Bloomfield Hills, USA: Lawrence Erlbaum.

Freisler, S. and Kesseler, M. (1997). *Document Engineering,* Schema GmbH. http://www.schema.de/doku/html-deu/schemapu/vortrag/-document.htm.

Fricke, D. (1990). *Einführung in die Korrespondenzanalyse*. Frankfurt: R. G. Fischer.

Froomkin, M. (1996). "Flood Control on the Information Ocean: Living With Anonymity, Digital Cash, and Distributed Databases", *University of Pittsburgh Journal of Law and Commerce,* 395(15): http://-www.pitt.edu/~jourlc/.

Fulk, J. and DeSanctis, G. (1995). "Electronic Communication and Changing Organizational Forms", *Organization Science,* 6(4): 337-349.

Furnas, G.W. (1981). *The Fisheye View: A New Look at Structured Files*. Technical Memorandum, New Jersey: Bell Laboratories.

Furnas, G.W. (1986). "Generalized Fisheye Views", *ACM Conference on Human Factors in Computing Systems (CHI-86)*. Boston, USA: Association for Computing Machinery. 16-23.

Gale, B.T. and Wood, R.C. (1994). *Managing Customer Value: Creating Quality and Service That Customers Can See*. New York: Free Press.

Garrett, P. and Bell, A. (1998). "Media and Discourse: A Critical Overview", *Approaches to Media Discourse*. Eds. A. Bell and P. Garrett. Oxford: Blackwell. 1-20.

Garzotto, F., Mainetti, L. and Paolini, P. (1995). "Hypermedia Design, Analysis, and Evaluation Issues", *Communications of the ACM*, 38(8): 74-86.

Garzotto, F., Mainetti, L. and Paolini, P. (1996). "Navigation in Hypermedia Applications: Modeling and Semantics", *Journal of Organizational Computing and Electronic Commerce*, 6(3): 211-237.

Garzotto, F., Paolini, P. and Schwabe, D. (1993). "HDM: A Model-based Approach to Hypertext Application Design", *ACM Transactions on Information Systems*, 11(1): 1-26.

Gay, G. and Lentini, M. (1995). "Use of Communication Resources in a Networked Collaborative Design Environment", *Journal of Computer-Mediated Communication*, 1(1): http://www.ascusc.org/jcmc/.

Gay, G., Sturgill, A., Martin, W. and Huttenlocher, D. (1999). "Document-centered Peer Collaborations: An Exploration of the Educational Uses of Networked Communication Technologies", *Journal of Computer-Mediated Communication*, 4(3): http://www.ascusc.org/jcmc/.

Gebauer, J. (1996). *Informationstechnische Unterstützung von Transaktionen*. Wiesbaden: Gabler.

Gebauer, J. and Scharl, A. (1999). "Between Flexibility and Automation: An Evaluation of Web Technology from a Business Process Perspective", *Journal of Computer-mediated Communication*, 5(1): http://www.ascusc.org/jcmc/.

Geldof, S. (1997). "Generating Text in Context", *PhD Workshop on Natural Language Generation (ESSLLI-97)*. Aix-en-Provence, France: http://www.lpl.univ-aix.fr/~esslli97/.

Giannoccaro, A., Shanks, G. and Darke, P. (1999). "Stakeholder Perceptions of Data Quality in a Data Warehouse Environment", *Australian Computer Journal*, 31(4): 110-116.

Gibson, W. (1984). *Neuromancer*. New York: Ace Books.

Gibson, W. (1992). *Agrippa: A Book of the Dead*. New York: Kevin Begos.

Ginsburg, M. (1998). "Annotate! A Tool for Collaborative Information Retrieval", *7th International Workshops on Enabling Technologies: Infrastructure for Collaborative Enterprises (WETICE-98)*. Stanford, USA: IEEE Computer Society Press.

Ginsburg, M. and Kambil, A. (1999). "Annotate: A Web-based Knowledge Management Support System for Document Collections", *32nd Hawaii International Conference on System Sciences (HICSS-32)*. Hawaii, USA: IEEE Computer Society Press.

Glushko, R.J., Tenenbaum, J.M. and Meltzer, B. (1999). "An XML Framework for Agent-based E-commerce", *Communications of the ACM*, 42(3): 106-114.

Gnaho, C. and Larcher, F. (1999). "A User Centered Methodology for Complex and Customizable Web Applications Engineering", *First ICSE Workshop on Web Engineering (WebE-99)*. Los Angeles, USA.

Godehardt, E. (1990). *Graphs as Structural Models: The Application of Graphs and Multigraphs in Cluster Analysis*. Braunschweig: Vieweg.

Gray, S.H. (1993). *Hypertext and the Technology of Conversation: Orderly Situational Choice*. Westport: Greenwood Press.

Greenacre, M. (1994). "Correspondence Analysis and its Interpretation", *Correspondence Analysis in the Social Sciences*. Eds. M. Greenacre and J. Blasius. London: Academic Press: 3-22.

Greenpeace (1999a). *Greenpeace Calls Upon the British, French and Japanese Governments to Ban the Imminent Shipment of Weapon-Usable Plutonium Fuel from Europe to Japan*. Press Release, Geneva: Greenpeace International. http://www.greenpeace.org/pressreleases/.

Greenpeace (1999b). *UK Government Imposes Draconian Ban on Greenpeace Vessel to Silence Opposition to Plutonium Transports*. Press Release, Geneva: Greenpeace International. http://www.greenpeace.org/pressreleases/.

Gresik, T. and Satterthwaite, M.A. (1989). "The Rate at which a Simple Market Converges to Efficiency as the Number of Traders Increases: An Asymptotic Result for Optimal Trading Mechanisms", *Journal of Economic Theory*, 48: 304-332.

Grover, P. and Evans, R. (2000). *Europe's Year of the Internet: Bricks and Clicks*, London: E-Audits. http://www.novell.com/corp/intl/uk/company/web100_2000.html.

Günther, O. (1998). *Environmental Information Systems*. Berlin: Springer.

Guthrie, J.T. and Kirsch, I.S. (1987). "Distinctions between Reading Comprehension and Locating Information in Text", *Journal of Educational Psychology*, 79: 220-227.

Guttman, R., Moukas, A. and Maes, P. (1998). "Agent-Mediated Electronic Commerce: A Survey", *Knowledge Engineering Review*, 13(2): 147-160.

Ha, L. and James, E.L. (1998). "Interactivity Reexamined: A Baseline Analysis of Early Business Web Sites", *Journal of Broadcasting and Electronic Media*, 42(4): 457-474.

Halasz, F. and Schwartz, M. (1994). "The Dexter Hypertext Reference Model", *Communications of the ACM*, 37(2): 30-39.

Haller, S. (1997). *Handels-Marketing*. Ludwigshafen: Kiehl.

Halliday, M.A. (1998). *Introduction to Functional Grammar*. London: Edward Arnold Press.

Hansen, H.R. (1995). "Conceptual Framework and Guidelines for the Implementation of Mass Information Systems", *Information & Management*, 28(2): 125-142.

Hansen, H.R. (1996a). *Klare Sicht am Info-Highway: Geschäfte via Internet & Co*. Vienna: Orac.

Hansen, H.R. (1996b). *Wirtschaftsinformatik I. Grundlagen betrieblicher Datenverarbeitung*. Stuttgart: Lucius & Lucius.

Hansen, H.R. and Scharl, A. (1998). "Cooperative Development of Web-based Mass Information Systems", *4th Americas Conference on Information Systems (AIS-98)*. Baltimore, USA: Association for Information Systems. 994-996.

Hansen, H.R. and Tesar, M.F. (1996). "Die Integration von Masseninformationssystemen in die betriebliche Informationsverarbeitung", *Fachtagung "Data Warehouse" an der Gerhard-Mercator-Universität GH Duisburg*. Duisburg, Germany.

Harpold, T. (1994). "Conclusions", *Hyper/Text/Theory*. Ed. G.P. Landow. Baltimore: Johns Hopkins University Press. 189-222.

Hars, A. (1994). *Referenzdatenmodelle: Grundlagen effizienter Datenmodellierung*. Wiesbaden: Gabler.

Hasler, F., Palaniappan, K., Manyin, M. and Dodge, J. (1994). "A High-Performance Interactive Image Spreadsheet (IISS)", *Computers Physics,* 8(3): 325-342.

Hemingway, C.J. (1999). "Toward a Socio-cognitive Theory of Information Systems: An Analysis of Key Philosophical and Conceptual Issues", *IFIP WG 8.2 and 8.6 Joint Working Conference on Information Systems: Current Issues and Future Changes.* Helsinki, Finland: IFIP. 275-286.

Hendley, R.J., Drew, N.S., Wood, A.M. and Beale, R. (1995). "Narcissus: Visualizing Information", *1st IEEE Symposium on Information Visualization (InfoVis-95).* Atlanta, USA: IEEE Computer Society. 90-96.

Henry, T.R. (1992). *Interactive Graph Layout: The Exploration of Large Graphs.* Doctoral Thesis, Tucson: University of Arizona.

Henry, T.R. and Hudson, S.E. (1991). "Interactive Graph Layout", *ACM Siggraph Symposium on User Interface Software and Technology.* Hilton Head, USA: Association for Computing Machinery. 55-64.

Herman, I., Melançon, G., de Ruiter, M.M. and Delest, M. (1999). *Latour - A Tree Visualization System,* Amsterdam: National Research Institute for Mathematics and Computer Science. http://www.cwi.nl-/InfoVisu/papers/LatourOverview.pdf.

Herring, S.C. (1999a). "Interactional Coherence in CMC", *Journal of Computer-Mediated Communication,* 4(4): http://www.ascusc.org/-jcmc/.

Herring, S.C. (1999b). "Interactional Coherence in CMC", *32nd Hawaii International Conference on System Sciences (HICSS-32).* Hawaii, USA: IEEE Computer Society Press.

Hess, T. and Brecht, L. (1995). *State of the Art of Business Process Redesign: Description and Comparison of Existing Methods (in German).* Wiesbaden: Gabler.

Ho, J. (1997). "Evaluating the World Wide Web: A Global Study of Commercial Sites", *Journal of Computer-Mediated Communication,* 3(1): http://www.ascusc.org/jcmc/.

Hochheiser, H.S. and Shneiderman, B. (1999). *Understanding Patterns of User Visits to Web Sites: Interactive Starfield Visualizations of WWW Log Data.* Technical Report, College Park: University of Maryland, Department of Computer Science. http://www.cs.umd.-edu/hcil/pubs/.

Hoffer, J.A., George, J.F. and Valacich, J.S. (1999). *Modern Systems Analysis and Design.* Reading: Addison-Wesley.

Hoffman, D.L., Novak, T.P. and Chatterjee, P. (1997). "Commercial Scenarios for the Web: Opportunities and Challenges", *Journal of Computer-Mediated Communication.* 1(3): http://www.ascusc.org/-jcmc/.

Hoffman, D.L., Novak, T.P. and Peralta, M. (1999). "Building Consumer Trust Online", *Communications of the ACM,* 42(4): 80-85.

Hohl, H., Böcker, H.-D. and Gunzenhäuser, R. (1998). "Hypadapter: An Adaptive Hypertext System for Exploratory Learning and Programming", *Adaptive Hypertext and Hypermedia.* Eds. P. Brusilovsky et al. Dordrecht: Kluwer Academic Publishers. 117-142.

Holland, J.H. (1995). *Hidden Order: How Adaptation Builds Complexity.* Reading: Perseus Books.

Höök, K., Karlgren, J., et al. (1998). "A Glass Box Approach to Adaptive Hypermedia", *Adaptive Hypertext and Hypermedia.* Eds. P. Brusilovsky et al. Dordrecht: Kluwer Academic Publishers. 143-170.

Hopkins, S. (1992). "Camels and Needles: Computer Poetry Meets the Perl Programming Language", *Usenix Winter 1992 Technical Conference.* San Francisco.

Horn, R.E. (1989). *Mapping Hypertext: The Analysis, Organization, and Display of Knowledge for the Next Generation of On-line Text and Graphics.* Lexington: Lexington Institute.

Hornback, R. (1995). *An EDI Cost/Benefits Framework,* Electronic Commerce World. http://www.ecworld.org/Resource_Center/Case-_Studies/hornback.html.

Hüttner, M. (1997). *Grundzüge der Marktforschung.* Munich: Oldenbourg.

IEEE (1999a). *IEEE Web Publishing Guide,* Institute of Electrical and Electronics Engineers. http://www.ieee.org/web/developers/style/index.html.

IEEE (1999b). *Volume 1: Customer and Terminology Standards.* Piscataway: IEEE Computer Society Press.

Inform (1997). *FuzzyTech 5.0 User's Manual.* Aachen: Inform Software Corporation.

Ipsen, G. (1997). "Linguistic Orientation in Computational Space", *Semiotics of the Media: State of the Art, Projects, and Perspectives.* Ed. W. Nöth. Berlin: Mouton de Gruyter. 559-573.

Isakowitz, T., Stohr, E.A. and Balasubramanian, P. (1995). "RMM: A Methodology for Structured Hypermedia Design", *Communications of the ACM,* 38(8): 34-44.

Ishai, A. and Sagi, D. (1995). "Common Mechanisms of Visual Imagery and Perception", *Science,* 268: 1772-1774.

Jackson, M.H. (1997). "Assessing the Structure of Communication on the World Wide Web", *Journal of Computer-Mediated Communication,* 3(1): http://www.ascusc.org/jcmc/.

Jacobson, I., Booch, G. and Rumbaugh, J. (1999). *The Unified Software Development Process.* Reading: Addison-Wesley.

Jamali, N., Thati, P. and Agha, G.A. (1999). "An Actor-based Architecture for Customizing and Controlling Agent Ensembles", *IEEE Intelligent Systems,* 14(2): 38-44.

Jasper, J.E., Ellis, R.D. and Wajahath, S. (1998). *Towards a Discourse Analysis of User Clickstreams on the Web,* Institute of Gerontology, Wayne State University. http://giw.iog.wayne.edu/manuscripts/web-discourse/.

Jaspersen, T. (1997). *Computergestütztes Marketing: Controllingorientierte DV-Verfahren für Absatz und Vertrieb.* Munich: Oldenbourg.

Jensen, J.F. (1998). "Interactivity: Tracing a New Concept in Media and Communication Studies", *Nordicom Review,* 19: 185-204.

Johnson, B. and Shneiderman, B. (1991). "Tree-Maps: A Space-Filling Approach to the Visualization of Hierarchical Information Structures", *IEEE Visualization '91 Conference.* San Diego, USA: IEEE. 284-291.

Jones, M. (1999). "Information Systems and the Double Mangle: Steering a Course between the Scylla of Embedded Structure and the Charybdis of Strong Symmetry", *IFIP WG 8.2 and 8.6 Joint Working Conference on Information Systems: Current Issues and Future Changes.* Helsinki, Finland: IFIP. 287-302.

Joyce, M. (1992). "A Feel for Prose: Interstitial Links and the Contours of Hypertext", *Writing on the Edge,* 4(1): 83-101.

Jutla, D., Bodorik, P., Hajnal, C. and Davis, C. (1999a). "Making Business Sense of Electronic Commerce", *Computer,* 32(3): 67-75.

Jutla, D., Bodorik, P. and Wang, Y. (1999b). "Developing Internet E-Commerce Benchmarks", *Information Systems,* 24(6): 475-493.

Kambil, A., Ginsberg, A. and Bloch, M. (1996). *Re-Inventing Value Propositions.* Working Paper, New York: Leonard N. Stern School of Business.

Kaplan, C., Fenwick, J. and Chen, J. (1998). "Adaptive Hypertext Navigation Based on User Goals and Context", *Adaptive Hypertext and Hypermedia.* Eds. P. Brusilovsky et al. Dordrecht: Kluwer Academic Publishers. 45-69.

Katerattanakul, P. and Siau, K. (1999). "Measuring Information Quality of Web Sites: Development of an Instrument", *20th International Conference on Information Systems (ICIS-99).* Charlotte, USA: International Conference on Information Systems. 279-285.

Kaukal, M. and Simon, B. (1999). "Redesign von WWW-basierten Masseninformationssystemen", *Electronic Business Engineering: 4. Internationale Tagung Wirtschaftsinformatik.* Saarbrücken: Physica. 51-66.

Kay, J. and Kummerfeld, B. (1997). "User Models for Customized Hypertext", *Intelligent Hypertext: Advanced Techniques for the World Wide Web.* Eds. C. Nicholas and J. Mayfield. Berlin: Springer. 47-69.

Kelle, H., (1995). *Computer-Aided Qualitative Data Analysis. Theories, Methods and Practice.* London: Sage.

Kelly, S. (1994). *Data Warehousing: The Route to Mass Customization.* Chichester: John Wiley & Sons.

Kendall, K.E. and Kendall, J.E. (1999). *Systems Analysis and Design.* Upper Saddle River: Prentice Hall.

Kent, R.E. and Neuss, C. (1997). "Conceptual Analysis of Hypertext", *Intelligent Hypertext: Advanced Techniques for the World Wide Web.* Eds. C. Nicholas and J. Mayfield. Berlin: Springer. 70-89.

Kieser, A. and Kubicek, H. (1992). *Organization (in German).* Berlin: de Gruyter.

Kitching, R.L. (1983). *Systems Ecology: An Introduction to Ecological Modelling.* St. Lucia: University of Queensland Press.

Klapsing, R. and Neumann, G. (2000). *Applying the Resource Description Framework to Web Engineering.* Working Paper, Essen: University of Essen.

Klein, S. (1999). "Designing for Customer Interaction on the Web", *IEEE Internet Computing*, 3(1): 32-35.

Kleinberg, J., Papadimitriou, C. and Raghavan, P. (1998). "A Microeconomic View of Data Mining", *Data Mining and Knowledge Disovery*, 2(4): 311-324.

Knott, A., Mellish, C., Oberlander, J. and O'Donnel, M. (1996). "Sources of Flexibility in Dynamic Hypertext Generation", *8th International Workshop on Natural Language Generation*. Herstmonceux Castle, UK. 151-160.

Koblick, R. (1999). "Concordia", *Communications of the ACM*, 42(3): 96-97.

Kohonen, T. (1988). "The 'Neural' Phonetic Typewriter", *Computer*, 21(30): 11-22.

Kohonen, T. (1997). *Self-Organizing Maps*. Berlin: Springer.

Kolb, D. (1994). "Socrates in the Labyrinth", *Hyper/Text/Theory*. Ed. G.P. Landow. Baltimore: Johns Hopkins University Press. 323-344.

Kotler, P. and Armstrong, G. (1998). *Principles of Marketing*. London: Prentice Hall.

Kratzer, K.P. (1990). *Neuronale Netze - Grundlagen und Anwendungen*. Munich: Hanser.

Kress, G. and Leeuwen, T.v. (1998). "Front Pages: (The Critical) Analysis of Newspaper Layout", *Approaches to Media Discourse*. Eds. A. Bell and P. Garrett. Oxford: Blackwell. 186-219.

Krippendorf, K. (1980). *Content Analysis: An Introduction to Its Methodology*. Beverly Hills: Sage.

Krulwich, B. (1997). "Lifestyle Finder: Intelligent User Profiling Using Large-Scale Demographic Data", *AI Magazine*, 18(2): 37-56.

Kuhn, T.S. (1996). *The Structure of Scientific Revolutions*. Chicago: University of Chicago Press.

Kumar, H.P., Plaisant, C. and Shneiderman, B. (1997). "Browsing Hierarchical Data with Multi-level Dynamic Queries and Pruning", *International Journal of Human-Computer Studies*, 46(1): 103-124.

Labrou, Y., Finin, T. and Peng, Y. (1999). "Agent Communication Languages: The Current Landscape", *IEEE Intelligent Systems*, 14(2): 45-52.

Lamont, C. (1997). "Annotating a Text: Literary Theory and Electronic Hypertext", *Electronic Text: Investigations in Method and Theory*. Ed. K. Sutherland. Oxford: Clarendon Press. 47-66.

Lamping, J. and Rao, R. (1996). "The Hyperbolic Browser: A Focus + Context Technique for Visualizing Large Hierarchies", *Journal of Visual Languages and Computing*, 7(1): 33-55.

Landow, G.P. (1992). *Hypertext: The Convergence of Contemporary Critical Theory and Technology*. Baltimore: Johns Hopkins University Press.

Landow, G.P. (1994). "What's a Critic to Do?: Critical Theory in the Age of Hypertext", *Hyper/Text/Theory*. Ed. G.P. Landow. Baltimore: Johns Hopkins University Press. 1-48.

Landow, G.P. (1997). *Hypertext 2.0*. Baltimore: Johns Hopkins University Press.

Lang, A. (1990). "Involuntary Attention and Physiological Arousal Evoked by Structural Features and Emotional Content in TV Commercials", *Communication Research*, 17(3): 275-299.

Lange, D.B. and Oshima, M. (1999). "Seven Good Reasons for Mobile Agents", *Communications of the ACM*, 42(3): 88-89.

Langenohl, T. (1993). *Systemarchitekturen Elektronischer Märkte*. Doctoral Thesis, St. Gallen: University of St. Gallen.

Lassila, O. (1998). "Web Metadata: A Matter of Semantics", *IEEE Internet Computing*, 2(4): 30-37.

Lebart, L. (1994). "Complementary Use of Correspondence Analysis and Cluster Analysis", *Correspondence Analysis in the Social Sciences*. Eds. M. Greenacre and J. Blasius. London: Academic Press. 162-178.

Lebart, L., Salem, A. and Berry, L. (1998). *Exploring Textual Data*. Dordrecht: Kluwer Academic Publishers.

Ledgerwood, M.D. (1997). "Hypertextuality and Multimedia Literature", *Semiotics of the Media: State of the Art, Projects, and Perspectives*. Ed. W. Nöth. Berlin: Mouton de Gruyter. 547-558.

Lee, J., Hoch, R., et al. (1999). *Analysis and Visualization of Metrics for Online Merchandising*. Technical Paper, Yorktown Heights: IBM Institute for Advanced Commerce. http://www.ibm.com/iac/.

Lee, J. and Podlaseck, M. (2000). *Visualization and Analysis of Click-stream Data of Online Stores for Understanding Web Merchandising.* Technical Paper, Yorktown Heights: IBM Institute for Advanced Commerce. http://www.ibm.com/iac/.

Lee, K. and Speyer, G. (1999). *Platform for Privacy Preferences Project (P3P) & Citibank,* Citibank Advanced Development Group. http://www.w3.org/P3P/Lee_Speyer.html.

Lelii, S.R. and McCright, J. (1999). *With DG Acquisition, EMC Stakes Claim for Mid-range Storage Market*: PC Week Online. http://www.zdnet.com/pcweek/.

Leung, Y.K. and Apperley, M.D. (1994). "A Review and Taxonomy of Distortion-Oriented Presentation Techniques", *ACM Transactions on Computer-Human Interaction,* 1(2): 126-160.

Levoy, M. (1994). "Spreadsheets for Images", *Computer Graphics (Proceedings of ACM Siggraph-94),* 28(4): 139-146.

Lieberman, H. (1995). "Letizia: An Agent That Assists Web Browsing", *14th International Joint Conference on Artificial Intelligence (IJCAI-95).* Montreal, Canada: Morgan-Kaufmann. 924-929.

Lieberman, H. (1997). "Autonomous Interface Agents", *ACM Conference on Human Factors in Computing Systems (CHI-97).* Atlanta, USA: ACM Press. 67-74.

Lieberman, H., Van Dyke, N.W. and Vivacqua, A.S. (1999). "Let's Browse: A Collaborative Web Browsing Agent", *International Conference on Intelligent User Interfaces.* Redondo Beach, USA: ACM Press. 65-68.

Liestøl, G. (1994). "Nonlinearity and Literary Theory", *Hyper/Text/Theory.* Ed. G.P. Landow. Baltimore: Johns Hopkins University Press. 87-120.

Lindemann, M.A. and Runge, A. (1998). "Electronic Contracting within the Reference Model for Electronic Markets", *6th European Conference on Information Systems (ECIS-98).* Aix-en-Provence, France: Euro-Arab Management School. 44-59.

Link, J. and Hildebrand, V.G. (1995). "Wettbewerbsvorteile durch kundenorientierte Informationssysteme: Konzeptionelle Grundlagen und empirische Ergebnisse", *Journal für Betriebswirtschaft,* 45(1): 46-62.

Lohse, G.L., Biolsi, K., Walker, N. and Rueter, H.H. (1994). "A Classification of Visual Representation", *Communications of the ACM,* 37(12): 36-49.

Lohse, G.L. and Spiller, P. (1998). "Electronic Shopping", *Communications of the ACM,* 41(7): 81-87.

Lowe, D. and Hall, W. (1999). *Hypermedia and the Web: An Engineering Approach.* Chichester: John Wiley & Sons.

Luqi (1989). "Software Evolution Through Rapid Prototyping", *IEEE Computer,* 22(5): 13-25.

Lyardet, F., Rossi, G. and Schwabe, D. (1999). "Discovering and Using Design Patterns in the WWW", *Multimedia Tools and Applications,* 8(3): 293-308.

Mackinlay, J.D. (1986). "Automating the Design of Graphical Presentations of Relational Material", *ACM Transactions on Graphics,* 5(2): 111-141.

Maes, P., Guttman, R.H. and Moukas, A.G. (1999). "Agents that Buy and Sell", *Communications of the ACM,* 42(3): 81-91.

Maglio, P.P. and Barrett, R. (1997). "How to Build Modeling Agents to Support Web Searchers", *6th International Conference on User Modeling (UM-97).* Chia Laguna, Italy: Springer. 5-16.

Mahler, A. and Göbel, G. (1996). "Internetbanking: Das Leistungsspektrum", *Die Bank,* 8: 488-492.

Mahling, D.E. (1994). "Cognitive Systems Engineering for Visualization", *Cognitive Aspects of Visual Languages and Visual Interfaces.* Eds. M.J. Tauber et al. Amsterdam: North-Holland. 41-75.

Mainzer, K. (1997). *Thinking in Complexity: The Complex Dynamics of Matter, Mind, and Mankind.* Berlin: Springer.

Malchow, R. and Thomsen, K. (1997). "Web-Tracking", *Screen Multimedia, Sep 1997:* 57-61.

Mani, I. and Bloedorn, E. (1999). "Summarizing Similarities and Differences Among Related Documents", *Information Retrieval,* 1(1/2): 35-67.

Marchionini, G. (1995). *Information Seeking in Electronic Environments.* Cambridge: Cambridge University Press.

Marcus, S. (1997). "Media and Self-Reference: The Forgotten Initial State", *Semiotics of the Media: State of the Art, Projects, and Perspectives.* Ed. W. Nöth. Berlin: Mouton de Gruyter. 15-47.

Martin, J. (1996). *Cybercorp: The New Business Revolution*. New York: Amacom.

Masters, T. (1993). *Practical Neural Network Recipes in C++*. San Diego: Academic Press.

Mathé, N. and Chen, J.R. (1998). "User-Centered Indexing for Adaptive Information Access", *Adaptive Hypertext and Hypermedia*. Eds. P. Brusilovsky et al. Dordrecht: Kluwer Academic Publishers. 171-207.

Maturana, H.R. and Varela, F.J. (1980). *Autopoiesis and Cognition: The Realization of the Living*. Dordecht: D. Reidel Publishing.

Maule, W.R. (1997). "Cognitive Maps, AI Agents and Personalized Virtual Environments in Internet Learning Experiences", *Internet Research: Networking Applications and Policy*, 8(4): 347-358.

Mayfield, J. (1997). "Two-Level Models of Hypertext", *Intelligent Hypertext: Advanced Techniques for the World Wide Web*. Eds. C. Nicholas and J. Mayfield. Berlin: Springer. 90-108.

McGann, J.J. (1997). "The Rationale of Hypertext", *Electronic Text: Investigations in Method and Theory*. Ed. K. Sutherland. Oxford: Clarendon Press. 19-46.

McLuhan, M. (1964). *Understanding Media: The Extension of Man*. London: Routledge and Kegan Paul.

McMillan, S.J. (1999a). "Four Models of Cyber-Interactivity", *49th Annual Conference of the International Communication Association (ICA-99)*. San Francisco, USA.

McMillan, S.J. (1999b). "The Microscope and the Moving Target: The Challenge of Applying a Stable Research Technique to a Dynamic Communication Environment", *49th Annual Conference of the International Communication Association (ICA-99)*. San Francisco, USA.

McMullin, E. (1993). "Rationality and Paradigm Change in Science", *World Changes: Thomas Kuhn and the Nature of Science*. Ed. P. Horwich. Cambridge: MIT Press. 55-78.

McQuail, D. (1994). *Mass Communication Theory: An Introduction*. London: Sage.

McTear, M.F. (1993). "User Modelling for Adaptive Computer Systems: A Survey of Recent Developments", *Artificial Intelligence Review*, 7: 157-184.

Mecca, G., Merialdo, P., Atzeni, P. and Crescenzi, V. (1999). *The Araneus Guide to Web-Site Development*. Working, Rome, Italy: University of Rome. http://www.dia.uniroma3.it/Araneus/articles.html.

Medsker, L.R. (1995). *Hybrid Intelligent Systems*. Boston: Kluwer Academic Publishers.

Meffert, H. (1992). *Merketingforschung und Käuferverhalten*. Wiesbaden: Gabler.

Melucci, M. (1999). "An Evaluation of Automatically Constructed Hypertexts for Information Retrieval", *Information Retrieval*, 1(1/2): 91-114.

Mena, J. (1999). *Data Mining Your Website*. Boston: Digital Press.

Meyer, J.A. (1996). "Wirkung bildlicher Darstellungen auf das Informations- und Entscheidungsverhalten von Managern: Erweiterung der bisherigen Forschung auf bewegte Bilder", *Schmalenbachs Zeitschrift für betriebswirtschaftliche Forschung*, 96(07-08): 738-760.

Meyer, J.A. (1997). "Informationsüberlastung im (Marketing-) Management", *Werbeforschung & Praxis*, 42(1): 10-14.

Meyer, J.A. and Grundei, J. (1995). "Akzeptanz visueller Informationsdarstellung im Management", *Journal für Betriebswirtschaft*, 45(5-6): 366-380.

Miles, G.E., Howes, A. and Davies, A. (2000). "A Framework for Understanding Human Factors in Web-based Electronic Commerce", *International Journal of Human-Computer Studies*, 52(1): 131-163.

Miller, D. (1991). "A Logic Programming Language with Lambda-Abstraction, Function Variables, and Simple Unification", *Journal of Logic and Computation*, 1(4): 497-536.

Milosavljevic, M. (1998). "Electronic Commerce via Personalised Virtual Electronic Catalogues", *2nd Annual Collaborative Electronic Commerce Technology and Research Conference (CollECTeR-98)*. Sydney, Australia: University of Wollongong. 26-37.

Milosavljevic, M. and Oberlander, J. (1998). "Dynamic Hypertext Catalogues: Helping Users to Help Themselves", *9th ACM Conference on Hypertext and Hypermedia (HT-98)*. Pittsburgh, USA. 123-131.

Misic, M.M. and Johnson, K.L. (1999). "Benchmarking: A Tool for Web Site Evaluation and Improvement", *Internet Research: Networking Applications and Policy*, 9(5): 383-392.

Mitra, A. (1999). "Characteristics of the WWW Text: Tracing Discursive Strategies", *Journal of Computer-Mediated Communication,* 5(1): http://www.ascusc.org/jcmc/.

Mladenic, D. (1998). *Machine Learning on Non-homogeneous, Distributed Text Data.* Doctoral Thesis, Ljubljana: University of Ljubljana.

Mladenic, D. (1999). "Text-Learning and Related Intelligent Agents: A Survey", *IEEE Intelligent Systems,* 14(4): 44-54.

Moody, D. and Walsh, P. (1999). "Measuring the Value of Information: An Asset Valuation Approach", *7th European Conference on Information Systems (ECIS-99).* Copenhagen, Denmark: Copenhagen Business School. 496-512.

Moore, G.A. (1999a). *Crossing the Chasm: Marketing and Selling High-Tech Products to Mainstream Customers.* New York: Harper Business.

Moore, G.E. (1965). "Cramming More Components Onto Integrated Circuits", *Electronics Magazine,* 38(8): 114-117.

Moore, J.F. (1993). "Predators and Prey: A New Ecology of Competition", *Harvard Business Review,* 71(3): 75-85.

Moore, J.F. (1997). *The Death of Competition: Leadership and Strategy in the Age of Business Ecosystems.* New York: Harper Collins.

Moore, S.A. (1999b). "KQML & FLBC: Contrasting Agent Communication Languages", *32nd Hawaii International Conference on System Sciences (HICSS-32).* Hawaii, USA: IEEE Computer Society Press.

Morris, M. and Ogan, C. (1996). "The Internet as Mass Medium", *Journal of Computer-Mediated Communication,* 1(4): http://www.ascusc.org/jcmc/.

Morrison, M. (1998). "A Look at Interactivity from a Consumer Perspective", *Developments in Marketing Science.* Eds. J.B. Ford and E.D. Honeycutt. Norfolk, USA: Academy of Marketing Science. 149-154.

Müller-Schneider, T. (1994). "The Visualization of Structural Change by Means of Correspondence Analysis", *Correspondence Analysis in the Social Sciences.* Eds. M. Greenacre and J. Blasius. London: Academic Press. 267-279.

Munzner, T. (1998). "Exploring Large Graphs in 3D Hyperbolic Space", *IEEE Computer Graphics and Applications,* 18(4): 18-23.

Munzner, T. (1999). "Drawing Large Graphs with H3Viewer and Site Manager", *Graph Drawing: 6th International Symposium (GD-98)*. Ed. Sue Whitesides. London: Springer. 384-393.

Munzner, T. and Buchard, P. (1995). "Visualizing the Structure of the World Wide Web in 3D Hyperbolic Space", *1st Annual Symposium on Virtual Reality Modeling (VRML-95)*. San Diego, USA. 33-38.

Murray, J.H. (1997). *Hamlet on the Holodeck: The Future of Narrative in Cyberspace*. New York: Free Press.

Murugesan, S., Deshpande, Y., Hansen, S. and Ginige, A. (1999). "Web Engineering: A New Discipline for Development of Web-based Systems", *First ICSE Workshop on Web Engineering (WebE-99)*. Los Angeles, USA. 1-9.

Nambisan, S. and Wang, Y.-M. (1999). "Roadblocks to Web Technology Adoption?", *Communications of the ACM*, 42(1): 98-101.

Nanard, J. and Nanard, M. (1995). "Hypertext Design Environments and the Hypertext Design Process", *Communications of the ACM*, 38(8): 49-56.

Nation, D.A., Plaisant, C., Marchionini, G. and Komlodi, A. (1997). "Visualizing Websites Using a Hierarchical Table of Contents Browser: WebTOC", *3rd Conference on Human Factors & the Web*. Denver, USA: US West Communications.

Naumann, E. (1994). *Creating Customer Value: The Path to Sustainable Competitive Advantage*. Cincinnati: Thomson Executive Press.

Naumann, J.D. and Jenkins, A.M. (1982). "Prototyping: The New Paradigm for Systems Development", *MIS Quarterly*, 6(3): 29-44.

Nelson, T.H. (1965). "A File Structure for the Complex, the Changing and the Indeterminate", *Association for Computing Machinery's 20th National Conference*. New York: Association for Computing Machinery. 84-100.

Nelson, T.H. (1992). "Opening Hypertext: A Memoir", *Literacy Online: The Promise (And Peril of Reading and Writing With Computers)*. Ed. M.C. Tuman. Pittsburgh: University of Pittsburgh Press: 43-57.

Netscape (1998). *Persistent Client State HTTP Cookies: Preliminary Specification*, Netscape Communications Corporation. http://home.netscape.com/newsref/std/cookie_spec.html.

Newhagen, J.E. and Rafaeli, S. (1996). "Why Communication Researchers Should Study the Internet: A Dialogue", *Journal of Computer-Mediated Communication*, 1(4): http://www.ascusc.org/jcmc/.

Nguyen, T.-L. and Schmidt, H. (1999). "Creating and Managing Documents with LifeWeb", *5th Australian World Wide Web Conference (AusWeb-99)*. Ballina, Australia: Southern Cross University Press. 95-106.

Nielsen, J. (1990). *Hypertext and Hypermedia*. San Diego: Academic Press.

Nielsen, J. (1995). *Multimedia and Hypertext: The Internet and Beyond*. Boston: AP Professional.

Nielsen, J. (1997). *Be Succinct: How to Write for the Web*. http://www.useit.com/alertbox/9703b.html.

Nielsen, J. (1999). "User Interface Directions for the Web", *Communications of the ACM*, 42(1): 65-72.

Norman, D.A. (1998). *The Invisible Computer: Why Good Products Can Fail, the Personal Computer Is So Complex, and Information Appliances Are the Solution*. Cambridge: MIT Press.

Norman, D.A. and Draper, S.W. (1986). *User Centered System Design: New Perspectives on Human-Computer Interaction*. Hillsdale: Lawrence Erlbaum Associates.

Norman, K., Weldon, L. and Shneiderman, B. (1986). "Cognitive Layouts of Windows and Multiple Screens for User Interfaces", *International Journal of Man-Machine Studies*, 25: 229-248.

North, C. and Shneiderman, B. (1999). *Snap-Together Visualization: Coordinating Multiple Views to Explore Information*. Technical Report, College Park: University of Maryland, Department of Computer Science. http://www.cs.umd.edu/hcil/pubs/.

Norton, K.S. (1999). "Applying Cross-functional Evolutionary Methodologies to Web Development", *First ICSE Workshop on Web Engineering (WebE-99)*. Los Angeles, USA.

Novak, T.P. and Hoffman, D.L. (1997). "New Metrics for New Media: Toward the Development of Web Measurement Standards", *World Wide Web Journal*, 2(1).

Noyes, J. and Baber, C. (1999). *User-centred Design of Systems*. London: Springer.

O´Keefe, R.M. and McEachern, T. (1998). "Web-based Customer Decision Support Systems", *Communications of the ACM*, 41(3): 71-78.

O´Sullivan, P.B. (1999). "Personal Broadcasting: Theoretical Implications of the Web", *49th Annual Conference of the International Communication Association (ICA-99)*. San Francisco, USA.

Olsina, L., Godoy, D., Lafuente, G.J. and Rossi, G. (1999). "Specifying Quality Characteristics and Attributes for Websites", *First ICSE Workshop on Web Engineering (WebE-99)*. Los Angeles, USA.

Olson, G.M. and Olson, J.S. (1991). "User-centered Design of Collaboration Technology", *Journal of Organizational Computing*, 1(1): 61-83.

Österle, H. (1995). *Business Engineering: Prozeß- und Systementwicklung, Band 1: Entwurfstechniken*. Berlin: Springer.

Ozanne, J.L., Brucks, M. and Grewal, D. (1992). "A Study of Information Search Behavior During the Categorization of New Products", *Journal of Consumer Research*, 18(4): 452-463.

Palmer, J.W. (1997). "Retailing on the WWW: The Use of Electronic Product Catalogs", *International Journal of Electronic Markets*, 7(3): 6-9.

Paltridge, S. (1999). "Mining and Mapping Web Content", *Journal of Policy, Regulation and Strategy for Telecommunications Information and Media*, 1(4): 327-342.

Parker, R.C. (1997). *Roger C. Parker's Guide to Web Content and Design*. New York: MIS Press.

Pask, G. (1992). "Different Kinds of Cybernetics", *New Perspectives on Cybernetics: Self-Organization, Autonomy and Connectionism*. Ed. G. Van de Vijver. Dordrecht: Kluwer Academic Publishers. 11-31.

Paternò, F. (1999). *Model-based Design and Evaluation of Interactive Applications*. London: Springer.

Payne, G. (2000). "Intelligent Transportation Systems (ITS): Opportunities for Bicycle Transportation", to appear in: *Bicycle Forum*, 50.

Pearce, C. and Miller, E. (1997). "The TELLTALE Dynamic Hypertext Environment: Approaches to Scalability", *Intelligent Hypertext: Advanced Techniques for the World Wide Web*. Eds. C. Nicholas and J. Mayfield. Berlin: Springer. 109-130.

Phillips, D. (1995). *Correspondence Analysis (= Social Research Update, Issue 7)*, Guildford: University of Surrey. http://www.soc.surrey.ac.uk/sru/sru7.html.

Picot, A. and Reichwald, R. (1987). *Bürokommunikation - Leitsätze für den Anwender*. Hallbergmoos: Angewandte Informationstechnik.

Pitasi, A. (1999). "Visualisation as Design Strategy for Communication Research", *49th Annual Conference of the International Communication Association (ICA-99)*. San Francisco, USA.

Poddig, T. (1992). *Künstliche Intelligenz und Entscheidungstheorie*. Wiesbaden: Deutscher Universitätsverlag.

Pollack, M.E., Hirschberg, J. and Webber, B.L. (1982). "User Participation in the Reasoning Processes of Expert Systems", *National Conference on Artificial Intelligence*. Pittsburgh, USA: AAAI Press. 358-361.

Porter, M.E. (1998). *Competitive Advantage: Creating and Sustaining Superior Performance*. New York: Free Press.

Potter, J.W. and Levine-Donnerstein, D. (1996). "Content Analysis Methodology: Assessing Reliability for Multiple Coders", *46th Annual Conference of the International Communication Association (ICA-96)*. San Francisco, USA.

Potter, J.W. and Levine-Donnerstein, D. (1999). "Rethinking Validity and Reliability in Content Analysis", *Journal of Applied Communication Research*, 27(3): 258-284.

Potter, R.F. (1999). "Measuring the "Bells & Whistles" of a New Medium: Using Content Analysis to Describe Structural Features of Cyberspace", *49th Annual Conference of the International Communication Association (ICA-99)*. San Francisco, USA.

Powell, P. (1992). "Information Technology Evaluation: Is It Different?", *Journal of the Operational Research Society*, 43(1): 29-42.

Powell, T.A., Jones, D.L. and Cutts, D.C. (1998). *Web Site Engineering: Beyond Web Page Design*. Upper Saddle River: Prentice Hall.

Pressman, R.S. (1996). *Software Engineering: A Practitioner's Approach*. New York: McGraw-Hill.

Psoinos, A. and Smithson, S. (1999). *The 1999 Worldwide Web 100 Survey*, London: London School of Economics. http://is.lse.ac.uk/press_release.htm.

Pyle, D. (1999). *Data Preparation for Data Mining*. San Francisco: Morgan Kaufmann.

Rafaeli, S. (1988). "Interactivity: From New Media to Communication", *Advancing Communication Science*. Eds. R.P. Hawkins et al. Beverly Hills: Sage. 110-134.

Rafaeli, S. and Sudweeks, F. (1997). "Networked Interactivity", *Journal of Computer-Mediated Communication,* 2(4): http://www.ascusc.org/jcmc/.

Ramscar, M., Pain, H. and Lee, J. (1997). "Do We Know What the User Knows, and Does it Matter? The Epistemics of User Modeling", *6th International Conference on User Modeling (UM-97).* Chia Laguna, Italy: Springer. 429-431.

Raudaskoski, P. (1997). "Semiosis at Computer Media", *Semiotics of the Media: State of the Art, Projects, and Perspectives.* Ed. W. Nöth. Berlin: Mouton de Gruyter. 535-545.

Reagle, J. and Cranor, L.F. (1999). "The Platform for Privacy Preferences", *Communications of the ACM,* 42(2): 48-55.

Reeves, B. and Nass, C. (1996). *The Media Equation: How People Treat Computers, Television, and New Media like Real People and Places.* New York: Cambridge University Press.

Reiß, M. and Beck, T.C. (1995). "Performance-Marketing durch Mass Customization", *Marktforschung & Management,* 39(2): 62-67.

Remenyi, D., Money, A.H. and Twite, A. (1993). *A Guide to Measuring and Managing IT Benefits.* Manchester: NCC Blackwell.

Renear, A. (1997). "Out of Praxis: Three (Meta)Theories of Textuality", *Electronic Text: Investigations in Method and Theory.* Ed. K. Sutherland. Oxford: Clarendon Press. 107-126.

Rheinfrank, J., Evenson, S. and Wulff, W. (1994). "Design as Common Ground", *Cognitive Aspects of Visual Languages and Visual Interfaces.* Eds. M.J. Tauber et al. Amsterdam: North-Holland. 77-102.

Robertson, G.G., Mackinlay, J.D. and Card, S.K. (1991). "Cone Trees: Animated 3D Visualizations of Hierarchical Information", *Conference on Human Factors in Computing Systems (CHI-91).* New Orleans, USA: Association for Computing Machinery. 189-194.

Robinson, H. (1990). "Towards a Sociology of Human-Computer Interaction: A Software Engineer's Perspective", *Computers and Conversation.* Eds. P. Luff et al. London: Academic Press.

Rockart, J.F. and Short, J.E. (1991). "The Networked Organization and the Management of Interdependence", *The Corporation of the 1990s: Information Technology and Organizational Transformation.* Ed. M.S.S. Morton. NewYork: Oxford University Press. 189-219.

Rogers, E.M. (1995). *Diffusion of Innovations.* New York: The Free Press.

Rosello, M. (1994). "The Screener's Maps: Michel de Certeau's "Wandersmänner" and Paul Auster's Hypertextual Detective", *Hyper/Text/Theory*. Ed. G.P. Landow. Baltimore: Johns Hopkins University Press. 121-158.

Rosenfeld, L. (1997). *Organizing Your Site from A-Z: Creating an Index for Users Who Know What They Are Doing*, Argus Associates. http://webreview.com/wr/pub/97/10/03/arch/.

Rosenschein, J. and Zlotkin, G. (1994). *Rules of Encounter: Designing Conventions for Automated Negotiation among Computers*. Boston: MIT Press.

Rosie, A.M. (1969). "Cybernetics and Information (Information Theory Problems)", *Survey of Cybernetics: A Tribute to Dr. Norbert Wiener*. Ed. J. Rose. New York: Gordon and Breach. 145-162.

Rubinstein, R. and Hersh, H.M. (1984). *The Human Factor: Designing Computer Systems for People*. Burlington: Digital Press.

Rumpradit, C. and Donnell, M.L. (1999). "Navigational Cues on User Interface Design to Produce Better Information Seeking on the World Wide Web", *32nd Hawaii International Conference on System Sciences (HICSS-32)*. Hawaii, USA: IEEE Computer Society Press.

Sampson, J.R. (1976). *Adaptive Information Processing: An Introductory Survey*. New York: Springer.

Schaeffer, P. (1995). La Communiation c'est la Guerre. *Le Monde*. Paris.

Schaller, R.R. (1997). "Moore's Law: Past, Present, and Future", *IEEE Spectrum*, 34(6): 52-59.

Scharl, A. (1997a). "Referenzmodelle für die Entwicklung von Masseninformationssystemen: ein Fallbeispiel aus der Branche Informationstechnik", *Journal für Betriebswirtschaft*, 47(5-6): 282-294.

Scharl, A. (1997b). *Referenzmodellierung kommerzieller Masseninformationssysteme: Idealtypische Gestaltung von Informationsangeboten im World Wide Web am Beispiel der Branche Informationstechnik*. Frankfurt: Peter Lang.

Scharl, A. (1998a). "Reference Modeling of Commercial Web Information Systems Using the Extended World Wide Web Design Technique (eW3DT)", *31st Hawaii International Conference on System Sciences (HICSS-31)*. Hawaii, USA: IEEE Computer Society Press. 476-484.

Scharl, A. (1998b). "Removing Communication Barriers with a Transaction-Oriented Derivative of the Extended World Wide Web Design Technique (eW3DT)", *Business Information Technology Management: Closing the International Divide.* Ed. P. Banerjee. New Delhi: Har Anand. 249-264.

Scharl, A. (1999a). "A Conceptual, User-Centric Approach to Modeling Web Information Systems", *5th Australian World Wide Web Conference (AusWeb-99).* Ballina, Australia: Southern Cross University Press. 33-49.

Scharl, A. (1999b). "Reference Modeling as the Missing Link between Academic Research and Industry Practice", *Journal of Scientific and Industrial Research,* 58(3/4): 211-220.

Scharl, A. (2000a). "A Classification of Web Adaptivity: Tailoring Content and Navigational Systems of Advanced Web Applications", *Web Engineering.* Eds. S. Murugesan and Y. Deshpande. Berlin: Springer. Forthcoming.

Scharl, A. (2000b). "The Five Stages of Customizing Web-based Mass Information Systems", *Managing Web-enabled Technologies in Organizations: A Global Perspective.* Ed. M. Khosrowpour. Hershey: Idea Group Publishing. 103-121.

Scharl, A. and Bauer, C. (1998). "Informational Requirements for Participating in Electronic Business Ecosystems", *Western Australian Workshop on Information Systems Research (WAWISR-98).* Perth, Australia: Curtin University of Technology. 79-86.

Scharl, A. and Bauer, C. (1999). "Explorative Analysis and Evaluation of Commercial Web Information Systems", *20th International Conference on Information Systems (ICIS-99).* Charlotte, USA: International Conference on Information Systems. 534-539.

Scharl, A., Bauer, C. and Kaukal, M. (1999). "From Static Worlds to Complex Negotiations: A (Commercial) Agent's Perspective on Customizable Transactions", *12th International Bled Electronic Commerce Conference.* Bled, Slowenia: Moderna organizacija. 33-45.

Scharl, A. and Brandtweiner, R. (1998a). "A Conceptual Research Framework for Analyzing the Evolution of Electronic Markets", *International Journal of Electronic Markets,* 8(2): 39-42.

Scharl, A. and Brandtweiner, R. (1998b). "Maximizing the Customer Delivered Value with Web-based Mass Information Systems", *4th Americas Conference on Information Systems (AIS-98).* Baltimore, USA: Association for Information Systems. 453-455.

Scharl, A., Gebauer, J. and Bauer, C. (2000). "Matching Process Requirements with Information Technology to Assess the Efficiency of Web Information Systems", *Information Technology and Management*: Forthcoming.

Scheruhn, H.-J. (1996). "Maßgeschneidert: Referenzmodelle: Hilfe bei der Einführung von Standardsoftware", *iX: Magazin für Professionelle Informationstechnik*, 96(01): 112-119.

Schiepers, C.W.J. (1980). "Response Latency and Accuracy in Visual Word Recognition", *Perception and Psychophysics*, 27: 71-81.

Schiffrin, D. (1989). "Conversation Analysis", *Language: The Sociocultural Context*. Ed. F.J. Newmeyer. Cambridge: Cambridge University Press. 251- 276.

Schmid, B. (1993). "Elektronische Märkte", *Wirtschaftsinformatik*, 35(5): 465-480.

Schmid, B.F. and Lindemann, M.A. (1998). "Elements of a Reference Model for Electronic Markets", *31st Hawaii International Conference on System Sciences (HICSS-31)*. Hawaii, USA: IEEE Computer Society Press. 193-201.

Schubert, C., Zarnekow, R. and Brenner, W. (1998). "A Methodology for Classifying Intelligent Software Agents", *6th European Conference on Information Systems*. Aix-en-Provence, France: Euro-Arab Management School.

Schultz, T. (1999). "Interactive Options in Online Journalism: A Content Analysis of 100 U.S. Newspapers", *Journal of Computer-Mediated Communication*, 5(1): http://www.ascusc.org/jcmc/.

Schwabe, D. and Rossi, G. (1995). "The Object-oriented Hypermedia Design Model", *Communications of the ACM*, 38(8): 45-46.

Schwabe, D., Rossi, G. and Barbosa, S. (1996). "Systematic Hypermedia Application Design with OOHDM", *7th ACM Conference on Hypertext*.

Segev, A., Beam, C. and Gebauer, J. (1997). *Impact of the Internet on Purchasing Practices: Preliminary Results from a Field Study (= CMIT Working Paper 97-WP-1024)*. Berkeley: Fisher Center for Management and Information Technology University of California.

Segev, A., Wan, D. and Beam, C. (1995). *Designing Electronic Catalogs for Business Value: Results of the CommerceNet Pilot (= CMIT Working Paper)*. Berkeley: Fisher Center for Management and Information Technology University of California.

Selz, D. and Schubert, P. (1997). "Web Assessment: A Model for the Evaluation and Assesment of Successful Electronic Commerce Applications", *International Journal of Electronic Markets,* 7(3): 46-48.

Senn, J.A. (1987). *Information Systems in Management.* Belmont: Wadsworth.

Seta, K., Ikeda, M., Kakusho, O. and Mizoguchi, R. (1997). "Capturing a Conceptual Model for End-User Programming: Task Ontology As a Static User Model", *6th International Conference on User Modeling (UM-97).* Chia Laguna, Italy: Springer. 203-214.

Shannon, C.E. and Weaver, W. (1964). *The Mathematical Theory of Communication.* Urbana: University of Illinois Press.

Shepherd, M. and Watters, C. (1999). "The Functionality Attribute of Cybergenres", *32nd Hawaii International Conference on System Sciences (HICSS-32).* Hawaii, USA: IEEE Computer Society Press.

Shneiderman, B. (1997a). "Designing Information-abundant Web Sites: Issues and Recommendations", *International Journal of Human-Computer Studies,* 47(1): 5-29.

Shneiderman, B. (1997b). *Designing the User Interface: Strategies for Effective Human-Computer Interaction.* Berkeley: Addison-Wesley.

Shneiderman, B., Shafer, P., Simon, R. and Weldon, L. (1986). "Display Strategies for Program Browsing: Concepts and an Experiment", *IEEE Software,* 3(3): 7-15.

Sierra, C., Faratin, P. and Jennings, N.R. (1997). "A Service-Oriented Negotiation Model between Autonomous Agents", *8th European Workshop on Modeling Autonomous Agents in a Multi-Agent World (MAAMAW-97).* Ronneby, Sweden. 17-35.

Silipo, R. (1999). "Neural Networks", *Intelligent Data Analysis: An Introduction.* Eds. M. Berthold and D.J. Hand. Berlin: Springer. 217-268.

Singh, M.P. (1999). "Agent Communication Languages: Rethinking the Principles", *Computer,* 31(12): 40-47.

Slatin, J. (1991). "Reading Hypertext: Order and Coherence in a New Medium", *Hypermedia and Literary Studies.* Eds. P. Delany and G.P. Landow. Cambridge: MIT Press. 153-169.

Smith, P.A., Newman, I.A. and Parks, L.M. (1997). "Virtual Hierarchies and Virtual Networks: Some Lessons from Hypermedia Usability Research Applied to the World Wide Web", *International Journal of Human-Computer Studies,* 47(1): 67-95.

Smithson, S. (2000). *The Web 2000 Growth Report: Exploring the Links between Company Growth and Electronic Business*, London: London School of Economics. http://www.lse.ac.uk/Press/Web2000/.

Snyder, I. (1996). *Hypertext: The Electronic Labyrinth*. Melbourne: Melbourne University Press.

Solutions, B.I. (1999). *Open Sesame Technical White Paper*, Cambridge: Bowne Internet Solutions. http://www.opensesame.com/.

Someya, Y. (1998). *e_lemma.txt*. http://www.ndirect.co.uk/~lexical/-downloads/e_lemma.zip.

Sommer, U. and Zoller, P. (1999). "WebCon: Design and Modeling of Database Driven Hypertext Applications", *32nd Hawaii International Conference on System Sciences (HICSS-32)*. Hawaii, USA: IEEE Computer Society Press.

Sonesson, G. (1997). "The Multimediation of the Lifeworld", *Semiotics of the Media: State of the Art, Projects, and Perspectives*. Ed. W. Nöth. Berlin: Mouton de Gruyter. 61-77.

Sperber, D. and Wilson, D. (1986). *Relevance: Communication and Cognition*. Cambridge: Harvard University Press.

Spool, J.M., DeAngelo, T., et al. (1998). *Web Site Usability: A Designer's Guide*. North Andover: Morgan Kaufmann Academic Press.

SPSS (1999). *SPSS Base 9.0 Applications Guide*. Chicago: SPSS Inc.

SRI_Consulting (2000). *Values and Lifestyles: Psychographic Segmentation*, Stanford Research Institute. http://future.sri.com/vals/actuali-zers.shtml.

St. Laurent, S. (1998). *Cookies*. New York: McGraw-Hill.

StatSoft (2000). *Correspondence Analysis*, Tulsa: StatSoft Inc. http://-www.statsoftinc.com/textbook/stcoran.html.

Stein, A., Gulla, J.A. and Thiel, U. (1997). "Making Sense of Users' Mouse Clicks: Abductive Reasoning and Conversational Dialogue Modeling", *6th International Conference on User Modeling (UM-97)*. Chia Laguna, Italy: Springer. 89-100.

Stout, R. (1997). *Web Site Stats: Tracking Hits and Analyzing Traffic*. Berkeley: Osborne / McGraw-Hill.

Strachan, L., Anderson, J., Sneesby, M. and Evans, M. (1997). "Pragmatic User Modeling in a Commercial Software System", *6th International Conference on User Modeling (UM-97)*. Chia Laguna, Italy: Springer. 189-200.

Strader, T.J. and Shaw, M.J. (1999). "Consumer Cost Differences for Traditional and Internet Markets", *Internet Research: Networking Applications and Policy*, 9(2): 82-92.

Suchman, L.A. (1987). *Plans and Situated Actions: The Problem of Human-Machine Communication*. Cambridge: Cambridge University Press.

Sullivan, T. (1997). "Reading Reader Reaction: A Proposal for Inferential Analysis of Web Server Log Files", *3rd Conference on Human Factors & the Web*. Denver, USA: US West Communications.

Sutherland, K. (1997). "Introduction", *Electronic Text: Investigations in Method and Theory*. Ed. K. Sutherland. Oxford: Clarendon Press. 1-18.

Swick, R.R. (1999). "RDF: Weaving the Web of Discovery", *netWorker*, 3(2): 21-25.

Tai, H. and Kosaka, K. (1999). "The Aglets Project", *Communications of the ACM*, 42(3): 100-101.

Taylor, P. (1999). "Statistical Methods", *Intelligent Data Analysis: An Introduction*. Eds. M. Berthold and D.J. Hand. Berlin: Springer. 67-127.

Tenenbaum, J.M. (1998). "WISs and Electronic Commerce", *Communications of the ACM*, 41(7): 89-90.

Terveen, L.G., Hill, W.C. and Amento, B. (1999). "Constructing, Organizing, and Visualizing Collections of Topically Related Web Resources", *ACM Transactions on Computer-Human Interaction*, 6(1): 67-94.

Tesch, R. (1990). *Qualitative Research: Analysis Types and Software Tools*. New York: Falmer Press.

Thioulouse, J., Chessel, D., Dolédec, S. and Olivier, J.-M. (1997). "ADE-4: A Multivariate Analysis and Graphical Display Software", *Statistics and Computing*, 7(1): 75-83.

Timmermans, D. (1993). "The Impact of Task Complexity on Information Use in Multi Attribute Decision Making", *Journal of Behavioral Decision Making*, 6(2): 95-111.

Titscher, S., Wodak, R., Meyer, M. and Vetter, E. (1998). *Methoden der Textanalyse: Leitfaden und Überblick*. Opladen: Westdeutscher Verlag.

Treloar, A. (1999). "Just Another Technology? How the Dynamics of Innovation Can Help Predict the Future of the Browser", *5th Australian World Wide Web Conference (AusWeb-99)*. Ballina, Australia: Southern Cross University Press. 152-160.

Trigg, R. (1983). *A Network-Based Approach to Text Handling for the Online Scientific Community*. Doctoral Thesis, College Park: University of Maryland.

Truex, D.P., Baskerville, R. and Klein, H. (1999). "Growing Systems in Emergent Organizations", *Communications of the ACM*, 42(8): 117-123.

Tu, H.-C., Lyu, M.L. and Hsiang, J. (1999). "Agent Technology for Website Browsing and Navigation", *32nd Hawaii International Conference on System Sciences (HICSS-32)*. Hawaii, USA: IEEE Computer Society Press.

Tufte, E.R. (1983). *The Visual Display of Quantitative Information*. Cheshire: Graphics Press.

Tufte, E.R. (1990). *Envisioning Information*. Cheshire: Graphics Press.

Tufte, E.R. (1997). *Visual Explanations: Images and Quantities, Evidence and Narrative*. Cheshire: Graphics Press.

Turban, E. and Aronson, J.E. (1998). *Decision Support Systems and Intelligent Systems*. Upper Saddle River: Prentice-Hall.

Turoff, M., Hiltz, S.R., et al. (1999). "Collaborative Discourse Structures in Computer Mediated Group Communications", *32nd Hawaii International Conference on System Sciences (HICSS-32)*. Hawaii, USA: IEEE Computer Society Press.

Tweedie, L. (1997). "Characterizing Interactive Externalizations", *ACM Conference on Human Factors in Computing Systems (CHI-97)*. Atlanta, USA: ACM Press. 375-382.

Ueda, N. and Nakano, R. (1994). "A New Competitive Learning Approach Based on an Equidistortion Principle for Designing Optimal Vector Quantizers", *Neural Networks*, 7(8): 1211-1227.

Ulmer, G.L. (1994). "The Miranda Warnings: An Experiment in Hyper-rhetoric", *Hyper/Text/Theory*. Ed. G.P. Landow. Baltimore: Johns Hopkins University Press. 345-377.

Utterback, J.M. (1996). *Mastering the Dynamics of Innovation*. Boston: Harvard Business School Press.

Uzilevsky, G. (1994). "Ergosemiotics of User Interface Research and Design: Foundations, Objectives, Potential", *4th East-West International Conference on Human-Computer Interaction (EWHCI-94)*. St. Petersburg, Russia: Springer. 1-10.

Van der Heijden, P.G.M., Mooijart, A. and Takane, Y. (1994). "Correspondence Analysis and Contingency Table Models", *Correspondence Analysis in the Social Sciences*. Eds. M. Greenacre and J. Blasius. London: Academic Press. 79-111.

Varian, H.R. (1992). *Microeconomic Analysis*. New York: Norton.

Vassileva, J. (1998). "A Task-Centered Approach for User Modeling in a Hypermedia Office Documentation System", *Adaptive Hypertext and Hypermedia*. Eds. P. Brusilovsky et al. Dordrecht: Kluwer Academic Publishers. 209-247.

Vasudevan, V. and Palmer, M. (1999). "On Web Annotations: Promises and Pitfalls of Current Web Infrastructure", *32nd Hawaii International Conference on System Sciences (HICSS-32)*. Hawaii, USA: IEEE Computer Society Press.

Von Bertalanffy, L. (1974). "The History and Status of General Systems Theory", *System Analysis Techniques*. Eds. J.D. Couger and R.W. Knapp. New York: John Wiley & Sons. 9-26.

Von Glasersfeld, E. (1992). "Cybernetics", *Cybernetics and Applied Systems*. Ed. C.V. Negoita. New York: Marcel Dekker. 1-5.

W3C (2000). *Resource Description Framework (RDF) Schema Specification 1.0 - W3C Candidate Recommendation 27 March 2000*, World Wide Web Consortium (W3C). http://www.w3.org/TR/2000/CR-rdf-schema-20000327/.

Waern, A., Averman, C., Tierney, M. and Rudström, Å. (1999). "Information Services Based on User Profile Communication", *7th International Conference on User Modeling*. Banff, Canada: Springer. 319-321.

Walczak, S. and Sincich, T. (1999). "A Comparative Analysis of Regression and Neural Networks for University Admission", *Information Sciences*, 119(1-2): 1-20.

Walther, E. (1997). "The Sign as Medium, the Medium Relation as the Foundation of the Sign", *Semiotics of the Media: State of the Art, Projects, and Perspectives*. Ed. W. Nöth. Berlin: Mouton de Gruyter. 79-85.

Ware, J.P. (1998). *The Search for Digital Excellence*. New York: McGraw-Hill.

Weinberg, J. (1997). "Rating the Net", *Hasting Communications and Entertainment Law Journal*, 19(2): 453-482.

Weitzman, E.A. and Miles, M.B. (1995). *Computer Programs for Qualitative Data Analysis: A Software Sourcebook*. Thousand Oaks: Sage.

Wenz, K. (1997). "Principles of Spatialization in Text and Hypertext", *Semiotics of the Media: State of the Art, Projects, and Perspectives*. Ed. W. Nöth. Berlin: Mouton de Gruyter. 575-586.

Werthner, H. and Klein, S. (1998). *Information Technology and Tourism - A Challenging Relationship*. Vienna: Springer.

Werthner, H., Scharl, A. and Bauer, C. (2000). "The Online Tourism Industry - Measuring Success Factors", *World Automation Congress (WAC-2000)*. Maui, USA. Forthcoming.

Wexelblat, A. (1999). "History-based Tools for Navigation", *32nd Hawaii International Conference on System Sciences (HICSS-32)*. Hawaii, USA: IEEE Computer Society Press.

Whitaker, R. (1995). *Self-Organization, Autopoiesis, and Enterprises*, ACM Special Interest Group on Supporting Group Work. http://www.acm.org/sigois/auto/Main.html.

Wiener, N. (1961). *Cybernetics or Control and Communication in the Animal and the Machine*. New York: MIT Press / John Wiley & Sons.

Wilde, K.D. (1992). "Database-Marketing für Konsumgüter", *Handbuch des Electronic Marketing: Funktionen und Anwendungen der Informations- und Kommunikationstechnik im Marketing*. Eds. A. Hermanns and V. Flegel. Müchen: Beck. 791-805.

Wilson, R.J. (1996). *Introduction to Graph Theory*. Harlow: Longman.

Winograd, T. (1997). "The Design of Interaction", *Beyond Calculation: The Next Fifty Years of Computing*. Eds. P.J. Denning and R.M. Metcalfe. New York: Copernicus. 149-174.

Witherspoon, E.M. (1999). "A Pound of Cure: A Content Analysis of Health Information on Web Sites of Top-Ranked HMOs", *49th Annual Conference of the International Communication Association (ICA-99)*. San Francisco, USA.

Wittgenstein, L. (1953). *Philosophical Investigations*. Oxford: Basil Blackwell.

Wong, D., Paciorek, N. and Moore, D. (1999). "Java-based Mobile Agents", *Communications of the ACM*, 42(3): 92-102.

WRI (1999a). *Detroit: A City in Transition*, Washington: World Resources Institute. http://www.igc.org/wri/enved/.

WRI (1999b). *Jakarta: A Booming Magacity*, Washington: World Resources Institute. http://www.igc.org/wri/enved/.

WRI (1999c). *Problems and Priorities in Jakarta and Detroit: A World of Differences*, Washington: World Resources Institute. http://www.igc.org/wri/enved/.

Wright, W. (1995). "Information Animation Applications in the Capital Markets", *1st IEEE Symposium on Information Visualization (InfoVis-95)*. Atlanta, USA: IEEE Computer Society. 19-25.

Wright, W. (1998). "Business Visualization Adds Value", *IEEE Computer Graphics and Applications*, 18(4): 39.

Wurman, P.R., Walsh, W.E. and Wellman, M.P. (1998). "Flexible Double Auctions for Electronic Commerce: Theory and Implementation", *Decision Support Systems*, 24(1): 17-27.

Yang, Y., Carbonell, J.G., et al. (1999). "Learning Approaches for Detecting and Tracking News Events", *IEEE Intelligent Systems*, 14(4): 32-43.

Yoo, J. and Bieber, M. (2000). "Towards a Relationship Navigation Analysis", *33rd Hawaii International Conference on System Sciences (HICSS-33)*. Hawaii, USA: IEEE Computer Society Press.

Yule, G. (1996). *Pragmatics*. Oxford: Oxford University Press.

Zacharia, G., Moukas, A. and Maes, P. (1999). "Collaborative Reputation Mechanisms in Electroinc Marketplaces", *32nd Hawaii International Conference on System Sciences (HICSS-32)*. Maui, USA: IEEE Computer Society Press.

Zakon, R.H. (1999). *Hobbes' Internet Timeline v4.1*. http://info.isoc.org/guest/zakon/Internet/History/HIT.html.

Zukerman, I., Albrecht, D.W. and Nicholson, A.E. (1999). "Predicting Users' Requests on the WWW", *7th International Conference on User Modeling*. Banff, Canada: Springer. 275-284.

Index

browser, 5, 8, 28, 67-69, 100f., 109, 115, 121, 196
brushing, 91, 227
bulletin board, 44
business ecosystem, 37-39, 58-60, 216, 247-249
business model, 12, 42-44, 140, 184f., 247
business process, v, 33, 53, 56, 75f., 106, 171
business sector, vi, 36, 53, 96, 108f., 113, 116-119, 147f., 165, 248
business-to-business, 12, 48
business-to-consumer, vii, 12, 50, 56, 106, 233

C

caching, 103, 195
Cadence Design Systems, 120, 141, 145, 147
canning, 212
CASE (Computer-Aided Software Engineering), 32
CERN (European Laboratory for Particle Physics), 8
certification, 74, 197
chat room, 44
chi-square distance, 174
chi-square test, 166
circular tree, 222
circular visualization, 225
city traffic, 99
classic loop of adaptation, vii
clickstream, 72, 103, 202f.
cluster analysis, 118, 129, 141, 146, 177f.
cluster tree, 129, 146
coding unit, 161f., 164
co-evolution, 37, 249
cognition, 77f., 98
cognitive load, 77, 214
cognitive process, 78, 232
cognitive style, 217
coherence, 3, 21, 90, 170f., 213

cohesion, 28, 171, 216
collaborative filtering, vii, 232-234, 236f.
collinearity, 129
collocation display, 170, 173
color coding, 208, 215f., 226, 230-232
CoM (Center-of-Maximum Method), 135
communication model, 12, 27, 34, 41-44, 49, 52f., 71, 84, 195, 242, 248
Compaq Computer, 120, 141
compatibility, 9, 48, 104, 109, 124, 174
complexity, 1, 15, 20, 27, 46-50, 55, 75, 77f., 83, 86, 89, 109, 112, 152, 173, 183, 189, 198, 238, 244
comprehension, 19, 78, 158f., 195
Computer Associates, 120, 145
computer-mediated communication, 3, 43, 188
Compuware, 120, 141, 145-147
concordance, 170f.
conditionalization, 212
cone tree, 224f., 231
connectivity, 33, 54, 74, 210
consistency, 18, 54, 73, 88, 109, 187-189, 204, 230
consumer behavior, 49, 191
consumer-to-consumer, 12
content analysis, 71, 115, 126, 156, 160
content-based filtering, 238
context unit, 115, 161
contingency table, 160, 174
convergence, v, 20, 25, 37, 63
conversation analysis, 156
cookies, 91, 102, 196
coopetition, 37
corporate identity, 69
correctness, 95
correspondence analysis, 117f., 160, 174-181
co-text, 170
critical mass, 40, 238
cross-sectional analysis, 73, 108, 152, 248